Counterurbanization

Counterurbanization

the changing pace and nature of
population deconcentration

**EDITED BY
A.G. CHAMPION**

Edward Arnold
A division of Hodder & Stoughton
LONDON NEW YORK MELBOURNE AUCKLAND

© 1989 Edward Arnold

First published in Great Britain 1989

Distributed in the USA by Routledge, Chapman and Hall, Inc.
29 West 35th Street, New York, NY 10001

British Library Cataloguing in Publication Data

Counterurbanization: the changing face and nature of
  population deconcentration.
  1. Counterurbanization
  I. Champion, A.G. (Anthony Gerard)
  307'.2

  ISBN 0–7131–6573–1

Library of Congress Cataloging-in-Publication Data

Counterurbanization: the changing face and nature of population
deconcentration/edited by A.G. Champion.
     p.   cm.
  Bibliography: p.
  Includes index.
  ISBN 0–7131–6614–2
  1. Population density.   2. Population forecasting.   3. Rural
population.   4. Urbanization.   I. Champion, A. G. (Anthony Gerard)
HB1953.C68   1990   89–15100
304.6'1 – dc20   CIP

Typset in Linotron Palatino by Wearside Tradespools, Fulwell,
Sunderland
Printed and bound in Great Britain for Edward Arnold, the educational
academic and medical publishing division of Hodder and Stoughton
Limited, 41 Bedford Square, London WC1B 3D1 by
Biddles Ltd, Guildford and King's Lynn

For
Marilyn, Katherine and Victoria

Contents

List of Tables

List of Figures

The Contributors

TONY CHAMPION is Senior Lecturer in Geography at the University of Newcastle upon Tyne. He received his doctorate in geography from the University of Oxford in 1972 with a thesis on land-use change and its relationship to population growth. His principal research interests lie in the monitoring and analysis of population distribution trends in advanced Western countries, particularly Great Britain. He is co-editor, with Ross Davies, of *The future for the city centre* (London: Academic Press, 1983); co-editor, with John Goddard, of *The urban and regional transformation of Britain* (London: Methuen, 1983) and the co-author of *Changing places: Britain's demographic, economic and social complexion* (London: Edward Arnold, 1987).

YVONNE COURT is currently a consultant with the Property Group at CACI Market Analysis. She graduated in geography at Portsmouth Polytechnic and took her MA in Urban and Regional Studies at the University of Sussex. She obtained her doctorate at Portsmouth Polytechnic in 1988 with a thesis which focused on alternative explanations of counterurbanization in Denmark. She has published several papers on population change and regional development in Denmark.

GIUSEPPE DEMATTEIS is Professor in Urban and Regional Geography and Head of Dipartimento Interateneo Territorio, Università e Politecnico di Torino. His research interests lie in urban geography and its applications in town and regional planning. He has written extensively on counterurbanization and the new types of regional urban network emerging in Italy.

WILLIAM H. FREY is a Faculty Associate at the Population Studies Center, University of Michigan. He holds the doctorate in Sociology which he received from Brown University in 1974. His main research interests are migration and population redistribution in the United States and the demography of metropolitan areas. He is author, with Alden Speare, of *Regional and metropolitan growth and decline in the United States* (New York: Russell Sage, 1988); co-author, with Larry H. Long, of *Migration and* *settlement: United States* (Laxenburg, Austria: IIASA, 1982); and co-author, with Alden Speare and Sidney Goldstein, of *Migration, residential mobility, and metropolitan change* (Cambridge, Mass.: Ballinger, 1975). Dr Frey is currently directing the Michigan Metropolitan Migration Project which has assembled comparable metropolitan migration data for fourteen industrialized nations.

JENS CHRISTIAN HANSEN is Professor at the Department of Geography in the University of Bergen, Norway. His research interests are in the monitoring and analysis of population and employment trends in the marginal areas of Norway and evaluating the effectiveness of government regional policy. He is the author of several papers on the spatial disparities in economic development, regional policy and the urban turnaround in Norway.

GRAEME HUGO is Reader in Geography, Flinders University of South Australia, and Visiting Professor in Geography, University of Hawaii. He completed his doctorate in Demography at the Australian National University in 1975. As well as researching population issues in South East Asia, he has worked extensively on Australian population issues and problems, especially on issues relating to the ageing of the population. He is the author of *Australia's changing population: trends and implications* (Melbourne: Oxford University Press, 1986).

THOMAS KONTULY is a faculty member in the Department of Geography, University of Utah, Salt Lake City, a Research Associate with the Center for Public Affairs and Administration, and an Associate Director of the Survey Research Center. He obtained his doctorate at the Department of Regional Science at the University of Pennsylvania, where working with Daniel R. Vining, Jnr, he was the first to show how widespread was the metropolitan migration turnaround of the early 1970s across the advanced Western world. He has worked for several years with Roland Vogelsang on patterns of population deconcentration in the FRG and has co-authored several papers on this subject.

TOSHIO KURODA is Director Emeritus of the Population Research Institute, Nihon University, Tokyo. His principal areas of interest are urbanization and internal migration in Asia, especially in Japan, and population ageing in East Asia. His recent publications include contributions to the NUPRI Research Papers Series, including one with K. Suzuki on the spatial distribution of urban population in Japan and one with P.M. Hauser on the ageing of the Japanese population and its implications. In 1974–76 Dr Kuroda was Director of the Institute of Population Problems, Japan Ministry of Health and Welfare.

PHILIP OGDEN is Senior Lecturer in Geography at Queen Mary College, University of London. His main research interests are in population studies, particularly migration, and he has worked on both the nineteenth and the twentieth centuries. Dr Ogden has spent long periods in France, particularly at the Institut National d'Etudes Demographiques (INED) in Paris, and has also worked on the French Caribbean and on Britain. His books include *Migration and geographical change* (CUP, 1984), *Europe's population in the 1970s and 1980s* (CUP, 1985, with Ray Hall), *Economy and society in the EEC* (Saxon House, 1976, edited with Roger Lee) and *Migrants in modern France: population mobility in the nineteenth and twentieth centuries* (Unwin Hyman, 1989, edited with Paul White).

PETROS PETSIMERIS is Associate Lecturer in Urban Social Geography at the Faculty of Architecture of Turin and also Maître de Conferences Associé in Urban Geography at the University of Caen, France. He obtained his Doctorate de 3me cycle in Geography at the University of Caen in 1988 with his thesis on the urbanization of the Piedmont region of Italy.

NORIKO O. TSUYA is Research Associate at the Population Research Institute at the Nihon University, Tokyo. After obtaining a Ph.D. in Sociology from the University of Chicago, she was a Research Fellow at the Population Institute, East–West Center, Honolulu, Hawaii. Dr Tsuya's main interests lie in fertility and infant mortality, focusing especially on the Far East.

ROLAND VOGELSANG is Professor in the Department of Geography at the University of Paderborn, and also holds the Chair of Regional Geography of Canada at the Institute for Canadian Studies at the University of Augsburg. He obtained his doctorate from the University of Munster in 1972. He has published widely on aspects of population geography and the geography of the FRG, including several papers based on his recent work with T. Kontuly on counterurbanization trends in the FRG.

HILARY WINCHESTER is Lecturer in Geography, Department of Geography, the University of Wollongong, NSW, Australia. She obtained her doctorate from Oxford University and, before moving to Australia, was Lecturer in Population Geography at Plymouth Polytechnic, UK. Dr Winchester's research interests are primarily focused on the changing population geography of France, with particular reference to migration and rural change. She is the author of a number of articles on migration in France and is currently preparing a degree-level textbook on France to be published by Longman.

Preface

Over the last ten years a great deal of attention has been focused on the phenomenon of the rural population turnaround and on the patterns and processes of urban deconcentration with which it seems to have been associated. In particular, census-based studies have shown that the rates of population loss sustained by the large cities of the majority of the most advanced Western countries accelerated between the 1960s and 1970s, while the more remote rural parts of many of these countries achieved population growth through net in-migration, reversing a decades-old tradition of depopulation. Coupled with evidence of changes in the organization of production and the distribution of employment, these observations have prompted suggestions that national settlement systems have entered a revolutionary period of counterurbanization that is just as fundamental as the main phase of urbanization and industrialization, and will eventually result in a 'post-industrial' pattern of settlement based largely on medium-sized and small cities distributed much more evenly over national territory. The latest population estimates, however, indicate that the pace of population deconcentration has declined markedly since the early 1970s, raising questions about the inevitability of counterurbanization and about the nature and significance of the factors underlying it. The purpose of this book is to investigate in some detail the recent experience of a number of countries and attempt to provide answers to these questions.

The approach which this book adopts for its examination of the counterurbanization phenomenon is primarily through a series of national case studies. These review the actual trends observed in each country against the background of the academic literature on the conceptual and methodological problems of studying counterurbanization and within the context of national attitudes on the causes and significance of these changes. The countries covered in this book have been selected to represent a wide range of counterurbanization experiences, partly reflecting the actual scale and timing of the new population trends and partly related to differences in the nature of the inherited patterns of population density and distribution upon which they have been superimposed. All nine countries have at some time over the past twenty years registered some movement towards counterurbanization, though not all have recorded a sustained reversal of traditional migration flows from more remote rural regions to major metropolitan centres. The national essays are preceded by two overview chapters which set the context. The first introduces the counterurbanization experience, documenting the 'discovery' of the rural population turnaround and reviewing the statistical evidence relating to the patterns and trends in urban deconcentration for a wide range of international contexts. The second chapter outlines the main research issues which have been raised in the counterurbanization debate, including the vexed question of the real meaning of the term and the way in which the process should be measured. The concluding chapter is designed to draw together the principal findings of the national case studies in order to outline and justify a general model of changes taking place in the degree and nature of counterurbanization. It ends by discussing the probable implications of these findings for the future development of settlement patterns and the needs for further research.

The perspective adopted for this book is primarily that of population geography. This is a conscious decision which is an obvious one in certain respects but is also one which has implications for the style and depth of the analysis which should be made plain at the outset. This is a study in population geography because, first and foremost, my personal interests and experience lie principally in monitoring the changing patterns of population distribution within the urban and regional systems of advanced Western countries. The academic justification for the importance of this line of work lies in the fact that the principal manifestion of counterurbanization is the migration of people from one type of place to another. The recognition and analysis of this phenomenon requires a careful approach to the definition of settlements as well as the examination of the socio-demographic characteristics of the migrants and the impact which they have on the population composition of the settlements. In this way the intellectual case for this approach rests on the same arguments as those put forward three decades ago by Trewartha (1953) and Hooson (1960), when they made their classic statements on the case for population geography and on the importance of population distribution as the essential geographical expression. From this viewpoint, changes in the size, distribution and composition of population represent the starting point for inquiry in human geography, and their successful analysis the ultimate goal. It goes without saying, however, that other branches of human geography have their parts to play in the explanation of the patterns observed by population geographers, alongside the contribution made by the latter in terms of investigating the role of demographic and related social factors. This wider contribution is drawn upon by the authors of the national case studies in the later sections of their essays and features in the concluding chapter of the book, but the primary emphasis is on the documentation of recent population trends and their understanding in terms of the demographic components of change and the relative performance of the different elements of the national settlement systems.

The principal role of the book will be as a resource for second- and third-year undergraduates reading geography. Because these students should not only try to assimilate the main findings of recent research but should also be encouraged to assess their validity and question the means by which they have been derived, the book does not shirk from describing methodological issues nor from outlining outstanding research problems. In both the two introductory chapters and the national essays, therefore, considerable attention is given to the conceptual difficulties encountered in testing for the existence of counterurbanization and to the technical problems of assembling up-to-date statistics in a satisfactory form. Nevertheless, bearing in mind the breadth of the counterurbanization theme and its relevance for a wider readership in the essentially multidisciplinary areas of urban studies, population studies and environmental studies including town and country planning, the more technical sections have been kept separate as far as possible and can be skipped by the more general reader whose main interest is in the substantive results of the studies. It is hoped that both sets of readers will find this book not only informative but also an inspiration for further reading and investigation, given the potential importance of the phenomenon and the number of questions that remain only partially resolved.

In bringing this book to fruition, I have many causes for gratitude. In an edited book of this kind, the largest debt is always to the contributors. This is particularly true in this case, not only for the usual reasons of keeping broadly to schedule and of acceding willingly to the editor's whims but for two further reasons. First, rather than follow their own devices and desires, they all agreed to fashion their chapters around quite a precise set of guidelines which was provided by the editor in order to ensure a reasonable degree of conformity and comparability between the national case studies. Secondly, several of the contributors do not have English as their first language, yet they produced clearly written manuscripts that required relatively little redrafting. They have also lightened the editor's task by arranging for the preparation of their illustrations and by obtaining permission to reproduce tables and figures from copyright-holders.

I would also like to take this opportunity of acknowledging several others who, either knowingly or unwittingly, helped towards the inception and preparation of this book. It was in discussions with Mike Coombes that the seeds of the idea of an edited book along these lines were sown. It was my trouble-free experiences in the preparation of a previous book, *Changing places: Britain's demographic, economic and social complexion*, for Edward Arnold that prompted this idea to germinate. I am grateful to my editor at Edward Arnold for taking on this proposal and being very patient during the book's preparation, and for seeing it through its production stages so efficiently. I must also thank Professor Peter Hall and three theoretically anonymous reviewers who all made useful suggestions at the proposal stage.

Acknowledgements go to the University of Newcastle upon Tyne, which allowed me study leave during the period when the main part of the work was undertaken, and particularly to my colleagues in the Geography Department for taking on extra burdens during my absence. The British Academy and the Economic and Social Research Council both provided grants to cover additional research expenses during this period. The biggest burden of all, however, has been shouldered by my wife, Marilyn, who not only had to put up with me around the house for much of this time (without me being 'at home' as far as the children were concerned) but was also heavily involved in the typing of the manuscript, the compilation of the bibliography and the preparation of the index. She has earned her dedication in this book several times over.

Newcastle upon Tyne   A.G. Champion
December 1988

Acknowledgements

The editor and publishers would like to thank the following for permission to reproduce copyright material:

Figure 1.1 from Vining, D.R. and Strauss, A. 1977: A demonstration that the current deconcentration of population in the United States is a clean break with the past, *Environment and Planning A* 9, Figure 2, p. 754, by permission of Pion.

Figure 1.2: based on Figure 1 from Cochrane, S.G. and Vining, D.R. 1986: Recent trends in migration between core and peripheral regions in developed and advanced developing countries, Working Paper 108 (Philadelphia: Regional Science Department, University of Pennsylvania), p. 16.

Table 1.3: based on Table 1 from unpublished paper by Richard Engels, presented at the 1986 Annual Meeting, Population Association of America.

Figure 2.1: based on Figures 1 and 3 from Fielding, A.J. 1982: Counterurbanization in Western Europe, *Progress in Planning* 17(1) pp. 8 and 10, by permission of Pergamon.

Figure 6.3 reproduced by permission of Statistisk Sentralbyrå, Oslo.

Table 6.2 reprinted from "The analysis of the settlement pattern in relation to planning problems", by J. Byfuglien, from *Norsk Geografisk Tidsskrift* 40 (1986) p. 191 by permission of Norwegian University Press (Universitetsforlaget AS), Oslo.

Table 6.3 reprinted from Ohls-Packalén, G. 1987: Hovudstadsregionernas befolkningsutveckling æren 1971–1985, *NordREFO* 17: 2–3, 25–37, by permission of Nordiskt institut för regionalpolitisk forskning.

Tables 7.2 and 7.3 provided by Sven Illeris, at Amtskommunernes og kommunernes Forskningsinstitut, Copenhagen.

Figure 7.1 and Table 7.5 reprinted from Illeris, S. 1988: *Local economic development in Denmark*, Figure 5, page 16, and Table 1, page 64, by permission of Amtskommunernes og Kommunernes Forskningsinstitut, Copenhagen.

Table 7.4 taken from Maskell, P. 1985: Redistribution of Denmark's manufacturing industry 1972–82, *Scandinavian Housing and Planning Research* 2, 79–83.

Figure 9.2 reprinted from Pumain, D. 1983: Déconcentration urbaine, *Population et Sociétés* 166, Figure 1, by permission of Institut National d'Etudes Demographiques, Paris.

Figure 9.3 reprinted from Boudoul, J. and Faur, J.-P. 1982: Renaissance des communes rurales ou nouvelle forme d'urbanisation? *Economie et Statistique* 149, I–XVI, by permission of Institut National de la Statistique et des Etudes Economiques and the author.

Figure 9.5 reprinted from Fielding, A.J. 1986: Counterurbanization in Western Europe, in Findlay, A. and White, P. (eds.) *West European Population Change*, Figure 3.2, p. 38, by permission of Croom Helm.

Figure 9.7 reprinted from Boudoul, J. and Faur, J.-P. 1986: Trente ans de migrations intérieures, *Espace, Populations, Sociétés* 1986-II, 283–92, by permission of the author.

1

Introduction:

the counterurbanization experience

A.G. CHAMPION

Barely fifteen years have elapsed since the attention of the academic community was drawn to a very remarkable development taking place in the geography of population change in the USA. Calvin L. Beale, a researcher in the Economic Development Division of the US Department of Agriculture, observed from population estimates that between 1970 and 1973 population was growing faster in the non-metropolitan counties in aggregate than in the metropolitan areas. It appeared that the vast rural-to-urban migration of the people that was the common pattern of US population movement in the first two decades after the Second World War had been halted and, on balance, reversed. More detailed investigation showed that a large number of rural counties which had been experiencing population loss in the 1960s had undergone a population turnaround.

This observation and a number of similar sightings of what quickly became known variously as the 'rural population turnaround' and 'counterurbanization' triggered off a flurry of population monitoring studies and engendered widespread intellectual excitement about the possibility of a fundamental change taking place in patterns of population distribution. The revival of rural population growth in the USA was confirmed by several studies and shown to be the result not merely of the lateral extension of existing metropolitan areas but also of developments occurring in more remote locations. As the 1970s progressed, similar trends were identified in a large number of more developed countries around the world, including not only other New World countries like Canada and Australia, but also smaller and more densely populated countries in Western Europe and even Japan. While the pace of urban population growth was accelerating rapidly across the Third World, the urbanization process – at least in terms of the increasing concentration of population into large agglomerations – appeared to be going into reverse in the First World. These changes fitted in very neatly with contemporary ideas of a shift from an industrial to a 'post-industrial' society, providing a physical and easily measurable manifestation of more complex and deep-seated changes believed to be taking place in economic and social structures.

It is this switch from urbanization to counterurbanization – from population concentration to deconcentration – that is the focus of this book. Its primary aim is to discover more precisely what has been happening in a number of separate countries. In each of the case-study chapters the authors describe the latest trends in population distribution and compare them with previous experience in order to establish whether population deconcentration has been occurring in recent years and, if so, whether this marks a significant departure from the past. They have an advantage over the first commentators on counterurbanization in that they are aware that, since the early 1970s, population deconcentration has slowed in several countries and that some have even reverted to traditional urbanization patterns. This development serves a very useful purpose, both in promoting great care in the analysis and interpretation of the data and in providing an extra angle from which the counterurbanization phenomenon can be examined.

Before the case studies, however, it is important to outline the context into which they fit. The counterurbanization debate of the last fifteen years has been plagued by a plethora of concepts and terms which have been advanced by different commentators. The manner in which the debate has evolved, and the misunderstandings which have arisen along the way, provide a fascinating insight into the erratic nature of intellectual progress, but equally it is important to provide some clarification of the principal research questions which the national studies have been asked to address. The remainder of this chapter therefore provides an account of the way in which the rural population turnaround was discovered and of how our awareness of the widespread nature of the counterurbanization phenomenon evolved from a variety of different sources. The task of Chapter 2 is to produce some degree of order out of all this information. The aim there is to work towards a relatively specific definition of 'counterurbanization' which can provide at least a working hypothesis about geographical patterns of population change suitable for testing in the subsequent chapters. It is left to the final chapter of the book to evaluate the success of this framework, as well as to assess the practical implications of the observed trends.

The discovery of the rural population turnaround in the USA

The observations based on the annual county-level population estimates made by the US Bureau of the Census in the early 1970s provided the trigger which unleashed the counterurbanization debate. Though it is now known that counterurbanization tendencies had already developed in some other countries by this time and in some cases had been cited in the literature, these other sightings had by no means the same impact on the course of population research as Beale's 1975 paper and the publications on the American scene which appeared over the next two years. This readiness to announce these developments as a major change in the history of US settlement can no doubt be attributed in part to America's 'love of newness' (Berry 1976) and its equating of change with progress, but can also be related to the fact that changes along these lines had already been anticipated in a number of more speculative studies. Nevertheless, the speed with which the new trend appeared, and its pervasiveness across the American continent, helped to guarantee the warmth of the reception which it received.

The results of Beale's (1975) analysis make impressive reading. In the 1960s non-metropolitan America lost almost 3 million people through net out-migration, but in the first three years of the 1970s alone it gained more than 1.1 million people through net in-migration. As late as the 1960s the rate of metropolitan growth was double that for non-metropolitan areas, but in 1970–73 the latter grew faster than the national average, its rate of 4.2 per cent for the three-year period contrasting with one of only 2.9 per cent for metropolitan areas. Admittedly, there were still nearly 600 non-metropolitan counties declining in population during 1970–73, particularly in the Great Plains, but this was less than half as many as the nearly 1,300 declining in 1960s and many formerly large groups of declining counties in the Old South and southern Appalachian coalfields had been broken up.

To some extent, these observations accorded with the way in which researchers had been visualizing the development of urban America. In his classic study on residential neighbourhoods, Homer Hoyt (1939) pointed to the inexorable outward movement of the urban periphery as householders sought new housing. In an equally well-known study, Vernon (1960) forecast a time when the New York metropolitan area would no longer be growing. Berry (1970) quoted extensively from H.G. Wells's reflections in his 1902 book *Anticipations*, including 'The city will diffuse itself until it has taken up considerable areas and many of the characteristics of what is now country'. Berry identified extensive 'inter-urban peripheries' whose economies and populations were declining, but concluded that by the year 2000 the geography of the USA would be radically altered by an acceleration in the outward movement of people from central cities to the expanding outer edges of urban regions.

Just as Berry (1970, 23) observed that the pace of change during the twentieth century had proceeded more rapidly than Wells expected, so too the events of the early 1970s were bearing out Berry's anticipations almost straightaway. This is reflected not only in the occurrence of the rural population turnaround at this time, but also in its geographical spread. Beale (1975) found that, though counties lying adjacent to metropolitan areas were growing more rapidly than those at greater distances, the difference between the two – 4.7 and 3.7 per cent respectively for 1970–73 – was relatively small and very much narrower than it had been during the previous decade. Moreover, it was the entirely rural counties not adjacent to metropolitan areas that had experienced the most marked upward shift in population change rate between the 1960s and early 1970s, along with non-metropolitan counties with a tradition of strong retirement in-migration (Table 1.1). Subsequent studies by Morrison and Wheeler (1976), Beale (1977), Sternlieb and Hughes (1977) and McCarthy and Morrison (1978) confirmed these conclusions and also demonstrated their validity for an even wider range of county types including those dominated by employment in energy extraction, recreation and government-related activities as well as manufacturing and retirement counties.

Table 1.1 United States: Population change and net migration rates for various categories of metropolitan and non-metropolitan counties, 1960–73

County category	Annual population change rate (%)		Annual net migration rate (%)	
	1960–70	1970–73	1960–70	1970–73
USA Total	1.3	1.1	0.2	0.3
Metropolitan	1.7	1.0	0.5	0.1
Non-metropolitan	0.4	1.4	−0.6	0.7
Metropolitan[1]				
SMSAs over 3 m. people in 1970	1.7	0.3	0.5	−0.4
SMSAs 1–3 m. people in 1970	2.1	1.2	0.9	0.4
SMSAs under 1 m. people in 1970	1.6	1.4	0.3	0.4
Non-metropolitan counties				
With 20% or more commuters to SMSAs	1.1	2.2	0.2	1.5
With 10–19% commuters to SMSAs	0.7	1.5	−0.2	0.8
With under 10% commuters to SMSAs	0.3	1.3	−0.7	0.6
With city of 25,000 or more	1.1	1.4	−0.1	0.5
With no city of 25,000 or more	0.1	1.4	−0.7	0.7
Enitrely rural not adjacent to SMSAs	−0.5	1.4	−1.2	1.0
With 35% or more employed in agriculture	−1.2	−0.1	−1.9	−0.4
With 40% or more employed in manufacturing	0.7	1.1	−0.4	0.3
With a senior state college	1.3	1.9	0.1	1.1
With 10% or more net in-migration at retirement ages[2]	1.9	3.3	0.9	2.7
With 50% or more black population	−0.9	−0.2	−2.4	−1.3

Notes: 1 Standard Metropolitan Statistical Areas (SMSAs) as defined in 1974
2 For white persons 60 years and over, 1970, during 1960–70
Source: Calculated from Berry (1976), Table 1, and Beale (1975), Table 2 (incorporating amendments supplied by author). Based on data from Current Population Reports, US Bureau of the Census

For these reasons most American commentators were in no doubt about the great significance of the rural population turnaround. Morrison and Wheeler (1976) referred to it as a 'rural renaissance'. Beale (1975), while he did not believe that the system of cities was being dismantled, observed the sharply diminished attraction of the more massive metropolitan areas and interpreted the changes in terms of a population shift down the scale of settlement to both the smaller metropolitan areas and the small towns and rural areas – 'another aspect of the demographic transition ..., in which the distribution of population is no longer controlled by an unbridled impetus to urbanization' (Beale 1975, 14). Berry (1976) went a step further by coining the term 'counterurbanization' and announcing that, 'A turning point has been reached in the American urban experience. Counterurbanization has replaced urbanization as the dominant force shaping the nation's settlement patterns' (Berry 1976, 17).

Further proof of a break from past trends was provided by several subsequent studies. Probably the best known and most controversial was

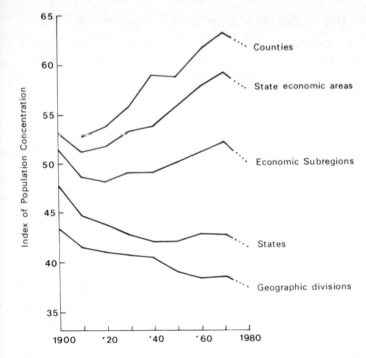

Figure 1.1 United States: Trends in index of population concentration for various systems of areal subdivision, 1900–1974. Note that the trends for 1970–74 have been projected to 1980 for illustrative purposes only. Source: Vining and Strauss, 1977.

that by Vining and Strauss (1977) who applied the Hoover index of concentration to population data at five different scales ranging from broad geographical division down to the individual county (Figure 1.1). For the county scale, this exercise revealed that the long-term trend towards greater concentration between each Census from 1900 and 1970 had been reversed. Indeed between 1970 and 1974 all five geographical scales indicated deconcentration, this being the first time that they had all pointed in the same direction and signifying for Vining and Strauss 'a clean break with the past'. Gordon (1979) challenged this conclusion on the grounds that the Hoover index results were not incompatible with continued metropolitan spread, but the 1980 Census provided more detailed evidence in support of the new interpretation. Long (1981) confirmed that deconcentration was now the rule at all three basic spatial scales – the broad regional level and the scale of suburbanization as traditionally, but now also the intermediate metropolitan/non-metropolitan scale. Moreover, according to Long and DeAre (1982), the dispersion of population growth beyond metropolitan areas was not so much a movement to smaller towns as a movement to the open countryside, suggesting a new shift towards rural life-styles.

The search for the migration turnaround worldwide

The apparently revolutionary nature of events in the USA stimulated a wider search for signs of similar developments across the Developed World and some of the newly industrialized countries. Several of these studies were multi-national in nature, amassing information on population trends in many countries and comparing their individual experience against *a priori* expectations of what should constitute the new pattern of population redistribution. Many other studies were national in focus; some merely involving a reinterpretation of existing research results in the light of the American observations, others, directly stimulated by the desire to refine or to refute the conclusions of the wider comparative studies which sometimes seemed to perceive individual countries in rather a superficial or cavalier way. A good impression of the sheer weight and range of the new interest in the basic dimensions of changing national population geographies can be obtained from the references cited in the case-study chapters in this book. In this section attention is focused primarily on the multi-national studies, because these provide a useful introduction to the widespread nature of the counterurbanization phenomenon in the 1970s. Moreover, since they vary considerably in their aims and approaches, these studies are sufficient to raise most of the conceptual and methodological issues that are addressed in more detail in Chapter 2. The studies reviewed here are primarily those of Berry (1976), Vining and Kontuly (1978a), Fielding (1982) and Hall and Hay (1980).

Berry's (1976) book *Urbanization and Counterurbanization* is distinct from the other comparative studies in that it is an edited collection of essays on recent urbanization experiences in various parts of the world and does not apply a consistent framework for testing for the existence of centripetal or centrifugal trends in population distribution. Nevertheless, though appearing only a year after the International Geographical Union's (1975) report *Essays in World Urbanization* had stated that 'Urbanization is no longer a phenomenon peculiar to certain regions of the world: it is a really worldwide phenomenon' (Kiuchi, in Jones 1975, xi), Berry's book was able to assemble some impressive evidence that the new era of population dispersal was not confined to the USA. For instance, it was reported that, 'Urbanization in Australia and Canada appears to have entered a new period. . . . Internal migration streams have shifted away from the two dominant major metropolitan areas in each country towards medium-sized cities and to small centres just outside the metropolitan regions' (Bourne and Logan 1976, 136). In her review of the changing nature of European urbanization, Lichtenberger (1976, 81) referred to 'the comeback of the medium-sized city', noting that 'In the West the small towns have been the most successful ones, especially in the German-speaking countries' (ibid, 99). In their analysis of metropolitan change in Britain, Drewett, Goddard and Spence (1976) also observed the relatively faster growth of medium-sized and smaller urban areas at the expense of the largest cities and concluded that the dominant trend in the national urban system was accelerating decentralization. At the same time, however, it is important to record that the overall tone of these essays was more cautious than Berry's introductory remarks, because at various points they refer to the basic stability of the urban system, the emergence of new metropolitan centres in previously non-metropolitan space and the strong degree of continuity from the 1950s and early 1960s evident in many of the aspects of urban change noted in the 1970s. This is a critical issue to which we will return later.

It was, however, Vining and Kontuly (1978a) that first demonstrated the widespread nature of the slowdown in metropolitan growth rates. Applying a relatively consistent approach to eighteen countries, they found that eleven of them had experienced either a reversal in the direction of net population flow from their sparsely populated, peripheral regions to their densely populated core regions or, at least, had seen a dramatic reduction in the level of this inflow. These countries comprised Japan, Sweden, Norway, Italy, Denmark, New Zealand, Belgium, France, West Germany, East Germany, and the Netherlands. By contrast, six of their sample – Hungary, Spain, Finland, Poland, South Korea and Taiwan – had not shown any significant reduction in the rate of migration into their most densely populated regions. With the data available to them at the time, they also concluded that Great Britain was also an exception to the general rule, though subsequently more detailed information led them to change their minds (Vining and Kontuly 1978b).

This study was updated and extended by Vining and his colleagues at the University of Pennsylvania (Vining, Pallone and Plane 1981; Vining, Pallone and Yang 1982). Their most comprehensive study (Vining and Pallone 1982) covered 22 countries and was able to add several more cases of metropolitan migration reduction or reversal. This survey included the USA and Canada, which had been omitted from the 1978 study but which were characterized by substantial levels of net out-migration from core regions. This paralleled the experience of most countries in north-western Europe – Belgium, Denmark, France, the Netherlands and West Germany – in which moderate net out-migration from the core regions was found. By this time, too, they observed that Finland, Spain and Iceland were also showing clear signs of a slowdown in metropolitan growth. These three countries were akin to other countries on the periphery of Western Europe, which had experienced a sharp decline in levels of net migration towards the core regions since the 1960s but not to the point where a sustained net flow of population away from these regions had been observed; the others being Norway, Sweden, the UK and Italy, together with similar patterns in Japan and New Zealand. No such development, however, was yet observable in Eastern Europe or for South Korea and Taiwan (Vining and Pallone, 1982).

The Vining studies, following closely on the heels of Berry's pronouncement of the end of urbanization in the USA, proved extremely influential in terms of stimulating further research on the geography of recent population change. In particular, they led Fielding (1982) to check whether counterurbanization had really replaced urbanization as the dominant force in Western Europe. The need for such a test arose because the Vining studies were principally concerned with the distinction between core and periphery regions in each country rather than with population redistribution across the urban system – with the result that, though they revealed trends that could be associated with counterurbanization, they did not measure them in a way that could prove this connection. Fielding therefore adopted a framework of geographical areas which represented the structure of the urban settlement system as closely as the available data sources would allow. He also developed a precise test for counterurbanization based on the statistical relationship between net migration rate and settlement size; though in practice, he used a measure of population density in place of size because of problems of obtaining data for properly defined settlements.

With this relatively rigorous approach, Fielding (1982) was able to confirm the widespread nature of counterurbanization in Western Europe. By the 1970s urbanization, defined as a positive relationship between net migration and settlement size (or population density) had ceased in almost all of the countries of Western Europe. This was proved clearly for nine of the fourteen major countries in the study – Belgium, Denmark, France, Italy, the Netherlands, Norway, Sweden, the United Kingdom and West Germany – and looked probable for Austria and Switzerland as well. Only in three countries (Ireland, Spain and Portugal) did it appear from the available data that a broadly positive relationship between net migration and settlement size continued into the 1970s. Moreover, in seven of the nine countries where urbanization had clearly been shown to have ceased, counterurbanization appeared to be fully developed, with metropolitan and principal industrial cities showing signs of net migration loss in the 1970s and rural regions containing small and medium-sized towns showing signs of net migration gain. In addition, paralleling the observations of Vining and Pallone (1982), even in a country like Ireland where urbanization appeared to be continuing, there had been a significant diminution in the level of urbanization between the 1960s and the 1970s.

At the same time, Fielding urged caution in the interpretation of these results, because inspection of the full data sets revealed considerable complexity. For instance, where it was possible to disaggregate net migration into its internal (domestic) and international components, it was found that in some countries like Ireland and Italy international migration – presumably return migration – was contributing to population growth in more rural areas, whereas in most countries it was working against counterurbanization and was thus causing an understatement of the real level of population deconcentration produced by internal migration processes. A second consideration was the immense complexity of the regional and local situations within countries – something that needs to be taken into account when the level of spatial disaggregation allows the identification of sub-systems within the national settlement system. Thus, for Italy, Fielding observed that, while there was a fairly developed tendency towards counterurbanization in the north in the late 1970s, central and southern parts of the country were still experiencing the opposite trend, albeit only weakly (Fielding 1982, 15). Nevertheless, these observations do not undermine Fielding's (1982, 9) overall conclusion that, 'Every country in Western Europe has experienced major changes in their (sic) migration patterns during the 1950–80 period and . . . , in every case, these changes can be shown to have been away from urbanization and towards counterurbanization.'

A more detailed picture of urban change in Europe since the 1950s can be obtained from several cross-national studies which have used specially defined 'functional urban regions'. These areas, which are based on recognizable urban centres and include their commuting hinterlands, have the advantage of providing a realistic representation of the settlements making up the urban system – something that Fielding could not manage because of his reliance on data for official statistical areas – but also face the drawback that sufficiently detailed population data are normally available only for Census years. Hall and Hay (1980) identified 539 separate urban systems (or 'metropolitan areas') in fifteen countries, plus 351 non-metropolitan residual areas, and then examined population and employment trends for broadly 1950–60, 1960–70 and 1970–75. Cheshire and Hay (1986) updated this study to include 1975–81 for the 438 urban systems of the first nine members of the European Economic Community (i.e. excluding Greece, Portugal and Spain). Meanwhile, work at the Vienna Centre (the European Co-ordination Centre for Research and Documentation in Social Sciences) examined the larger urban centres of 14 countries in both Eastern and Western Europe, using a different set of 189 Functional Urban Regions and dealing with trends relating to 1950–75 (Berg *et al.*, 1982).

It should be stressed that these studies place more emphasis on the internal development of population trends for the inner (core) and outer (ring) parts of each metropolitan area than on its overall level of population change, but they are valuable because they do provide some information on the latter and also because their results can be used to explore the links between population redistribution across a national settlement system and developments within each element of it. On this basis these studies are able to identify a major transformation in European patterns of population shift between the 1950s and 1970s. Hall and Hay (1980) showed at the aggregate European level that, while population was concentrating remarkably into the cores of metropolitan areas in the 1950s, by the 1960s a reversal had taken place for, though metropolitan areas were still growing, they were decentralizing people from cores to rings. After 1970 this process accelerated, so that the cores virtually ceased to grow and the rings accounted for more than the entire net gain of the population on the basis of this evidence. Hall and Hay (1980, 87) concluded that 'something like a clean break' had occurred in population trends during the 1960s and early 1970s.

Moreover, these studies revealed that a number of these metropolitan areas, particularly the larger ones, were by the early 1970s experiencing not merely decentralization from core to ring but overall population decline. In these cases the absolute growth in their rings was not large enough to compensate for the scale of population loss sustained by their cores. This pattern was interpreted as a natural development in the evolution of an urban region, following the 'stages of urban development' model originally developed by Hall (1971) and subsequently extended into cyclic form by Klaassen *et al.* (1981). This particular stage was termed 'decentralization during decline' by Hall and Hay (1980) and 'desurbanization' (*sic*) by Berg *et al.* (1982). As clearly chronicled by Cheshire and Hay (1986) it represented the situation in less than 5 per cent of the EEC9's 438 urban systems in the 1950s and 1960s, but the proportion had risen to over 10 per cent in 1970–75 and around one-quarter by 1975–81. It was concluded that the European urban system was passing steadily through the various stages of the urban development model over these three decades – a process which appeared initially in northwest Europe, particularly West Germany and the United Kingdom, but spread southwards to have a significant effect on Italy by 1975–81. According to Berg *et al.* (1982), the only countries which by 1970–75 had not progressed out of the stage which they had reached in the 1950s were Bulgaria, Hungary and Poland.

While the European experience of population deconcentration thus seemed generally to parallel developments in the USA, however, Hall and Hay (1980) noticed one important contrast: in Europe there had not been a reversal in the relative population growth performance of metropolitan and non-metropolitan areas, at least not before 1975. Admittedly, this observation was based on rates of overall population change rather than net migration and unfortunately, because neither Berg *et al.* (1982) nor Cheshire and Hay (1986) present data specifically for non-metropolitan areas, it is not possible to use their results to corroborate or update this analysis. Nevertheless, as Table 1.2 shows, the differences in growth rate

Table 1.2 Europe: Metropolitan and non-metropolitan population change, 1950–75

Geographical divisions (and number of countries)	Population change rate (% per year)		
	1950–60	1960–70	1970–75
Europe (9)	0.76	0.89	0.50
Metropolitan	0.91	1.08	0.65
Non-metropolitan	0.06	−0.09	−0.46
Atlantic Europe (1)	0.49	0.54	0.10
Metropolitan	0.52	0.54	0.12
Non-metropolitan	−0.16	0.54	−0.45
Northern Europe (3)	0.70	0.81	0.46
Metropolitan	0.81	1.00	0.50
Non-metropolitan	0.32	0.15	0.28
Western Europe (3)	1.04	1.13	0.72
Metropolitan	1.20	1.25	0.74
Non-metropolitan	0.22	0.47	0.59
Southern Europe (2)	0.74	0.94	0.54
Metropolitan	1.00	1.37	1.00
Non-metropolitan	−0.05	−0.49	−1.22

Note: Composition of the geographical divisions is as follows: Atlantic – Great Britain; Northern – Denmark, Norway, Sweden; Western – Belgium, France, Netherlands; Southern – Italy, Spain. Central Europe is excluded because no non-metropolitan areas were recognized there.
Source: Calculated from Hall and Hay (1980), Table 4.7

between metropolitan and non-metropolitan areas found by Hall and Hay were extremely wide at the aggregate European level and applied to all four of the continental divisions which their study was able to use for this analysis. Moreover, the overall figures showed no major diminution of the gap between the two types of areas between the 1960s and early 1970s. Though it had shrunk in the cases of their Northern and Western Europe divisions, it was found to have widened in the 1970s for Southern Europe (Spain and Italy) and Atlantic Europe (Great Britain). Indeed, in the latter case, this analysis indicated that non-metropolitan areas had managed to achieve the national rate of population growth in the 1960s, only to slip back into population decline in the early 1970s (Table 1.2).

The failure of Hall and Hay (1980) to detect a significant non-metropolitan population turnaround in Europe not only contrasts with the American experience but also runs counter to the results of some other studies which have examined population trends for individual countries or parts of them. In relation to Denmark, for instance, Court (1986) found that it was the Danish municipalities with urban areas of less than 2000 inhabitants which experienced the highest rates of annual population increase between 1965 and 1974, representing a major change from earlier population loss. Dean (1986) noted a very significant migration reversal in many smaller and more remote settlements in Brittany, though here the most marked swing occurred in the later 1970s. Calculations based on the work of Kennett and Spence (1979) have revealed a clear switch from loss to gain for Britain's non-metropolitan areas between 1961–71 and 1971–74 (Champion 1981a), while a series of local studies have identified a marked change in the fortunes of areas well beyond metropolitan influence (Bolton 1988; Dean *et al.*, 1984b; Jones *et al.*, 1984; 1986).

There have also been reports of rural revival accompanying metropolitan decline from other parts of the world besides the USA and Europe. For Canada, Bourne and Simmons (1979) commented on the population resurgence in more remote rural areas that was part of a major shift in the distribution of population growth away from the Toronto and Montreal regions, while Hodge (1983) specifically highlights the renaissance of small towns in the Prairies. In Australia, Burnley (1981) observed comparable shifts across the urban system, while Holmes (1981) and Smailes and Hugo (1985) identified parts of rural Australia which had seen the cessation of population decline or a switch to a positive migration balance. Even Japan – the most recently urbanized country of the developed world – was displaying signs of a fall in the level of migration losses from its more remote, non-metropolitan areas (Yamaguchi 1984).

It would therefore appear that population deconcentration was well established by the 1970s not only in the USA but in a large number of other countries across the Developed World. It is certainly clear that the growth rates of the larger metropolitan centres in these countries fell sharply after the 1960s and that, in many cases, net migration gains turned to losses. It is equally clear that some of the fastest growth rates in the 1970s were experienced by medium-sized and smaller cities and that these included not just places situated close to the main metropolitan centres but also some in relatively remote locations. There seems, however, to be less agreement over the extent, and indeed existence, of a non-metropolitan population revival outside the USA, particularly in Europe. The contradictory signs coming from a variety of studies may reflect real differences in the recent experience of different parts of the world, or alternatively may result from differences in the objectives and methods of these studies. Shedding further light on the extent of the rural turnaround forms one of the principal aims of this book, along with obtaining a better appreciation of the scale and nature of the changes taking place in and between urban areas.

Population trends in the 1980s

The debate over counterurbanization has been given an additional twist over the last ten years by revelations that the pace of population deconcentration has diminished since the 1970s. In some of the countries that recorded a metropolitan migration reversal and rural population turnaround in that decade, those trends would now themselves appear to have been overturned to give a reversal of the original reversal, or a 'turnbackaround' in Fuguitt's terminology (Fuguitt 1987). Indeed, more detailed investigation of annual population estimates suggests that in some cases the counterurbanization trend had already peaked and begun to wane even before the mid 1970s, i.e. before the phenomenon had first been identified. On the other hand, whereas the deconcentration patterns of the 1970s appear to have been recorded fairly uniformly across the Developed World, the national experiences of the 1980s – as far as they can be monitored from the available data – present a much more varied picture, in that counterurbanization does not appear to have slowed in all countries. This observation is extremely important, because while it indicates a considerably greater degree of complexity in population redistribution trends than do the developments in the 1970s, it also provides the range of different temporal and geographical experiences that through comparative analysis can potentially yield greater insights into the nature of the phenomenon. As the review in this section shows, the choice of national case studies included in this book embraces at least one example of each of the main types of experience.

As with the initial 'discovery' of the population turnaround, the first signs of a fresh reversal came from America. Engels and Healey (1979) noted that several of the USA's largest cities were beginning to recover from the heavy losses that they had experienced in the early 1970s, while Richter (1985) found that the growth of non-metropolitan America had slowed down considerably during the last three years of that decade. Monitoring population estimates for the years since the 1980 Census, Forstall and Engels (1984) demonstrated that by 1982 the USA's metropolitan population was again growing faster than the non-metropolitan population. Engels (1986) was also able to show that, on the basis of the metropolitan areas as defined in June 1984, the rate of non-metropolitan growth had been below the metropolitan rate every year since 1980 and that the margin had widened progressively as the decade advanced (see Table 1.3). Further details of the 1980–85 population trends at regional and

Table 1.3 United States: Population change rates for metropolitan and non-metropolitan areas, 1970–85

Year	Metropolitan % per year	Non-metropolitan % per year	Met/non-met ratio
1970–80	1.0	1.3	0.8
1980–85	1.2	0.7	1.6
1980–81	1.1	0.9	1.2
1981–82	1.1	0.8	1.4
1983–84	1.0	0.7	1.4
1984–85	1.1	0.3	3.7

Note: 1982–83 is excluded because of a lack of comparability in the population estimates for that pair of years
Source: Engels, 1986

metropolitan scales are presented in Chapter 3 of this book by Frey, with particular attention to the extent to which these represent a return to the pre-turnaround patterns of the 1960s.

Signs of a slowdown in the pace of population deconcentration were also picked up early on in Britain. An analysis of 'remoter, largely rural' local government districts revealed a clear peaking of population growth in 1971–73, followed by significantly lower rates of growth during the rest of the decade. From yearly data it was also possible to show that the above-average growth rate for this type of area dated from the beginning of the 1960s (Champion 1981a; 1981b). Subsequent examination of population and migration trends for all types of districts indicated a parallel reduction in the rate of decline for Britain's largest cities between the early 1970s and the early 1980s (Champion 1987b). Particularly dramatic was the stabilization of Greater London's population in the mid 1980s, when small increases in population took place in marked contrast to the massive losses registered in the late 1960s and early 1970s (Champion 1987a; Champion and Congdon 1988). Nevertheless, at no time during this period was it possible to detect an actual reversal of internal migration flows back towards the principal metropolitan areas, but rather a conspicuous narrowing of the change rate differentials between more urban and more rural areas. Population deconcentration trends in the UK since the early 1960s thus appear to have been dominated by a cyclic pattern – a point which is explored further in Chapter 5.

Just as the initial observations of a rural population turnaround in the USA generated a series of studies round the world, so too has the more recent slowdown or reversal of migration from large metropolitan centres stimulated investigations to find out how common this trend has been across the Developed World. Again Vining has been one of the leaders in the field, updating the earlier analyses to the mid 1980s for 17 of the 22 countries included in Vining and Pallone (1982). According to Cochrane and Vining (1986), all three of the country groupings which Vining and Pallone (1982) had shown to have experienced a shift in migration patterns in favour of peripheral regions in the 1970s have subsequently recorded some movement back towards pre-existing patterns. The generalized

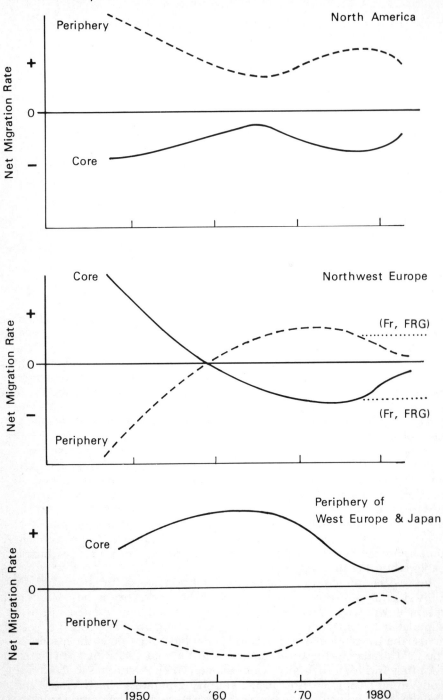

Figure 1.2 Generalized trends in net internal migration for three groups of countries.
Source: Cochrane and Vining, 1986.

trends for the three types are shown in Figure 1.2. For North America, the latest population estimates indicated a fall in the net migration losses of the core regions of both the USA and Canada, leading to a narrowing of the migration rate differential between core and periphery. A similarly consistent pattern was evident for the peripheral European countries and Japan, in that Norway, Sweden, Finland, Spain, Italy and Japan have all recorded an increase in the migration attractiveness of their core regions. The main difference from the North American experience is that in most of these European cases their core regions did not lose migrants to their peripheral regions for a sustained period during the 1970s and, as a result, the latest trends have brought a renewed divergence between core and periphery growth rates. The countries of Northwest Europe lie in an intermediate position between these two types, and exhibit less uniformity, according to Cochrane and Vining. The Netherlands and Denmark follow the generalized trend shown in Figure 1.2, whereby their peripheries were gaining migrants from the cores in the 1970s and have more recently shown a switch back to faster core growth. By contrast, in the Federal Republic of Germany it was found that the core region was continuing to lose migrants in the 1980s, while in France the rate of population losses from the core region was accelerating.

Secondly, Illeris (1988a) has studied 11 countries in central and north-western Europe at a similar macro-region scale. He confirms the widespread tendency towards the recovery of national core regions, but gives greater prominence to the existence of variation between and within countries than Cochrane and Vining. In relation to the trends experienced in the 1980s by national capital regions, Illeris distinguished two groups of countries. In Finland, Iceland, the Netherlands, Norway, Sweden and the UK, he found that the core regions had more or less resumed their former growth above the national average. By contrast, in Belgium, Denmark, France, the FRG and Switzerland, the major metropolitan areas continued to show growth rates below or around the national averages, lower or only slightly higher than in the 1970s. The agricultural/rural peripheries more or less form a mirror images of these trends. Extra variety is added by Illeris's recognition of two other types of region. Old industrial and mining regions, which experienced above-average growth in most countries in the 1950s, were in general showing population decreases or below-average growth in the 1970s and, if anything, experienced further deterioration since then. A fourth category of 'mixed regions', by contrast, exhibit the greatest diversity of growth trends. Normally containing a number of medium-sized towns, this category was characterized by below-average growth in most countries in the 1950s and average or above-average growth in the 1970s, but in the 1980s its growth rate dropped back in some countries but not in others. There is also marked diversity in this category *within* countries; in France, the FRG and the UK, for instance, the southern representatives of this category have consistently shown higher growth rates than their northern–central ones and have recorded the highest growth rates of all regions in the 1980s (Illeris 1988a; see also Champion and Illeris 1989).

A third national comparative analysis of developments in the early 1980s

Table 1.4 Western Europe: National trends in urbanization and counterurbanization in the 1970s and early 1980s

Country (number of regions)	1970s tendency[1]		1980s tendency[1]		Direction of shift[2]
	Period	r	Period	r	
Austria (16)	1971–81	+0.38			?
Belgium (9)	1971–81	−0.36	1981–83	−0.41	−
Denmark (11)	1975–78	−0.79	1981–83	+0.16	+
France (22)	1968–75	−0.26			?
Ireland (Eire) (9)	1971–79	+0.50	1979–81	−0.07	−
Italy (13)	1978	+0.12	1981–83	−0.08	⎱ −
(69)	1978	−0.00	1981–83	−0.25	⎰
Netherlands	1976–78	−0.83	1981–83	−0.12	+
Norway (8)	1976–79	+0.21	1981–83	+0.53	+
Portugal (18)	1970–71	+0.36	1979–81	+0.53	+
Spain (46)	1970–81	+0.53			?
Sweden (12)	1976–79	−0.26	1981–83	+0.37	+
Switzerland (11)	1970–80[3]	−0.49	1981–83	−0.51	no change
United Kingdom (?)[4]	1971–81[3]	−0.65			?
West Germany (FRG) (30, 50)	1978	−0.29	1981–83	−0.45	−

Notes: 1 Correlation coefficient of relationship between net migration rate and population density
2 + = shift towards 'urbanization'; − = shift towards 'counterurbanization'
3 for overall population change
4 for England and Wales only; number of regions not stated
Also note that the correlation coefficients should be interpreted with care because their significance level depends on the number of regions.
Source: compiled from Fielding 1982, 1986a

is provided by Fielding (1986a), updating the results of his 1982 study using the same framework of finer-grained spatial units as previously. Table 1.4 presents some key statistics extracted from Fielding's 1982 and 1986 reports. The available comparisons between the 1970s and 1980s indicate a number of significant changes and, paralleling Illeris's conclusions, suggest a remarkable lack of uniformity. Half the countries are shown to have experienced a relative swing towards greater population concentration ('urbanization') or at least slower deconcentration ('counterurbanization'). Particularly dramatic changes in this direction are evident for Denmark and Sweden, but the Netherlands has also seen a major fall in rate of counterurbanization and Norway and Portugal have recorded smaller increases in the rate of urbanization. The other five countries, by contrast, have either seen a switch from urbanization to counterurbanization (Italy and Ireland, the latter admittedly based on 1979–81 for the latest trends), or experienced an increase, or at least no diminution, in their earlier rate of counterurbanization (Belgium, Switzerland and the FRG). A separate analysis also appears to put France into this latter category (Fielding 1986a).

Two conclusions arise from this review of developments since the 1970s. In the first place, the evidence suggests that the slowdown or reversal of the original population turnaround is not confined to the USA and the UK. Secondly, however, it is clear that the situation in the 1980s is rather complex. There are both examples of countries that are experiencing population concentration and cases of population deconcentration. This variety does not arise because of methodological differences between researchers, because it is evident within each of the three comparative studies reviewed. Nor does it merely reflect the legacy of positions reached in the 1970s, overlain by a general shift away from counterurbanization – several countries have experienced a shift towards (greater) deconcentration since then. At the same time, the various sources seem to find less scope for agreement with each other in the 1980s than previously, and indeed each appears to have met greater problems categorizing individual countries. Herein lies an important task for this book, namely to provide a more detailed picture of recent population developments in the selected countries as well as trying to identify the factors responsible for the patterns of the 1970s and the reasons for any subsequent changes.

Summary

Population redistribution patterns in the advanced Western world have entered a period of largely unexpected turmoil since the 1960s. Following the massive levels of rural–urban migration earlier this century and the relatively recent decline in national population growth rates, it was not unreasonable twenty years ago to believe that the foreseeable future would represent a period of consolidation, involving relatively small changes to basically mature and well-balanced national settlement systems. Yet, as seen in the evidence presented in this chapter, a major switch in the general patterns of population redistribution took place during the 1970s. Virtually all countries recorded a slowdown in their rate of population concentration or a complete reversal of the migration trends affecting their core regions and larger metropolitan centres, though for some countries there appear to be discrepancies between studies as to whether a rural population turnaround occurred or not. A further complication is that for the 1980s the available literature suggests a fairly widespread swing back away from the new centrifugal patterns, but there is also evidence that some countries experienced continued counterurbanization or even an intensification of it. In general, the more recent developments appear less uniform than those of the 1970s not only in the variety of trends recorded at the national scale but also in terms of diversity within countries. The broad dichotomies between large and small settlements and between core and periphery regions no longer seem to provide such powerful explanations of differential rates of population growth in many countries as during the previous decade. A central question therefore is whether the events of the 1970s constitute a temporary anomaly or form the harbinger of a longer-term tendency towards population dispersal that will reverse the effects of a century or more of urbanization.

The aim of this book is to check the validity of the observations reviewed in this chapter and to explore the background to them in more detail than was possible in the cross-national surveys which have been drawn upon so far. The medium for undertaking these tasks is through a series of national case studies. Together, the nine countries selected for this book cover a wide range of the different population experiences noted above. The USA,

Australia, the UK, Denmark, France and the FRG are included as representatives of those countries which experienced a metropolitan migration turnaround in the 1970s, whereas Norway, Italy and Japan allow the opportunity to investigate situations in which the swing away from urbanization took only a more muted form. As regards developments in the 1980s, the USA, the UK, Norway and Japan provide examples of a slowdown or reversal of counterurbanization trends in contrast to the situation of continued or intensified deconcentration observed for France, the FRG and Australia, while Denmark and Italy are two cases on which the studies reviewed above appear to disagree. Before getting into the detail of the case studies, however, it is important to clarify what is meant by the term 'counterurbanization' and establish exactly what it is that the national case studies should be trying to recognize and explain.

Further reading

The two studies which initiated the study of the rural population turnaround and counterurbanization in the USA are: Beale, C.L. 1975: *The revival of population growth in non-metropolitan America* (Washington DC: US Department of Agriculture ERS-605), and Berry, B.J.L. 1976: The counterurbanization process: Urban America since 1970, in Berry, B.J.L. (ed.) *Urbanization and counterurbanization* (Beverly Hills, Ca.: Sage), 17–30. A more accessible, and somewhat extended, version of the former can be found in Beale, C.L. 1977: The recent shift of United States population to non-metropolitan areas, 1970–75, *International Regional Science Review* 2, 115–22.

Also prominent among the early studies was the explicit attempt to prove that the latest population trends were revolutionary: Vining, D.R. and Strauss, A. 1977: A demonstration that the current deconcentration of population in the United States is a clean break with the past, *Environment and Planning A* 9, 751–8.

The principal studies which explored the evidence for population deconcentration in several countries in the 1970s were: Berry, B.J.L. (ed.) 1976: *Urbanization and counterurbanization* (Beverly Hills, Ca.: Sage); Vining, D.R. and Kontuly, T. 1978: Population dispersal from major metropolitan regions: an international comparison, *International Regional Science Review* 3, 49–73; Hall, P. and Hay, D. 1980: *Growth centres in the European urban system* (London: Heinemann); Berg, L. van den *et al.* 1982: *Urban Europe Vol. 1: A study of growth and decline* (Oxford: Pergamon); and Fielding, A.J. 1982: Counterurbanization in Western Europe, *Progress in Planning* 17(1), 1–52.

Studies of the slowdown or reversal of deconcentration trends in the later 1970s and 1980s in the USA and Britain include: Richter, K. 1985: Non-metropolitan growth in the late 1970s: the end of the turnaround? *Demography* 22, 245–63, and Champion, A.G. 1987: Recent changes in the pace of population deconcentration in Britain, *Geoforum* 18, 379–401.

The cross-national studies which compare the 1980s with previous experience are: Fielding, A.J. 1986: Counterurbanization in Western Europe, in Findlay, A. and White, P. (eds.), *West European population change* (London: Croom Helm), 35–49; Cochrane, S.G. and Vining, D.R. 1988: Recent trends in migration between core and peripheral regions in developed and advanced developing countries, *International Regional Science Review* 13, 215–43; and Champion, A.G. and Illeris, S. 1989: Population redistribution trends in Western Europe: a mosaic of dynamics and crisis, in Hansen, J.C. and Hebbert, M. (eds.), *Unfamiliar territory: the reshaping of European geography* (Aldershot: Gower).

2

Counterurbanization:

the conceptual and methodological challenge

A.G. CHAMPION

The discovery and further examination of the counterurbanization phenomenon has engendered a major debate in academic circles concerning
the nature of these developments, the reasons underlying them, the
prospects for the future and their implications for public policy. The
question which has aroused the greatest controversy is whether or not the
developments of the last twenty years actually represent a 'turning point'
in the urban experience, as Berry (1976) concluded from his examination of
the American evidence. For many commentators the key issue here is
whether the recent trends in population deconcentration form an extension of suburbanization and local metropolitan decentralization or constitute a process of adjustment to a radically different pattern of settlement
resulting from a switch in preferences by residents and employers alike
towards smaller urban places and rural regions. Several studies have
attempted to resolve this issue by examining patterns of population change
with reference to the existing framework of metropolitan areas and urban
centres, but their 'proof' of the newness of recent trends has been
challenged in many quarters.

This chapter outlines the various interpretations which have been put on
the developments in population redistribution described in Chapter 1. The
primary reason for doing this is to provide an introduction to the concepts
and ideas which will be drawn upon by subsequent chapters. One of the
tasks of the national case studies is to review population changes in each
country in the light of the wider literature on counterurbanization. In a
sense, therefore, this chapter is designed to provide a 'showcase' of models
that can be tried on for size to see how closely each one – individually or in
combination with others – fits a particular national experience. For this
purpose the following review casts its net widely to include aspects of
population redistribution which some commentators do not consider to
constitute counterurbanization, as well as the stricter interpretations of the
'clean break' school.

The main evaluation of the counterurbanization debate is left until the
final chapter when the findings of the national case studies can be drawn
upon, but it is impossible to present this review without some reference to

the arguments for and against each viewpoint. Looking back over the early literature, perhaps the most notable feature is the lack of precision in Berry's (1976) original statement, in that it contained no detailed definition of counterurbanization nor an exact indication of which aspect(s) of population development constituted the 'turning point'. It is perhaps not surprising that this statement has sired such a variety of studies adopting different frames of reference and often talking at cross-purposes, leading to the state of great confusion which was detected by Dean *et al.* (1984a). This chapter therefore begins with a closer look at Berry's original presentation of the counterurbanization thesis, before going on to examine alternative ways in which it has been interpreted by subsequent studies and finally outlining the way in which the case-study chapters will approach the study of counterurbanization trends in their individual national contexts.

Berry's counterurbanization thesis

For Berry, counterurbanization represented the direct antithesis of urbanization. In both his 1976 statement and his more detailed presentation in 1980, Berry refers to the key feature of urbanization as being the tendency for increasing population concentration. He cites Weber (1899, 1) as concluding that, 'The most remarkable social phenomenon of the present century is the concentration of population in cities'. He quotes Hope Tisdale's (1942) description of urbanization as follows: 'Urbanization is a process of population concentration. It proceeds in two ways: the multiplication of the points of concentration and the increase in size of individual concentrations ... It implies a movement from a state of less concentration to a state of more concentration.' According to Berry, therefore, 'Counterurbanization is a process of population deconcentration; it implies a movement from a state of more concentration to a state of less concentration' (Berry 1976, 17; 1980, 14).

No more elaborate definition is offered. On the other hand, Berry's (1976) paper provides an opportunity for inferring the principal features of counterurbanization because, in Berry's words, '(It) lays out the facts of the change' that constitutes the switch away from urbanization. Drawing on an analysis of population data by Forstall (1975), Berry (1976, 21) highlights five 'facts';

1 Since 1970, US metropolitan areas have grown more slowly than the nation as a whole, and substantially less rapidly than non-metropolitan America, a development that stands in strong contrast to all preceding decades back to the early nineteenth century.

2 On a net basis, metropolitan areas are now losing migrants to non-metropolitan territory, although they still show a slight total increase in immigration because of recent immigrants from abroad.

3 The decline in metropolitan growth is largely accounted for by the largest metropolitan areas, particularly those located in the North-east and North Central regions. The eight metropolitan areas exceeding three million people have lost two-thirds of a million net migrants since 1970, and their central counties have declined in population absolutely by more than a quarter of a million. Altogether the central cities of the nation's SMSA's (Standard

Metropolitan Statistical Areas) grew at an average annual rate of 0.6 per cent between 1960 and 1970, but declined at an average annual rate of −0.4 per cent after 1970 (annexations excluded). . . .

4   Rapid growth has taken place in smaller metropolitan areas, particularly in Florida, the South, and the West; in exurban counties located outside SMSAs as currently defined, but with substantial daily commuting to metropolitan areas; and in peripheral counties not tied into metropolitan labour markets.

5   Particularly impressive are the reversals in migration trends in the largest metropolitan areas and in the furthermost peripheral counties: the metropolitan regions with populations exceeding 3 million gained migrants between 1960 and 1970 but have lost since 1970; the nation's peripheral non-metropolitan counties lost migrants between 1960 and 1970 but have gained since 1970. The balance of migration flows has been reversed.

Berry goes on to draw attention to the accompanying restructuring of the older metropolitan regions. Using the example of Cleveland, Ohio, he points both to the outward thrust of the city's commuting field between 1960 and 1970 and to the dramatic decreases in daily commuting to the city from zones close to the city which had experienced active suburban and exurban development during the decades. New residential and employment complexes were enabling people to seek out new life-styles and to cut their ties to the older central city. As a result, 'The intermetropolitan periphery was now displaying newly found independence as one of the region's new growth centres – not in the form of a traditional concentrated industrial-urban mode, but rather in a low-slung and far-flung form . . . North-eastern Ohio had always been a multicentred urban region. During the 60s it became more thoroughly dispersed as the older central cities declined, decentralization proceeded apace, metropolitan regions were restructured internally, and more amenity-rich outlying areas were brought into daily interaction with other parts of metropolitan America by expressway-related accessibility changes . . .' (Berry 1976, 23).

   There can be little doubt from this review that, for Berry, all these 'facts' constitute evidence of population deconcentration and, by definition, counterurbanization. Though the patterns on the ground appear multi-faceted, they are all related to the same phenomenon. This is made clear in the second half of Berry's (1976) paper which speculates on the nature of the process. After rejecting the notion that the observed changes constitute merely a 'temporary perturbation' caused by economic recession, Berry explains how they accord with all the trends of the twentieth century; for instance, H.G. Wells's forecast of the outward diffusion of the city almost to the point of obliteration, Lewis Mumford's call for a new reintegration of men and nature in dispersed urban regions, and the countless public opinion surveys indicating that popular preferences are for smaller places, lower densities and richer environmental amenities. Indeed, what was being observed in the 1970s was 'not something new, but something old – the reassertion of fundamental predispositions of the American culture' including the love of newness, the desire to be near nature, the frontier spirit, the freedom to move, and the wish to maintain the individuality of the homogeneous subgroup (Berry 1976, 24–8). These original preferences expressed by American settlers and their descendants had been overwhelmed by the process of urban concentration unleashed by the technologies of the Industrial Revolution, but were now at last able to dominate once again as the latter waned in power.

It is necessary to turn to Berry's (1980) statement on counterurbanization for a fuller elaboration of the way in which the forces of urban concentration have relaxed. In explaining the breakdown of the classic regionalization of the USA, Berry writes, 'The glue of centrality that restricted innovative new developments to the core cities of the industrial heartland has been dissolved. Regions throughout the nation are sharing in the newer forms of employment growth. Transportation improvements and new forms of communication have virtually eliminated the classic localizing effects of transport inputs and the significance of proximity in speedy transmission of new ideas and practices. The economy's rapid growth industries are dispersed throughout the former exurban, non-metropolitan and sunbelt peripheries, and they are being followed by the post-industrial management and control functions of the private sector' (Berry 1980, 17–18). Gone are the strict locational imperatives of the industrial era, replaced by much greater flexibility in locational choice for firms and a much stronger role for the residential preferences of their very mobile, higher-income staff. The key factor is 'time–space convergence' which has produced a differentiated but highly interconnected national society and economy and has led to the emergence of a truly national settlement system, as reflected in the growth of the periphery and decline of the core – the hallmarks of counterurbanization (Berry 1980, 20).

At this stage it may be appropriate to recall the purpose of this review of Berry's counterurbanization thesis. In fact, there are three related aims: to discover what Berry originally meant by the term 'counterurbanization', to identify the sources of imprecision which have apparently led to confusion over the term, and finally to provide a basis from which to work up an operational definition which can be applied in the national case studies later in this book. On the face of it, nothing could be clearer than Berry's original definition of counterurbanization as 'a process of population deconcentration'. All the evidence which he draws upon to illustrate the dominance of counterurbanization in the America of the 1970s involves shifts of people from a state of greater concentration to a state of lesser concentration – the faster growth of the West and South relative to the North-east and North Central regions, the decline of the large metropolitan centres in the North-east and the rapid growth of smaller metropolitan centres in the sunbelt, the reversal of the traditional net migration flow out of non-metropolitan America, the outward extension of city commuting fields and the emergence of more dispersed and multi-modal urban regions.

Despite this apparent clarity and simplicity, however, confusion and inconsistency have abounded in the subsequent counterurbanization debate. Moreover, they arise from two major problems concerning the way in which Berry presented his thesis in 1976. One relates to Berry's assertion of a 'turning point' being reached in the American urban experience. The dating of this event is very precisely documented by reference to the comparison of population trends for 1960–70 and for the early 1970s. Yet what exactly was it that prompted Berry to identify 1970 as the time when counterurbanization came to replace urbanization as the dominant force shaping the USA's settlement patterns? It could not be the dispersal of population from the north-eastern corner of the nation to the South and West, because that tendency had been recorded for decades earlier. Nor could it be the related processes of suburbanization, local metropolitan decentralization and the expansion of the commuting fields of individual urban centres; these, too, had been in progress for a very long time. Of all the 'facts' that Berry cited, there was essentially only one instance of a switch from concentration to deconcentration around 1970. This was the reversal of migration trends for the largest metropolitan areas and the non-metropolitan counties lying outside metropolitan labour markets, with its accompanying effects on the overall growth rate and net migration rate for the aggregates of metropolitan and non-metropolitan areas. One should obviously not underestimate the importance of this change, as Long (1981) stresses very properly, but one must be aware of the implications of this observation: is it the change at this scale – intermediate between national-scale dispersal and local decentralization – that in reality is the counterurbanization phenomenon? Alternatively, can counterurbanization be said to be taking place only when decentralization is evident at all geographical scales, as was certainly the case in the USA in the early 1970s? Berry does not say, though the way in which he presents his argument suggests the latter interpretation. If this is the case, does it mean that for any country counterurbanization cannot be recognized until deconcentration is the prevailing tendency at all spatial scales? Moreover, does it mean that the search for counterurbanization is appropriate only for national territories as a whole and not for sub-national areas?

It might be thought that some light could be shed on this question by the second half of Berry's 1976 paper, where he speculates on the nature of the process. This, however, is not the case; instead, this section gives rise to a second source of confusion. The key question here is whether counterurbanization should be considered to be a process or a pattern, or indeed both. Though in the first part of his paper Berry recognizes counterurbanization in terms of statistical analyses of inter-area population redistribution, he defines it as 'a *process* of population deconcentration' and goes on in the second half of his paper to describe its nature as rooted in the residential preferences of individual people and households which are seen to be essentially anti-urban in orientation. This interpretation sheds little extra light on the 'turning point' question, since as Berry points out, popular preferences for small-town and rural life have a long history and have dominated residential movement in the twentieth century, albeit principally over relatively short distances. The change of the 1970s seems, for Berry, to be that this factor is leading to a much more far-flung pattern of population deconcentration than previously, but from his comments it appears that the latter is less due to a change in the intensity of anti-urban feeling and more to do with the relaxation of constraints traditionally imposed by other locational influences. It is also necessary to question whether the broad regional shifts to the South and West over many decades are primarily the result of residential preferences. In reality, as

Fielding (1982) has more recently stated, the antipathy towards urban life is only one of several processes that could account for population deconcentration. The counterurbanization process, as defined in terms of residential preferences, should therefore not automatically be treated as synonymous with the patterns of population deconcentration observed in the USA and many other countries round the world.

Enough has now been said to demonstrate why Berry's apparently simple definition of counterurbanization is not in the least straightforward. On the one hand, Berry seems to adopt an extremely broad-minded attitude towards the patterns of counterurbanization, since he describes population redistribution at all geographical scales from suburban moves to inter-regional shifts under this heading. On the other hand, however, he focuses almost exclusively on the innate desire for low-density living as the process underlying population deconcentration. While this may be the only process which is common to deconcentration at all spatial scales it hardly seems likely to be the only factor responsible for it. The task for the remainder of this chapter is to explore further the issues surrounding these twin problems of 'turning point' and 'pattern/process distinction' and thereby clarify what the subsequent chapters should be seeking by way of signs of counterurbanization patterns on the ground.

Conceptual issues

It is the issue over the 'turning point' idea which must receive most attention here, though having concluded that it constitutes a valid hypothesis this section must proceed to establish the precise rules for testing it. As noted in Chapter 1, Berry was not alone in suggesting that a new era had dawned. His statement echoed the conclusions of Beale (1975), while Vining and Strauss (1977) were convinced that their test using the Hoover index of concentration proved beyond all shadow of doubt that the trends of the early 1970s constituted 'a clean break from the past' (see Chapter 1). Yet this notion has been challenged on several grounds, each of which contains more exacting criteria for the recognition of counterurbanization than Berry and the 'clean break' school appear to consider necessary. In order of ascending strictness, these maintain that a 'clean break' should be recognized only if the relevant growth (1) is not merely metropolitan 'spillover'; (2) is not leading to the emergence of new metropolitan areas; (3) is not taking place in the form of urbanized areas or urban settlements; and (4) is not leading merely to the relocation of urban ways of life but involves a change from an urban to a rural or neo-rural life style. These will be considered in turn, drawing on the reviews by Fielding (1982; 1986b), Perry et al. (1986) and Coombes et al. (1989) as well as from original sources.

The 'spillover' school represents the first, and least restrictive, step in narrowing down the definition of counterurbanization from the very wide intepretation which we have seen that Berry gave to it in his original 1976 statement. The argument is that any population growth taking place within the commuting fields of existing metropolitan centres cannot be considered as a break from past trends, but merely a continuation of the long-established process of suburbanization and local metropolitan decentralization involving shifts of people and jobs from core to ring in each urban region. This approach also points out that the prevailing tendency is for individual metropolitan centres to extend their spheres of influence over progressively wider areas, as transport improvements increase accessibility to the metropolitan core from more distant places and as the process of metropolitan restructuring leads more people to orientate their journeys to suburban nodes rather than to the central city. According to this viewpoint, this type of development cannot be defined as counterurbanization or any form of 'clean break' because it is leading to an increase in both the physical extent and population size of the same metropolitan areas by effectively annexing the surrounding territory and its existing settlements.

This level of restriction on the term 'counterurbanization' is accepted very widely in the literature. Indeed, as mentioned in Chapter 1, the importance of this distinction was recognized in the studies of the rural population turnaround right from the outset. For the USA Beale (1975) was careful to distinguish between non-metropolitan counties which were adjacent to metropolitan areas as currently defined and those which were not adjacent, while Berry (1976) compared population growth and migration trends for non-metropolitan counties classified according to their level of commuting allegiance to metropolitan areas (see Table 1.1). This lead was followed by other studies such as Sternlieb and Hughes (1975), Morrison and Wheeler (1976) and McCarthy and Morrison (1978). According to this research, it was clear that, while the most accessible non-metropolitan counties were recording the highest rates of population growth in the early 1970s, something rather dramatic was taking place in the remoter rural areas because the latter had recorded the largest upturn in population change rates since the 1960s. This much was accepted by even the sternest critics of the 'clean break' idea such as Wardwell (1977) and Gordon (1979), but these maintained that remote rural growth was relatively unimportant in terms of population numbers and that it arose from the acceleration of retirement migration and recreational activity rather than from any major rejection of metropolitan areas. The fundamental question which this perspective poses is the relative importance of the population changes that result from spillover and those that are something more than spillover – a question which raises some difficult methodological issues and to which we will return later in this section.

The second step in restricting the meaning of counterurbanization raises similar methodological problems, though its conceptual basis may be considered rather different. It involves the idea that, even though population growth may be taking place in more remote and peripheral areas, this does not constitute a long-term switch to a new type of settlement pattern dominated by small towns and villages, but instead forms part of a continuous process of urban decline and growth across the urban system. As noted by Coombes *et al.* (1989), population movements in England during the early days of the Industrial Revolution might well have suggested a counterurbanization pattern, if they had been measured in ways similar to those used in much of the counterurbanization literature;

for instance, with data capturing the decline of established textile towns in East Anglia and the Cotswolds and the movement of workers into the initially small towns and villages on the flanks of the Pennines. In the American context, Borchert (1967) has shown how the evolution of the metropolitan system can be conceived as a series of 40–60 per year 'eras', each leading to the eclipse of some established centres and the emergence of new ones.

As with the first step, there is clear evidence that part of the new population growth taking place in non-metropolitan areas is contributing towards the emergence of new metropolitan centres. This is even the case in England and Wales, where it might have been thought that the urban network was already so dense as to prevent the appearance of major new centres. Here Spence *et al.* (1982), applying the same criteria to 1971 data as Hall *et al.* (1973) had to 1966 data, identified 116 Standard Metropolitan Labour Areas, compared to Hall's 100. For the USA, however, the figures are very much more impressive, with the number of metropolitan areas rising from 169 in 1950 to 212 in 1960, 243 in 1970 and 318 in 1980. Admittedly, part of this increase results from the criteria being relaxed, but even after allowing for this, the growth in numbers is still steep – 195, 240, 281 and 318 for the four years respectively. Forstall (1981) shows that, as a result both of the increase in the number of metropolitan areas and of the extension of the boundaries of existing metropolitan areas, the total number of people classified as living in non-metropolitan areas was substantially lower in the 1980 US Census than in 1970, 57.1 million people as opposed to 63.8 million. In other words, non-metropolitan America in 1980 was significantly smaller than ten years before in both its territorial coverage and its population. Recalling Hope Tisdale's (1942) dictum that one of the two ways in which urbanization proceeds is by the 'multiplication of the points of concentration', a case can thus be made that a part of the apparent non-metropolitan growth is the result of continued urbanization, or at least metropolitization.

The third step leads on from this argument, principally by focusing on the concept of 'urban' as opposed to 'metropolitan'. In this interpretation, counterurbanization is seen as the direct antithesis of urbanization, where the latter is defined in geographical terms by reference to the proportion of the population living in urban areas. From this perspective counterurbanization can be said to exist only when the proportion of the population living outside urban places is on the increase at the expense of urban dwellers. This approach, however, needs very careful handling for several reasons. One is the movement of people to exurban locations within easy travel distance of urban centres – the *raison d'être* for using functional rather than physical criteria to define settlements in the modern world. Another is the fact that methods for delineating settlements and defining them as urban or rural vary considerably from country to country, particularly in terms of minimum threshold population size, and may take on different meanings in different population contexts. In some studies, however, 'urban' measures have been used alongside other criteria to indicate the geographical background behind recent population redistribution. For the USA, for instance, Richter (1985) compared population change rates for non-metropolitan counties grouped according to size of 'largest place', a similar approach to that mentioned by Court on Denmark in Chapter 7 of this book. For Norway, Byfuglien (1986) has examined the trends in population growth for communes that lie beyond a reasonable commuting distance from urban settlements of at least 200 inhabitants – a really remote situation that is not uncommon in the very sparsely populated north of that country. Does this have to be the situation before counterurbanization can be said to be taking place?

The final interpretation of counterurbanization is the most restrictive because it is based on a combination of both geographical and sociological criteria. In brief, to be a true 'counterurbanite', a person or household not only has to take up residence in a remote rural area but also has to assume a life-style which, if not identical with the traditional rural way of life, should essentially be the modern equivalent of it. Berry (1976) appears to give some support to this perspective, in that – as noted earlier in the chapter – he identifies deep-seated yearnings for the qualities associated with rural residence as the principal motivating force behind the counterurbanization phenomenon – 'not something new but something old'. Unfortunately, in practice, it is as hard to define rural in sociological as in spatial terms, as perceptively forecast by H.G. Wells's (1902) statement that 'The country will take itself many of the qualities of the city'. Counterurbanization studies have been particularly interested to discover the extent to which urban–rural movements have involved the classic urban drop-out who seeks non-work life in cheaper and more congenial surroundings, either in the form of the 'hippy' communities associated with the post-1968 mini-revolution era or in terms of people forced out of work by the various economic recessions from 1967 onwards. A wider interpretation would perhaps include the elderly, other retired people and certain types of self-employed people working from home or, more particularly, at home. Amongst the latter could be numbered not only those engaged in supplying the growing market for hand-produced arts and crafts, but also those taking work on own-account or sub-contracted bases from distant clients. As far as this involves manufactured goods, this development is reminiscent of the pre-factory arrangements for 'putting out' work to people's homes, but according to some sources (see Hepworth 1987) this practice is even more suitable for the basic processing of information using computers and advanced telecommunications. It may, of course, be argued that such developments do not involve any real return to traditional rural life-styles, but perhaps this criterion is not realistic and should be modified in the light of the present-day life-styles of those who continue to engage in the traditional rural occupations such as farming and forestry. Against this background, one of the most important diagnostic features is the extent of regular (i.e. daily) journeys to large towns and cities. Home-working, the school bus, the travelling shop, the freezer, and the wide range of gadgetry like washing machines and televisions that provide services in-house rather than relying on imported domestic servants or externally provided facilities, all these have served to increase the independence of households from employment and service centres without a significant decrease in quality of life.

This four-fold division of conceptual issues in the counterurbanization debate, as just outlined, may seem somewhat arbitrary and forced, but does serve to demonstrate the ambiguous nature of the concept. A natural reaction would be to say that the term '*counter*urbanization', and the notion of the 'turning point' or 'clean break' which it implies, has caused much more trouble than it is worth. Indeed, since its originator appears to use it to denote all forms of population deconcentration, there is a strong case for the broadest of approaches towards studying recent trends in population distribution and playing down the more dramatic questions about whether they constitute revolutionary or evolutionary change. Against this view, however, it could be argued that merely posing the possibility of a 'clean break' of some sort can help to clarify the principal issues which research on population decentralization should address. This is the attitude adopted in this book, namely that the individual national studies should strive to identify how realistic each of these four interpretations is in making sense of deconcentration tendencies in the respective countries.

Towards a working definition

Against the background of the alternative conceptual frameworks outlined above and of the earlier discussion of population deconcentration trends, it is now necessary to work towards an operational definition which can be used to test for the existence of counterurbanization and explore its extent, nature and fluctuations over time. A key challenge is to find a satisfactory way of distinguishing metropolitan spillover from other forms of decon-centration, but questions also arise concerning the precise manner in which counterurbanization should be recognized, including the specifica-tion of the variables involved and the scale at which the tests should be applied.

There is considerable agreement in the counterurbanization literature about the best way of dealing with spillover effects. As outlined by Fielding (1982), each urban region should be defined in terms of its identity as a functional labour market area so that an urban centre is assigned all the territory which is regarded as lying within its commuting catchment. On this basis any shifts in population distribution within each region will be regarded as suburbanization and local decentralization in contrast to longer-distance shifts which transfer population between urban regions. Robert and Randolph (1983) stress the importance of this distinction by calling them 'decentralization' and 'deconcentration' respectively, though this creates its own problems because of the various contexts in which these terms have been used previously. This approach is supported by other researchers such as Bolton (1988), Champion (1987b), Coombes *et al.* (1989) and Perry *et al.* (1986). The spirit of this approach has also been followed in the US analyses from the outset, though the fact that a fair number of non-metropolitan counties supply 20 per cent or more of their employed residents to jobs in the SMSAs indicates that the latter are underbounded in functional terms. To be a fully effective discriminator of the two types of population shift, the urban regions should be delimited accurately and on the basis of the situation existing at the end of the study period, so that the outward extension of the commuting field is not counted as non-metropolitan growth.

Similar considerations apply to the problem created by the emergence of new metropolitan areas, described in the previous section as the second step in refining the definition of counterurbanization. The most obvious cases can be dealt with by using a framework of metropolitan areas defined at the end of the study period. Any growth taking place within these areas over the study period will then be attributed to the metropolitan aggregate rather than artificially inflating the rate of non-metropolitan growth. More difficult to deal with, however, are cases where embryonic metropolitan areas have not grown large enough to be recognized as 'metropolitan' even by the end of the study period. In these circumstances the best approach is again to draw upon the concept of labour market areas and to extend the functional regionalization procedure across the whole of national space, thereby leaving no unclassified, or 'non-metropolitan', territory. This is achieved by allowing relatively small places to be explored as potential centres of labour market areas and by playing down the rather arbitrary distinction between metropolitan areas and smaller labour market areas.

This approach may not be accepted readily by those who subscribe to one of the more restrictive interpretations of counterurbanization outlined in the previous section. As we have seen previously, the early American literature placed particular emphasis on the rural population turnaround. In a somewhat later critique, however, Engels and Healey (1979, 17) question the importance of such a clear break by observing, 'Only those SMSAs over two million people had more people leave than arrive. Furthermore, for 1970–76 the level of migration to SMSAs below 2 million people was approximately double the level of migration to non-metropolitan areas.' Indeed relatively few of the studies reviewed in Chapter 1 squarely addressed the question of population redistribution across the urban system. The Vining studies and Illeris (1988a) were orientated to the broader scale of national core–periphery comparisons, while Hall and Hay (1980) were concerned primarily with intra-urban shifts between cores and rings and with aggregations of trends across entire urban systems rather than with shifts between urban regions of different sizes.

Yet Berry (1976) included the rapid growth of smaller and medium-sized metropolitan areas as part of his evidence on counterurbanization and implied that, as urbanization was associated with increasing concentration into the largest urban centres, its antithesis should embrace redistribution away from the largest concentrations towards smaller ones. In that sense, the rural population turnaround should be viewed merely as one manifestation of a much wider process of urban-system restructuring rather than as an isolated phenomenon with its own separate internal dynamic. This is also the approach adopted by Fielding (1982; 1986a) whose analyses of Western Europe described in Chapter 1 have gone virtually unchallenged. The principal conclusion therefore is that the study of counterurbanization should give at least as much attention to shifts in population down the urban hierarchy as to transfers of people across a somewhat arbitrary boundary out of labour market areas that are

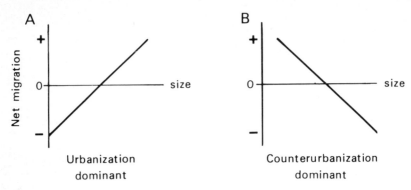

Figure 2.1 Models of urbanization and counterurbanization based on the relationship between net migration and settlement size. Source: Fielding, 1982.

considered urban (or metropolitan) into other areas.

A way in which this approach can be used in the study of counterurbanization has been developed and applied by Fielding (1982). As already described in Chapter 1, the existence of counterurbanization can be tested statistically by examining the correlation between indicators of growth and urban status for all labour market areas in a national settlement system. As shown in Figure 2.1, where a positive relationship is found between growth and settlement size, then urbanization is deemed to be the prevailing tendency at work, whereas counterurbanization is identified where the rate of growth is greater for progressively smaller sizes of places. Fielding suggested that for Western Europe as a whole the former situation was prevailing in the 1950s and hypothesized that the 1980s would see the completion of the reversal in this relationship. The intervening period would be characterized by a much less significant relationship between the two indicators, while the trends in population redistribution were in the process of turning around.

It is this interpretation that is adopted as the working definition of counterurbanization for the purposes of this book. Having said this, however, there remains room for discussion about the precise manner in which the two indicators are measured. Though Fielding develops his model with settlement size as the measure of urban status, in practice he uses population density in testing for the balance of concentrating and deconcentrating tendencies in each country. This is because for many countries the available data do not relate specifically to functional urban regions and because in these circumstances Fielding considers density a more reliable measure of urban status than the population size of rather arbitrarily defined regional units. Density measures are, however, extremely sensitive to the position of the boundary line with respect to the amount of open countryside included, as is freely admitted by Fielding (1982, 33, note 7), and must therefore be considered a very poor second best to the accurate measurement of a settlement's population size. Nevertheless, this discussion does raise the possibility of using other measures of urban status which reflect the hierarchical ordering of a national settlement system, such as the relative importance of higher-order services, professional and managerial employment or establishments exercising particular levels of command and control functions.

The measurement of the growth (or change) indicator offers a similar degree of room for manoeuvre – not surprisingly, since a case can be made for using the same criterion for change as for urban status. Thus the most basic test for counterurbanization would involve the correlation of overall population change rate against population size. As shown in Figure 2.1, Fielding preferred to use net migration rate, which can be justified on the grounds that it provides a more direct measure of the current forces affecting population redistribution since the natural change component (the surplus of births over deaths) can be considered either relatively autonomous or to be affected by earlier patterns of age-selective migration. On the other hand, Perry *et al.* (1986) have argued that a true test of the shift to a new type of settlement structure should go further than this and investigate whether redistribution of economic activity is occurring alongside the shift in population. One way of doing this would be to exclude retired and other economically inactive people and restrict the measure to change in the size of the labour force. A logical progression of this argument is to use change in jobs (recorded at the workplace rather than at workers' places of residence in order to eliminate commuting effects), in which case it would be appropriate to alter the measure of urban status to an aspect of a settlement's strength in employment terms.

The resolution of these types of measurement issue depends entirely on the way in which counterurbanization is conceptualized and on what this means for the balance between description and explanation. If counterurbanization is viewed as essentially a demographic phenomenon, then it is most appropriate that the test should be couched in terms of net migration, or even overall population change, and that change in the employment base is merely one of several possible explanations. If however, in order to be recognized as a distinctive development, counterurbanization is required to involve the more even spread of economic activity (or some particular element of it) across the national settlement system, then this interpretation will strongly dictate the measures to be used and at the same time restrict the range of explanations to those relating to the location of production and servicing activities. This book follows the lead provided by the majority of the early counterurbanization literature in viewing counterurbanization as a tendency in the distribution of population and therefore adopts the first of these two approaches.

Summary: a starting point for the national case studies

The purpose of this chapter has been to air the principal issues relating to the conceptualization of counterurbanization, so as to guide the approach to be used in the ensuing country-by-country examinations of recent trends in population distribution. Chapter 1 has already indicated the range of experience of different countries in terms of the timing of a significant change in the pace of population concentration, the degree to which rural population turnaround and metropolitan migration reversal took place, and the extent to which these new patterns themselves went into reverse in the 1980s. The emphasis in the present chapter has been on the development of a conceptual and methodological framework which can provide a basis for the identification and measurement of counterurbanization and related aspects of population deconcentration.

This step is important because even a cursory view of the literature reveals the diversity of viewpoints which have been taken by studies in this field. It is perhaps surprising that the umbrella heading of 'counterurbanization' can embrace all the types of studies described in chapter 1, ranging as they do from the broad scales of population redistribution between national capital regions and peripheral regions of national space down to core–ring shifts within individual urban areas. As seen at the beginning of the present chapter, however, Berry, in coining the term 'counterurbanization', uses it to refer to all types of population deconcentration and, moreover, appears to consider them as part of one single process, in which residential preferences constitute the primary motivating force while economic and technological factors act essentially in a permissive role influencing the speed with which these new patterns can unfold. Nevertheless, other commentators have argued that, if recent developments are to be recognized as something very different from the long-established process of urbanization, then a considerably narrower definition of counterurbanization must be adopted.

Having explored four progressively more restrictive definitions of what might be considered necessary to constitute a clean break from past trends, this chapter has proceeded to opt for a 'working definition' which lies in the middle of this range. In brief, counterurbanization is deemed to be the prevailing tendency when the distribution of population is shifting from larger to smaller places, where 'places' are defined in terms of relatively self-contained areas comprising an urban centre and its commuting and servicing catchment. On this basis counterurbanization does not require the abandonment of all types of urban settlements in favour of the villages and isolated dwellings traditionally associated with the countryside, nor does it necessitate a return to rural life-styles in the sense of giving up the trappings of a modern materialistic society. It does, however, require the faster growth of those smaller places that are not linked to major cities by significant commuting ties or other frequent journeys than those that are, and therefore specifically excludes the long-established processes of suburbanization and metropolitan expansion. Contrary to the more liberal interpretation conveyed by Berry (1976), this criterion must be satisfied if the developments of the 1970s are to be seen as qualitatively different from earlier experience. On the other hand, this model is set up merely as a hypothesis to be tested and does not rule out the possibility of undertaking more rigorous tests or of exploring alternative interpretations of population trends.

To carry out this test, each of the nine national case studies is organized in broadly the same way. Recognizing that each country has inherited a distinctive settlement pattern, the case-study authors have been encouraged to start their essays by outlining what counterurbanization would mean in terms of expected patterns of population change in their countries.

The main part of the test is to compare these predictions with the observed patterns of population change, insofar as the availability of data and suitability of the statistical reporting areas allow. The subsequent stages of each analysis are designed to pin down more exactly the nature of the counterurbanization patterns revealed. Where possible, the overall patterns of population change are disaggregated into their natural change and migration components in order to ensure that the latter has played a significant role. Analysis of population change or net migration flows by age is then used to examine the degree to which retirement migration has contributed to the growth of smaller and more remote places. To the extent that people of working age have been involved in these population shifts, the task is then to explore the rate of change in the economically active and employed population and to discover whether any such growth has resulted from greater out-commuting or from an increase in the availability of work locally. Each of these steps involves direct explanations in the form of an accounting approach to understanding recent trends, but finally authors are encouraged to draw on the evidence of other studies, particularly relating to changes in the size and composition of local economies, to probe the nature and relative importance of the factors underlying the observed trends in population distribution. Their findings are brought together in Chapter 12, where they are set within a broader discussion of the alternative explanations of counterurbanization, thus enabling conclusions to be drawn about the nature and likely longevity of the phenomenon.

Further reading

For Berry's original statement on counterurbanization, see Berry, B.J.L. 1976: The counterurbanization process: Urban America since 1970, in Berry, B.J.L. (ed.) *Urbanization and counterurbanization* (Beverly Hills, Ca.: Sage), 17–30. This was developed further by Berry, B.J.L. 1980: Urbanization and counterurbanization in the United States, *Annals of the American Academy of Political and Social Science* 451, 13–20.

Reviews of the conceptual issues raised by the counterurbanization debate can be found in: Coombes, M.G., Dalla Longa, R. and Raybould, S. 1989: Counterurbanization in Britain and Italy: a comparative critique of the concept, causation and evidence, *Progress in Planning* 32, 1–70; Dean, K. *et al.* 1984: The conceptualization of counterurbanization, Area 16, 9–14; Fielding, A.J. 1982: Counterurbanization in Western Europe, *Progress in Planning* 17(1), 1–52; Fielding, A.J. 1986: Counterurbanization, in Pacione, M. (ed.) *Population geography: progress and prospects* (London: Croom Helm), 224–56; and Perry, R., Dean, K. and Brown, B. 1986: *Counterurbanization* (Norwich: Geo Books).

3

United States:

counterurbanization and metropolis depopulation

WILLIAM H. FREY

Introduction

For much of the nation's history – certainly since the onset of industrialization – population redistribution in the United States could be characterized by three dominant patterns. First, there has been a westward regional redistribution of the population as the nation's initial eastern seaboard settlement continued to 'fill in' its unsettled territory. Of the four standard census regions, Northeast, Midwest, South, and West, the latter region has consistently displayed the highest rates of growth. The second dominant pattern has redistributed the nation's population from rural territory to urban places and from non-metropolitan to metropolitan areas. This pattern accelerated after the turn of the century, when the transition from a rural agricultural economy to an urban industrial economy attracted large streams of migrants into metropolitan areas in each of the four census regions. The third dominant trend is related to the second and involves redistribution 'up the size hierarchy' as the metropolitanization process evolved. Larger metropolitan areas gained in their migration exchanges with smaller metropolitan areas *and* non-metropolitan areas. The turn-of-the-century immigration also contributed to this pattern. Greatest gains, therefore, tended to accrue to the nation's largest industrial centres located primarily in the Northeast and Midwest census regions.

Although these three patterns characterized most of the nation's recent redistribution history (Taeuber and Taeuber 1971; Hawley 1971; Long 1981), significant alterations in these patterns appeared with the 1970s decade. Indeed, a detailed review of these changes suggests that the 1970s might be considered a 'transition decade' in United States redistribution patterns (Frey and Speare 1988). Regional redistribution patterns became altered such that the South – in addition to the West – exhibited high rates of population growth. This contrasts with earlier decades when the South was considered to be something of a lagging region. Yet the more fundamental changes occurring with the 1970s involved metropolitan population redistribution shifts. For the first time since the onset of industrialization, the population of the nation's non-metropolitan territory grew faster than that of its metropolitan territory. Moreover, the long-standing up-the-size-hierarchy redistribution that occurred across metropolitan areas began to reverse for much of the nation. Some of the largest industrial metropolitan areas sustained losses from their exchanges with smaller metropolitan areas and non-metropolitan areas, leading to unprecedented population declines in these large areas.

Possible explanations

These reversals in metropolitan redistribution are consistent with 'counterurbanization' patterns observed in other developed countries during the 1970s. This raises the question: What do the 'transition decade' redistribution patterns imply for future population changes across regions, metropolitan areas, and non-metropolitan territory? The question is particularly relevant for the largest industrial metropolitan areas, whose agglomeration tendencies weakened considerably during the 1970s decade. The answer to this question depends on what is seen as the primary explanation of the 1970s redistribution transitions.

Period explanations

One set of explanations attributes the 1970s counterurbanization patterns to *period* influences specific to that decade. These include economic factors such as the energy crisis and the decade's recessions. The oil shortage associated with the former precipitated extensive development of extractive industries in western non-metropolitan areas. The mid-decade recession and continued economic stagnation served to reduce the job-generating capacity of large metropolitan areas. Hit particularly hard were manufacturing areas that faced increased competition on the international market.

New demographic developments are also cited as period explanations. It was during the 1970s that large birth cohorts progressed into the college enrolment ages (the post-war 'baby boom' cohorts) and retirement ages (those born in the 1910s and 1920s). These developments, respectively, facilitated the expansion of state universities and community colleges in non-metropolitan territory; and raised demands for non-metropolitan-located retirement residences. In short, these period explanations treat the 1970s redistribution patterns as aberrations which should subside after the short-term economic and demographic dislocations become stabilized.

In contrast to those who view the 1970 counterurbanization tendencies as a period phenomenon, other writers suggest that they represent the beginning of new evolutionary redistribution tendencies. Indeed, two distinctly different evolutionary perspectives can be identified. These can be termed the 'regional restructuring perspective' and the 'deconcentration perspective', respectively (Frey 1987).

The regional restructuring perspective

The regional restructuring perspective follows from recent writings of an array of social scientists who attribute the post-1970 population redistribution patterns to significant period economic shifts coupled with fundamental changes in the organization of production that occurred within many of the world's industrialized nations (Noyelle and Stanback 1984; Castells 1985; Scott and Storper 1986). These developments led to declines in the industrial sectors that comprise the economic basis for large metropolitan areas in these nations' core industrial regions. At the same time, they suggest that a new functional differentiation of space is developing such that some metropolitan areas will serve as regional, national, or even worldwide centres of corporate decision-making and thus will continue to grow over the long run. Still other areas, according to these scholars, will develop as centres of 'high tech' innovation and will also exhibit agglomeration tendencies. Indeed, the regional restructuring perspective of post-1970 spatial growth and decline does *not* foresee a permanent dismantling of large metropolitan areas in developed countries. Metropolitan loss in industrial 'core' regions is seen, rather, to be specific to the 1970s period and to metropolitan areas whose economies have been tied to labour-intensive industrial production. In the long run, this perspective suggests that continued agglomeration will occur in selected large metropolitan areas with both 'core' and 'peripheral' regions.

Noyelle and Stanback (1984) suggest that the foundation of recent redistribution reversals lies with the enhanced role of services – particularly business services – and the diminished role of labour-intensive manufacturing production in national economies. A large part of this transformation, as they view it, has occurred within the service sector itself. Services are seen less as final products and more as 'inputs' in the production process – in knowledge-based activities like engineering, research and development, and planning. Such activities, they believe, will continue to expand and also benefit from certain economies of agglomeration. Moreover, they see the multi-locational corporation as a key agent in this transformation, because it facilities a division of labour across an international network of places, and leads to a centralization of higher-level service activities in specific metropolitan areas. Finally, the regional restructuring perspective does not foresee continued growth for smaller metropolitan areas and non-metropolitan areas that engage in routine production and consumer service activities. Growth which might occur in these 'subordinate' areas is likely to be constrained by the vagaries of external decision-making on the part of absentee corporations with centres located in larger metropolitan areas.

The deconcentration perspective

The deconcentration perspective draws from the writings of sociologists and geographers of the human ecology tradition (Hawley 1978; Wilson 1984; and Berry 1976) in their attempts to explain the emerging tendencies toward counterurbanization and redistribution down the metropolitan hierarchy. Like the regional restructuring perspective, the deconcentration perspective takes cognizance of changes in the developed economies' industrial structures and the effects of technological innovation on production activities. However, in addition to these influences, this perspective attributes considerable importance to the role of resident-consumer preferences in location decisions. It takes the view that long-standing residential preferences toward lower-density locations are becoming less constrained by institutional and technological barriers. The changing industrial structure, rising standard of living, and technological improvements in transportation, communication, and production are leading to a convergence – across size and place categories – in the availability of amenities that were previously accessible only in large places. As a consequence, deconcentration theorists suggest that the post-1970 counterurbanization tendencies represent the beginning of a long-term shift toward the depopulation of urban agglomerations in both core and peripheral regions. This may eventually result in the disintegration of geographically separated labour market units so that a more 'diffuse' urbanization may come into being (Hawley 1978). Because the peripheral regions in most countries possess a greater reserve of undeveloped, high-amenity areas than their industrial 'core' regions, this perspective expects an increased redistribution toward the periphery.

The deconcentration perspective, therefore, suggests that a much more fundamental redistribution shift is under way than that which was suggested by the regional restructuring perspective. Perhaps the only area of agreement across the two perspectives lies with the short-term decline that both predict for core–region manufacturing centres. Yet the deconcentration perspective anticipates similar long-term redistribution tendencies for large metropolitan areas of all types, in both the core and peripheral regions in developed nations. The sustained depopulation of these large areas is attributed to more than just transitional phasing out of unprofitable economic sectors, but rather to a general convergence in the availability of employment opportunities and modern urban amenities across all areas in the country. In short, the deconcentration perspective toward long-term redistribution tendencies implies the following: reduced long-term growth in virtually all large metropolitan areas, a greater redistribution toward the periphery, and an increased growth within small urban areas and in territory that lies beyond the boundaries of current metropolitan areas.

Evaluating the counterurbanization process

Each of the explanations just discussed implies different future redistribution tendencies for US metropolitan redistribution patterns. The period explanation suggests that the 1970s 'aberration' will terminate and redistribution will, again, become consistent with long-term historical patterns. At the other extreme, the deconcentration perspective suggests that the 1970s represent the beginning of a new era dominated by the counterurbanization process wherein the largest metropolitan areas will sustain reduced growth and decline, while smaller and non-metropolitan areas gain. The regional restructuring perspective suggests neither a reversion to long-term historical redistribution patterns, nor continued counterurbanization. Rather, it suggests that a new functional hierarchy of metropolitan areas will develop along with the changing organization of production. These explanations will be used to orient the evaluation of recent US redistribution changes across regions and metropolitan areas. The sections that follow will contrast the redistribution tendencies that were evident in the 1960s, 1970s, and the early 1980s in order to ascertain whether the counterurbanization tendencies that were so evident in the 1970s are likely to persist.

Identifying urbanization and counterurbanization tendencies

This evaluation of urbanization and counterurbanization tendencies will centre around the metropolitan area concept that is employed in US census publications. These areas generally consist of central cities with populations greater than 50,000, as well as those surrounding counties that are economically and socially linked to the city.[1] Within the six New England states this definition is slightly modified such that surrounding towns, rather than counties, make up the building blocks for the metropolitan area unit. Metropolitan areas, so defined, were designated as Standard Metropolitan Statistical Areas (SMSAs) at the time of the 1980 census. A second type of unit, termed a Standard Consolidated Statistical Area (SCSA), was also designated in the 1980 census. These SCSAs represent groupings of individual SMSA units, with coinciding boundaries, that were determined to be economically unified. The 'metropolitan areas' used in the present analysis consist, for the most part, of 1980 census-designated SCSAs and the remaining freestanding SMSAs. An exception lies in the six New England states where, departing from census procedures (that employed town boundaries for such areas), metropolitan areas will be defined on the basis of county boundaries. For the nation as a whole, this results in 278 metropolitan area units. The non-metropolitan area, examined in this study, pertains to the territory that lies outside the boundaries of these 278 individual areas (see Figure 3.1).

These definitions and metropolitan units will be used to evaluate the nature of the 1970s counterurbanization phenomenon in the United States and also to assess whether the post-1980 redistribution process represents a return to the past, continued counterurbanization, or new stage in the urban evolution process. The investigations focus on population growth rates associated with metropolitan and non-metropolitan territory and with metropolitan areas of the different sizes. Distinct counterurbanization tendencies are occurring when non-metropolitan areas exhibit higher growth than metropolitan territory, and when an inverse relationship exists between a metropolitan area's size and its rate of population growth. This contrasts with urbanization patterns, when opposite growth

1. While this characterization applies to most US census-defined metropolitan areas, there are exceptions. For example, under various circumstances, multiple central cities – each with populations less than 50,000 – can form the basis of a metropolitan area. For a more complete discussion of the metropolitan area concept, as it has evolved in census publications, see: Frey, W.H. and Speare, A. Jr. 1988: *Regional and metropolitan growth and decline in the United States*: A 1980 Census Monograph (New York: Russell Sage), Chapter 2.

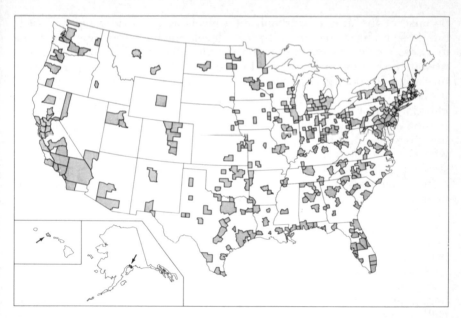

Figure 3.1 United States: Standard Metropolitan Statistical Areas, as defined in 1980.

tendencies prevail. The next section of this chapter will compare such non-metropolitan, metropolitan, and size-of-metropolitan-area growth differences over the periods 1960–70, 1970–80, and 1980–85. Additional focus will be given to growth in the 35 largest individual metropolitan areas. Many of these areas possess economic bases with which the regional restructuring perspective associates further agglomeration tendencies in the post-1980 period. A close look at these areas permits an evaluation of that perspective's forecasts of future urbanization tendencies.

Two methodological points should be kept in mind prior to reviewing these comparisons. First, all of these cross-period trend analyses are based on the same metropolitan and non-metropolitan units and areas, consistent with the 1980-based definitions discussed above. Because, over time, officially defined metropolitan areas tend to become altered (usually expanded) and additional metropolitan areas are created, this consistent use of 1980-based boundaries tends to overstate actual metropolitan territory (and understate non-metropolitan territory) in the decades prior to 1980. This approach, however, holds the advantage of estimating area growth rates that are not confounded by metropolitan area definitional changes. More important, for the present investigation, it permits a conservative measure of counterurbanization redistribution tendencies, because growth that occurs within soon-to-be-designated metropolitan territory will not be counted as non-metropolitan growth. (An alternative approach to the one adopted here would be the 'floating' metropolitan definition approach advanced by Fuguitt *et al.* (1988).)

The second methodological point involves the consideration of broad geographic regions in an analysis of US counterurbanization tendencies.

Because of the different urbanization levels and growth rates that each broad region has experienced over its development history, it is important to assess recent urbanization patterns *within* the regional context. For this reason, the present analysis examines redistribution patterns separately for the broad regional groups: North, South, and West. The North, for the purposes of this study, will consist of the census Northeast and Midwest regions. This region is generally considered to be the core industrial portion of the United States. It possesses a higher level of metropolitanization than the other two regions. Nevertheless its regional population, as a whole, and its metropolitan population have sustained significant growth slowdowns in recent decades. The West also possesses a high level of metropolitanization, largely as the result of recent, high levels of metropolitan and regional growth. In contrast, the South's population has historically been more rural and non-metropolitan than the other regions. Since the 1960s, however, it has begun to attract high levels of regional and metropolitan growth. As a consequence, the 1970s counterurbanization patterns are less evident in the South than in the other two regional categories.

A later section of this chapter will focus more specifically on the migration processes that are affecting internal redistribution patterns. It will examine the changing structure of migration streams, both across regions and metropolitan categories. Since there is a strong inter-regional redistribution from the North to the South and West (or from the 'snowbelt' to the 'sunbelt'), it is important to consider how these inter-regional migration streams – apart from intra-regional migration patterns – affect overall urbanization tendencies. The role of international migration in internal redistribution patterns will also be explored. Another underlying dynamic in the redistribution process involves the migration patterns of specific population subgroups, so attention is also paid to the migration and redistribution patterns of key age and race population groups. Finally, the chapter's concluding section returns to the original question: Do recent redistribution tendencies in the United States represent a return to the urbanization patterns of the past, or a continuation of the counterurbanization patterns that were initiated in the 1970s, or a shift to a newly evolving urbanization process?

Metropolitan and non-metropolitan population change, 1960–1985

How distinct were the 1970s redistribution patterns from those of the immediately preceding decade? What types of patterns do the estimated post-1980 population changes imply? Some initial answers can be gleaned from the data presented in Table 3.1. Shown here are annualized rates of population change for metropolitan-area size classes and non-metropolitan areas over the periods 1960–70, 1970–80, and 1980–85. As with other data presented in this chapter, these rates were compiled from population counts in the 1960, 1970, and 1980 US Censuses of Population, and post-censal estimates undertaken by the US Census Bureau for the year 1985. The rates are presented in annualized form (i.e., converted into single

Table 3.1 United States: Annualized per cent population change 1960–85, for regional and metropolitan categories[a]

Region and metropolitan category	1980 Population (millions)	Annualized per cent population change		
		1960–70	1970–80	1980–85[b]
METROPOLITAN CATEGORIES BY REGION				
NORTH				
Metropolitan	*85.0*	*+1.1*	*+0.1*	*+0.2*
Large metropolitan	58.7	+1.1	−0.2	+0.2
Medium metropolitan	17.9	+1.1	+0.5	+0.3
Small metropolitan	8.4	+1.1	+0.7	+0.2
Non-metropolitan	*23.5*	*+0.3*	*+0.8*	*+0.2*
SOUTH				
Metropolitan	*49.8*	*+2.0*	*+2.0*	*+2.0*
Large metropolitan	19.8	+2.8	+2.1	+2.3
Medium metropolitan	20.8	+1.6	+1.9	+1.8
Small metropolitan	9.2	+1.3	+1.9	+1.6
Non-metropolitan	*25.0*	*+0.2*	*+1.6*	*+1.0*
WEST				
Metropolitan	*35.5*	*+2.5*	*+2.1*	*+2.1*
Large metropolitan	26.0	+2.6	+1.8	+2.1
Medium metropolitan	6.2	+2.4	+2.6	+2.3
Small metropolitan	3.4	+2.0	+3.3	+2.1
Non-metropolitan	*7.6*	*+0.9*	*+2.7*	*+1.8*
REGIONAL TOTALS				
North	108.5	+0.9	+0.2	+0.2
South	74.8	+1.3	+1.9	+1.7
West	43.2	+2.2	+2.2	+2.1
METROPOLITAN CATEGORY TOTALS				
Metropolitan	*170.5*	*+1.6*	*+1.0*	*+1.1*
Large metropolitan	104.5	+1.7	+0.7	+1.1
Medium metropolitan	44.9	+1.5	+1.4	+1.3
Small metropolitan	21.0	+1.3	+1.6	+1.1
Non-metropolitan	*56.1*	*+0.3*	*+1.4*	*+0.8*
US TOTAL	226.5	+1.3	+1.1	+1.1

[a] Defined according to 1980 census definitions: SCSAs and SMSAs that lie outside of New England and county approximations to SCSAs and SMSAs in New England (see text). Large, medium, and small metropolitan size categories pertain to 1980 populations of 1,000,000 and over, 250,000–1,000,000, and under 250,000, respectively
[b] Based on post-censal estimates of 1985 population
Source: Compiled from data made available by the US Bureau of the Census

year rates) to facilitate comparisons of population change across time periods of unequal length.

The answer to the first question posed above is quite clear. The 1970s counterurbanization redistribution tendencies differ markedly from the more traditional urbanization patterns of the 1960s. The shift is most distinct in the West. Here, 1960s metropolitan change was significantly greater than non-metropolitan change and change rates increased with metropolitan size. This situation was reversed with the 1970s, when the West's non-metropolitan areas grew at a faster rate than its combined metropolitan categories. Within the three metropolitan categories, growth rates declined for larger-sized areas. Even more significant evidence of the West's shift toward counterurbanization lies with the comparison of 1960s and 1970s rates for each category. At the one extreme, non-metropolitan areas grew three times faster in an average 1970s year than they did in an average 1960s year; while at the other extreme, large metropolitan areas grew a third more slowly in an average 1970s year.

Similar, although less striking, counterurbanization shifts took place within the North. Unlike in the West, all broad categories of metropolitan areas in the North grew at about the same rate in the 1960s. Yet like the West (and South), the North's non-metropolitan area growth rates were then far lower than those observed in metropolitan areas. For the 1970s, one observes a higher growth rate for non-metropolitan areas than for the metropolitan area categories combined. Furthermore, the North's large metropolitan areas are distinct in exhibiting negative growth during this decade. It is significant to note that all three of the North's metropolitan area categories displayed lower rates of growth in the 1970s than they did in the 1960s, while non-metropolitan growth rates almost tripled.

The experience within the South is different from that of the other two regions. Here one finds no true reversal of urbanization tendencies between the 1960s and the 1970s. In both decades, the largest metropolitan category grew the most rapidly and the aggregated non-metropolitan territory grew more slowly than the aggregated metropolitan territory. Nevertheless, the urbanization pattern moderated in the South during the 1970s. This is evident primarily within the region's non-metropolitan areas which increased their annualized growth rate from 0.2 per cent to 1.6 per cent between the two decades. At the same time, the region's large metropolitan areas saw a fall in their high rate of growth from 2.8 to 2.1 per cent. As a consequence, the growth disparities between large metropolitan areas and non-metropolitan areas became narrower in the 1970s. It should be realized that the South still remains the least urbanized of the three regions and the strong urbanization tendencies that took place during the 1960s and 1970s represent a recent development in the region's redistribution history.

The general redistribution patterns that are evident within the broad metropolitan categories of Table 3.1 are also evident in finer-grained geographical analyses. Work by Glenn Fuguitt and Calvin Beale indicates that in the 1970s gains were evident within most of the 26 non-metropolitan sub-regions of the United States; and that, within individual non-metropolitan counties, unincorporated territory grew to a greater degree than smaller-sized places or larger-sized places (Fuguitt 1985; Beale and Fuguitt 1978a; 1978b). This research indicates that sub-regions with greatest growth were involved with recreation and retirement-related industries, with energy extraction, and with the decentralization of industry.

More detailed analyses of metropolitan area change also confirm the broad patterns that are summarized within the size of place categories in Table 3.1. The plots in Figure 3.2 provide a picture of the relationship between metropolitan area size and its annualized rate of population

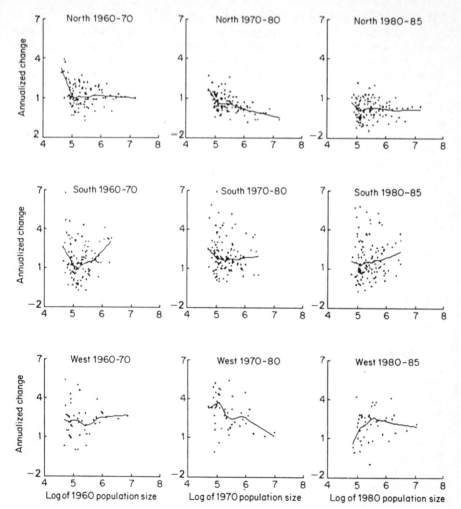

Figure 3.2 United States: Metropolitan Area population change rates (% per year) for 1960–70, 1970–80 and 1980–85, plotted against log of population size, for North, South and West regions.

change. Separate plots are shown for each region, where the metropolitan area's size (on the horizontal axis) is converted to natural log form. Superimposed on each plot is a fitted line using the LOWESS smoothing procedure based on Cleveland (1979, 1981) as incorporated in the SYSTAT (1987) statistical package. While there is a good deal of variation in growth among small and medium-sized metropolitan areas in all regions, the overall relationships suggest a 1960s-to-1970s shift toward counterurbanization. In particular, the West's regression line shifts from a slight positive slope in the 1960s decade to a strong negative slope in the 1970s decade. A similar but less distinct shift is suggested within the South. In the North, smaller metropolitan areas showed greater growth already in the 1960s, but a more general negative slope appears in the 1970s.

The patterns just reviewed serve to confirm what a number of other studies have shown, namely that in the decade 1970–80 the counterurbanization phenomenon was real, pervasive, and significant in the United States (see Fuguitt 1985, for an extensive review of these studies). Now, to the second question posed above: What urbanization or counterurbanization tendencies are implied by population developments over the five-year period since 1980? The examination of the data in Table 3.1 suggests that the answer is not straightforward. For example, the 1980–85 changes within the West suggest a re-emergence of urbanization. The non-metropolitan area growth rate lies below the aggregate growth rates of all three metropolitan area categories. Yet within metropolitan categories there is no relationship between size category and growth rate. Furthermore, when one compares the earlier 1960–70 growth rates with those for the 1980–85 period, one finds a decrease in growth for the largest two metropolitan area categories, and a substantial increase in growth for non-metropolitan areas. Hence, the urbanization tendency is not nearly as strong in the most recent period as it was prior to the 1970s decade. The range in growth rates across metropolitan area categories has narrowed considerably.

The narrowing of growth across categories in the 1980s is particularly evident in the North. The moderate counterurbanization tendencies of the 1970s have now changed toward relatively homogeneous growth rates in each broad category. The largest changes in this region have occurred with the smaller metropolitan areas and with non-metropolitan areas, where growth rates have fallen by the largest margin. At the same time, the North's large metropolitan areas have undergone a positive shift in growth rates between the 1970s and early 1980s.

The variation in growth rates across the metropolitan categories in the South for 1980–85 conform, as previously, to the urbanization model. Moreover, disparities across categories are greater in the 1980s than they were during the 1970s. Even so, the growth rate of the South's non-metropolitan areas remains significantly higher than before 1970, such that the sharp metropolitan–non-metropolitan growth disparities for that period are no longer evident.

Clearly, the strong counterurbanization tendencies of the 1970s have become moderated in the early 1980s. This is confirmed in other, more finely grained geographical analyses of non-metropolitan growth patterns (Engels and Forstall 1985; Beale and Fuguitt 1985; Forstall 1987). One such study has tracked the recent growth pattern for what have been termed the 'turnaround counties', i.e. non-metropolitan counties that sustained population declines during the decades of the 1950s and the 1960s but displayed growth during the 1970s. Of these 674 counties, only 430 were still growing in the 1980–85 period, and 323 of the latter were growing at a slower annualized rate than was the case in the 1970s (Engels 1986). The move away from counterurbanization in 1980–85 is also evident in the plots of individual metropolitan area growth patterns shown in Figure 3.2. The fitted lines that suggested a negative relationship between a metropolitan area's growth rate and its population size in the 1970s shifted in the

1980–85 period, so as to indicate a less distinct relationship between size and growth. However, it should again be noted that these fitted lines constitute summary measures of broad patterns, and that there is significant individual metropolitan area variation around these regression slopes.

Although the counterurbanization tendencies have become significantly reduced in the early 1980s, one cannot conclude that redistribution patterns are reverting to the strong urbanization tendencies of the 1960s and earlier decades. Evidence for this has already been cited and suggests that while growth differences *between* the broad regions remain distinct, growth differentials across metropolitan categories *within* regions are becoming less significant. Further, it should be noted that the two most extreme growth changes that occurred during the 1970s transition decade show no signs of reverting to pre-1970s patterns. The first was the significant diminution of growth sustained by the largest metropolitan areas in the nation's 'core' region. The second was the unprecedented acceleration in growth rate for the non-metropolitan territory of the 'peripheral' regions. In the early 1980s, large metropolitan areas in the North displayed some positive shift in their growth, and non-metropolitan areas in the South and West were growing at a slower rate than in the previous decade. Yet these recent shifts are relatively small in comparison to the ones that occurred between the 1960s and 1970s and have not pushed the pattern of growth *levels* for these metropolitan categories very far back towards the patterns recorded in the 1980s.

The latter point is verified by examining single-year growth rates over the period 1971–72 through 1984–85 for these three categories (see Figure

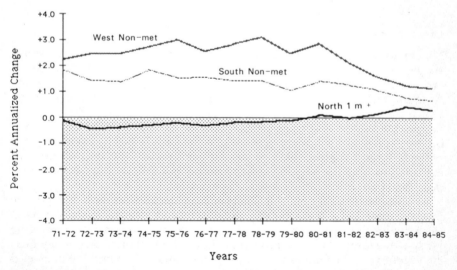

Figure 3.3 United States: annual population change rate, 1971–85, for selected regional and metropolitan groupings.

3.3). Clearly, the mid-1970s was the period of the greatest disparity between the growing peripheral non-metropolitan areas and the declining core metropolises. These accentuated differences were certainly influenced by many of the 'period' explanations discussed earlier. Non-metropolitan growth was spurred on by increased resource exploration and development and by the growing retirement population which was attracted to low-density amenity-laden areas in the South and West. The mid-decade recession, coupled with increased competition from foreign markets, led to significant cutbacks in manufacturing production and concomitant declines in the job-generating capacity of large industrial centres. The effects of these period influences began to subside with the late 1970s and early 1980s (Richter 1985; Fuguitt 1985; Frey and Speare 1988). As the de-industrialization process played itself out, some large industrial areas sustained moderate growth. Similarly, non-metropolitan counties involved in energy extractive activities sustained significant growth slow-downs, while even recreation and amenity areas became less attractive, having already absorbed a significant share of the larger elderly cohorts.

Yet Calvin Beale has observed that the reduction in non-metropolitan growth in the early 1980s might also be attributable to period effects (Beale and Fuguitt 1985). He observes that the recession around 1980 affected the economies of non-metropolitan areas more adversely than those of metropolitan areas, particularly areas engaged in agriculture, timber and mining, and manufacturing plants linked to declining heavy industries. Despite these post-1980 shifts, non-metropolitan growth rates in the South and West continue to lie above those for large northern metropolises. This contrasts sharply with the situation of the 1960s and earlier decades. It implies that some deconcentration of residences and workplaces is continuing, irrespective of whatever period effects may be operating.

Large individual metropolitan areas

The regional and metropolitan redistribution patterns reviewed above suggest that the period 1980–85 cannot be characterized conclusively as one of either continued counterurbanization or as a return to urbanization. As in the 1970s, it is subject to both period-specific influences and a pattern which suggests some continued deconcentration into the nation's peripheral regions and non-metropolitan areas. Further light can be shed on the explanations that are operating in the early 1980s by examining the nation's largest metropolitan areas. This is because the deconcentration explanation and the regional restructuring perspective foresee different post-1980 patterns for these areas, in particular.

As indicated earlier in this chapter, the deconcentration perspective predicts that large metropolitan areas will continue to sustain growth slow-downs and population declines, while the regional restructuring perspective forecasts a new functional differentiation of metropolitan areas consistent with the changing organization of production and the increased role of advanced services as 'inputs' to production process. The spatial restructuring associated with this industrial restructuring involves the

Table 3.2 United States: Annualized per cent population change 1960–85, for individual large metropolitan areas[a]

Region and metropolitan area	Functional classification[b]	1980 population (millions)	Annualized per cent population change		
			1960–70	1970–80	1980–85[c]
NORTH					
New York	DS	15.8	+1.1	−0.6	+0.4
Chicago	DS	7.8	+1.1	+0.2	+0.4
Philadelphia	DS	5.5	+1.1	−0.1	+0.3
Boston	DS	3.7	+1.0	−0.1	+0.3
Cleveland	DS	2.8	+0.9	−0.6	−0.4
St Louis	DS	2.4	+1.2	−0.2	+0.3
Minn-St Paul	DS	2.1	+2.1	+0.7	+1.1
Cincinnati	DS	1.7	+1.0	+0.3	+0.2
Kansas City	DS	1.3	+1.4	+0.4	+0.8
Indianapolis	DS	1.3	+1.6	+0.4	+0.5
Columbus	DS	1.1	+1.9	+0.7	+0.7
Detroit	SS	4.6	+1.3	−0.1	−0.7
Pittsburgh	SS	2.3	−0.0	−0.6	−0.7
Milwaukee	SS	1.6	+1.0	−0.0	−0.3
Hartford	SS	1.1	+2.0	+0.2	+0.4
Dayton	SS	1.0	+1.6	−0.3	−0.2
Providence	P	1.3	+1.0	+0.3	+0.3
Buffalo	P	1.2	+0.3	−0.8	−0.9
SOUTH					
Houston	DS	3.1	+3.3	+3.6	+3.2
Dallas-Ft Worth	DS	2.9	+3.2	+2.3	+3.7
Miami	DS	2.6	+4.1	+3.4	+1.7
Baltimore	DS	2.2	+1.4	+0.5	+0.5
Atlanta	DS	2.0	+3.2	+2.4	+3.0
New Orleans	DS	1.2	+1.4	+1.3	+0.9
Washington, DC	SS	3.1	+3.3	+0.5	+1.4
San Antonio	P	1.1	+1.9	+1.9	+2.9
Tampa-St Pet	C	1.6	+3.0	+3.7	+2.7
WEST					
LA-Long Beach	DS	11.5	+2.6	+1.4	+2.1
SF-Oakland	DS	5.2	+2.4	+1.1	+1.6
Seattle-Everett	DS	2.1	+2.5	+1.3	+1.4
Denver-Boulder	DS	1.6	+2.9	+2.7	+2.5
Phoenix	DS	1.5	+3.9	+4.5	+4.1
Portland	DS	1.2	+2.1	+2.1	+0.8
Sacramento	SS	1.0	+2.5	+2.4	+2.6
San Diego	P	1.9	+2.8	+3.2	+2.8
US TOTAL		226.5	+1.3	+1.1	+1.1

Notes: [a] Metropolitan areas with 1980 populations exceeding 1,000,000. Defined according to 1980 census definitions: SCSAs and SMSAs that lie outside of New England and county approximations to SCSAs and SMSAs in New England
[b] Following Noyelle and Stanback, 1984. DS = Diversified Service; SS = Specialized Service; P = Production; C = Consumer
[c] Based on post-censal estimates of 1985 populations
Source: Compiled from data made available by US Bureau of the Census

continued 'filtering down' of old-line manufacturing production activities to peripheral areas, non-metropolitan areas, and producer sites in other developing countries, along with an increased concentration of business service activities in large metropolitan areas that serve as headquarters for multi-locational corporations.

Noyelle and Stanback (1984) identify types of metropolitan areas that they believe will become advanced service centres. Areas which they class as Diversified Service Centres hold the greatest potential for such growth. These areas possess diversified economies and have accumulated substantial banking resources, well-developed concentrations of business services (advertising, legal, accounting, etc.) and have served as sites for a disproportionate share of the nation's largest corporations. Areas classed as Specialized Service Centres also hold some potential for gain. However, because their advanced services tend to be oriented to particular industries in which the metropolitan area specializes (e.g., automobiles in Detroit), their growth potential as advanced service centres is dependent on the success of that specialized industry. Finally, there are two classes of areas that hold little potential to gain as advanced service centres. These include areas wherein the economies are heavily tied to production activities (Production Centres) and those whose bases are centred on providing residential or amenity-related services (Consumer Centres).

According to the regional restructuring perspective, the decline of large industrial metropolitan areas in the 1970s was a transitory phenomenon, associated with the 'filtering down' of manufacturing activities that have located in such areas. Yet, aside from possessing large manufacturing bases, many of these areas hold a diversity of other economic activities which will serve to offset manufacturing-related population loss after the de-industrialization process has run its course. These Diversified Service Centres would be expected to fare better in the 1980s than they had during the 1970s decade. Other Diversified Centres, located primarily in the South and West, did not possess large heavy manufacturing components and therefore did not sustain significant losses through de-industrialization during the 1970s. These areas should be particularly well positioned for future growth according to the regional restructuring perspective.

The population change patterns exhibited for the nation's 35 largest individual metropolitan areas provide qualified support for this perspective (Table 3.2). Clearly, the population growth slow-downs and declines of the 1970s were most accentuated in metropolitan areas with strong manufacturing bases. These include northern Specialized Service Centres and Production Centres, such as Detroit, Pittsburgh, and Buffalo. Many northern Diversified Service Centres, possessing strong manufacturing components, also experienced significant declines. Yet, although such decline was most accentuated in areas with strong manufacturing bases, *all* large northern metropolitan areas experienced a downward shift in their population growth rate in the 1970s compared to the previous decade. Moreover, several of the 17 South and West metropolises grew more slowly in the 1970s than in the 1960s, and this group included most of these regions' largest Diversified Service Centre areas. The pervasiveness of decline or slower growth suggests that more general deconcentration influences are operating along with effects of industrial restructuring.[2]

The shifts observed between the 1970s and early 1980s are more consistent with what would be expected from the regional restructuring perspective. Eleven of the 18 large northern metropolitan areas display increased growth (or reduced decline) over the 1980–85 period and most of this growth occurs in Diversified Service Centres. In particular, New York City, by far the nation's largest Diversified Service Centre, displayed a strong upward shift in annual rate from −0.6 per cent to +0.4. In contrast, most northern Specialized Service Centres and Production Centres continued slow growth or declines into the 1980s. In the South and West as well, significant post-1980 gains are shown in the largest Diversified Service Centres (Los Angeles–Long Beach, San Francisco–Oakland, and Dallas–Forth Worth). The exception is Houston, where oil-related growth subsided in the early 1980s. Still, there are mixed patterns of change among other South and West areas. Large gains are observed for Washington, DC (a Specialized Service Centre) and San Antonio (a Production Centre); while the relatively strong growth observed in Miami and Portland (two Diversified Service Centre areas) over 1970–80 became far more moderate in 1980–85.

While the shifts from the 1970s to the early 1980s provide some support for the regional restructuring perspective, it should be observed that the latter period's annualized growth rates lie significantly below those of the 1960s for all large northern metropolitan areas. The 1980s growth is lower, as well, in the two largest sunbelt Diversified Service Centre areas (Los Angeles–Long Beach and San Francisco–Oakland). Of the 35 metropolitan areas listed in Table 3.2, only a few exhibit early 1980s growth rates that exceed those of the 1960s decade. Clearly, there is a regional restructuring-related influence that leads to some concentration of activities in selected advanced service centres. However, this appears to be operating in the contexts of strong period-specific influences and a pervasive tendency toward population deconcentration.

Migration patterns: 1965–70 and 1975–80

The population change figures reviewed in the previous section combine both natural increase and migration contributions. However, the overall impact of natural increase has declined since the mid-1960s due to lower levels of national fertility.[3] The deconcentration influences that affected the strong counterurbanization tendencies of the 1970s and the more mixed

2. Due to higher natural increase levels, annualized national growth rates of 1960–70 exceeded those for 1970–80 and 1980–85 (Table 3.2). However, adjusted data (not shown) indicate that the metropolitan area comparisons just cited are not explained away by these national growth shifts.
3. The nation's annualized rate of natural increase per 1000 mid-year population declined from 15.3 in the 1950s to a range between 5.8–7.2 over 1975–85. Of course, natural increase levels are not uniform across all sub-national areas. Non-metropolitan areas, due to their older age composition (and higher mortality levels), tend to display lower natural increase levels than metropolitan areas. However, as non-metropolitan areas began to attract younger in-migrants in the 1970s, differences in natural increase between metropolitan and non-metropolitan areas have diminished (Richter 1985).

redistribution tendencies of the early 1980s reflect underlying migration patterns which shifted sharply between the 1960s and 1970s. This section evaluates two aspects of these changing migration patterns – shifts in migration stream contributions and accompanying shifts in migrant selectivity. These analyses draw from migration stream data that are collected by the US census. As in the past, both the 1970 and 1980 censuses queried respondents on their place of residence five years prior to the census date. Such data provide us with the means for comparing the migration patterns that occurred over the period 1965–70 with those that occurred in the 1975–80 period.

Migration stream contributions

In evaluating migration stream contributions, it is important to distinguish internal migration from international migration contributions to redistribution because each exhibits different patterns and changes in those patterns between the late 1960s and the late 1970s.

Internal migration

The net effects of internal migration on regional and metropolitan categories are shown in the first two columns of Table 3.3, indicating strong 1960s-to-1970s reversals. During the 1965–70 period, non-metropolitan territory for all three regions exhibited net out-migration as a result of internal migration. Significant internal net out-migration was also

Table 3.3 United States: Net internal migration, and immigration and total net migration (including immigration) for regional and metropolitan categories, 1965–70 and 1975–80, thousands

Region and metropolitan categories	Net internal migration[a] 1000s		Immigration[b] 1000s		Total net migration[c] 1000s	
	1965–70	1975–80	1965–70	1975–80	1965–70	1975–80
NORTH						
Large metropolitan	−1055	−2774	+1061	+1040	+ 6	−1734
Other metropolitan	+ 43	− 338	+ 238	+ 239	+ 281	− 99
Non-metropolitan	− 366	− 64	+ 124	+ 128	− 242	+ 64
SOUTH						
Large metropolitan	+ 868	+ 539	+ 383	+ 529	+1251	+1068
Other metropolitan	+ 294	+ 827	+ 325	+ 432	+ 619	+1259
Non-metropolitan	− 531	+ 632	+ 110	+ 155	− 421	+ 787
WEST						
Large metropolitan	+ 730	+ 328	+ 544	+1051	+1274	+1379
Other metropolitan	+ 157	+ 448	+ 160	+ 253	+ 317	+ 701
Non-metropolitan	− 141	+ 402	+ 67	+ 106	− 74	+ 508

Notes: [a] In-migrants – Out-migrants
        [b] Immigrants
        [c] In-migrants + Immigrants – Out-migrants
Source: Compiled from data made available by US Bureau of the Census

sustained during this period by the North's large metropolitan areas. Nevertheless, migration gains were displayed by all other metropolitan area categories – particularly by the large metropolitan areas in the South and West. The late 1960s migration patterns shown for the latter regions served to reinforce long-term urbanization tendencies.

The shifts in these internal migration patterns observed with the 1975–80 period are consistent with the post-1970 counterurbanization redistribution tendencies. Within the North both sizes of metropolitan areas sustained greater net out-migration, and non-metropolitan territory exhibited less net out-migration, than was the case during the later 1960s. In the South and West, substantially greater migration gains were registered for non-metropolitan and small metropolitan areas, as compared with the late 1960s. Moreover, the large metropolitan areas in the South and West received considerably fewer net in-migrants over the 1975–80 period. Of all nine metropolitan categories, the greatest numerical shifts in internal migration occurred for the large metropolitan areas in the North, and for the non-metropolitan territory in the South and West. The former saw their population fall by 2.7 million as a consequence of net internal migration between 1975 and 1980, compared to a reduction of only slightly over one million in 1965–70. In contrast, while the combined non-metropolitan areas in the South and West lost almost 700,000 people through internal migration during the late 1960s, during the late 1970s they gained over one million people.

Greater insight into the shifts that occurred with the post-1970 internal migration processes can be gleaned from the migration exchange measures

Table 3.4 United States: Net internal migration for three regional and metropolitan categories, decomposed into exchanges with other groupings, 1965–70 and 1975–80, thousands

Region and metropolitan categories	NORTH Large metropolitan		SOUTH Non-metropolitan		WEST Non-metropolitan	
	1965–70	1975–80	1965–70	1975–80	1965–70	1975–80
Net internal migration, of which:	−1056	−2773	−531	+632	−141	+402
NORTH						
Large metropolitan	—	—	− 67	+238	+ 13	+ 62
Other metropolitan	− 158	− 321	− 17	+ 85	+ 3	+ 36
Non-metropolitan	− 128	− 421	+ 6	+ 82	+ 21	+ 45
SOUTH						
Large metropolitan	− 348	− 587	−114	+204	− 16	+ 6
Other metropolitan	− 106	− 480	−308	− 11	− 20	− 1
Non-metropolitan	+ 67	− 238	—	—	− 8	− 7
WEST						
Large metropolitan	− 325	− 526	− 29	+ 19	− 49	+254
Other metropolitan	− 45	− 138	− 9	+ 8	− 85	+ 7
Non-metropolitan	− 13	− 62	+ 8	+ 7	—	—

Note: all figures are rounded to nearest thousand
Source: Compiled from data made available by US Bureau of the Census

displayed in Table 3.4. Shown here for the North's large metropolitan areas and for the non-metropolitan areas in the South and West are their total net internal migration changes decomposed into migration exchanges with the other metropolitan categories. The migration exchanges represent contributions associated with in- and out-migration streams with each of the other geographic categories. These exchange measures provide a glimpse into the changing structure of migration streams between 1965–70 and 1975–80. They show how shifts in an area's total net migration results from shifts in that area's exchanges with other geographic areas.

The migration exchange data point up the pervasiveness of the post-1970 counterurbanization tendencies – which appear to stretch across regions *and* across metropolitan categories within regions. For example, the higher level of overall net out-migration observed for the North's large metropolitan areas in 1975–80 (compare 1965–70 with 1975–80 levels in columns 1 and 2 of Table 3.4) is the result of increased net out-migration exchanges with every other region and metropolitan category (rows 2 through 10). Particularly noteworthy in 1975–80 are the strong negative exchanges that the North's large metropolitan areas experienced with small metropolitan areas and non-metropolitan areas in each region. This contrasts sharply with the 1965–70 experience when this category's losses were attributable primarily to negative exchanges with the large metropolitan areas in the other two regions. The more recent migration exchanges are consistent with the 'down the size hierarchy' redistribution process.

Columns 3 through 6 of Table 3.4 show the migration exchanges that contribute to the internal migration balance of the non-metropolitan areas in the South and West. Here again, the migration exchanges indicate a shift towards a 'down the size hierarchy' migration process for the 1975–80 period. As discussed earlier, overall net migration for these areas shifted from negative to positive levels between 1965–70 and 1975–80. Yet the migration processes underlying these overall shifts have also altered. In 1965–70 the internal migration losses sustained by non-metropolitan areas in both regions resulted primarily from large negative exchanges with large and small metropolitan areas within the same region, though the South's non-metropolitan areas also lost migrants in their exchanges with metropolitan areas in the other regions. This pattern had shifted dramatically by 1975–80. During this period non-metropolitan areas in the South and West gained large numbers of migrants in their exchanges with large metropolitan areas in their same regions, and both also gained in their exchanges with large metropolitan areas in the North. Indeed, with only a few exceptions, 1975–80 migration patterns across all nine metropolitan categories (including those not shown) indicate a consistent 'down the size hierarchy' migration process coupled with the North-to-South-and-West regional redistribution of the population. This pattern underlies the overall 1975–80 figures which show greatest net out-migration for the North's large metropolitan areas and significant net in-migration to small metropolitan areas and non-metropolitan areas in the South and West.

This systematic 'down the size hierarchy' migration process is consistent with the deconcentration perspective's explanation of post-1970 counterurbanization in the United States. The perspective, it will be recalled, suggests that continually higher growth levels for smaller places and non-metropolitan areas pervade all parts of the country, irrespective of geographic location or economic function. While the nine-area metropolitan typology used here represents a relatively crude one, a more fine-grained geographical analysis of 1975–80 migration processes adds further confirmation to this perspective. In a separate study which examined trends in migration stream exchanges for individual large metropolitan areas between 1965–70 and 1975–80 (Frey 1987), it was found that in almost every case the large metropolitan areas sustained greater losses (or reduced gains) with the smaller metropolitan areas and non-metropolitan territory within its own region. South and West large metropolitan areas that registered net migration gains over the 1975–80 period received these gains primarily from their exchanges with the North. Within their own regions, these areas sustained losses (or reduced gains) in their exchanges with smaller metropolitan areas and non-metropolitan territory. These patterns point up the pervasiveness of the 'deconcentration-related' migration process of the late 1970s. They represent a substantial reversal of those processes characterized by regional and metropolitan population redistribution prior to the 1970s decade.

International migration

The immigration component of population redistribution needs to be considered separately because it observes different geographical patterns from internal migration. The destination selections of immigrants are less responsive to the kinds of economic forces and environmental attractions that affect internal migrants' choices. Many immigrants tend to locate in areas near their 'entry port' cities or in areas where earlier immigrants from their country of origin have settled. As a consequence, immigrants tend to locate disproportionally in large metropolitan areas, particularly on the eastern and western seaboards.

This geographical pattern is evident for immigrants in both 1965–70 and 1975–80 (shown in columns 3 and 4 of Table 3.3), with the greatest number of immigrants to be found in the large metropolitan areas, particularly in the North and West. Nevertheless, some changes can be noted between the two periods. There have been substantial increases in the numbers of immigrants arriving from Latin America and Asia, enhancing the importance of the large West Coast metropolitan areas as entry ports. In 1975–80 greater net immigration was also being directed to large and medium-size southern cities that tend to attract migrants from Latin American origins.

The distinctly different destination patterns of international immigration tended to 'cushion' the strong counterurbanization tendencies displayed by internal migrants. As a consequence of immigration, the overall net out-migration shown for the North's large metropolitan areas (columns 5 and 6 of Table 3.3) is 40 per cent lower than for internal migration for 1975–80. Moreover, immigration accounts for 50 per cent and 76 per cent, respectively, of total net in-migration to large metropolitan areas in the South and West. The continued rise in immigrants from Latin America and Asia serve to reinforce metropolitan growth in the South and West, while the substantial number of immigrants that still opt for the large metropolitan areas in the North serve to counter the impact of deconcentration-related internal migration processes there.

Migrant selectivity

Are the new deconcentration-related migration processes represented among all population subgroups? Or do they reflect a redistribution of migrants with particular social and demographic characteristics? The answers to these questions provide insight to the generality of the counterurbanization phenomenon in the United States. While an exhaustive inventory of migrant selectivity is beyond the scope of this chapter, the following discussion focuses on two significant dimensions of selective migration in America – selectivity by age, and selectivity by race.

Age selectivity

During the initial migration surges toward the southern and western sunbelt regions and toward amenity-laden counties within those regions, a good deal of attention focused on the importance of the so-called 'footloose' population for this growth. The latter population represents those who are out of the labour force entirely, as well as individuals whose work is not permanently tied to a particular employment location. The retired elderly represent a significant component of the footloose population. This population was thought to contribute heavily to the counterurbanization phenomenon that was beginning to emerge.

Subsequent research has verified that elderly migration did indeed play a pioneering role in the counterurbanization phenomenon (Fuguitt and Tordella 1980; Lichter *et al.* 1981; Heaton 1983; and Longino *et al.* 1984). Non-metropolitan counties that attract large numbers of elderly migrants have registered higher rates of growth and net in-migration than almost any other class of non-metropolitan counties (Beale and Fuguitt 1978a; Beale and Fuguitt 1985). The strong participation of this footloose segment of the population raises the question of the generality of the counterurbanization phenomenon across other age categories.

In many respects, the 25–34 age group represents a much more significant segment of the population with regard to its migration behaviour and attachment to the labour force. It is during these ages, after all, that migration levels are high and the destinations migrants select tend to be relatively permanent (Frey 1986). The strong attachment to the labour force of these migrants is also significant. A greater tendency toward counterurbanization, displayed by this group, would suggest that the 'down the size hierarchy' redistribution is linked to a similar redistribution of employment opportunities.

Net internal migration rates for the nation's elderly (ages 65 and above) and 25–34 year olds are shown in Table 3.5. The last two columns indicate the net migration rates of each age category for the 1965–70 and 1975–80 periods, respectively. Already in the 1960s, the elderly population displayed some hint of a 'down the size hierarchy' redistribution. This can

Table 3.5 United States: in-, out-, and net migration rates, 1965–70 and 1975–80, for regional and metropolitan categories, ages 25–34 and 65+

Region and metropolitan categories/ Age at 1970, 1980	In-migration rate[a]		Out-migration rate[b]		Net internal migration rate[c]	
	1965–70	1975–80	1965–70	1975–80	1965–70	1975–80
AGES 25–34						
NORTH						
Large metropolitan	+26.0	+26.2	−25.9	−30.4	+0.1	−4.2
Other metropolitan	+29.2	+27.4	−29.2	−31.4	0.0	−4.0
Non-metropolitan	+30.9	+31.1	−34.0	−32.0	−3.1	−0.9
SOUTH						
Large metropolitan	+38.5	+37.6	−29.5	−31.4	+9.0	+6.2
Other metropolitan	+33.5	+33.8	−37.1	−34.1	−3.6	−0.3
Non-metropolitan	+27.3	+28.4	−33.2	−26.8	−5.9	+1.6
WEST						
Large metropolitan	+35.7	+33.5	−30.1	−29.7	+5.6	+3.8
Other metropolitan	+38.0	+36.7	−40.0	−33.2	−2.0	+3.5
Non-metropolitan	+43.1	+44.7	−48.1	−36.8	−5.0	+7.9
AGE 65+						
NORTH						
Large metropolitan	+ 6.9	+ 6.2	−10.9	−11.2	−4.0	−5.0
Other metropolitan	+ 7.2	+ 6.2	− 8.1	− 7.6	−0.9	−1.4
Non-metropolitan	+ 9.3	+ 8.3	− 9.1	− 8.1	+0.2	+0.2
SOUTH						
Large metropolitan	+17.3	+13.5	−10.6	− 9.8	+6.7	+3.7
Other metropolitan	+11.3	+11.1	− 8.2	− 7.1	+3.1	+4.0
Non-metropolitan	+ 8.5	+ 9.1	− 8.0	− 6.6	+0.5	+2.5
WEST						
Large metropolitan	+14.0	+12.2	−12.1	−11.3	+1.9	+0.9
Other metropolitan	+14.0	+12.9	−10.4	− 8.8	+3.6	+4.1
Non-metropolitan	+14.2	+14.7	−13.8	−11.9	+0.4	+2.8

Notes: [a] (In-migrants/Beginning-of-period population) × 100
[b] (Out-migrants/Beginning-of-period population) × 100
[c] (In-migrants − Out-migrants/Beginning-of-period population) × 100
Source: Compiled from data made available by US Bureau of the Census

be seen in the strong out-migration shown for the North's large metropolitan areas and the net in-migration associated with non-metropolitan areas in the South and West. South large metropolitan areas – particularly Miami, Florida – attracted large numbers of elderly as well. This counterurbanization-related migration of the elderly in the late 1960s was not shared by the 25–34 year old population. The latter population's migration patterns during this period were generally consistent with the long-standing urbanization model. In each region, non-metropolitan areas experienced net out-migration and the greatest migration gains were enjoyed by the large metropolitan areas in the region.

By the later 1970s the patterns for the 25–34 year olds had changed in such a way that both elderly and 'prime age' populations exhibited counterurbanization-related patterns then. Within each region except the South, 25–34 year olds registered greater net in-migration (or reduced net out-migration) in non-metropolitan areas than in the large or small metropolitan area categories in the region. Although in the South large metropolitan areas still exhibited net in-migration, this rate is lower than that observed in the late 1960s. Furthermore, non-metropolitan areas in the South have experienced a switch from significant net out-migration of 25–34 year olds in 1965–70 to net in-migration in 1975–80. The elderly population displays an even more accentuated 'down the size hierarchy' redistribution with the late 1970s. Particularly in the South and West, small metropolitan areas and non-metropolitan areas show significant increases in net in-migration as compared with the late 1960s.

These late-1970s net migration rates are consistent with the view that the counterurbanization process is a general one that includes both the elderly footloose population as well as individuals in their prime mobility and labour force ages. This pervasive 'down the size hierarchy' redistribution of residence and employment opportunities is also consistent with the deconcentration perspective's view of post-1970s redistribution patterns in the United States.

Race selectivity

Another important selectivity dimension involves the differences in migration patterns of blacks from the remainder of the population. The black population in the United States has, historically, displayed migration and distribution patterns that differed from the remainder of the population. Initially concentrated in the rural South, blacks migrated in great numbers to selected metropolitan areas in the North and later the West since the 1920s. Within metropolitan areas, blacks were generally confined to segregated centrally located neighbourhoods and communities, while the rest of the population proceeded to suburbanize. These unique redistribution patterns of blacks have to do, in part, with their lower levels of education and income which limited their access to housing and employment opportunities. However, more important than their relative economic status, blacks had been subject to widespread discrimination in labour and housing markets which led to their concentration in particular neighbourhoods, metropolitan areas, and regions (Taeuber and Taeuber 1965; Taeuber 1975; Frey and Speare 1988).

Since the mid-1960s, the black population has achieved significant social and economic gains and has, as well, received greater legal protections against discrimination in education, employment, and housing (Farley 1984). Nevertheless, their spatial redistribution patterns still tend to lag behind the majority of the population (Heaton *et al.* 1982; Lichter *et al.* 1986). It is for this reason that an evaluation of black participation in the post-1970 counterurbanization process will provide insights into the generality of that process. The net migration rates in Table 3.6 permit such an assessment. Here, migration rates for the black population and the non-black population can be contrasted for the 1960s and late 1970s.

In the 1965–70 period, black migration patterns conform more closely to the traditional urbanization model than do those of the remainder of the population. Largest metropolitan areas in all three regions experience net in-migration of blacks and the non-metropolitan territories of each region sustain net out-migration. The black net out-migration is especially high for non-metropolitan areas in the South during this period – although rates of net out-migration for blacks in all three regions' non-metropolitan territories is greater than that for non-blacks in those territories. While non-black redistribution patterns in the late 1960s generally conform to the urbanization model, one finds an exception for the large metropolitan areas in the North. Already in this period, these areas display a significant net out-migration for non-blacks.

By the late 1970s, both blacks and non-blacks were exhibiting counterurbanization-related migration patterns (Table 3.6). These patterns are more consistent for non-blacks where, even in the South, non-metropolitan

Table 3.6 United States: Internal in-, out-, and net migration rates, 1965–70 and 1975–80, for regional and metropolitan categories, Blacks and Non-blacks

Region and metropolitan categories/ Race	In-migration rate		Out-migration rate		Net internal migration rate	
	1965–70	1975–80	1965–70	1975–80	1965–70	1975–80
BLACK						
NORTH						
Large metropolitan	+ 8.5	+ 8.1	− 6.7	−10.8	+1.8	−2.7
Other metropolitan	+14.8	+13.0	−10.3	−12.7	+4.5	+0.3
Non-metropolitan	+23.3	+27.2	−25.8	−23.8	−2.5	+3.4
SOUTH						
Large metropolitan	+12.1	+13.6	− 9.3	−11.6	+2.8	+2.0
Other metropolitan	+ 9.9	+12.9	−11.7	−10.6	−1.8	+2.3
Non-metropolitan	+ 7.5	+ 9.4	−14.2	−11.4	−6.7	−2.0
WEST						
Large metropolitan	+16.2	+16.5	− 9.4	−12.0	+6.8	+4.5
Other metropolitan	+25.7	+29.4	−23.5	−22.1	+2.2	+7.3
Non-metropolitan	+32.9	+37.6	−36.2	−33.3	−3.3	+4.3
NON-BLACK						
NORTH						
Large metropolitan	+13.9	+13.9	−16.2	−19.0	−2.3	−5.1
Other metropolitan	+15.9	+15.7	−15.9	−17.2	−0.0	−1.5
Non-metropolitan	+17.1	+17.6	−18.8	−17.9	−1.7	−0.3
SOUTH						
Large metropolitan	+26.0	+24.6	−19.9	−21.7	+6.1	+2.9
Other metropolitan	+23.4	+23.3	−21.5	−20.4	+1.9	+2.9
Non-metropolitan	+18.2	+19.4	−19.6	−15.9	−1.4	+3.5
WEST						
Large metropolitan	+22.3	+20.6	−19.2	−19.6	+3.1	+1.0
Other metropolitan	+24.4	+24.0	−22.2	−19.4	+2.2	+4.6
Non-metropolitan	+25.6	+27.9	−28.0	−22.6	−2.4	+5.3

Note: see Table 3.5 for notes on rates
Source: Compiled from data made available by US Bureau of the Census

growth exceeds metropolitan growth, but similar tendencies are seen for the black population in all three regions. The role of net out-migration from non-metropolitan areas fell sharply between the late 1960s and the late 1970s in the South, and switched to net gain in the North and West. Although black metropolitan gains still outdistance non-metropolitan gains (or losses) in the South and West, the disparities between metropolitan and non-metropolitan categories have become considerably reduced. Moreover, in the North a consistent 'down the size hierarchy' migration process is observed for the black population in the late 1970s. Here large metropolitan areas sustained a significant net out-migration of both blacks and non-blacks. Clearly, the black population has participated in the same counterurbanization distribution tendencies as the total population. This provides additional support for the thesis that the late 1970s counterurbanization phenomenon was a pervasive one.

Conclusion

What can be concluded about the future of counterurbanization in the United States? Do the patterns of the early 1980s possess elements of the strong counterurbanization tendencies of the 1970s? Or is there a reversion to the more traditional urbanization tendencies that characterized American population redistribution for most of the prior century? How can the post-1970 patterns be explained? Are they influenced largely by period-specific events? Do they follow from a more fundamental deconcentration of residence and employment opportunities? Or do they represent new economic restructuring of regions and places? The data and studies that were reviewed in this chapter can provide only tentative answers to these questions, but they do allow for some speculations about the future of regional and metropolitan area change.

The strong counterurbanization tendencies of the 1970s have, indeed, subsided in the early 1980s. What began as a redistribution of population 'down the size hierarchy' of metropolitan areas has turned into a redistribution of population across regions. As the North sustained reduced levels of population growth and the South and West enjoyed increases, the growth differences across metropolitan categories *within regions* have narrowed. Still, the early 1980s redistribution patterns in the North and West only faintly resemble the traditional urbanization model of pre-1970 decades, while the continued urbanization displayed in the South is far less accentuated than was the case in the 1960s, despite not having reached such a high level of metropolitanization as the other two regions. Another significant difference between the early 1980s and the 1960s is the higher rate of growth shown for non-metropolitan areas. Clearly, there are elements of the counterurbanization phenomenon still evident in the early 1980s but they are most apparent when contrasted with pre-1970 redistribution patterns.

Each of the three redistribution explanations has been given some support in this analysis. Period-specific influences have accounted for some of the early 1970s non-metropolitan growth of counties engaged in resource extraction and those which served as retirement locations for the large cohorts who entered into their elderly years during this decade. The mid-decade recession and stiffer international competition for manufac-tured goods led to the accentuation of out-migration from many large industrial metropolitan areas during the 1970s. The regional restructuring perspective appears also to be helpful in explaining the early 1980s growth upturns in several northern corporate, financial, and diversified service centres, as well as in explaining the continued decline of other metropoli-tan and non-metropolitan areas that specialize in old-line industrial activities.

Yet, beyond these period and regional restructuring influences, a more pervasive deconcentration influence has continued to affect the nation's broad redistribution tendencies. While the 1980s brought some upward shift in population growth in several large metropolitan areas in the nation's 'core region' these growth rates were generally significantly lower than the levels these northern areas enjoyed in the 1960s and in earlier decades. Furthermore, the 1980s growth rates displayed by non-metropolitan areas in the South and West 'peripheral' regions remain considerably higher than the negligible or negative population growth rates these areas encountered prior to 1970.

A fundamental post-1970 shift in the nation's redistribution processes is particularly evident in the changes which took place in internal migration streams between the late 1960s and the late 1970s. The underlying structure of internal migration switched almost completely from a predominantly 'up the size hierarchy' redistribution of population to one that filters migrants in the opposite direction. This reversal in the migration process is evident in analyses of broad region and metropolitan categories, in the analyses of flows which affect individual metropolitan areas, and in the selectivity patterns of specific population subgroups. Until the results of the 1990 census are available, it will not be possible to assess the structure of the late 1980s internal migration streams. However, given the fun-damental changes that took place with the 1970s and the apparent continuation of counterurbanization-related growth patterns, it does not appear likely that a consistent 'up the size hierarchy' redistribution process has returned. Rather, some combination of the two earlier processes has probably come into being.

This being the case, it is instructive to compare the long-term redistribution implications of these two 'ideal type' internal migration processes. This comparison is possible from the alternative projections shown in Figure 3.4. Displayed here are two alternative projections of population size for each of the nine metropolitan categories used in the earlier analysis. Each of the two projections, for each area, begin in the year 1980 and project that area's population size over the 50-year period 1980–2030. One of these projections assumes that the 1965–70 age-specific migration rates will be followed by population cohorts over the 50-year period. The second projection assumes that the 1975–80 migration rates will be followed by these same cohorts. Both projections begin with the same (actual) 1980 area population and assume the same fertility and mortality rates. They differ only in the migration assumptions that are used.

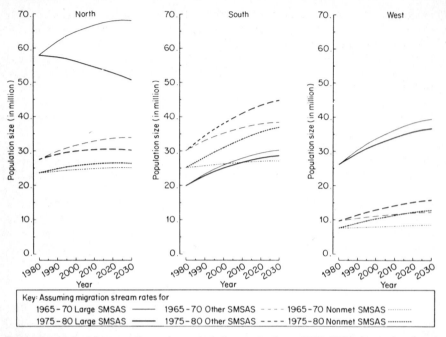

Figure 3.4 United States: alternative population projections, 1980–2030, for regional and metropolitan groupings, assuming 1965–70 and 1975–80 migration rates (see text for further details of method). Source: Frey, 1987.

It is clear that the late 1960s-based projection leads to continued growth of large metropolitan areas in the North and negligible growth in non-metropolitan territory for all three regions. In contrast, the late 1970s-based projections lead to a significant decline for large metropolitan areas in the North over the 50-year period. They also lead to projected gains for non-metropolitan areas and small metropolitan areas in the South and West. While a continued urbanization of the nation's population is projected with the late 1960s rates, a significant counterurbanization is projected with the late 1970s rates. If the *actual* migration rates conform to the mixed redistribution patterns of the early 1980s, it is likely that future regional and metropolitan redistribution will lie somewhere in-between.

It is the view here that the 1970s represented a 'transition decade' in the history of US regional and metropolitan population redistribution. The strong counterurbanization observed during this decade constitutes, in part, a response to period-specific economic shocks and the beginning of some economic restructuring of the nation's regions and places. Yet continued improvements in transportation, communication, and production technologies have freed production organizations, employers and residents from the friction of space that fostered earlier urbanization tendencies. Although the prediction of a continued and pervasive counterurbanization of the population may not be warranted, it is clear that both residents and employers have at their disposal a greater degree of locational flexibility than ever before. While future redistribution tendencies in the United States may evolve in directions now unforeseen, they will not be subject to the same proximity and location constraints that dictated the patterns of the past.

Acknowledgements

The analyses presented in this chapter were supported by Grant No. HD17168 from the Centre for Population Research of the National Institute of Child Health and Human Development and by the Russell Sage Foundation in association with the National Committee for Research on the 1980 Census. The author has benefited from discussions with Alden Speare, drawing from their collaboration on the volume *Regional and metropolitan growth and decline in the United States* (New York: Russell Sage, 1988). Computer programming assistance was rendered by Cathy Sun.

Further reading

Three volumes from the 1980 Census Monograph Series, 'The Population of the United States in the 1980s', provide the reader with additional details of the regional, metropolitan, and rural–urban population redistribution patterns that have occurred within the United States during the 1970s and early 1980s: Frey, W.H. and Speare, A. Jr. 1988: *Regional and metropolitan growth and decline in the United States* (New York: Russell Sage); Long, L.H. 1988: *Migration and residential mobility in the United States* (New York: Russell Sage); and Fuguitt, G.V. and Beale, C.L. 1989: *Rural and small town America* (New York: Russell Sage).

Recent developments in the non-metropolitan turnaround are examined by: Fuguitt, G.V. 1985: The non-metropolitan population turnaround, *Annual Review of Sociology* 11, 259–80; and Richter, K. 1985: Non-metropolitan growth in the late 1970s: the end of the turnaround? *Demography* 22, 245–62.

4

Australia:

the spatial concentration of the turnaround

GRAEME HUGO

Since 1970 there have been several major, and largely unanticipated, shifts in Australia's demography – unprecedented declines in fertility, increases in longevity of older people, ageing of the overall population structure, massive changes in family structure, and the transformation of international migration flows, to name but a few. Perhaps none have been so unexpected, however, as the phenomenon which has come to be known as 'The Turnaround' or 'Counterurbanization'. In the early 1970s Burnley (1974, 12) accurately summarized Australia's postwar experience with respect to changing patterns of population distribution between the various levels of the settlement hierarchy as follows . . .

> Australia has clearly emerged in the postwar world as one of the most urbanized countries in the world, whatever indices of urbanization are used as a measurement. The basic pattern has been the further increase in primacy of the metropolitan capital cities within their respective States; the rapid growth of two industrial non-metropolitan cities (Wollongong and Geelong) and the very rapid growth of the national capital, Canberra, with a notable absence of any intermediate-sized centres in the urban hierarchy of the respective States.

This chapter shows that in postwar Australia prior to 1970 there was a pattern of increasing concentration of population characterized not only by a growing percentage of national populations living in urban areas but also by growth in the share of that urban population residing in the largest centres. It is demonstrated that in common with most developed nations this pattern was reversed during the 1971–76 intercensal period, continued in the late 1970s and, unlike several other nations, was maintained into the 1980s. However, the turnaround in Australia is strongly concentrated in the most ecologically favourable parts of the non-metropolitan sector and vast areas continue to experience rural depopulation. A range of hypotheses regarding the turnaround is examined in the Australian context and it is concluded that any satisfactory explanation should include elements of expanded-urban-field, employment-led, welfare-led and lifestyle-led arguments. Finally, some of the impacts of the turnaround upon Australia's non-metropolitan population are examined and the growing convergence in the characteristics of metropolitan and non-metropolitan populations is demonstrated.

The nature and timing of counterurbanization in Australia

The long-term tendency toward concentration of the Australian population has shown a consistent pattern over the century prior to 1971 (Hugo 1986a). At the 1933 census, 37.4 per cent of Australians lived in rural areas but by 1961 this proportion had halved and in 1976 only 14.2 per cent of the population was classified as rural. The postwar pattern depicted in Table 4.1 was not just one of concentration in urban centres up to 1971 but a growing dominance of the largest metropolitan centres. Indeed the non-metropolitan share of the total national population progressively declined in the half century following 1921 from 57 to 40 per cent so that by 1971 three-fifths of all Australians lived in the large metropolitan capital cities. Between 1971 and 1976, however, the proportion of the population living in rural areas continued to decline (albeit marginally) but there was also a decline in the metropolitan areas' share of the total national population. Hence in the early 1970s the only sector to gain ground was that of non-metropolitan urban areas. In the 1976–81 intercensal period

Table 4.1 Australia: Population distribution and change, 1954–86, by type of settlement

Census year	Metropolitan total	Non-metropolitan			Australia total
		Total	Other urban	Rural	
SHARE (%)					
A. Floating boundaries					
1954	53.6	46.4	24.6	21.8	100.0
1961	56.0	44.0	25.7	18.3	100.0
1966	58.0	42.0	24.9	17.1	100.0
1971	60.4	39.6	25.0	14.6	100.0
1976	59.7	40.3	26.1	14.2	100.0
1981	58.3	41.7	27.4	14.4	100.0
1986	62.9	37.1	22.4	14.5	100.0
B. Fixed boundaries					
1976	63.9	36.1	22.1	13.9	100.0
1981	63.2	36.8	22.6	14.2	100.0
1986	62.9	37.1	22.4	14.5	100.0
PERIOD CHANGE RATE (%)					
A. Floating boundaries					
1954–61	22.3	10.8	21.8	− 1.6	16.9
1961–66	14.4	5.4	7.1	3.0	10.4
1966–71	14.3	3.7	10.3	− 6.0	9.8
1971–76	5.2	8.0	10.9	3.1	6.3
1976–81	5.0	11.5	12.9	9.0	7.6
1981–86	15.6	− 5.2	−12.2	8.2	6.9
B. Fixed boundaries					
1976–81	6.3	9.5	9.7	9.3	7.5
1981–86	6.7	7.8	6.4	9.8	7.1

Sources: Bowie, 1987: ABS, 1976, 1981, 1986 Censuses of Population and Housing

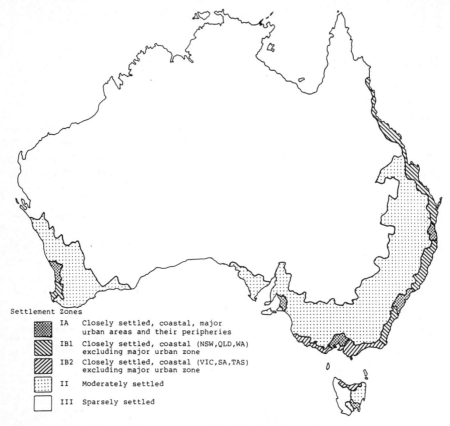

Settlement Zones

	IA	Closely settled, coastal, major urban areas and their peripheries
IB1		Closely settled, coastal (NSW,QLD,WA) excluding major urban zone
IB2		Closely settled, coastal (VIC,SA,TAS) excluding major urban zone
II		Moderately settled
III		Sparsely settled

Figure 4.1 Australia: settlement zones (after Goddard, 1983).

urban areas continued to increase their share at the expense of the largest metropolitan centres. However, for the first time this century the proportion of the total population living in non-metropolitan areas increased. In percentage terms these are fairly small changes but it is clear that they do represent a significant break with past trends.

Panel B in Table 4.1 adopts common boundaries to examine the distribution of population between cities with more than 100,000 residents, and other urban and rural areas over the decades 1976–86. It shows that there has been a slowdown in counterurbanization during the 1981–86 intercensal period. The intercensal population growth rate in metropolitan areas increased from 6.3 to 6.7 per cent from the late 70s to the early 80s while that of non-metropolitan areas fell from 9.5 to 7.8 per cent. This discrepancy between the official census figures in Panel A and those in Panel B is caused by the reclassification of five formerly separate urban centres on the central northern coast of New South Wales as a single metropolitan centre between 1981 and 1986. It is interesting to note in Panel B of Table 4.1 that there was a slight increase in the rate of rural population growth in the early 1980s but a significant reduction in the growth of non-metropolitan urban centres. Indeed the latter grew slightly more slowly than the metropolitan population between the 1981 and 1986 censuses.

It is important to note that the population turnaround has by no means been universal throughout Australian non-metropolitan areas. This can be readily demonstrated with reference to trends in various settlement zones identified by Goddard (1983). These were defined according to patterns of land use and associated population density levels and provide a useful framework for examining metropolitan/non-metropolitan population change. The zones and a brief description of them are shown in Figure 4.1.

The fastest growing areas are in the non-metropolitan but closely settled parts of coastal Queensland, New South Wales and southwest Western Australia (Zone IB1). Table 4.2 shows that the population of this zone grew at more than twice the national rate and three times as fast as the major metropolitan areas (Zone IA) at the height of the turnaround over the 1976–81 period. It should be stressed that the metropolitan areas are 'overbounded' by Goddard to take account of metropolitan overspill problems. Clearly the turnaround is spatially concentrated. Indeed the closely settled areas of South Australia, Victoria and Tasmania (Zone IB2) and the moderately settled wheat/sheep belt of all states (Zone II) recorded lower population growth rates than the metropolitan sector.

Table 4.2 also indicates the demographic components of the turnaround. There is a small but significant natural increase element involved, in that over the 1976–81 period natural increase rates were higher in each of the non-metropolitan sectors than in the overbounded metropolitan areas. This is a function of the intrinsically lower mortality levels in non-metropolitan areas (Hugo 1986a, Chapter 2), the higher fertility levels in the non-metropolitan sector (Hugo 1986a, Chapter 3) and the youthful age structure of non-metropolitan areas, especially the more remote areas (Category III) and closely settled parts of Queensland, New South Wales and Western Australia (Category IB1) (Hugo 1986a, Chapter 7). Nevertheless it is clear from Table 4.2 that net migration was the major component in the population turnaround in the major sector in which it has occurred – namely the closely settled (IB1) areas. In the remainder of non-metropolitan Australia net migration gains were lower than in the large metropolitan centres.

Table 4.2 Australia: Annual average population change and its components, by settlement zone, 1976–81, % per year

Settlement zone (see Fig. 4.1)	Natural increase	Net migration	Total change
IA	0.7	0.4	1.1
IB1	0.9	2.5	3.3
IB2	0.8	0.2	1.0
II	0.9	−0.1	0.9
III	1.5	0.2	1.8
Australia	0.8	0.5	1.2

Source: Goddard, 1983; Hugo, 1983a

Table 4.3 Australia: Annual average population change 1981–86, for metropolitan and non-metropolitan parts of States and Territories

State/Territory	Metropolitan (%)	Non-metropolitan (%)
New South Wales	0.90	1.53
Victoria	0.80	1.35
Queensland	2.25	2.57
South Australia	0.96	0.77
Western Australia	2.04	1.89
Tasmania	0.79	0.87
Northern Territory	3.50	5.78
Australian Capital Territory	2.42	−4.02
Australia	1.19	1.74

Source: ABS, 1981 and 1986 Censuses

The slowdown in counterurbanization during the 1980s has also been uneven in its spatial distribution. Table 4.3 shows that in most States and Territories the non-metropolitan population grew much faster than did metropolitan areas. Indeed in the three largest States along the eastern seaboard the non-metropolitan population grew substantially faster than that of the cities of Brisbane, Melbourne and Sydney. It is only in Western and South Australia that population growth rates in the capital exceeded those in non-metropolitan areas. In Western Australia this distinctive pattern may have been a function of the exceptional growth of Perth associated with the building and tourism booms linked with the America's Cup challenge. A second likely factor is the downturn in mining and agriculture which will have been felt especially hard in non-metropolitan Western Australia, since much of the growth of the 1970s was founded on the 'minerals boom'. In South Australia, too, these arguments would apply with Adelaide experiencing a building boom largely associated with tourism. The virtual city-state of Canberra has a negligible non-metropolitan population and little notice should be taken of its growth rate.

Further light can be shed upon non-metropolitan population change by adopting local areas as units of analysis. Table 4.4 summarizes the growth trends over the last decade for non-metropolitan Local Government Areas (LGAs) in each of the States. The top panel of the table indicates that the dominant trend has been for population growth in non-metropolitan areas to be sustained from the late 1970s into the early 1980s. The number of LGAs which experienced the 'flip-flop' of growth in the late 1970s and decline in the early 1980s was in fact slightly smaller than those which recorded a turnaround from decline to growth between the two periods (80 and 82 respectively). It is perhaps significant to note that Queensland was the State with the highest incidence of LGAs switching from growth to decline after being one of the major locations of the turnaround in the late 1970s. The lower panel of Table 4.4 focuses upon the non-metropolitan LGAs which recorded growth during both periods. This shows that the areas which increased their rate of growth (170) were somewhat fewer than those in which the rate decreased (211), though this can be explained in part by the lower level of population growth nationally (see Table 4.1).

Table 4.4 Australia: Proportion of non-metropolitan Local Government Areas (LGAs) with specified population change experiences, 1976–86, by States

Population change rates for 1976–81 and 1981–86 compared	Vic %	NSW %	Qld %	WA %	SA %	Tas %	Australia %	(N)
All LGAs	100	100	100	100	100	100	100	(695)
Growth in both periods	61	61	60	45	43	56	55	(383)
Growth, then decline	8	9	14	13	13	13	12	(80)
Decline, then growth	8	3	19	7	23	20	12	(82)
Decline in both periods	23	27	8	36	23	11	22	(150)
LGAs growing in both periods	100	100	100	100	100	100	100	(383)
Acceleration in growth	51	29	45	41	53	56	44	(170)
Deceleration in growth	48	71	54	59	47	44	55	(211)
No change	1	—	1	—	—	—	1	(2)

Note: The final column gives the number of LGAs in each category for Australia. The Australian totals include the LGAs of the Northern Territory and Australian Capital Territory
Source: ABS 1976 and 1981 Censuses; Resident population estimates by state offices of ABS

Overall, then, the data suggest some slowing down in the deconcentration trends since the late 1970s and early 1980s but there is much less evidence of renewed population concentration than in the United States. This is in spite of the existence in Australia of some new tendencies which would appear to be working toward population concentration and are perhaps responsible for the US pattern. These include increased fossil fuel prices (which are substantially higher than in the US), increased immigration from overseas (immigrants settling disproportionately in large cities), an agricultural crisis of similar severity to that being experienced in the US heartland, and the revival of inner cities through gentrification, policies of urban renewal and urban consolidation, and other factors.

The role of international migration in metropolitan growth

One-fifth of Australia's population was born overseas. Only Israel among the world's nations has a higher proportion of foreign-born residents. Accordingly, where immigrants settle has a significant impact upon spatial variations in population growth within Australia. It is important to stress that postwar immigrants have settled in disproportionately (in relation to the total population) large numbers in the largest urban centres. Table 4.5A shows that during the first two decades after the Second World War half of the population growth of Australia's urban centres was attributable to the net gain of migrants from overseas, while only 7 per cent was due to net gains from elsewhere in Australia. When it is considered that a substantial part of the natural increase component of metropolitan growth was children born to overseas immigrants, it can be conservatively estimated that more than two-thirds of the growth in the State capital cities was attributable to immigration. It is apparent from Table 4.5a that there were

Table 4.5 Australia's major capital cities: Components of population change, 1947–66 and 1976–81

Statistical division		Natural increase	Net migration			Total population increase
			Overseas	Internal	Total	
A. 1947–66						
Sydney	000s	379	441	17	457	836
	%	45.3	52.7	2.0	· 54.7	100.0
Melbourne	000s	366	485	6	491	857
	%	42.7	56.6	0.7	57.3	100.0
Brisbane	000s	124	79	84	163	287
	%	43.1	27.5	29.4	56.9	100.0
Adelaide	000s	104	171	42	213	318
	%	32.9	54.0	13.1	67.1	100.0
Perth	000s	93	105	33	138	231
	%	40.3	45.4	14.3	59.7	100.0
Hobart	000s	29	16	4	20	49
	%	58.5	32.8	8.7	41.5	100.0
Total	000s	1094	1297	186	1483	2578
	%	42.5	50.3	7.2	57.5	100.0
B. 1976–81						
Sydney	000s	115	78	−58	21	136
	%	84.9	57.8	−42.6	15.1	100.0
Melbourne	000s	103	35	−56	−20	83
	%	124.9	42.7	−67.2	−24.5	100.0
Brisbane	000s	41	26	29	55	95
	%	42.7	27.4	29.9	57.3	100.0
Adelaide	000s	29	5	−4	1	30
	%	95.4	16.9	−12.3	4.6	100.0
Perth	000s	39	31	19	50	89
	%	44.2	35.0	20.8	55.8	100.0
Hobart	000s	9	0	−2	−2	7
	%	134.9	1.5	−36.4	−34.9	100.0
Total	000s	336	176	−72	104	440
	%	76.4	40.1	−16.5	23.6	100.0

Note: Absolute numbers have been rounded to nearest thousand
Source: Commonwealth Bureau of Census and Statistics, 1962, 1967; Burnley, 1974; ABS, Vital Statistics State Offices and 1976 and 1981 Censuses of Population and Housing

substantial variations between the State capitals in the significance of net immigration gains in postwar population growth. The importance of immigration in the growth of the nation's two major metropolitan centres, Sydney and Melbourne, is readily apparent. Adelaide, too, was an important focus of international migration with the considerable expansion of its manufacturing industries during the early postwar years. Brisbane, on the other hand, was the only capital city to record larger net gains from internal migration than from international migration.

If we turn to the peak period of the turnaround (1976–81) it can be seen from Table 4.5B that net overseas migration was a major component in population growth in all State capitals except the smallest, Hobart. In particular, it contributed more than half of the intercensal increase in Sydney and over two-fifths in Melbourne. In Sydney this net gain more than counterbalanced the net loss of population due to internal migration. In Melbourne, however, net international migration gains were only half as large as in Sydney, while the internal migration loss was of similar dimensions, so that an overall net migration loss was sustained.

This pattern contrasts sharply with that prevailing over the 1947–66 period shown in Table 4.5A in the following ways. First, Sydney's absolute population growth was substantially higher than Melbourne's in 1976–81, while Melbourne grew slightly faster in the earlier period. Secondly, both recorded small net internal migration gains over 1947–66, while both had major net losses in 1976–81. Thirdly, Melbourne recorded more net population gains due to international migration than Sydney in the early period, in contrast to the situation in 1976–81. Lastly, overall net migration accounted for more than half of the population growth in 1947–66, but in the later period it accounted for only 15 per cent of Sydney's growth while Melbourne had a net loss.

It is interesting to note in Table 4.5B that population increases in both Perth and Brisbane were greater than that in Melbourne between 1976 and 1981. In both of these cities net internal migration gains were a significant element of growth while in all the other capitals net losses were sustained. These two cities are also distinctive in the 1976–81 period in the comparatively low proportion of their population growth which was due to natural increase. Clearly Table 4.5B supports the contention that the turnaround has been achieved by persons already established in Australian major cities moving to non-metropolitan localities or those already residing in such areas deciding not to move out to the metropolitan sector.

The role of international migration can be best illustrated by examining the components of postwar growth in the two largest cities of Sydney and Melbourne. Figure 4.2 shows that up to 1971 in Sydney and 1966 in

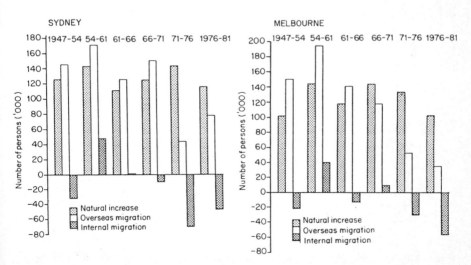

Figure 4.2 Australia: components of population change, 1947–81, for the Sydney and Melbourne statistical divisions. Source: ABS.

Melbourne net international migration was the most important component of population growth. In the subsequent intercensal periods, although natural increase has assumed the mantle of the predominant component of growth, immigration has remained significant, even though the 1970s was a period of significant downturn in Australia's intake of immigrants (Hugo 1986a). On the other hand, we can note from Figure 4.2 the substantial net losses incurred by the two cities through internal migration during the 1970s. The net losses by internal migration of 1947–54 in Figure 4.2 appear aberrant but are due to the expansion of both cities well beyond their official boundaries during this period. Sydney and Melbourne suffered a combined net loss of over 100,000 persons due to net internal migration in 1976–81. Those cities, however, experienced a slightly larger net migration gain from international migration. This points to the 'switchover function'

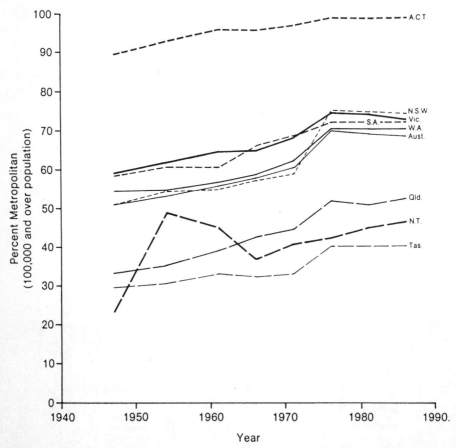

Figure 4.3 Australian States and Territories: proportion of total population living in cities with 10,000 or more inhabitants at each Census year, 1947–86. Source: Bowie, 1987; ABS Censuses.

(Maher and McKay 1986) of Australia's major cities, especially Sydney and Melbourne, whereby a net loss of migrants in exchange with other parts of Australia is more than counterbalanced by an inflow of overseas migrants.

The end result of these patterns is that, while in 1986 58 per cent of the Australian-born population lived in the major urban centres, these cities housed 79 per cent of the overseas-born. Moreover, while there was a fall of two percentage points between 1976 and 1986 in the proportion of the Australian-born living in major cities, the fall for overseas-born was only one percentage point. Hence, the metropolitan turnaround has clearly impinged more upon the Australian-born than the overseas-born population.

Spatial concentration of the turnaround

The extent and nature of urbanization and counterurbanization has varied considerably between different regions of Australia during the postwar period. Figure 4.3 shows the proportion of the population of each State and

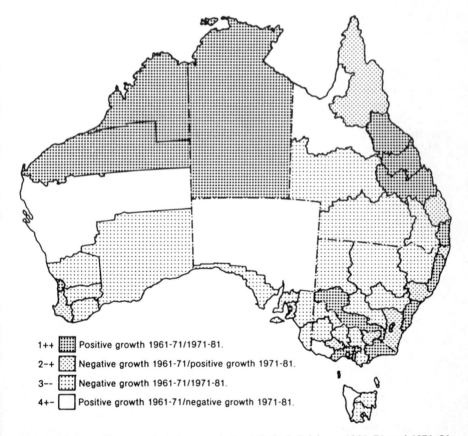

1++ Positive growth 1961-71/1971-81.

2-+ Negative growth 1961-71/positive growth 1971-81.

3-- Negative growth 1961-71/1971-81.

4+- Positive growth 1961-71/negative growth 1971-81.

Figure 4.4 Australia: net migration trends in statistical divisions, 1961–71 and 1971–81. Source: Hugo and Smailes, 1985.

Territory living in metropolitan centres. Clearly there are significant variations ranging between the virtual city-state of the Australian Capital Territory and Tasmania with its non-primate urban system (Scott 1964). In all cases, however, a levelling off or decline in the proportion of the population living in large cities is in evidence after 1976. The pattern is most marked in New South Wales and Victoria, the two largest States.

Turning to a spatial breakdown of the turnaround, the overall pattern of regional net migration trends in Australia during the 1960s and 1970s is shown in Figure 4.4. In this map estimates of net migration derived using life-table survival-ratio techniques (Hugo 1984) for all Australian statistical divisions during the 1960s and 1970s have been divided into four categories of trends. The first category shows statistical divisions which recorded an overall net migration gain in both the 1961–71 and 1971–81 decades. Dominant here are the metropolitan statistical divisions, Perth, Adelaide, Hobart, Melbourne, Canberra, Sydney and Brisbane, but it was pointed out earlier that in recent years these net gains in metropolitan areas have declined somewhat. Most striking on the map, however, is the northwest-ern quadrant of the continent comprising the northern part of Western Australia and the Northern Territory. This is a little misleading since, although these areas are huge, the numbers of people involved are small. The third area with consistent net migration gains is also in the north and is the cluster of statistical divisions in central coastal Queensland. There are several other statistical divisions strung along the east coast further to the south which also recorded net migration gains over the past two decades. Several of these are divisions adjoining the three largest Australian cities. In these 'adjacent' areas the net gains during the 1970s were much greater than those recorded in the 1960s. The final region recording net migration gains over the last twenty years was the Murray River Valley which forms much of the boundary between New South Wales and Victoria.

The second category on the map represents areas which experienced a 'turnaround' from net migration losses between 1971 and 1981. These types of region are confined to a few coastal non-metropolitan divisions along the eastern, southeastern and southwestern coasts. Again, as with the areas of consistent net migration gain several are located in the adjacent areas, i.e. those areas near major metropolitan centres on the margins of, and slightly beyond, the commuting zones of those cities. It will be noted in Figure 4.4 that the central east coast as well as three nuclei around Melbourne, Adelaide and Perth experienced either consistent net migration gains or a turnaround to net gains in the 1970s. In Victoria there were two inland statistical divisions that recorded net losses in the 1960s but net gains in the 1970s. These were the regions focused on the growing regional centres of Ballarat and Albury-Wodonga.

The third category in Figure 4.4 includes a broad continuous belt of statistical divisions inland of the coastal net gains zone. This is an area of consistent net migration losses through both the 1960s and 1970s and covers almost the entire wheat/sheep agricultural zone of Australia. It should be noted that the net migration losses in this region were generally smaller during the 1970s than in the 1960s. This zone is particularly extensive in southern Queensland, western New South Wales, western

Victoria and southern parts of South and Western Australia. No Tasmanian non-metropolitan statistical divisions recorded net migration gains in the 1960s or the 1970s and the eastern half of the island recorded consistent net migration losses throughout the 1960s and 1970s.

The final category of a reversal from net migration gains in the 1960s to net migration losses in the 1970s covers extensive areas, predominantly in the sparsely settled arid zone of central Western Australia, northern South Australia and central northern Queensland. In the latter area a major element has been the fortunes of Mount Isa where the expansion of mining activity in the 1960s saw its population double from 13,358 in 1961 to 25,497 in 1971. Population growth based on expansion of mining activity is notoriously fragile as fluctuations in world markets and/or exhaustion of local ore deposits can produce abrupt reversals to which Australia's large number of mining ghost towns bear mute testimony. The downturn in activity at Mount Isa has seen its population decline to 24,390 in 1981. This volatility of mining-based population growth must be borne in mind in considering the recent population expansion across the north of Australia. The reversal in central Western Australia and the unincorporated area of South Australia was also partly associated with a decline in mining activity, but in the latter case it was predominantly due to the virtual closure of the Woomera-Maralinga defence research area during the 1970s after it had grown rapidly during the 1960s. The reversal of net gain in western Tasmania was also associated with a downturn in mining activity. The southwest of Victoria was the only statistical division recording this type of population change which was not in an arid and/or mining zone.

Hence it is clear that the non-metropolitan renaissance in Australia is very uneven spatially, being concentrated predominantly in the well-watered and attractive areas of the south-east and east coast. On the other hand, while net migration data show the areas which have experienced population growth and decline due to migration, they do not give any indication of the origin of in-migrants and the destination of out-migrants. To gain some impression of these flows we will focus upon the peak 'turnaround' period of 1976–81. If we examine gross migration flows for the IB1 zone which was shown above to account for the majority of non-metropolitan net migration gains, it is clear that there is a high degree of reciprocity with other settlement zones. Figure 4.5 shows that the major source of in-migrants to the closely settled non-metropolitan coastal areas of New South Wales, Queensland and Western Australia is the major metropolitan areas of those States which provide some 60 per cent of all in-migrants. Again, however, it should be noted that there is a substantial, albeit significantly smaller, flow in the opposite direction.

Having established the dominance of outward flow from metropolitan areas in the migration into these 'adjacent' zones, a crucial question becomes the extent to which these migrants maintain work based within the metropolitan area. It is also important to note the relative smallness of the inflow of persons from overseas to Zone IB1, especially since against it we should put an unknown number of residents of the zone who have subsequently moved overseas. The diagram shows that there were also significant inflows and net gains from the moderately and sparsely settled

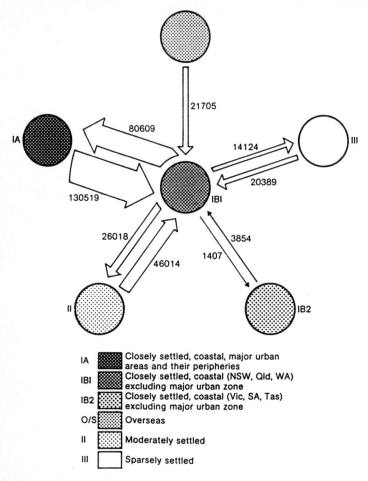

21705

80609

14124

20389

130519

IBI

26018

3854

46014

1407

II

IB2

IA	Closely settled, coastal, major urban areas and their peripheries
IBI	Closely settled, coastal (NSW, Qld, WA) excluding major urban zone
IB2	Closely settled, coastal (Vic, SA, Tas) excluding major urban zone
O/S	Overseas
II	Moderately settled
III	Sparsely settled

Figure 4.5 Australia: migration to and from Settlement Zone IB1, 1976–81. Source: 1981 Census Internal Migration Tapes.

agricultural zones. Certainly in the non-metropolitan areas adjoining the capital cities back-commuting is of significance. To take one example, the small but growing LGA of Mallala, north of Adelaide, experienced a 38 per cent increase between 1976 and 1981 in the number of residents who worked in Metropolitan Adelaide and an 8 per cent decline in those working within the LGA. Several case studies have documented the expansion of hobby farming (often in association with extra-urban commuting over extended distances) in the areas surrounding Australia's major cities (Menzies and Bell 1981; McQuinn 1978; Paterson *et al.* 1978; Williams 1972).

Explaining population deconcentration in Australia

Greater population retention by non-metropolitan areas

An understanding of shifts in the balance of growth rates between Australia's metropolitan and non-metropolitan areas needs to take account not only of shifts in patterns of net internal migration but also of the fact that non-metropolitan areas have been much more successful during the 1970s in retaining people who, if the 1960s patterns would have continued, would have moved to large metropolitan areas. Whether this has been due to increased job, educational and other opportunities outside the metropolitan areas or a decline in perceived opportunities in the large cities has not been established definitively by empirical research. Nevertheless, there are indications that there has been greater retention of population in non-metropolitan areas. This especially applies to school leavers. Wright (1982) made a study of school leavers in the south-east region of South Australia, using school records, a survey of the class of 1982 and census data, and established that there was a significant increase in the retention rate of school leavers in the 1970s. During the 1966–71 intercensal period there was a net out-migration of more than 10 per cent of persons aged 10 to 19 (a net loss of 1,015 persons). However, in the 1971–76 period the net loss was reduced to around 3 per cent of the age group (229 net loss). *Non-migration* is thus a significant factor in the turnaround in Australia. The impact of this element is reinforced by the fact that the retained people are selectively from the young adult age groups and so they are likely to have a positive impact on natural increases when they begin family formation.

Nevertheless, the major demographic element in the turnaround has been the reversal of the gradient of the metropolitan/non-metropolitan net migration balance. It is therefore the explanation of this phenomenon to which the main part of this section is devoted. The major forces which have increased metropolitan to non-metropolitan moves and/or reduced the flow in the opposite direction in Australia have been reviewed by several authors (e.g. Bell 1978; Jarvie 1981; Hugo and Smailes 1985; Hugo 1987). Four lines of explanation seem most relevant to the Australian context, namely the 'expanding urban fields' approach, the 'job-led' structural change hypothesis, the 'life-style' hypothesis relating to residential preferences, and the 'welfare-led' approach.

The expanding urban fields approach

This line of explanation 'postulates a scaled-up continuation of the same basic processes of suburbanization and extension of metropolitan commuting hinterlands as occurred in the 1950s and 1960s, with the metropolis exerting a perhaps more tenuous but still dominant influence on the location of new employment opportunities and residential choices' (Hugo and Smailes 1985, 12). The fact that, as has been demonstrated above, much of the non-metropolitan population growth and net migration gain has been recorded in the IB1 and IB2 densely settled zones must lend some support to this theory. It has been demonstrated elsewhere (Hugo 1988) that during the last decade or so in Australia there has been a major increase in the forces which have produced this rural–urban convergence. These forces are manifold and well known. Especially important are the greatly increased levels of individual mobility which have been afforded by exponential increases in motor vehicle ownership; great improvements in, and widened access to, a range of modes of public transport (including air travel); road building and improvement programmes, real increases in personal incomes and real reductions in the unit costs of virtually all forms of travel.

The influences of this personal mobility revolution are many, affecting both urban and rural populations. Rural residents can travel more frequently to urban centres to purchase services and be influenced by the different life-styles and attitudes, the reverse applying for urban residents. It has also allowed people to live in rural areas at the edge of the city and well beyond it and yet still work and engage in other activities in the city centre, 'Working in the city but living in the country' is an option open to many as is the alternative of 'working in the country but living in a city'.

There can be no doubt that the rapid development of transport and communication systems has greatly extended the distances over which businesses and people can maintain linkages with the city centre and has greatly expanded their options for location. In addition, much of the population growth in the 'adjacent' areas of the margins and immediately beyond the limit of daily commuting to major centres has involved the establishment of enterprises and households, the location of which is strongly influenced by proximity to the major centre (Smailes and Hugo 1985). Nevertheless, this technological factor is a 'facilitator' of the population growth in this zone rather than a fundamental explanation of it. Hence, even within a zone of 100 to 200 km around each major city, it is likely that more fundamental causative processes are at work.

The job-led hypothesis

There is considerable debate over the extent to which deconcentration of population is occurring due to the movement of employment. Jarvie (1981) has argued forcefully on the basis of her analysis of the 1971–76 period in Australia that the process is predominantly employment-led. Some support for this position can be gained through examination of changes in the employment characteristics of people residing in metropolitan, urban and rural areas between the 1976 and 1986 censuses. There was a greater numerical increase in the number of employed people living in non-metropolitan locations (372,551) than in cities with more than 100,000 inhabitants (302,297), in spite of the fact that in 1976 two-thirds of all employed persons lived in large cities. Over the same ten-year period the rate of increase in employed persons in cities with under 100,000 inhabitants in 1981 was, at 23 per cent, nearly three times the 7.9 per cent increase in the larger cities.

Moreover, significant changes in the structure of employment were also taking place over this period, not just nationally but also between urban and rural areas. For Australia as a whole, while the total number of jobs increased by 6.9 and 5.3 per cent in 1976–81 and 1981–86 respectively, there were declines of 6.2 and 4.0 per cent in agriculture and 2.1 and 12.4 per cent in manufacturing. These were more than offset by the gains in mining (22.2 and 2.7 per cent for the two periods), utilities and transport (15.7 and 4.8) and trade, finances, administration, retailing and other services (9.3 and 21.1).

Among the settlement types, the rural areas were distinctive in that the only decline in jobs occurred in agriculture, the traditional mainstay of the rural economy, while they were the only settlement type to experience a sustained increase in manufacturing workforce and had easily the largest percentage increases in employment in the transport, utilities and tertiary sectors. In the non-metropolitan urban areas there was rapid growth in mining and transport/utilities in 1976–81 but slower growth in the 1980s, and in manufacturing a gain in the late 1970s was transformed into a net loss in the 1980s. Here the most rapid sustained growth was in the tertiary sector. Over this decade therefore there was a significant growth and restructuring taking place in non-metropolitan Australia, particularly its rural areas.

Note, however, that employment change data from the census are a little misleading in that they relate to the place of residence of the worker and not the location of the job, so that an important question remains as to the proportion of workers living in rural or other urban localities but commuting to jobs located within major urban areas. It must also be borne in mind that between the 1976 and 1986 censuses, the percentage of all workers employed in major urban areas declined only from 66.3 to 64.0 per cent. However, in all zones there was a substantial decline in employment in agriculture and the patterns of employment gain in the non-metropolitan zones heavily favour tertiary industry and tend to point towards a deconcentration of employment in Australia.

An examination of articulated motives of persons moving from metropolitan to non-metropolitan areas helps to gauge the importance of employment factors in producing counterurbanization in Australia. According to the 1987 national survey of internal migration (ABS, 1988), some 37 per cent of persons who moved from metropolitan to non-metropolitan areas did so for employment-related reasons. While this supports the argument for a significant employment-led element in the turnaround, it is interesting to note that employment-related reasons accounted for an even greater proportion of migrants from non-metropolitan to metropolitan areas (46 per cent). Meanwhile, a greater share of metropolitan to non-metropolitan migrants moved for location-related reasons (27 per cent) than did migrants going in the opposite direction (23 per cent). The largest differences in the distribution of reasons for moving between the two types of movers, however, is in the retirement/health category which accounts for a tenth of all metropolitan to non-metropolitan movers but only 3 per cent of those moving in the opposite direction.

Residential preferences

It is clear from this ABS (1988) survey that life-style factors play a significant role in the outward movement of population from Australia's major cities. This line of explanation suggests that there is an 'enhanced locational freedom (which) implies a rise in the degree to which jobs follow people, as opposed to the somewhat more traditional process whereby the creation of jobs more clearly preceded the movement of individuals' (Long and Hansen 1979, 28). Evidence such as that presented above points to the growing significance of migrations to non-metropolitan areas which are little influenced by economic considerations. The growing volume of movements of retirees (Murphy 1979; Prinsley *et al.* 1979; Cook 1980; Wait 1979; Hugo *et al.* 1981), hobby farmers (McQuinn 1978; Menzies and Bell 1981), long-distance commuters (Paterson *et al.* 1978) and people seeking alternative life-styles (Lindblad 1976) all testify to this. While Jarvie (1984) rejects net migration of the aged as a significant element in the turnaround at the statistical division level for the 1971–76 period, there can be no doubt that the growth of the older population in non-metropolitan areas is having a significant impact in particular local areas (Hugo 1989a).

Case studies in non-metropolitan areas experiencing the turnaround also provide some support to this behavioural hypothesis. One study in rural South Australia (Smailes and Hugo 1985), for example, concludes that there is strong evidence of life-style considerations in migration decision-making. This is not to deny, of course, that the particular community in which people live and the bulk of inter-regional migration is strongly shaped by the availability of job opportunities. The growth or decline of population in most communities is still largely influenced by the changing spatial distribution of employment of various types and hence by the structural changes which are occurring in the Australian economy.

The welfare-led or income-transfer hypothesis

A final argument which has been put forward as a partial explanation of turnaround has been titled the 'welfare-led hypothesis' (Hugo 1989b). This suggests that a significant element associated with in-migration into Australian non-metropolitan areas and the retention of long-standing residents in the latter sector has been people who receive some form of transfer payments. The number of Australians receiving some form of income transfer is large and growing. According to the Department of Social Security (1988, 8), in 1983 22 per cent of males and 31 per cent of females aged 16 and over were the recipients of a government pension or benefit. These included age pensioners, invalid pensioners, widows, supporting parent beneficiaries, sheltered employment allowees, rehabilitation allowees and recipients of a wife's pension and carer's pension. In 1986 20.5 per cent of the nation's total population (all ages) were in receipt of some form of pension from Social Security or Veterans Affairs, compared to only 14.5 per cent in 1976 (Department of Social Security n.d.). On this basis, in 1986 there were 43 persons receiving benefits for every 100 employed persons, up from 32.4 in 1976. Even without including recipients of some special government benefits (e.g. for Aboriginal people) and private superannuation schemes, it can be seen that transfer payments form a very significant element in the overall income of Australians, and one that has risen over time as a result of the ageing of the population, the introduction of new benefits, the widening of eligibility and the trebling of unemployment rates in the 1970s (Hugo 1986a; 1986b).

The hypothesis argues that people in receipt of government or private pensions and benefits are disproportionately clustering in certain types of non-metropolitan areas for a number of reasons. In the first place, people use the locational freedom afforded by receiving an income which is not fixed to a particular place (all pensions in Australia are totally portable) to locate in a congenial environment. Some areas tend to be more scenically attractive in mountains, riverside or coastal areas, often in the sections of Australia that are warm throughout the year. Secondly, in many country areas housing is considerably cheaper than in the large metropolitan areas, so people on a fixed income can more readily afford it. For instance, the average cost of single-unit housing in country towns in South Australia was 35 per cent lower than in the Adelaide metropolitan area in March 1986, that of flats 57 per cent lower (South Australia Department of Lands 1986). Moreover, in some country towns which have suffered severe population decline in the early postwar years due to mechanization of farming, increased centralization of manufacturing and retailing in Adelaide, and so on, the costs of housing can be very cheap indeed. Thirdly, in non-metropolitan areas the chances of supplementing benefits or pensions with seasonal work in agriculture and with participation in informal sector activities are often a significant factor. Moreover, this may often be done in such a way that it does not come to the notice of the Department of Social Security or the taxation authorities. A fourth reason is that some movers have little choice. For example, the South Australian Housing Trust makes housing available for single mothers and other welfare groups on a priority basis, but this housing may often be available only in a country location. Finally, in some cases the movers out to rural areas, while receiving benefits or pensions, may be seeking alternative life-styles.

The enormous significance of transfer payments is often overlooked in examinations of non-metropolitan regional economies which tend to focus only upon employed persons. The inflow of cash benefits from the Federal and State governments to individuals can be a major element in the local economy, since the bulk of such monies are spent locally. For example, Drakakis-Smith (1984, 134) estimated that more than a third of the economy in the city of Alice Springs was reliant upon cash transfers from the Federal Government to Aboriginals living in the city. McDonald (1986, 41) reports that in the city of Broome, Western Australia, 40 per cent of the workforce are receiving unemployment benefits. Again Aboriginals are significant, but so too are '... well educated young people taking a leisurely holiday at the taxpayer's expense', camping in the sandhills lining the attractive beach. Clearly, if some areas gain a disproportionate share of welfare recipients, their population growth will not only benefit through in-migration and population retention, but also through the multiplier effects of the injection of those monies in the local economy.

It is therefore suggested that a welfare-led hypothesis of explanation of the turnaround has considerable validity. Definitive testing must await detailed survey work, but all the evidence points to it being one of the elements which have been working towards bringing about a deconcentration of population. It certainly is not a complete explanation but in the Australian context it is an essential element, if Hugo and Smailes's (1985) suggestion that an eclectic approach has to be adopted in the explanation of the turnaround, given our current state of knowledge and understanding.

Some impacts of the turnaround

Counterurbanization in Australia is selective not only with respect to the areas which it has affected but also the sub-groups in the population that have been involved. Accordingly, the process has wrought significant change in the composition of the non-metropolitan population as well as the rate of growth of that population. There is insufficient space here to detail the selectivity of out-movement from metropolitan to non-metropolitan areas but the following generalizations can be made. In the first place, the overseas-born tend to be underrepresented (Hugo 1986a; ABS 1988). Secondly, the migration is selective of young adults in the 25–39 age group and their children. It tends to involve established young families rather than school leavers and others in the peak mobility age group of 15–24 which dominates in non-metropolitan to metropolitan migration. In certain non-metropolitan communities (especially towns along the eastern and southeastern coasts), there is heavy in-migration of persons in their late 50s and 60s (Hugo 1989b). Thirdly, the out-migration is selective of unemployed persons. In general, the unemployed are more mobile than the employed population (ABS 1988). Finally, among the employed population, persons working in tertiary, service-type occupations are strongly represented.

These tendencies have contributed to a blurring of the characteristics of metropolitan and non-metropolitan populations in Australia. This convergence has also been facilitated by the greatly increased mobility of the 'native' non-metropolitan population. This enhanced mobility has also been a significant factor in the retention of non-metropolitan populations. It has, for example, greatly extended the area over which farm dwellers can range in seeking off-farm employment. One of the most striking changes in rural Australia in recent years has been the diversification of sources of farm income, an important element of which has been family members working on a part-time or even full-time basis in off-farm employment. In the River Murray irrigation areas of South Australia, for example, a study of 48 per cent of irrigators (Dwyer-Leslie and Maunsell 1983, Volume 2) found that fully 31 per cent of them were relatively independent of farm income because of their off-farm employment. The 1985–86 round of the Bureau of Agricultural Economics survey of broadacre, dairy and horticultural farms found that operators and spouses on 60 per cent of family farms earned off-farm income, that non-farm work was more frequently undertaken than work on other farms, and that in most cases this source of income was vital to the welfare of the families involved (Males *et al.* 1987).

The convergence taking place in the characteristics of Australia's metropolitan and non-metropolitan populations as a result of the turnaround can be demonstrated by reference to a range of indicators. Among the most impressive are the changes in industrial structure examined earlier, particularly the major decline in manufacturing employment and the rapid increase in the proportions of the rural workforce engaged in manufacturing, utilities and the service sector at the expense of agriculture. Clearly there has been a remarkable convergence occurring in the pattern of economic activity in metropolitan and non-metropolitan areas. In addition, there has been a substantial reduction of the differences between urban and rural areas with respect to their levels of fertility and mortality (Hugo 1986a). There has been a closing of the gap with respect to levels of educational attainment.

These changes carry substantial implications for planning and government policy. While the turnaround can be attributed partly to publicly funded infrastructural improvements as well as to explicitly spatial policies concerned with urban and regional development, there is a tendency in much planning to assume either that the spatial distribution of demand for particular goods and services changes very slowly or that any changes will be in the direction of those observed in the recent past. The new directions in population change which have emerged since the late 1960s are imposing fresh demands on both public and private sectors to provide infrastructure and services in areas of growth and to cope with problems of reduction in economic and social potential in the areas of decline. There can be no doubt that much of the existing planning and management structure is strongly orientated to the metropolitan cities and will need modifications if the existing tendencies towards population deconcentration continue.

Conclusion

Very clearly counterurbanization has emerged as a force to be reckoned with in Australia. It appears particularly dramatic in view of this nation's extraordinarily high level of population concentration in a few major metropolitan centres and the pervasive nature of urbanization trends right into the late 1960s. It is also clear that, though the migration turnaround peaked in the latter half of the 1970s, the following decade did not bring a return to metropolitan concentration. Unlike the experience of the United States in the early 1980s, non-metropolitan Australia continued to record faster population growth than the metropolitan sector.

At the same time, the analysis in this chapter has shown that the turnaround has not had anything like an even impact across the whole of Australia, but has itself been fairly highly concentrated, particularly in terms of absolute numbers of people. Extensive parts of the least densely populated areas of the continent continued to experience depopulation during the 1970s, while considerable variety over space and time characterized similar areas which were then recording overall growth, particularly those heavily dependent on the mining industry. The major part of the non-metropolitan renaissance was concentrated predominantly in the well-watered and attractive areas of the south-east and east coast, mostly in locations which are adjacent to and relatively accessible from the major metropolitan centres.

These observations must, however, be interpreted in the light of Australia's scale and distinctive geography, particularly in comparison with the majority of countries included in this book. Vast areas of the continent are, by their physical nature, extremely inhospitable and expensive to settle in, while it should be pointed out that the metropolitan areas are generously defined and that some of the so-called 'adjacent areas' are 400 km or more from the nearest city centre. The expansion of the urban fields of the major cities has undoubtedly played a part in the faster growth of the non-metropolitan population over the last two decades, but so too have the redistribution of jobs, the growing significance of income transfers and the increasing attention given to life-style considerations. Compared to the 1960s, more people have been prepared to leave the major cities and fewer non-metropolitan people seem to have been attracted by them.

Further reading

A detailed account of recent population trends in Australia is provided by Hugo, G.J. 1986: *Australia's changing population* (Melbourne: Oxford University Press). The 1970s experience is set in a longer historical perspective by Maher, C. 1985: The changing character of Australian urban growth, *Built Environment* 11(2), 69–82.

The counterurbanization debate is viewed from an Australian perspective in: Hugo, G.J. and Smailes, P.J. 1985: Urban–rural migration in Australia: a process view of the turnaround, *Journal of Rural Studies* 1(1), 11–30. This theme is developed further by Smailes, P.J. and Hugo, G.J. 1985: A process view of the population turnaround: an Australian case study, *Journal of Rural Studies* 1(1), 31–43. The most recent developments in Australia's experience of the turnaround are examined by Hugo, G.J. 1989: Counterurbanization in Australia, *Geographical Perspectives*.

5

United Kingdom:

population deconcentration as a cyclic phenomenon

A.G. CHAMPION

Introduction

The United Kingdom occupies a distinctive position in relation to most of the other countries treated in this book. Most important is its early history of large-scale urbanization, with over 50 per cent of its population living in urban settlements by the mid-nineteenth century and three-quarters by the beginning of this century – a result principally of the rapid rate of industrial expansion and the lack of employment opportunities in the countryside in this free-trade era. Related partly to the consequent lack of rural population pressure in the mid-twentieth century is the early date at which outward movement from the principal urban centres led to a net redistribution of population in favour of the smaller cities, towns and more rural areas. The forces of urbanization and counterurbanization had already moved into balance by the 1950s and the latter had become clearly dominant by the 1960s to the extent that the 1970s appear to represent the 'downwave' of a cycle of population deconcentration in Britain. The urban–rural shift, however, is by no means a spent force: while London has made an impressive recovery from the very high levels of migration loss that were recorded in the later 1960s and early 1970s, non-metropolitan Britain has continued to attract substantial net in-migration and indeed has seen its rate of overall population growth begin to rise again during the 1980s.

The relatively long period over which counterurban tendencies can be observed for Britain opens up wider opportunities for analysing these trends than are available for those countries with only recent experience of the phenomenon. In particular, the cyclic nature of population deconcentration in Britain – with its strongest acceleration in the 1960s and its subsequent waning – holds out the prospect of relating the trends in population distribution to periodicities in possible causal factors. The main part of this case study, however, is concerned – like the other chapters in this book – with providing more detail about the spatial patterns of population change in order to identify more precisely the types of places which have made the greatest contribution to the general deconcentration phenomenon and to discover the types of people involved and the reasons for their movement, particularly their age and socio-economic characteristics and the extent to which migration is related to changes in the distribution of employment opportunities. The first task, however, is to clarify what counterurbanization is taken to mean in the British context and to outline what measurements and tests for the existence of counterurbanization are permitted by the available data sources.

Approach, definitions and data

The existing body of literature broadly relating to the 'counterurbanization debate' in Britain contains a bewildering variety of approaches, most notably in the type and scale of spatial units used in the analyses. In most cases this reflects explicit differences in the aims of the studies, which though generally concerned with aspects of population concentration and deconcentration are not all designed specifically as tests for, or explanations of, counterurbanization *sensu strictu*. For instance, Vining and his colleagues have concluded that concentration has remained the prevailing force in Britain, albeit at a slower pace in the 1970s than previously, but their main analysis was based on a broad two-fold division between the national core region comprising the South East, East Anglia and the South West and the rest of the country (Vining and Kontuly 1978a; Vining and Pallone 1982). At the other extreme of spatial scales, it has been shown (e.g. by Weekley 1988) that a considerable number of the smaller settlements and civil parishes continued to experience depopulation in the 1970s, even where situated in areas of the country which were recording strong overall population growth.

It is, however, at the intermediate spatial scale that studies of counterurbanization should be located – almost by definition, since this is basically the scale of the urban system. The approach used here follows the broad framework set out by Berry (1976), Fielding (1982) and Perry *et al.* (1986). Counterurbanization is thus interpreted as involving a shift towards a less concentrated pattern of population distribution, during which a negative relationship between the population size of a place and its rate of net migration change will generally prevail. A more specific definition requires that this shift reflects a switch in net migration balance rather than merely a change in the differential patterns of natural increase. It is likely that, at the lower end of the settlement hierarchy, this phenomenon will be accompanied by a rural population turnaround, in which areas which have for decades experienced net outward migration move to a positive migration balance. In general, if population distribution is shifting in favour of larger urban places, then urbanization is deemed the dominant process, but if smaller places are generally growing faster than larger ones, then counterurbanization is occurring.

The key challenge is in defining 'place', not only in a conceptually appropriate way but in one which accords with the practicalities of data availability. The principal alternatives are between functionally defined urban regions, physically defined urban areas and administratively defined local authority (municipality) units. In the British context, Coombes *et al.*

(1982) and Champion *et al.* (1984; 1987) have argued strongly against the use of local authority areas, particularly since the reorganization of local government in 1974/75. Even before that time serious problems were posed by the fact that city boundaries had failed to keep up with the pace of suburban growth, but the reforms of the 1970s not only failed to address this problem adequately but also led to the amalgamation of separate urban systems into single units in some of the more sparsely populated parts of the country and generally paid rather little attention to the realities of the urban system. Because of these difficulties, over the last twenty years a substantial amount of academic research time has been expended in defining urban-centred regions along the lines pioneered for the USA by Berry (1967) and into providing data and analyses on these bases, primarily the Standard Metropolitan Labour Area framework developed by Hall (1971; see also Hall *et al.* 1973), extensions of this by Hall and Hay (1980) and Spence *et al.* (1982), and the Functional Regions family of areas developed by Coombes *et al.* (1982). The definition of settlements on the basis of built-up areas across the nation has generally been neglected in Britain, with the notable exceptions of Law's (1967) detailed examination of urban-areas change between 1801 and 1911 and the preparation of a set of 'Urban Areas' volumes from the 1981 Census (OPCS 1984).

In practice, however, data problems make it necessary to use a combination of geographical frameworks in order to build up a full picture of counterurbanization in Britain. The Functional Regions family forms the most comprehensive and up-to-date framework for studying urban change in Britain. Its key advantage for the present study is that it divides the whole territory of Great Britain into a set of 280 Local Labour Market Areas (LLMAs) on the basis of journey-to-work flows to employment centres (Figure 5.1). Moreover, it identifies a set of 20 higher-order 'Metropolitan Regions' comprising groupings of LLMAs which have relatively strong commuting ties between themselves in contrast to other LLMAs which are termed 'freestanding'. The LLMA framework, however, is very largely limited to the study of changes between Census years, because it is only the Census that can provide details for the small building blocks needed for the LLMAs. Since the 'Urban Areas' approach suffers from the same problem, the monitoring of trends between census years is possible only by reference to the mid-year population estimates prepared by the official statistical agencies for local authority areas. These can be classified on the basis of a basic criterion like population density (Champion 1983) or a mixture of administrative and socio-economic characteristics (OPCS 1981a, following Webber and Craig 1976).

Recent patterns for overall population change

The purpose of this section is to test for the existence of counterurbaniza-tion, prior to examining its characteristics in more detail and to attempting an explanation. Three principal questions need to be addressed, as follows: Have counterurbanization tendencies been evident during any recent period? If so, when did they emerge? Finally, have these trends continued up to the present time and indeed have they intensified? The evidence of

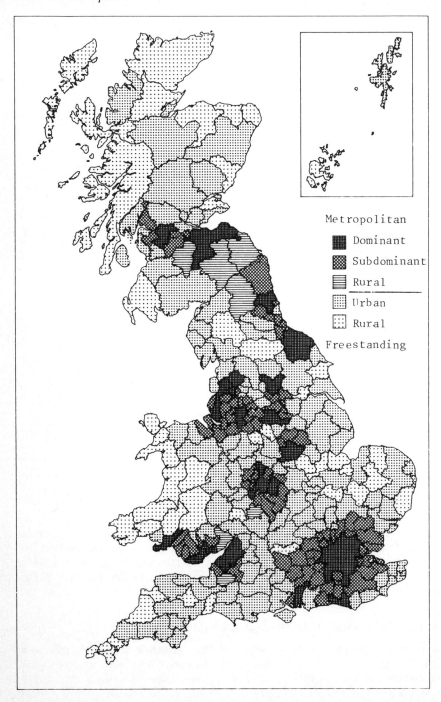

Figure 5.1 Great Britain: the 280 Local Labour Market Areas, by type. Source: Centre for Urban and Regional Development Studies, University of Newcastle upon Tyne.

the decennial Population Census can provide the basis for answering the first question and for giving a broad indication of the date of onset, but the third question requires the greater temporal detail that is available only from the annual population estimates for local authority districts.

Long-term trends

The evidence for the existence of a counterurbanization pattern of population redistribution in the 1971–81 intercensal period is overwhelming. A number of previous studies using the standard reporting units of the local authority areas have observed the heavy population losses sustained by many of Britain's larger cities over this period and have shown that most parts of rural Britain in general maintained or even increased their rates of population growth in the 1970s compared to the previous decade, contrary to the national trend towards a lower level of overall population increase (e.g. Champion 1981b; 1983; Hamnett and Randolph 1983; OPCS 1981b; Randolph and Robert 1981; Robert and Randolph 1983). These general observations have been confirmed by analyses based on the specially defined LLMA framework (e.g. Champion *et al.* 1984; Champion *et al.* 1987).

The results of one application of the LLMA framework are shown in Figure 5.2, where the LLMAs are grouped according to urban status and population size. Immediately apparent for the observations relating to 1971–81 change is the negative association between population growth and size of place that Fielding (1982) regards as the hallmark of counterurbanization. The London LLMA, with 8.58 million people in 1971, lost almost three-quarters of a million people during the decade, a reduction in population of 8.6 per cent. A similar average rate of loss was recorded by the five next largest LLMAs – the 'Conurbation Dominants' of Birmingham, Glasgow, Manchester, Liverpool and Newcastle upon Tyne – while futher down the size ladder there is a regular progression through lesser rates of loss and into greater rates of increase, with the Rural Areas adding 8.8 per cent to their aggregate population over the ten-year period.

Figure 5.2 also shows that the demographic dynamism of Britain's smallest places, as defined in functional terms, is a relatively recent phenomenon. The LLMA category of Rural Areas, which is dominated by places that are the most remote from the influence of the major metropolitan centres (see Figure 5.1), has in aggregate experienced a remarkable turnaround in its population change rate since the 1950s. At that time the Rural Areas were, in aggregate, losing population, albeit by the relatively small amount of 0.6 per cent for the decade but in sharp contrast to the 5.0 per cent increase in the national population. By the 1960s the Rural Areas had moved up to 5.4 per cent, almost identical to the 5.3 per cent national average for the decade. Their 8.8 per cent rate for 1971–81 indicates a further acceleration in population growth in actual terms, but represents an even greater increase relative to the national average than occurred between the two earlier decades. With the national rate of population growth falling to 0.6 per cent for 1971–81, the differential between Rural Areas and Great Britain as a whole totalled 8.2 percentage

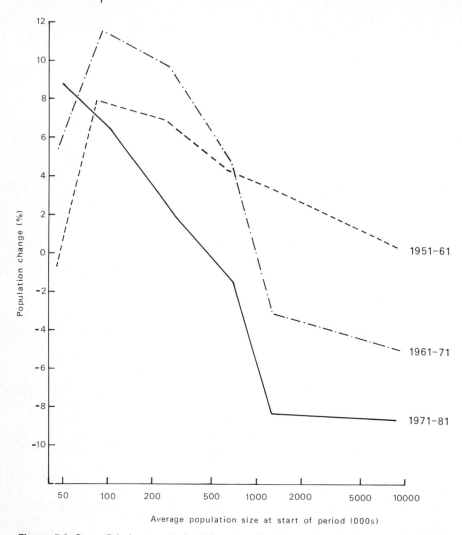

Figure 5.2 Great Britain: population change, 1951–81, by LLMA size category. Note: LLMAs are grouped by population size into six categories, with average 1971 population size (thousands) as follows: Rural Areas (49), Towns (103), Cities (279), Provincial Dominants (707), Conurbation Dominants (1246) and London (8577). Source: calculated from Population Census data.

points in this final period, compared with 0.1 in the previous decade and −5.6 in 1951–61. Clearly, the strong performance of rural Britain in the 1970s represents a major turnaround from earlier experience, but it can be seen that this transformation was already underway by the 1960s.

Reference to the other elements of the LLMA size ladder in Figure 5.2 provides further evidence indicating that broader counterurban tendencies were already deeply entrenched before the 1970s. It can be seen that even in the 1950s there was, at this aggregate level, a negative relationship between population size and growth rate spanning all the LLMA size groups except Rural Areas, though not characterized by such a steep gradient as subsequently. It is also noteworthy that the most significant changes across the main part of the urban system took place in the 1960s rather than later. This decade witnessed both an acceleration in the growth rate of Towns and Cities and the major switch into overall population decline of both London and the Conurbation Dominants. According to this analysis there was no further sharpening of this gradient of population deconcentration between the 1960s and the 1970s. Indeed, apart from the extension of the regular counterurbanization relationship to include the Rural Areas, the only noticeable difference in the 1970s was the improvement in London's change rate relative to the other non-rural categories, serving if anything to reduce the scale of differentials across the categories. A direct reading of Figure 5.2 suggests that the deconcentration process has tended to move down the LLMA hierarchy over time, though in reality the patterns are complicated by the variations in national growth rate and by other factors influencing population distribution, most notably the drift from North to South.

One issue which has not been addressed squarely so far is the extent to which the patterns could be produced by relatively local spillover from the major metropolitan centres rather than by a more widespread process of deconcentration across national space. In the aggregate analysis of Figure 5.2 the fast growth rate of the lower-order categories could be brought about entirely by exceptionally large gains made by relatively few LLMAs situated close to the large declining urban centres. To some extent the LLMA framework already overcomes this problem since each area is defined in such a way as to include its centre's primary commuting hinterland which forms the destination of more local decentralizing moves, but as pointed out by Hamnett and Randolph (1983) among others, a significant proportion of the longer-distance deconcentration shifts involve the surrounding LLMAs. Though these latter form urban nodes in their own right, they may also be linked strongly to the nearby metropolitan centres by commuting and other ties.

The classification of LLMAs shown in Figure 5.1 provides a mechanism for distinguishing the effects of urban deconcentration over shorter and longer distances, because the boundaries round the Metropolitan Regions are delineated so as to include all the LLMAs that (in 1971 at least) were linked together by strong journey-to-work flows. Table 5.1 shows the population trends across the three intercensal decades from 1951 for the four main types of LLMA (i.e. excluding the small category of the Metropolitan Rural Areas). Longer-distance deconcentration was clearly predominant in the 1970s, since the 20 Metropolitan Regions in aggregate saw their population decline by 2.4 per cent, while that of Freestanding Britain grew by 5.8 per cent. In terms of absolute numbers, the Dominants – the twenty 'capitals' of the Metropolitan Regions – lost over 1.3 million people during the decade, whereas the surrounding Subdominants grew by barely half a million people.

As with the size-based analysis of Figure 5.2, this longer-distance form of population deconcentration did not emerge suddenly in the 1970s. Already

Table 5.1 Great Britain: Population change, 1951–81, by LLMA type (%)

LLMA type	Actual rate			Above or below (−) GB rate		
	1951–61	1961–71	1971–81	1951–61	1961–71	1971–81
Freestanding rural	−0.5	5.8	9.4	−5.5	0.6	8.9
Freestanding urban	5.7	9.0	5.4	0.8	3.7	4.8
All freestanding	5.0	8.6	5.8	0.0	3.4	5.3
Metropolitan subdominant	9.4	12.4	3.9	4.4	7.2	3.3
Metropolitan dominant	2.8	− 1.4	−6.4	−2.2	−6.6	−6.9
All metropolitan*	5.0	3.5	−2.4	0.0	−1.8	−2.9
Great Britain	5.0	5.3	0.6	0.0	0.0	0.0

Note: * including 7 Metropolitan Rural LLMAs
Source: Calculated from Population Census

in the previous decade Metropolitan Britain, though growing, was not growing as fast as Freestanding Britain and thus, as shown by the right-hand part of Table 5.1, was experiencing a relative loss to the latter. As early as the 1950s these two halves of Britain were already evenly matched, suggesting that the drop in the Dominants' share of national population was in aggregate only just compensated for by the increase in the share accounted for by the Subdominants without recourse to longer-distance deconcentration. On the basis of this evidence, there would appear to have been no overall tendency towards population concentration in Britain since at least the 1950s. The centrifugal tendencies merely intensified over the two subsequent decades, both in terms of the numerical scale of net population redistribution and with respect to the extent of the impact down the LLMA hierarchy and across geographical space.

Short-term fluctuations

An examination of the annual population estimates for local authority districts, however, provides only partial corroboration of the picture of intensifying deconcentration painted by the Census statistics. This data source, which uses the districts introduced by the local government reorganization of 1974/75, can be used to trace district-level trends since 1961 for England and Wales. It confirms the early onset and continuous nature of population deconcentration, with relative shifts from the major metropolitan centres to less urbanized and more rural districts since the beginning of the 1960s at least. On the other hand, these data show that there has not been a regular and progressive intensification of this process over the past quarter of a century. Indeed, by contrast with the impression conveyed by the Census data of the 1970s being the period of most rapid counterurbanization, it appears that the urban–rural shift in population redistribution accelerated rapidly in the late 1960s and peaked in the first two or three years of the next decade, with most of the 1970s constituting a time of deceleration in the deconcentration process.

Table 5.2 England and Wales: Average annual population change rates, 1961–87, by type of district

Type of district	Annual growth rate per 1 000 people						
	1961–66	1966–71	1971–74	1974–77	1977–81	1981–84	1984–87
Greater London boroughs	− 4	− 9	−12	−12	−7	− 2	1
Inner London	− 8	−19	−21	−19	−15	− 5	0
Outer London	− 1	− 2	− 6	− 7	− 3	− 1	1
Metropolitan districts	2	− 0	− 4	− 5	− 4	− 4	− 3
Principal cities	− 8	− 8	−11	−10	− 8	− 5	− 4
Other districts	7	4	− 1	0	− 3	− 3	− 2
Non-metropolitan districts	13	10	8	4	5	3	6
Cities	1	− 2	− 2	− 4	− 3	− 3	− 4
Industrial	8	7	7	1	2	− 1	1
With New Towns	23	19	16	14	14	8	9
Resort, port & retirement	14	10	9	5	5	7	13
Other urban, etc	23	17	9	6	7	5	7
Remoter, largely rural	8	10	15	9	7	6	11
England and Wales	6	4	2	0	1	1	3

Note: 'Other urban etc.' refers to 'other urban, mixed urban–rural and more accessible rural'
Source: Calculated from OPCS mid-year population estimates

The evidence for this interpretation is presented in Table 5.2, which gives population change rates since the early 1960s for a district classification devised by the OPCS for England and Wales. It can be seen that, even at the beginning of the period covered by the data, the non-metropolitan part of the country was already growing more rapidly than the metropolitan part, the latter being defined in this case in terms of the administrative areas of the Greater London Council and the six Metropolitan County Councils (which were abolished in 1986). The differential between the two parts widened somewhat during the later 1960s and early 1970s, as the metropolitan growth rate, particularly that for Greater London, fell back more sharply than that for non-metropolitan districts. Indeed, the data show clearly that the most rural parts of the country, here labelled 'remoter, largely rural' districts, increased their growth rate at this time, moving against the national trend – the only category of districts to do this. By 1971–74 this category had emerged as one of the two fastest growing types, being surpassed only by 'districts with New Towns', which largely comprised planned metropolitan overspill schemes.

Table 5.2 also shows the subsequent slackening of the deconcentration trend. The growth rate of the remoter, mainly rural districts had fallen back significantly by the mid 1970s, and then levelled off at an average rate of around 6–7 persons per thousand towards the end of the decade and into the first part of the 1980s. This slowdown is also found for most of the other non-metropolitan district categories, being particularly abrupt for industrial districts after the 1974 oil price rise and related economic check and also for the New Town districts after the late 1970s decision to wind down the programme of planned overspill and attempt to rejuvenate inner city areas. At the other end of the urban hierarchy, London's rate of population loss had already peaked by 1971–74 and fell back markedly after the mid 1970s, as also occurred to a lesser extent for the principal cities of the Metropolitan Counties.

The rise and fall of population deconcentration over this period is displayed clearly at the two extreme ends of the national settlement hierarchy. Figure 5.3 shows the change rates for the remoter, largely rural districts and Inner London, expressed in terms of percentage point deviation from the national rate in order to allow for variations in the latter caused by fluctuations in natural increase and the overall level of migration with the rest of the world. The diagram enables the pinpointing of 1970–71 as the year of greatest population shift away from London, with virtually all the 1970s as well as the early 1980s constituting a period of almost unfaltering recovery. At the other end of the settlement spectrum, it can be seen that the most rural parts of the country began to exceed the national

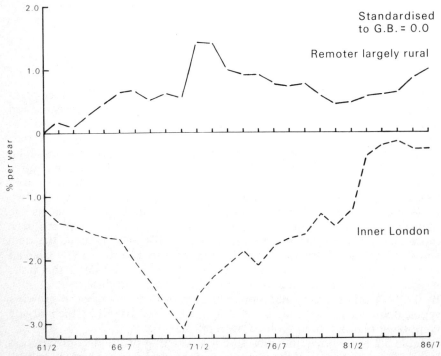

Figure 5.3 England and Wales: annual population change rate for Inner London and remoter, largely rural districts, 1961–87, expressed as percentage point deviations from the rate for Great Britain. Source: calculated from OPCS mid-year population estimates.

average growth rate at the beginning of the 1960s and experienced two periods of acceleration in growth – one during the first half of the 1960s and the second, more sudden surge in 1971–72 – followed by a steady decline in relative performance through the rest of the 1970s.

It would, however, be a mistake to conclude that population deconcentration is a spent force. The evidence from Table 5.2 and Figure 5.3 is that even in the early 1980s the remoter, largely rural districts continued to record an annual growth rate significantly above the national average. Moreover, the latest mid-year estimates reveal a substantial new surge in the rate of growth in this type of district, only partly due to a rise in the national growth rate. Several of the other elements of non-metropolitan settlement were also continuing to experience relatively strong growth in the mid 1980s, particularly the category containing smaller urban centres with specialized resort and retirement functions. This recent upturn in rural and non-metropolitan growth does not appear to be linked to a new round of population loss for London, but is associated with a further deterioration in the relative performance of the Metropolitan Counties and of Cities in the Non-metropolitan Counties.

The characteristics of urban deconcentration in Britain

The above analysis has confirmed the existence of counterurbanization in Britain, defined in terms of the shift in population distribution from larger and more densely inhabited settlements to smaller and more sparsely populated areas. The purpose of this section is to investigate the nature of this pattern of urban deconcentration and thereby provide a clearer idea of what counterurbanization involves in this country. The principal questions that are addressed here relate to the composition of these changes and their relationship to trends in the distribution of employment. More specifically, is the urban–rural shift in population distribution primarily due to migration or differential rates of natural increase? How significant is retirement migration? To the extent that working-age people are involved, is population growth outside the major metropolitan centres occurring alongside employment growth or are the growth areas essentially 'dormitory' settlements? Lastly, are the growing urban regions relatively self-contained or part of an extended metropolitan system?

The importance of migration

As with all types of population redistribution, urban deconcentration can potentially be the result of either net migration transfers or of spatial variations in natural change rates, or some combination of the two, even though the term 'counterurbanization' is normally interpreted with respect to migration shifts alone (Fielding 1982). In fact, previous studies which have distinguished the components of population change in Britain (e.g. Robert and Randolph 1983; Champion 1987b; Cross 1988) have demonstrated the prime importance of the migration components in long-distance deconcentration. They have shown that a considerably wider range of change rates across the nation exists for net migration than for natural

Table 5.3 England and Wales: Natural change and net migration, 1971–84, by type of district (per 1 000 people per year)

| Type of district | Natural change | | | Net migration | | |
	1971–78	1978–84	Shift	1971–78	1978–84	Shift
Greater London boroughs	1.0	2.0	+1.0	−12.0	− 6.5	+5.5
Inner London	0.7	2.2	+1.5	−19.5	−11.6	+7.9
Outer London	1.2	1.8	+0.6	− 7.0	− 3.4	+3.6
Metropolitan districts	1.0	1.1	+0.1	− 5.6	− 4.8	+0.8
Principle cities	1.6	1.5	−0.1	−10.3	− 6.3	+4.0
Other districts	−0.1	0.3	+0.4	− 3.3	− 4.1	−0.8
Non-metropolitan districts	1.1	0.8	−0.3	4.9	3.3	−1.6
Large cities	0.7	1.2	+0.5	− 5.1	4.1	+1.0
Smaller cities	0.0	0.6	+0.6	− 1.7	− 2.5	−0.8
Industrial	2.2	2.1	−0.1	1.6	− 1.4	−3.0
With New Towns	5.0	5.1	+0.1	10.7	5.3	−5.4
Resort, port & retirement	−6.4	−5.9	+0.5	12.6	11.6	−1.0
Other urban, etc.	3.1	2.3	−0.8	4.6	4.3	−0.3
Remoter, largely rural	−0.4	−1.0	−0.6	11.7	7.6	−4.1
England and Wales	1.0	1.0	1.0	− 0.2	0.0	+0.2

Note: As for Table 5.2
Source: Calculated from unpublished data provided by OPCS. First published in Champion (1987) Tables 7 and 8

increase. It is also clear from this work that, during the period of most rapid counterurbanization, migration rates displayed the more consistent urban–rural gradient, whereas the level of natural change tended to be relatively low at the two ends of the settlement spectrum (the largest cities and most rural areas) and highest at intermediate points in the urban hierarchy.

Unfortunately, data limitations make it impossible to look at components of change on the basis of the Functional Regions framework or for individual years before 1971, but Table 5.3 illustrates most of the points made by these previous studies. During the period 1971–78 which includes the time of most rapid deconcentration, migration was clearly the dominant process. Annual migration losses of 10 per thousand or more from London and the principal cities of the Metropolitan Counties and gains of similar proportions recorded by the three highest non-metropolitan categories contrast with a considerably narrower range of natural change rates. Indeed, for the rural and resort categories, the positive effects of migration were not reinforced by the natural change component, because here deaths were outnumbering births. It was also the migration component that was very largely responsible for the reduction in the rate of urban deconcentration in the later 1970s and early 1980s, though the shifts in natural change rate between 1971–78 and 1978–84 generally contributed towards this slowdown (Table 5.3).

The limited role of retirement migration

At first glance, observed variations in age composition across Britain

Table 5.4. Great Britain: Change in number of persons in broad age groups, 1971–81, by LLMA type (%)

LLMA type	Age group					Total
	0–15	16–24	25–44	45–PA	PA+	
Freestanding rural	− 1.2	15.3	20.0	1.1	15.7	9.4
Freestanding urban	− 6.8	12.6	15.8	− 2.5	12.8	5.4
All freestanding	− 6.2	12.9	16.3	− 2.1	13.1	5.8
Metrop subdominant	− 8.9	13.8	11.9	− 2.4	13.4	3.9
Metrop dominant	−19.1	2.5	1.5	−14.3	4.8	−6.4
All metropolitan*	−15.0	6.7	5.6	− 9.8	8.1	−2.4
Great Britain	−11.9	8.9	9.4	− 7.1	10.0	0.6

Note: PA = Pensionable age (65 for males, 60 for females)
* Including Metropolitan Rural
Source: Calculated from Population Census

suggest that retirement migration must have made a major contribution to counterurban shifts over the past quarter of a century. As noted by several studies (e.g. Dewdney 1968; Law and Warnes 1976; Lawton 1982; Champion *et al.* 1987), there exists a major contrast between a relatively youthful population in most of the more urbanized parts of Britain and an older population in virtually all the more rural and peripheral areas. As has been shown by Kennett (1983), this distinctive pattern results from the net out-migration of school-leavers and young adults from more rural areas to principally the largest centres, most notably London, and from the movement of older people in the opposite direction. Moreover, retirement migration can be expected to have become more important over time, as the number of elderly people has been increasing and because an increasing proportion of them are home owners and are usually able to realize a substantial sum of money through exchanging their family-size house in an expensive metropolitan location for a smaller one in a less congested part of the country.

The available evidence on counterurban migration flows, however, suggests that the contribution of retirement migration has been fairly modest. Though traditional resort and retirement areas were growing strongly in the 1970s and have shown a further surge in the mid 1980s, Warnes and Law (1984) found that many of these places were seeing a slowdown in the growth of their numbers of elderly and a restructuring of their population towards younger age groups. Survey work by Jones *et al.* (1984) on the Scottish Highlands and Dean *et al.* (1984b) on Cornwall revealed considerable place-to-place variation in the importance of retire-ment migration, but concluded that there was significant in-migration of pre-retirement groups and the 'middle-aged'. A case study set in North Devon (Bolton 1988) observed considerable inward movement by relatively young families, while in a study of 33 'rural growth districts' in England and Wales Cross (1988) observed that for the year 1980/81 the 15–29 age group accounted for fully a quarter of the net migration gain, whereas those of 60 year old and over were responsible for only around one-fifth.

These observations on the importance of migration by younger people is borne out by the more aggregate analysis for LLMA types shown in Table 5.4. Both categories of Freestanding Britain registered above-average growth in the size of all five age groups between 1971 and 1981. Though the population of pensionable age and over experienced strong growth in Freestanding Britain, the percentage point deviation from the national average was smaller than for all the other four groups. Furthermore, age-cohort analysis reported by Champion (1989) indicates the large number and wide spread of individual LLMAs which experienced by 1981 large gains of people aged 6–14 in 1971 – the school-leaving cohort that is traditionally associated with net movement to the major cities. In Britain therefore counterurbanization has by no means been restricted to the movement of the elderly, but appears to have involved all ages in fairly equal proportions.

The close links with employment change

One of the most crucial questions about the nature of counterurbanization is the extent to which it merely constitutes an extension of suburbanization and local metropolitan decentralization rather than a switch in population distribution towards smaller, relatively distinct settlements. It has just been shown that, in aggregate, people of working age constituted well over half the population growth recorded in rural and non-metropolitan areas. A key issue in this context is the degree to which this increase in residential population has been stimulated by the availability of extra local jobs as opposed to being the result of transport improvements which allow easier long-distance commuting into the larger metropolitan centres.

Several studies using data from the Census of Employment have shown conclusively that since the 1960s there has been a major redistribution of job opportunities paralleling the spatial patterns of population change. The

Table 5.5 Great Britain: Employment and population change, 1971–81, by LLMA size categories

LLMA size category	Employment (000s)		% GB employment		employment change (%)			population change (%)
	1971	1981	1971	1981	1971–78	1978–81	1971–81	1971–81
London	4 269	3 891	19.7	18.4	−5.9	−3.1	− 8.9	−8.6
Conurbation dominants	2 719	2 367	12.6	11.2	−3.6	−9.8	−12.9	−8.3
Provincial dominants	1 505	1 448	7.0	6.9	+2.6	−6.2	− 3.8	−1.5
Cities	6 469	6 430	29.4	30.5	+5.3	−5.6	− 0.6	+2.0
Towns	5 890	6 084	27.2	28.8	+8.1	−4.5	+ 3.3	+6.4
Rural areas	785	847	3.6	4.0	+9.7	−1.6	+ 7.9	+8.8
Great Britain	21 638	21 067	100.0	100.0	+2.7	−5.2	− 2.6	+0.6

Note: See caption of Figure 5.2 for details of LLMA type
Source: After Owen *et al.* 1986, Tables 2.2 and 2.6, based on data from Census of Employment via NOMIS; Population Census

urban–rural shift has been particularly marked for manufacturing employment. Fothergill and Gudgin (1979) found a strong negative relationship in the aggregate between the urban status of a place and rate of change in number of jobs in manufacturing industry, and Keeble (1980) highlighted the importance of within-region movements of manufacturing employment in producing the overall national tendency towards greater dispersion. The service sector has recorded more general growth across the different elements of the urban hierarchy, but taking all sectors of the economy together, Owen *et al.* (1986) identified a strong counterurban pattern on the basis of the same grouping of LLMAs as used in Figure 5.2. The pattern was particularly regular in the period of overall economic growth in 1971–78, but remained evident in the subsequent period of economic recession apart from the rather limited loss of jobs in London in 1978–81 (Table 5.5).

The commuting question

The final question raised at the beginning of this section is much more difficult to answer. It relates to the problematic issue of the 'clean break' discussed in Chapter 2. While there is no doubt that a geographical deconcentration of jobs has taken place alongside the centrifugal movement of population, the types of analysis outlined above do not make it clear whether the medium-sized and smaller LLMAs which are gaining people and jobs are relatively self-contained areas gaining as a result of their inherent advantages or whether they are being incorporated into an extended metropolitan system in which their principal attraction is improved accessibility to a major urban centre.

There appear to be two sides to any line of evidence that can be brought forward to resolve this issue. On the definitional side, as has been mentioned earlier, the LLMAs have been delineated so as to minimize the degree of inter-LLMA commuting, yet the identification of a set of Metropolitan Regions recognizes the fact that there are stronger journey-to-work flows across LLMA boundaries in certain more heavily populated areas than in others (Coombes *et al.* 1982). Secondly, through the application of a 'labour market accounts' approach to South East England, Congdon and Champion (1989) show that, while net in-commuting to London increased somewhat between the 1971 and 1981 Censuses, three counties – Berkshire, Surrey and West Sussex – recorded a decline in their absolute levels of net out-commuting and most of the others saw their scale of net out-commuting increasing more slowly than their numbers of employed residents. Yet this is not incompatible with a general increase in the level of gross journey-to-work movements into and out of individual LLMAs. Data provided by Anne Green show that, even in the more remote and rural parts of the country there are a few LLMAs where more than 1 in 5 of the employed residents worked outside their LLMAs of residence in 1981, while within the Metropolitan Regions the proportion was commonly more than 1 in 3. During the 1980s the incidence of long-distance commuting appears to have increased, not only for people working in major metropolitan centres like London but also in terms of suburb-to-suburb trips and journeys between smaller cities and towns in more rural regions (see Cross 1988, for a detailed study of South East England). On the other hand, some places which have recorded substantial job growth since the late 1960s are situated at a considerable distance from the major metropolitan centres and are relatively poorly served even by the local road network (Bolton 1988).

In summary, it seems to be very difficult to apply a specific label to describe the nature of urban deconcentration as it has been experienced in Britain over the past three or four decades. The phenomenon has certainly been stimulated largely by migration, but it has been reinforced to a certain extent by differences between places in natural change rates. It has by no means been restricted to retirement migration, but has also involved large numbers of economically active people of all ages and has been associated with a large-scale shift in the location of job opportunities. There has been strong population and employment growth on the margins of the Metropolitan Regions and in the more accessible places beyond, but equally many of the smaller LLMAs in the more remote parts of Britain have recorded substantial gains, particularly in percentage terms. It is therefore tempting to conclude that Britain has been experiencing a very general and widespread process of deconcentration.

Underlying explanations

Any explanation needs to be able to cope with the two principal observations made earlier in this chapter. The first is that urban deconcentration has been a very general process in Britain, involving a wide range of population sub-groups, affecting the distribution of jobs as well as people, and reaching out to more remote places as well as those closer to metropolitan centres. This raises the question as to whether many individual explanations should be sought or whether there could be a single fundamental factor at work. The second observation relates to the pace and timing of deconcentration. The fact that over the past quarter of a century the process appears to have followed a broad cyclic pattern offers pointers to the nature of the underlying explanation(s). It also suggests that in the British context the reasons behind counterurban shifts are more likely to be found in the circumstances of the 1960s when the process was accelerating than in those of the 1970s when it peaked and began to wane before beginning a further round of more rapid movement in the mid 1980s.

Many features of the 1960s appear conducive to urban deconcentration, some of which would particularly favour longer-distance redistribution between LLMAs. Building on the economic growth of the previous decade, it was a period of generally increasing employment and individual prosperity, though subject to short-term recessions of which the most severe occurred in 1967. House-building was proceeding at record levels, with a particularly strong contribution from the public sector, while the clearance of older sub-standard housing areas also peaked at this time, involving the displacement of people from inner city areas until the redevelopment of some of the cleared sites for housing could re-accommodate a proportion of them. This was the period when the first wave of New Towns, designated mainly between 1946 and 1950, reached its maximum level of construction activity and highest rates of increase in population and jobs, while it also saw the expansion of the New and Expanded Towns programme in response to the upward revision of national population projections resulting from an unexpected increase in fertility rates and an unprecedented surge in immigration from overseas. It was also the time when planning control on land for urban development began to bite in the more pressurized parts of Britain, particularly the inner parts of the South East where land allocated for a twenty-year plan period in the early 1950s had been largely exhausted within ten years, forcing private developers to look to more distant locations beyond the Green Belt. Urban containment policies were reinforced by regional policies which aimed to restrict the rate of employment growth in the more prosperous South and channel new manufacturing investment and office development to provincial locations, especially places affected by the contraction of jobs in coal mining and other traditional industries. This coincided with the onset of restructuring in many branches of manufacturing industry which involved the rise of the large national and multinational corporation and the boom in investment in branch-plant operations. The 1960s also saw the rapid expansion of motorway and trunk road construction, which permitted greater locational flexibility to firms and general public alike as both became increasingly orientated to private road transport, while public investment in higher education, health facilities and local services in general leapt ahead.

Some of these sources of development pressure continued into the 1970s, but the latter half of this decade was largely a period of consolidation and retrenchment, culminating in the severe recession of 1979–82. The restructuring of manufacturing industry continued apace, but after the economic crisis of 1974 the emphasis shifted progressively away from expansion of investment towards rationalization, with the older plant in traditional urban locations tending to be affected the most severely. A substantial growth of public employment took place around the time of local government reorganization in 1974/5, but local authority budgets were progressively trimmed back under the monetarist regime which was imposed on the UK by the International Monetary Fund in 1976 and was reinforced by the anti-inflation policies of the Conservative government from 1979. The birth rate had peaked in the mid 1960s, but as a consequence of this 'baby boom' the general process of family rearing was reaching its height in the early 1970s when the increasing number of school-age and adolescent children in the 'national household' put extra demands on housing space and boosted the demand for larger dwellings in lower-density environments. During late 1960s and the early 1970s a major change of housing policy took place, shifting the emphasis from slum clearance to the rehabilitation and improvement of older dwellings. Though to some extent this took the form of 'gentrification' involving replacement of the original occupants by wealthier and smaller households, it – along with the redevelopment of previously cleared sites – tended to reduce the need for long-distance overspill. So too did the emergence of central government concern for the 'inner city problem' in 1976, which led not only to a concerted effort at attracting investment to older urban areas but also to a decision to wind up the New and Expanded Towns programme.

This synopsis of factors influencing rates of population deconcentration in the 1960s and 1970s is by no means exhaustive, but is sufficient to indicate the multiplicity of individual explanations for this phenomenon. In the terminology used by Frey in Chapter 3, they are essentially 'period influences' because in one way or another they all help to account for the fact that deconcentration was running more strongly in the later 1960s and early 1970s than during the next few years. The list of even more specific factors – often highly specific in locational impact as well as in timing – could include the North Sea oil and gas boom, the re-opening of mineral workings during the resource shortage of the early 1970s, and the expansion of the nuclear power station construction programme on selected remote sites. Yet many of these factors are not autonomous, nor are they ephemeral, but instead are long-term in nature and are affected by fluctuations in national and international conditions. These underlying forces include long-term trends in socio-demographic structure of the population, the tendency towards lower-density urban development and the restructuring of the national economy away from the production of goods towards the handling of information. Their effect over time is conditioned by short-term pulsations relating to inherited population structures, the overall level of economic activity, and urban development and redevelopment cycles.

Against this background a new round of more rapid urban deconcentration in the UK in the mid-to-late 1980s is only to be expected. In the first place, the difficult economic conditions of the early 1980s, which depressed house-building levels and the general propensity for residential mobility, have led to pent-up pressures for new urban development, while the movement of the 'baby boom' cohorts of the late 1950s and early 1960s into peak household-forming age is now causing a sharp increase in the need for family-size houses in appropriate locations. Secondly, the relatively high level of private-sector investment in inner city areas in the early 1980s, encouraged by government policies and the shortage of alternative options, went a long way to exhausting the most viable sites and most lucrative market niches, prompting property developers to return to more traditional areas of activity. Thirdly, the recovery of the economy was so dominated by the growth of high-level service-sector jobs primarily orientated to central London that the cost gradients of office rents, house prices and land values across Britain became unprecedentedly steep, acting as a major incentive for a further round of centrifugal shifts.

Conclusion

This chapter has demonstrated conclusively the existence of counterurbanization in Britain, using that term in the same way as Berry (1976) to denote the process of population deconcentration. It has been shown that the pattern of centrifugal movement has gone far beyond suburbanization and local decentralization between core and ring of individual metropolitan areas or functional regions. It is also clear that this process of longer-distance deconcentration has been underway for most of the postwar period, with the largest LLMAs losing out in relative terms to smaller places as early as the 1950s and with the most rural parts of the country switching from absolute loss to substantial gain between the 1950s and the 1960s. The distinctive feature of the 1970s is that this was when the most remote and rural areas came to dominate population growth, at least in percentage terms. On the other hand, more detailed investigation indicates that the main part of the 1970s, as well as the early 1980s, were characterized by a downturn in the rate of deconcentration, while a more recent acceleration in net migration to less urbanized areas suggests that a new cycle in the urban–rural shift is underway.

The apparently cyclic behaviour of the deconcentration patterns provides both a challenge and an opportunity in terms of explanations. As outlined in the previous section, the upturn and subsequent downturn in the 1960s and 1970s respectively correlates with trends over time in a number of relevant factors, including demographic push, the state of the economy and government policy. At the same time, it has also been shown previously that deconcentration has been a very pervasive process, not only in its spatial impact but also in the types of people which it has involved and in the fact that employment trends have tended to parallel the urban–rural shift in population. It is tempting to conclude that, at least at the scale of inter-urban variations, the forces of deconcentration are extremely powerful, though their strength can fluctuate over time and their impact can be modified to a certain extent by a range of factors including government policy. At the same time, this is not to say that deconcentration is the only process responsible for recent developments in the national space economy, for it is possible to recognize other dimensions of population change, some very specific such as a closure of individual collieries or factories, others relating to a more general reorientation of the space-economy such as the growth of retirement areas or the emergence of environmentally rich areas as centres of the new service economy. Nor is there enough evidence available so far to prove that a completely new type of settlement pattern is emerging even though many of the more rural areas which experienced rapid growth in the 1970s are relatively remote and not readily accessible to the major metropolitan centres. One thing is certain, however, namely that in purely geographical terms the British population is now more evenly spread over national space than it was three decades ago, reversing a deep-seated trend of at least a century's standing. As such, counterurbanization in the UK demands serious attention by academics and decision-makers alike.

Further reading

More detailed treatments of recent trends in population distribution can be found in Britton, M. 1986: Recent population changes in perspective, *Population Trends* 44, 33–41; and Champion, A.G. 1983: Population trends in the 1980s, in Goddard, J.B. and Champion, A.G. (eds.) *The urban and regional transformation of Britain* (London,

Methuen), 187–221; and Champion, A.G. *et al.* 1987: *Changing places: Britain's demographic, economic and social complexion* (London: Edward Arnold).

Studies which focus specifically on counterurbanization issues include: Champion, A.G. 1987: Recent changes in the pace of population deconcentration in Britain, *Geoforum* 18, 379–401; Hamnett, C. and Randolph, W. 1983: The changing population distribution of England and Wales, 1961–81: clean break or consistent progression? *Built Environment* 8, 272–80; and Robert, S. and Randolph, W. 1983: Beyond decentralization: the evolution of population distribution in England and Wales, 1961–81, *Geoforum* 14, 75–102.

Three case studies are particularly recommended for an examination of changes in more remote rural areas: Jones, H. *et al.* 1986: Peripheral counterurbanization: findings from an integration of census and survey data in northern Scotland, *Regional Studies* 20, 15–26; Grafton, D.J. and Bolton, N. 1987: Counterurbanization and the rural periphery: some evidence from North Devon, in Robson, B.T. (ed.) *Managing the city* (London: Croom Helm), 191–210: and Dean, K.G. *et al.* 1984: Counterurbanization and the characteristics of persons migrating to West Cornwall, *Geoforum* 15, 177–90. The recovery of London's population change rate in the 1980s is examined by Champion, A.G. and Congdon, P.D. 1988: An analysis of the recovery of Greater London's population change rate, *Built Environment* 13, 193–211.

6

Norway:

the turnaround which turned round

JENS CHRISTIAN HANSEN

Three features of Norway's situation combine to provide a distinctive context for the study of counterurbanization tendencies. Norway is a peripheral country in the European context, and many Norwegians are sceptical about the economic and political power of continental, metropolitan Europe, as evidenced by the 'no' vote against entry into the European Community in 1972. Its geography is also one of vast peripheral or marginal regions, with more than 90 per cent of the national territory lying within the designated zones of development aid and entitled to regional policy support. Finally, Norway is a late-comer as an urbanized country compared with most West European nations, with its rural population not reaching its maximum size until around 1950 and with barely half its population living in urban settlements at that time.

Only since the late 1960s have the benefits of rapid urbanization been questioned in Norway. During the reconstruction of the Norwegian economy after the Second World War, urbanization was looked upon as a prerequisite for modernization, and economic policies encouraged growth in existing urban settlements as well as the development of new industrial settlements in peripheral areas in need of an urban focus. The change of attitudes twenty years ago was precipitated by the acceleration of population decline in peripheral areas, and led to the introduction of regional policy measures aimed at stemming these losses. When growth in the major urban regions slackened during the late 1960s and population decline in peripheral regions became less pronounced during the early 1970s, these trends were hailed as important developments by politicians and academics alike. When in 1973 North Norway had more in-migrants than out-migrants for the first time in over twenty years, this was heralded in the local press as a major event.

In retrospect, however, it can be seen that too much importance was attached to the observations of the early 1970s. In no year since 1973 has in-migration exceeded out-migration in North Norway, and by the mid 1980s its net migration losses were running as high as their peak level in the late 1960s. Even at the time it seemed that the urbanization process was more important than counterurbanization trends (Hansen 1979). Indeed, much of the regional 'consolidation' which took place in the 1970s resulted from migration from more rural areas into the urban settlements of the peripheral regions. The policy of so-called 'decentralized concentration' was not able to tackle the problems facing the marginal areas beyond the commuting range of urban centres and even within the commuting regions there were still many problem areas (Hansen 1975).

Norway's experience is an excellent example of the turnaround type observed by Cochrane and Vining (1986) for the peripheral countries of Western Europe and for Japan, involving the narrowing of the gap between growing core and declining periphery in the 1970s and then a renewed divergence (see Chapter 1). The turnaround was of a more muted form than in the United States of America and in several countries nearer the heart of Western Europe and from the end of the 1970s the turnaround itself turned round – it became a U-turn (Hansen 1985; 1986). This chapter documents the U-shaped pattern of population trends since the 1960s in Norway and describes the principal factors which were responsible for the events of the 1970s and 1980s. Nevertheless, this review points to the strong element of continuity which underlies the evolution of Norway's settlement patterns and raises some doubts about the value of a counterurbanization perspective in this context.

Approach

Any study of counterurbanization or turnaround in Norway must be shaped very strongly by the distinctive geography of the country. With 4.2 million people scattered over 320,000 km^2 – an area larger than Great Britain and Ireland combined – factors like distances, centrality and space loom large in the analysis of population change. Over large parts of the country population is so thinly spread that there are serious problems in maintaining even essential services like an elementary school or a local shop, let alone any higher-order services (Hansen 1983).

Previous studies of trends in the degree of population concentration in Norway have ranged across a wide gamut of scales. Myklebost (1984), for instance, recognized three levels of centre–periphery relations – at national level, the distinction between the Oslo urban region and the rest of the country; at regional level, the distinction between the main regional centre and the rest of the region; and at local level, the distinction between the main settlement and the surrounding countryside. Not surprisingly, however, in Norway's special geographical context, most attention has been given to the two ends of the spectrum – the growth of the capital region and the depopulation problems of the smallest settlements in the more remote and sparsely settled regions.

As the discussion in Chapter 2 has shown, however, counterurbanization is something more specific than population deconcentration. The approach adopted for this study is to examine the redistribution of population within the urban system and to relate these inter-urban changes to developments in the surrounding rural areas. These rural areas can be divided into two categories, those within and those beyond the daily commuting range of an urban centre. On this basis, counterurbanization can be said to occur when non-commuting areas show population growth while urban areas and their commuting hinterlands show population losses. This definition is not as liberal as the interpretation of counterurbanization outlined by the editor at the beginning of this book, for the latter includes shifts in population distribution down the urban hierarchy. In Norway's context, however, much of the recent growth of smaller settlements is due to in-migration from surrounding rural areas and is thus the outcome of continued urbanization rather than of deconcentration from higher levels of the urban hierarchy.

Even this relatively restricted definition of counterurbanization is difficult to apply in practice because of the internal heterogeneity of the statistical areas analysed. For instance, averages for extensive parts of the periphery carry little meaning in a situation where much of the growth there takes place in the urban centres, particularly given the fact that these centres are just as dominant in their own regional contexts as is the Oslo region in the national context. Equally, while it may seem reasonable to overbound the national core region or individual urban regions in order to counteract problems of urban overspill, as done by Vining and Kontuly (1978a), internal regional variations are collapsed into averages which may be meaningful in some contexts but not in others.

Data problems also impose certain constraints, even in a country as well endowed with basic population data as Norway. Data are most readily available for the administrative areas which comprise 19 counties and 454 communes, for which annual data on births, deaths, in-migration and out-migration, and age structure are published. The counties can be aggregated to form the macro-regions of the North, Trøndelag, West, South and East, the last containing the capital region of Oslo. On the other hand, for present purposes, there are some problems with the use of communes, not least that they are defined on administrative rather than functional criteria and vary greatly in size – from a mere 250 to 447,000 people and from 2.4 to 8,995 km². In addition since a new social security system was introduced in 1970, it has not been possible to monitor occupational trends at this scale.

For a more exact analysis of the urban system, several approaches have been adopted in the past. Some involve the grouping of communes for the study of centre–periphery relations, most notably the classification of communes on the basis of spatial (centrality) and structural (occupational) criteria by the Norwegian Central Bureau of Statistics (Statistisk Sentralbyrå, 1985). Byfuglien (1986) has identified 13,470 'basic units' in Norway and given each a centrality rating, while Myklebost (1984) has used data for urban settlements, defined in Norway as physically coherent places with at least 200 inhabitants. Past analyses at these levels rely very heavily on the spatial detail provided by the decennial census, the most recent being for 1980, though progress is being made towards providing annual data for basic units (Byfuglien 1986). Data for functionally defined areas are generally lacking, though Myklebost (1984) and Rasmussen (1986) report data for the urban regions of the larger centres and the 'centrality' measures described above provide a partial substitute.

Urbanization and settlement changes in Norway

As mentioned at the outset, Norway is a latecomer as an urbanized country. In 1950 little more than one half of the population lived in urban settlements (Table 6.1). Oslo was a city of half a million, Bergen was the second city, with 150,000 people, and only 27 of 450 urban settlements had a population of 10,000 or more. In North Norway, the three major towns had between 10,000 and 15,000 inhabitants (Myklebost 1979).

Moreover, as Table 6.1 shows, in the three intercensal decades since 1950, Norway's population continued to urbanize rapidly. Between 1950 and 1970 the urban population increased by 50 per cent, taking its share to two-thirds of the national population, while the rural population declined by 15 per cent. By 1970 Oslo had 700,000 inhabitants and Bergen 200,000 and the number of urban settlements increased to 520, though only 32 had more than 10,000 inhabitants. The fastest relative growth at this time took place in the smaller urban settlements. This reflects the need to fill in the gaps of a deficient system of service centres, another sign of a country which has not completed its process of urbanization. The urbanization process up to 1970 therefore was one of decentralized concentration, strengthening local and regional centres at the cost of the surrounding periphery.

Against this background, the events of the 1970s appear to be a mixture of continuity and change. The urban population continued to grow between 1970 and 1980, though at around half the rate in the previous decade, while the rural population maintained its decline, albeit again at a slower rate despite the downturn in the national growth rate (Table 6.1). Brox (1980) concluded from his study of population changes between 1970 and 1979 in the northern county of Troms that the settlement pattern was experiencing population 'consolidation' (i.e. stabilization), but when the hypothesis was tested in other parts of the periphery, the consolidation process was not evident at all (Imset 1982; Kanstad and Kindseth 1983; Båtevik 1987; Foss et al. 1987; Holt-Jensen 1987).

Both Myklebost (1984) and Byfuglien (1986) have pointed to the persistence of substantial population losses in more remote areas, particularly if the unit of analysis is reduced from the commune to the

Table 6.1 Norway: Change in rural and urban populations, 1950–80

Population (000s)	1950	1960	1970	1980
Total	3 275	3 590	3 875	4 090
Rural	1 565	1 540	1 320	1 200
Urban	1 710	2 050	2 555	2 890
(% urban)	(52)	(57)	(66)	(71)
Change %	1950–60	1960–70	1970–80	1950–80
Total	9.6	7.9	5.5	24.9
Rural	− 1.6	−14.3	− 9.1	−23.3
Urban	19.9	24.6	13.1	69.0

Source: Population census. 'Urban' refers to people living in urban settlements with at least 200 inhabitants.

'sub-area' or 'basic unit'. At the same time, Myklebost (1984) observed that 66 per cent of the total increase in Norway's urban population in 1970–80 occurred in urban settlements with less than 10,000 people. On the basis of this evidence it would appear that the filling in and strengthening of the urban hierarchy, so important during the 1950s and 1960s, continued in the 1970s. One could therefore argue that any population turnaround in Norway at this time was in reality a stage in the urbanization process where the lower levels of the urban hierarchy grew faster than the periphery. This urban growth was not the effect of migration from larger to smaller urban settlements.

On the other hand, a rather different picture emerges if one examines population change in the middle and upper levels of the urban hierarchy. A significant contrast between the 1960s and 1970s is evident from Byfuglien's (1986) study of communes classified according to their level of centrality, as measured by the size of the largest urban centre that can be reached within a given travel time. According to this analysis (Table 6.2), a strong positive relationship existed between centrality and population change in the 1960s, but in the following decade the relation was essentially negative, though admittedly rather weak and not embracing the 'periphery' communes for the reasons already given. Myklebost (1984) has also drawn attention to the major reduction in the population growth rates of the largest cities. In particular, the Oslo urban region, which had accounted for around one-third of national population growth in the late 1950s and 1960s, saw its contribution fall to barely 10 per cent by the mid 1970s and had virtually reached zero growth by the end of the decade. All nine of the largest urban regions except oil-rich Stavanger experienced a marked cutback in growth between the two decades, though equally none was plunged into the massive decline recorded by major cities in many other countries at this time.

The shift in population growth down the urban hierarchy in the 1970s takes on further significance in the light of subsequent developments.

Table 6.2 Norway: Population change in communes according to centrality 1961–1985

Type of commune	Average population change per year					
	1961–1970		1971–1980		1981–1985	
	total	%	total	%	total	%
1 High centrality	20 819	1.4	10 288	0.6	10 989	0.6
2 Medium centrality	9 269	0.9	7 735	0.7	3 338	0.3
3 Low centrality	1 069	0.4	2 326	0.9	617	0.2
4 Periphery	− 2 885	−0.3	1 376	0.2	− 1 546	−0.2
Total	28 885	0.8	21 725	0.6	13 399	0.3

Key to commune type:
1 Within 75 minutes (to Oslo 90 minutes) travel distance of urban settlement with 50 000 inhabitants or more
2 Within 60 minutes travel distance of urban settlement with 10 000–50 000 inhabitants
3 Within 45 minutes travel distance of urban settlement with 5 000–10 000 inhabitants
4 Beyond 45 minutes travel distance of urban settlement with at least 5 000 inhabitants
Source: Byfuglien, 1986

Table 6.3 Population change in the four Scandinavian capital regions as a percentage of the national change

Capital region	1971–1975	1976–1980	1981–1985	1985
Copenhagen (Denmark)	6	−36	−256	−64
Helsingfors (Finland)	73	40	46	73
Stockholm (Sweden)	29	37	130	99
Oslo (Norway)	16	10	37	69
Total	28	19	51	66

Source: Ohls-Packalén, 1987

Byfuglien's (1986) commune-level analysis reveals a switch back to a clear 'urbanization' relationship between population change rate and level of centrality in the first half of the 1980s. Whereas the 'periphery' slipped back into population decline, the 'high centrality' communes in aggregate maintained the same average rate of growth in 1981–85 as in the previous decade in spite of a fall in the national rate of growth (Table 6.2). Whereas these communes had contributed only 48 per cent of the national population increase in the 1970s, the proportion was 82 per cent in the first half of the 1980s. Moreover, according to Rasmussen (1986), the whole of Norway's population growth between 1980 and 1985 was concentrated on 45 city regions. Indeed, the proportion accounted for by the Oslo region alone rose from 10 per cent in 1976–80 to 37 per cent in 1981–85 and touched 69 per cent in 1985, generally paralleling the experience of other Scandinavian countries except Denmark (Table 6.3).

It is on the basis of this evidence that conclusions can be drawn about the significance of counterurbanization tendencies in Norway. It is clear that a complete population turnaround never took place, because the major urban centres did not switch into population loss at any stage during the 1970s nor did the rural settlements in aggregate register any concerted population gain. Set against this, however, is the fact that in the 1970s population growth became highly focused on urban settlements of under 10,000 people. Though this was probably due more to migration from surrounding rural areas than to population shifts down the urban hierarchy, it must be noted that the trends of the 1970s were taking place against the background of late urbanization. The differences between the 1970s and the previous decade, reinforced by the sudden resurgence of population concentration in the 1980s, indicate that Norway did not entirely escape the turnaround phenomenon of the 1970s. Something did indeed happen there during the 1970s which, though muted in scale, was not very different in pattern and timing from the counterurbanization experiences of several other countries and which, as in some other countries, has been rendered more visible by subsequent events.

The migration U-turn

A fuller understanding of recent trends in Norway's population geography requires a regional perspective. Shifts in the distribution of population growth between different levels of the urban hierarchy are closely related

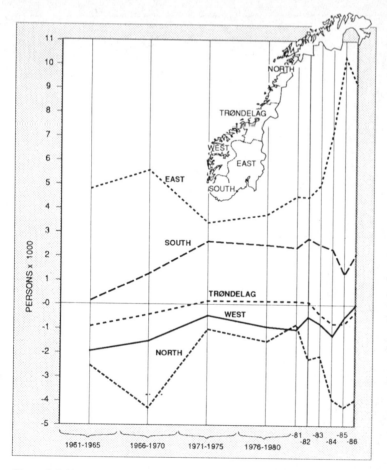

Figure 6.1 Norway: net migration, 1961–86, by major regions.

to regional change because of the very uneven pattern of urban development across Norway. Attention in this part of the chapter is focused on migration, because this component of population change has become more and more important as natural increase has declined and as geographical variations in natural growth rates have progressively diminished. Even more clearly than for trends in overall population change, migration rates have undergone a marked U-turn since the end of the 1960s, particularly for the regional extremes of the capital region and the North.

Figure 6.1 shows trends in net migration flows since 1961 for Norway's five major regions. This clearly reveals the wide margin between the declining North and the growing East in the early 1960s and the further divergence which took place later in this decade. Trøndelag and the West also experienced net out-migration at this time, though there was a relative improvement during the 1960s. In the first half of the 1970s there was a

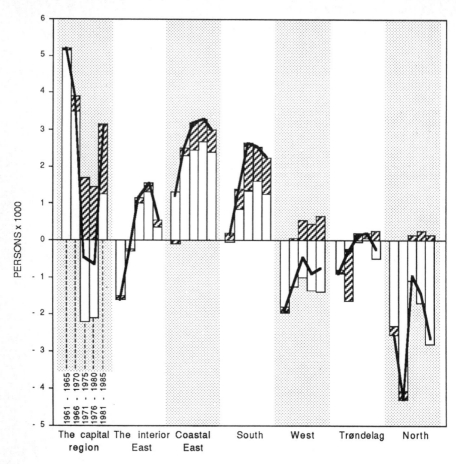

PERSONS x 1000

Figure 6.2 Norway: internal (unshaded), international (shaded) and total net migration, 1961–85, by region, annual average.

significant reduction in net in-migration to East Norway – the 'core region' of Vining and Kontuly (1978a). The South saw an increase in net in-migration, because of the growth of the oil industry in the Stavanger region. The West, Trøndelag and the North improved their migration balance, Trøndelag even turning into a net in-migration region. One could therefore claim that a relative regional consolidation had taken place, but one should not forget that the East still received more in-migrants than it lost out-migrants, and that the North still lost more migrants than it gained. The second half of the 1970s did not represent a significant change as compared to the first half: if anything, a trend towards less regional stability. In the 1980s, important changes have occurred, hesitatingly at first, but by 1983 there was clearly a return towards concentration. Indeed the core region had a much higher net in-migration than even that of the mid 1960s, while by 1985 the North was back where it had been in the late 1960s (Figure 6.1).

Figure 6.2 serves a double purpose. First, it divides the large and heterogeneous East – with 30 per cent of Norway's land and half its population – into three sub-regions: the capital region (Oslo and Akershus counties), the interior East or the periphery of the core (Hedmark and Oppland) and the coastal East. Secondly, it differentiates between internal and international migration. The latter, though involving only modest numbers of people by European standards, is important in the Norwegian context. Norway's international migration balance switched from loss to gain during the 1960s and surged ahead in the 1970s, influenced by oil activities, political refugees and movements within the open Scandinavian labour market. It increased further during the following decade, so that in 1987 net immigration contributed more than one half of the national population increase. Its regional significance can be seen by the fact that these gains have been concentrated very largely in East and South Norway, 85 per cent going there on average over the period 1961–85. Moreover, most immigrants go to urban areas, thus contributing to the centralization of the population.

Figure 6.2 shows very clearly how all regions, to a greater or lesser extent, bear signs of the migration turnaround and the subsequent U-turn, though the effect of international migration has at certain times and places tended to dampen this pattern, at others to reinforce it. In the capital region, the strong gains during the 1960s were almost exclusively a result of internal migration. During the 1970s – the turnaround period – this region had considerable net out-migration to the rest of the country, but net immigration almost compensated for this loss. During the 1980s, immigration from abroad persisted and its effect was reinforced by net in-migration from the rest of the country.

The coastal counties of the East, containing many of Norway's medium-sized industrial towns, have been receiving migrants from the rest of the country over the whole study period, and have also experienced an important net immigration. The two interior counties of the East had important migration losses in the early 1960s. The situation improved later in the decade and since 1970, this region has had net in-migration from the rest of Norway and from abroad, although at a lower rate in the 1980s. Here most of the migration gains were in a few communes in the southern parts of these counties. The South resembles the coastal East in its patterns of net gain from both other parts of Norway and from abroad. The importance of immigration was, however, greater here, partly due to return migration from North America and later due to the growth of oil-related jobs in the Stavanger area.

The other three regions, comprising marginal Norway, present a strong contrast to the East and South because, though the overall migration balance of each traces out a U-shaped trend over time, it was very largely negative throughout the period, particularly if international migration is not taken into account. The West experienced out-migration throughout the whole period, though immigration to some extent compensated for this, as oil activities moved northward to affect the Bergen area. Trøndelag, with the city of Trondheim, also clearly belongs to marginal Norway, although immigration during the 1970s led to population gain from

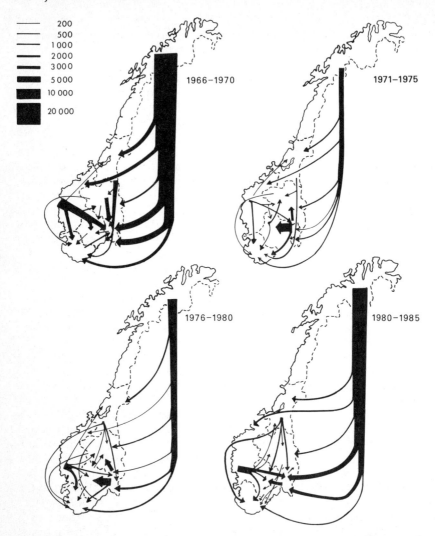

Figure 6.3 Norway: net migration flows between regions. Source: Norwegian Central Bureau of Statistics.

migration. In the 1980s, immigration could not compensate for the renewal of net out-migration to the rest of Norway, so Trøndelag returned to a situation of overall migration loss. Finally, the North never stopped being an out-migration area. Net immigration is far more modest than in the rest of the country, and the early 1970s did not really represent a turnaround trend, but only a temporary slowing down of net out-migration.

The internal net migration flows between the seven regions reinforce the U-turn impression of Norway's internal migration trends since the mid 1960s (Figure 6.3). The important shifts between the late 1960s and the early 1970s come out clearly, particularly the major reduction in net losses from the North and to a lesser extent the West and the change in the capital region's pattern of general gains to heavy losses to other parts of the East. So does the slow return towards old patterns in the late 1970s, before we get to the 1981–85 map which closely resembles the 1966–70 situation.

Net migration is, of course, merely the balance of gross migration inflows and outflows. More detailed data show that the surge in migration losses sustained by marginal Norway in the 1950s and 1960s was due to an increase in out-migration, whereas in-migration remained at its previous level. In the 1970s out-migration remained more or less at the same level as in the 1960s, but in-migration increased, partly because of return migration, which was particularly strong at the beginning of the decade – a direct consequence of the heavy out-migration in the late 1960s. In the 1980s the level of gross out-migration from marginal Norway has increased again, partly because whole households are moving, as contrasted to the 1970s, when most out-migrants were single, young people. In-migration to these areas has recently been on a lower level than in most of the 1970s, hence the widening of the net migration gap back towards its 1960s scale.

The local impact

From this analysis it can be seen that in the 1980s peripheral Norway is now back to the high levels of migration loss experienced in the 1960s. The principal difference is that this area now suffers the added disadvantage of having virtually no natural increase to compensate for these losses. The

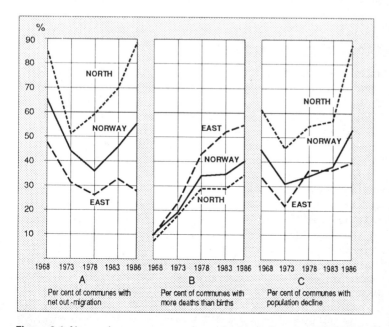

Figure 6.4 Norwegian communes: demographic indicators, 1968–86, for East and North regions.

implications of these developments for population change at the local scale are shown in Figure 6.4 for Norway as a whole and for the two extreme regions of the North and the East.

Figure 6.4A shows that two-thirds of the 454 communes in Norway experienced migration losses in 1968. This was the case for 85 per cent of the communes in the North, 47 per cent in the East. The turnaround still left one half of the communes of the North experiencing migration losses, and since then the U-turn has been so marked that by 1986 88 per cent of the northern communes had net out-migration. In the East only 28 per cent of the communes, most of which were located in the peripheral interior part of the region, had net migration losses in 1986.

Figure 6.4B introduces the effects of declining fertility and ageing. In 1968, very few communes experienced negative natural growth, but by 1986 this was the case in 40 per cent of them. The core was the leader in this process, the North the laggard, but even here one third of the communes had negative natural growth in 1986. Net out-migration was compensated for through a higher natural increase in many North Norwegian communes during most of the 1970s, but this advantage is becoming less and less marked, as the fertility decline reaches the north. At present it is West and South Norway which have the highest fertility in Norway.

Figure 6.4C shows the aggregate impact of these changes in migration and natural change, giving the percentage of communes experiencing population decline. The U-turn hypothesis seems to be supported by the graph. Nine out of ten communes in the North had population losses in 1986, five out of ten in the country as a whole, and four out of ten in the East.

Explaining the 1970s turnaround

The presentation so far has been limited to a description of what has been happening. The demographic processes have been discussed, with particular attention to migration. It has been shown that the turnaround in Norway was weak and did not last long, and that the 1980s marked a return to the dominant trend of centralization and the associated weakening of the periphery. The reduced fertility, the ageing population and the concentration of immigration on urban areas in the functionally central parts of Norway all contributed to this process. Demography thus is not only the outcome, but also part of the explanation. Nevertheless, in order to give a more comprehensive answer to the questions raised by recent trends in the geography of Norwegian population, it is necessary to look into economic development, economic policy and regional policy.

The Government policies developed during the 1960s and 1970s have had a profound effect on population change in Norway. These form a key element because the discovery of oil and gas in the North Sea made Norway rich enough during the 1970s to support policies aimed at preserving the settlement pattern which was seriously threatened by the centralization of population during the 1950s and 1960s. When unemployment rates began to rise in the late 1970s because of the world recession, Norway's politicians regarded the economic slump as a temporary setback and reinforced their existing measures by using part of the oil revenue to support unprofitable sectors of the economy and to create new jobs in public services. Even with the belated recognition of the fundamental nature of structural change in the economy and the drastic fall in oil prices in the mid 1980s, the political situation delayed the full-scale review of government measures. As outlined in the next few paragraphs, regional policy measures were directed mainly towards manufacturing industries but sectoral policies for primary activities and for the development of public services had very important regional consequences.

The industrialization of the periphery

The initial phase of industrialization of the Norwegian periphery was linked to exploitation of natural resources. Production units were small and geographically dispersed. New industries serving regional markets were established particularly during the inter-war years. Since the 1950s, the setting up of branch plants in designated development areas was encouraged as part of regional policy. The boom in ship-building in the 1960s, and later in oil rig and platform production, created new jobs in many small coastal shipyards, as well as ones based in the larger cities.

The combined effect of these developments was a relative and absolute increase in industrial employment in designated regional development areas during the 1970s and early 1980s. At the same time, employment decline in manufacturing industries in the large urban areas became more and more pronounced towards the end of the 1960s and throughout the 1970s. Norway did not have the large industrial regions that constitute the most serious regional problem in so many other Western countries during this period. Nevertheless, the three largest urban regions and the other main industrial centres taken together had a decrease of 15 per cent in manufacturing employment between 1970 and 1980, while the rest of the country had an increase of 16 per cent (Myklebost 1984).

This development has been interpreted as a positive effect of conscious regional policy, dating from the late 1950s. Promotion of industrial development in the regions has been regarded as the most effective policy measure. There can be no doubt about the positive effects of regional industrial policy. Indeed, according to shift-share analysis by Ahnström (1986), even before 1970 the capital region was losing significant numbers of jobs, particularly in manufacturing, due to geographical differentials in the performance of the various industries and only achieved strong growth at that time because its industrial structure was biased towards the nation's growth sectors. On the other hand, Ahnström's results for other countries suggest that the relatively stronger growth of the periphery in the 1970s resulted not just from a further increase in its locational advantages but also from a deterioration in the structural advantages of the core region. The latter was only partly due to the industrial restructuring caused by regional development measures and also reflected deep-seated changes in the national economy.

The periphery and the primary sector

Developments in the primary sector also played a part – although a very modest one – in the reduction in population losses in peripheral areas during the 1970s. At this time relatively buoyant market conditions combined with high levels of government support to increase incomes in these activities. Moreover, the time was right for a consolidation of employment in this sector, following the shake-out of the previous two decades.

In particular, the Norwegian farmer, by helping to sustain the settlement pattern in marginal regions, has been presented as a crucial actor in regional policy. The market for domestic agricultural products is protected from international competition through an elaborate set of import restrictions, while farmers also receive direct subsidies which are higher than in any other country, currently averaging around £10,000 per farmer each year. Even with all this support, however, the agricultural population continued to fall by 2–3 per cent a year during the 1970s nationally and by much more than this in peripheral areas.

Forestry, fishing and mining are also important to the marginal regions, but they do not constitute a stable element in the economy. Yet they performed more strongly in the early 1970s than during the 1960s because of the general upturn in international demand for raw materials.

The expanding service sector

The main cause of the temporary pause in the population decline in peripheral areas was the significant increase in the number of jobs in the service sector, and in particular in public services. This increase was strongest in areas which had a late take-off. The full impact of development of the welfare state came later in the periphery than in more central parts of the country. A conscious effort was made to satisfy people's needs as close to where they lived as possible. The range of services was extended with improvements in the communication system. The threshold was lowered for many public services, by decentralization in the organization of service systems. School centralization stopped. Health services were spread more evenly. Social welfare was offered at the door-step of those who needed it. Most of these elementary, locally based services were performed by women. The entry of the periphery's women into elementary service jobs contributed strongly to the consolidation of household economies in the periphery. The number of full-time employed men decreased in the 1970s, but the number of part-time jobs for women increased at a very rapid rate.

This development was not the result of a conscious regional policy, but the effect of the allocation of economic resources to sectoral policies of education, health and welfare. The periphery did not catch up fully with the centre as far as the provision of services is concerned. There are limits to decentralization. Many of the service activities were so specialized that they could only be located in centres of a certain minimum size. Private services were more selective in their locational choices because they had to be commercially viable in contrast to public services which were supported by taxpayers. This decentralized concentration led to rapid growth of regional and local centres during the 1970s, but sparsely populated areas surrounding these centres simultaneously experienced appreciable population losses.

In conclusion, it was the unprecedented expansion of employment in the public sector which was the primary cause producing the relative stabilization of the population in the Norwegian periphery in the 1970s. The traditional primary and secondary sectors contributed little to the consolidation of the settlement pattern. On the contrary, support for these sectors in the 1970s was the main factor in the scale of their decline in the 1980s because that support prolonged the survival of many unstable and otherwise unviable activities.

Forces at work in the 1980s

Those who told us, by the end of the 1970s, that the turnaround had come to stay in many countries have proved to be wrong. Part of the explanation for the U-turn in the 1980s can be traced to the reversal of the factors responsible for the turnaround. In particular, the economic difficulties which culminated in the deep world recession of 1979–82 led to a general reduction in the price of primary goods including foodstuffs, while the collapse of oil prices in 1985 further undermined the ability to subsidize primary producers and support investment and employment in public services. In contrast to the 1970s, the 1980s saw a much reduced availability of mobile capital for investment in new manufacturing plant in peripheral regions, while some activities faced particular problems, notably the rundown in fish stocks because of over-exploitation and ecological changes.

At the same time, however, the last ten years have been characterized by a restructuring towards new growth, which has favoured the Oslo region at the expense of the periphery. According to Spilling and Isaksen (1987), the capital region started the restructuring process earlier than the rest of the country and therefore was better prepared to face the economic downturn in the early 1980s and benefit from the subsequent recovery. The very reasons for the decline in its attractiveness between the 1960s and 1970s – scarcity of labour supply and land and their associated higher costs – led to a shake-out of less competitive activities, providing a firmer basis for growth in the 1980s. This contrasts with the 1970s situation in the peripheral areas, which increased their share of these less competitive activities and where traditional sectors were to some extent protected by public support from the need for restructuring.

Admittedly, much of the new growth has taken place in activities which positively seek out more central locations. The most dynamic sector of the Norwegian economy in the 1980s is that of private services linked to information processing, finance, technological consultancy and other 'post-industrial' functions, with most of its new jobs located in Oslo and the other major cities. Over the last few years there has been a vigorous discussion in Scandinavia about the geography of creativity (Andersson 1985; Oscarsson 1987; Törnqvist 1987). Though innovation is not necessarily an urban process – there are many examples of innovative environments in smaller communities in the periphery (Johannisson and Spilling 1986) – the results of creativity, as measured in terms of new jobs, tend to give an initial lead to the capital region, because much of the conversion of creative ideas through innovations to production takes place in the major centres.

What we do not know is whether the 1990s will bring structural changes in the economy which may lead once more to a turnaround trend. Foss *et al.* (1987) suggest that sheer demographic inertia will heavily influence the population distribution in Norway in the coming years. Only very dramatic shifts in migration patterns could bring about noticeable changes. Marginal Norway will probably see the negative employment effects of de-industrialization, whatever happens to the development of the capital region. If growth in the private service sector should come to an end in the most important cities, one must not expect this to cause a shift of activities towards the peripheral regions. The outcome may well be stagnation or decline of population in the capital region as well as in the periphery. Immigration will probably be reduced, and demographic vitality will not improve in the foreseeable future. Norway would soon be a zero growth country where both centre and periphery are losers.

As demonstrated earlier, the strengthening of regional and local service centres has been a dominant process in the changing population geography of Norway. Many observers continue to look upon 'decentral-ized concentration' as the only realistic policy for preventing a serious population decline in peripheral Norway. But Törnqvist (1989) recently has put the question: Will even the regional centres go on growing, or is this seemingly robust part of the settlement pattern now at risk? In his studies of changing contact networks using long-distance telephone calls, he found that the role of the regional centres has decreased considerably over the last ten years. The nodal functions of the regional centres are weakened because the individual firm relates directly to the national centre through a comprehensive set of data-bases monitoring both information flows and transfer of physical goods. The intermediary node loses important functions. If Törnqvist's findings can be generalized, one could expect an increasing polarization between the national centre and the remainder of the country, with the regional centres gradually losing their relay functions between the national centre and the rural periphery.

Such a development would greatly exacerbate the already serious problems posed by the lack of attractiveness of many smaller and more remote settlements. Even now some communities in the periphery do not possess resources considered worthwhile developing by the young generation. The most distressing aspect of the present demographic development is the diminishing return migration to peripheral communi-ties. The age cohorts of young people entering the labour market in the five to ten years to come will be much smaller than the present cohorts. The desertion of peripheral areas by the young may be interpreted as a reaction to traditional household organization in the periphery, where economic survival was based on income generated by migrant work, part-time local jobs and work in the informal sector. Communities organized in this way are poor by modern standards. They are dependent upon heavy external transfers, because their own taxable income cannot pay for standardized welfare state services. Dependency on welfare may be an acceptable solution for elderly people but it does not appeal to the young generation, and particularly young women. They hope for a better future. Their education alienates them from many of the traditional jobs available locally. Failure to provide the young with the kind of work to which they aspire spells doom for many peripheral communities.

This possibility raises serious questions concerning the future role and nature of regional policy. In the new environment of advanced technology and knowledge-based industries, the real question is not whether these growth industries can be used to develop the peripheral regions but whether Norway as a nation will be able to participate in them at all. Yet, if the centres of the periphery are declining, what prospects are there for the peripheries of the periphery? A meaningful regional policy for the periphery must focus on strengthening the urban settlements and developing them as centres which are acceptable to the young generations who are currently moving in large numbers to the central region. Selectivity must play an important role in such a policy, for preservation of the whole settlement pattern is a luxury that cannot be afforded and a minimum critical mass is needed before investment in new telecommunications infrastructure is viable. In the simplest terms, the settlement pattern should reflect the map of production. The long-term aim must be the involvement of the towns of the periphery as partners in a national production system. In Champion's terms, this would be an aspect of counterurbanization. In the Norwegian context, this represents a return to the policy of 'decentralized concentration', abandoned in the 1960s but perhaps worth taking up again today.

Conclusions

The process of counterurbanization, as defined by the editor of this book, had very little effect upon the changing population map of Norway in the 1970s. This sparsely populated and late industrialized country had not yet fully developed its urban system. The growth of medium-sized towns and small urban settlements for this reason persisted throughout the 1970s. This growth did not really represent a shift down the urban hierarchy. Although there was a decline in the growth rates of most of the larger urban labour market areas during the 1970s, the smaller towns got most of their growth through in-migration from rural areas. The observed consolidation of the Norwegian settlement pattern in the 1970s was in fact more an expression of this internal regional redistribution of people in less central areas, and not so much the result of the general turnaround trends observed in many other countries.

After 1982, the general picture of urbanization in Norway is one of increasing growth of the major cities, a stagnation of many medium-sized towns in less central parts of the country, and serious decline in most peripheral rural areas. The explanations for this development are partly economic like the switch from oil boom in the 1970s to oil bust in the 1980s. They are also partly demographic in terms of diminishing natural increase, increasing internal migration from peripheral areas, and increasing immigration, mainly to the most important urban regions.

The outlook is rather gloomy, when observed from the periphery. Regional policies, which were offensive in the 1970s, have been defensive in the 1980s, because the central goal of preserving the existing settlement pattern cannot be reached through large-scale economic intervention any longer. This author argues that population distribution is an effect of economic processes, not a goal in itself, and that regional policies of the 1990s should take this into account. Only then can a new offensive regional policy be worked out.

Further reading

Two comparative studies of counterurbanization include Norwegian data: Ahnström, L. 1986: The turnaround trend and the economically active population of seven capital regions in western Europe, *Norsk Geografisk Tidsskrift* 40, 55–64, and Vining, D.R. and Kontuly, T. 1978: Population dispersal from major metropolitan regions: An international comparison, *The International Regional Science Review*, 3, 49–73. The internal shifts within the Norwegian urban system are studied by Myklebost, H. 1984: The evidence for urban turnaround in Norway, *Geoforum* 15, 167–76. Recent data on the renewed centralization of population in the 1980s are given in Byfuglien, J. 1986: The analysis of the settlement pattern in relation to planning problems, *Norsk Geografisk Tidsskrift* 40, 187–94. The underlying causes of recent population changes in Norway are investigated by Hansen, J.C. 1983: Regional Policy in an oil economy, the case of Norway, *Geoforum* 14, 353–61, Hansen, J.C. 1985: Regional disparities in present-day Norway, *Norsk Geografisk Tidsskrift* 39, 109–24, and Hansen, J.C. 1989: Official policies in marginal regions: temporary relief or New Deal? In Byron, R. (ed.) *Public policy and the periphery: problems and prospects in marginal regions* (Halifax, Canada: International Society for the Study of Marginal Regions), 100–11.

7

Denmark:

towards a more deconcentrated settlement pattern

YVONNE COURT

For most of the twentieth century Denmark has demonstrated a general tendency towards urbanization. The first half of the century showed few major changes in the settlement system. All sizes of towns from Copenhagen, which has always played a dominant role in both the demographic and economic development of Denmark, to the small urban settlements grew more or less constantly. The big cities grew particularly fast during the 1930s as the level of industrialization increased, whereas the rural population began to decline not only in relative but also in absolute terms. In many towns, suburbs developed beyond the administrative boundaries of the central municipalities, though they were physically contiguous with the built-up areas (Hansen 1960). By the beginning of the 1960s the Danish urban system comprised the primate city of Copenhagen with half the country's urban population, and a series of towns with between 1,000 and 200,000 inhabitants, of which the three largest were clearly distinct from the rest (Illeris 1964; 1967).

Since 1960, however, the Danish urban system has changed radically in two ways (Illeris 1979b; 1980). Firstly, during the early 1960s the tendency towards non-contiguous suburban development which had previously affected only the metropolitan area of Copenhagen began to involve most other big cities such as Århus, and some mediun-sized towns, for instance Fredericia, while there was also a rapid growth of scattered settlements further out in the regions around these. Secondly, after 1970 counterurban tendencies became apparent, with population growth occurring in the remoter rural regions as well as with growth continuing in the regions of low settlement density adjacent to deconcentrating urban centres. In the early 1980s the Copenhagen region's population began to recover, suggesting that counterurbanization was slowing down, but the period since 1983 has shown this development to be short-lived (Illeris 1987a; 1987b).

The main purpose of this chapter therefore is to examine closely the population turnaround that occurred in the early and mid 1970s, though some attention will also be given to the subsequent fluctuations in the pace of deconcentration. As outlined in the next section, these changes should be studied both at the regional level and in terms of the urban settlement system. Population data in Denmark permit analyses at both these scales, including breakdowns in the components of population change and the study of net migration by age, but employment and related data are not so readily available. The penultimate section examines the various factors which have been put forward to explain counterurbanization trends in Denmark, including the deconcentration of manufacturing industry, the growth of employment in services, the extension of school and other facilities down the urban hierarchy, the expansion of owner-occupied housing, the influence of spatial planning and the indirect spatial effects of other government policies. The explanation lies not in one factor alone, but involves the interaction of several processes working at the same time, but not necessarily together or with the same degree of importance (Illeris 1979b; Court 1985a).

Approach

Even in a relatively small country like Denmark – at 43,000 km^2, not much more than half the size of Scotland and less than one-fifth of the UK – there are basically two scales for examining the existence of population deconcentration tendencies over and above that of suburbanization and local decentralization. One is the broad division between the core region based on Copenhagen and the rest of the country, though within the latter it is also possible to distinguish the less urbanized and more peripheral areas in the west, south and north of the country from the more heavily populated areas further east. Secondly, it is important to look at the changing structure of the settlement pattern in order to identify trends in the rural population and shifts in the distribution of the urban population between different levels in the settlement hierarchy.

In general, data on Denmark's population size, composition, distribution and movement are relatively good, although there has been no formal census since 1970. Information is provided on a regular basis by the Central Population Register (*Centrale personregister* or *CPR*) which contains data on all persons resident in Denmark. In 1976 and 1981 there was a 'census' of population and housing (*Folke- og Boligtællingen*) based on data obtained from a number of national registers including the CPR, but every year data are available for age, sex, marital status, occupation, number of migrations, birth-place and address before and after migrations. These data, relating to 1 January each year and migration over the previous twelve months, are produced quickly, but there are time lags in the publication of other data, particularly those for employment which take two to three years to appear.

Most data are collected only by administrative units, of which there are two – the municipality and the county. The problem of comparing areal units over time is particularly apparent in the case of Denmark, where there was a major reform of the administrative boundaries in 1970. Until 1970, the basic units were approximately 1,350 municipalities distributed over 25 counties. In April 1970 the number of municipalities was reduced to 275 in 14 counties on the guiding principle 'one town – one kommune'. This means that for towns of 10,000–250,000 inhabitants there is a good correspondence between the administrative unit and the urban area (including the main part of its commuting field). Urban settlements with under 10,000 inhabitants are overbounded, as they are included in municipalities which have a large rural population and may incorporate several urban settlements. The capital region and its total commuting field (which includes the area 50–70 km from the city centre) comprises three counties and some 50 municipalities, and will be examined as the metropolitan region.

Population change can be calculated for categories of settlements differentiated by population size. The standard Danish classification (*Geokode*) of municipalities by the size of the largest settlement within them enables the population trends to be tracked over time. Obviously the size category of a municipality will not remain constant throughout any time period, making detailed comparison over time difficult. One way of partially overcoming this problem is to classify the municipalities according to their size at one specific point in time. Whilst this overcomes the problem of comparison, it must to some extent obscure the dynamic nature of population change (Court 1985a).

The population turnaround in Denmark

The 1970s saw counterurbanization replacing urbanization as the dominant trend shaping settlement patterns in Denmark. This is not to say that the urban share of the population began to fall at this time, because, as in Norway and most countries where it is possible to monitor population change at a very localized scale, the proportion of people living in isolated dwellings and very small settlements (in this case those with less than 200 inhabitants) has continued to decline – from 25.9 per cent in 1960 to 20.1 per cent in 1970 and 15.7 per cent in 1985. What did occur in the 1970s, however, was a switch in the distribution of population growth away from the Copenhagen region in favour of the rest of the country at the broadest geographical scale, as well as a shift down the urban hierarchy in the incidence of the next most rapid rates of population growth – the latter not merely due to the decline of the metropolitan region but occurring widely over the rest of Denmark too.

The impact of these two features of the population turnaround is indicated in Table 7.1, which shows the overall level of population change for county groups and major towns between 1970 and 1986 (1985 for towns). It can be seen that the metropolitan region, which had grown strongly in the late 1950s and 1960s, experienced an overall decline during this period, with the two main settlements of Copenhagen and Frederiksberg together losing nearly a quarter of their initial population. By contrast, all three of the other broad territorial divisions recognized in Table 7.1 experienced substantial growth, not only in the islands category which, with the exception of Bornholm, lie adjacent to or around the metropolitan region, but in particular the eastern part of Jutland. Even peripheral Jutland, comprising the western, southern and northern parts of the peninsula, recorded a 7 per cent increase in population over this period. At the same time, within each of these three regions, the largest town

Table 7.1 Denmark: Population change, 1970–86, for geographical divisions and principal towns

	Total 1970	Total 1986[1]	Absolute change 1970–86	Per cent change 1970–86
Copenhagen region[2]	1 742 789	1 718 982	− 23 807	− 1.4
Copenhagen and Frederiksberg	739 826	566 645	−173 181	−23.4
Islands[3]	986 873	1 040 326	+ 53 453	+ 5.4
Odense	137 276	136 803	− 473	− 0.3
East Jutland[4]	827 463	912 910	+ 85 447	+10.3
Århus	198 981	194 348	− 4 633	− 2.3
Peripheral Jutland[5]	1 348 697	1 444 055	+ 95 358	+ 7.0
Ålborg	123 412	113 865	− 9 547	− 7.7
Denmark	4 905 822	5 116 273	+210 451	+ 4.3

Notes:
1   Town populations at 1985, change 1970–85
2   Includes Copenhagen and Frederiksberg, and the counties of Copenhagen, Frederiksborg and Roskilde
3   West Zealand, Storstrøm, Bornholm and Funen
4   Århus and Vejle counties
5   North Jutland, Viborg, Ringkøbing, Ribe and South Jutland
Source:Statistisk Årborg; various years

experienced population decline, indicating significant shifts in population distribution down the settlement hierarchy (Table 7.1).

A more comprehensive analysis of the penetration of population deconcentration tendencies down the regional and urban hierarchy is provided by Illeris (1979b; 1984b). He examined population growth in two time periods between 1965 and 1976. Some deconcentration of population could be observed during the late 1960s. The Copenhagen region saw a stagnation in its rate of population growth during the early 1970s, followed by a decrease. The greatest rates of population growth during the period 1965–1970 occurred in the medium-sized and small settlements both in those areas with a high level of out-commuting to large towns and cities and those located further afield.

More detailed evidence on the timing of trends is provided in Figure 7.1, which shows annual rates for 1970–86 for the Copenhagen region and three broad categories of municipalities elsewhere. It appears that the metropolitan region's growth rate had already begun to fall back from its 1960s level by the beginning of the 1970s and then it fell steeply during the first half of the decade, well in advance of the national trend. The Copenhagen region moved into overall population decline in 1974 and remained in that state through to the end of the study period, though no further significant deterioration took place after 1976 and indeed the region's rate relative to the national rate of change significantly improved during the late 1970s and early 1980s before the gap widened again after 1982.

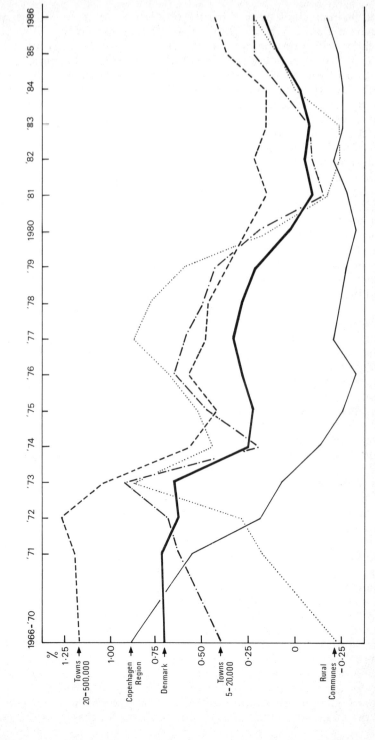

Figure 7.1 Denmark: annual population change rate, 1966–86, by type of municipality (after Sven Illeris).

Most of the main changes affecting the other three groups of municipalities shown in Figure 7.1 also took place during the early 1970s. The municipalities with principal towns of over 20,000 people constituted the most dynamic category in the late 1960s and early 1970s, but experienced a sudden drop in growth rate between 1972 and 1975 that was almost as large as that for the Copenhagen region. The change rate for this broad category did not become negative then or subsequently, but indeed remained above the national level, paralleling its fluctuations quite closely. The municipalities with towns of 5,000–20,000 at their centre have experienced wider oscillations in their change rate, performing strongly in 1972–73 and again in 1975–79 but dropping below the national level and into decline in 1981–83 before recovering again somewhat. This same pattern had been followed with even wider oscillations by the 'rural municipalities'. These are particularly distinctive both for the dramatic way in which they were affected by the population turnaround in the early 1970s and for the fact that this new-found demographic strength was maintained during the latter half of the 1970s, when they were the most rapidly growing of the four municipality groups (Figure 7.1).

To check the possibility that the turnaround picture in the 1970s presented by Figure 7.1 resulted merely because of the aggregate nature of the statistics, with strong growth in a few places offsetting widespread decline, Figure 7.2 maps population change at the municipality level for the main turnaround period 1970–79. While it was found that the largest single concentration of very rapid growth is located in the outer parts of the Copenhagen region and immediately adjacent parts of Zealand, many of the rural and small town areas of Jutland recorded substantial growth over the period, at least in relative terms, and the general picture is one of widespread population increases rather than depopulation. Indeed, only in north-west Jutland were there a significant number of cases of population decline amongst Denmark's more peripheral municipalities, while very high rates of population loss (10 per cent or more) are found only in Copenhagen's core area on the east coast of Zealand (Figure 7.2).

Clearly in the 1970s, a major turnaround affected the population fortunes of individual places in Denmark at both regional and urban scales. The metropolitan region experienced a particularly dramatic fall in its growth rate between the late 1960s and mid 1970s, while small towns and more rural areas – though not the smallest rural settlements – saw their aggregate positions changed from being the laggards of the 1960s to the most dynamic places of the middle and late 1970s. This effect was spread very widely across the more rural and peripheral parts of the country, though large-scale residential decentralization continued on a more local scale around the main cities, particularly the national capital. The early 1980s brought something of a reversal, with the decline in the change rate of the small-town and rural municipalities, and the improvement of the Copenhagen region and the larger towns relative to the national average, but the overriding impression of these few years is of a convergence of change rates around the national mean and a general slowdown in the process of population redistribution. The latter appears to have quickened again in the years since 1982, particularly with the widening of the gap

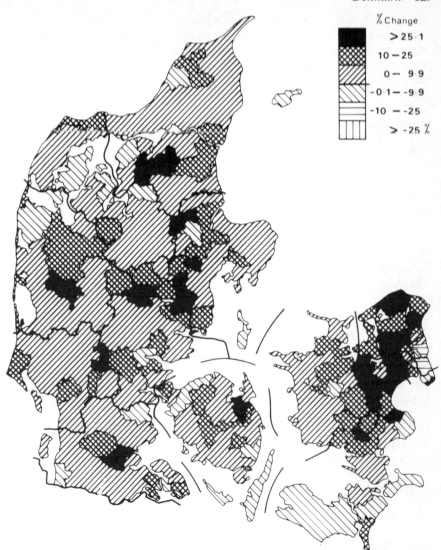

Figure 7.2 Denmark: population change, 1970–79, by municipality.

between the metropolitan region and the national rate, raising the possibility of a further period of more rapid counterurbanization.

Components of population change

Denmark has therefore been characterized by population deconcentration since the beginning of the 1970s, though the scale of population shifts from the Copenhagen region to the rest of the country has varied over time and the role of different parts of the latter has also fluctuated. The purpose of this section is to explain these patterns of deconcentration in terms of their demographic components – natural increase, international migration and internal migration. Each of these has been subject to changes at the national scale, but in addition individual regions and places have in some cases recorded substantial variations from the national trend, particularly for internal migration. Data are more readily available at the county level, but some mention is also made of trends for the different types of municipalities.

The key features of Denmark's national population development which help to explain the overall patterns in Figure 7.1 are as follows. First, the rate of natural change fell sharply from over 6 per thousand in the latter half of the 1960s to less than a third of this by 1976–78 and dropped below zero on average in the first half of the 1980s. Secondly, the international migration balance, though generally positive since 1970, has experienced two significant reversals associated with the periods of economic recession in 1974–75 and the early 1980s. Finally, the scope for internal population redistribution has been affected by the substantial decline which took place in internal migration propensities during the latter half of the 1970s. In all, the number of inter-municipality moves fell by 39 per cent between 1970 and 1981 and, though there was a slight upward turn in migration rates after 1981, it has by no means returned to the higher level of the late 1960s and early 1970s. In relation to the patterns in Figure 7.1, these three factors can be held responsible for, respectively, the overall downward trend in population change rates over time, the shorter-term downward kinks in this general profile around 1974–75 and 1981–82 and the tendency towards the convergence of the change rates of the four settlement categories at the end of the 1970s.

As regards population redistribution within Denmark, it is primarily the internal migration component that has been responsible for the changing levels and patterns of deconcentration since the late 1960s. Though not all parts of Denmark have closely paralleled the overall national trends in international migration and natural change, the extent of regional and local deviation is generally much smaller than for internal migration. Table 7.2 presents the net internal migration rates for the Copenhagen region and the remaining eleven counties for four periods between the latter half of the 1960s and the mid 1980s and allows the contribution of this component to overall population change to be compared with those of the other two components.

Table 7.2 shows clearly the dramatic change which took place in regional net migration patterns between the 1960s and 1970s. The period 1966–69 saw a continuation of the well-established pattern of migration losses from west Jutland, and net migration gains in the capital region and the urban areas of east Jutland, especially Århus. The early 1970s saw a major change in the situation, which is particularly evident in the downturn experienced in the internal migration balance of both the Copenhagen region and Århus. It is also clear that, at this county scale at least, the compensatory upturn was general across the rest of the country. It was greatest in the counties in the periphery (north, west and south Jutland), but was also strong in those more accessible to the capital region (west Zealand,

Table 7.2 Denmark: Population change and its components, 1966–86, for Copenhagen region and counties, annual rate per thousand people

Copenhagen region and counties	Internal migration				International migration				Natural growth				Total change			
	66–69	76–78	80–82	84–86	66–69	76–78	80–82	84–86	66–69	76–78	80–82	84–86	66–69	76–78	80–82	84–86
Copenhagen region	2.8	-3.9	-0.6	-1.5	0.8	0.9	-0.3	1.6	5.7	0.5	-1.9	-2.3	9.2	-2.5	-2.8	-2.2
West Zealand	2.6	6.5	1.2	4.4	0.3	1.2	0.0	2.1	5.1	1.1	-1.0	-1.1	8.1	8.8	0.2	5.4
Storstrøm	-2.4	4.7	1.4	2.2	0.4	0.8	0.1	1.7	2.8	-1.1	-3.2	-3.6	0.3	4.4	-1.7	0.3
Bornholm	-9.3	1.8	-1.4	-1.5	0.3	0.7	-4.9	0.8	3.7	0.8	-1.3	-2.1	-5.2	3.3	-7.6	-2.8
Funen	-2.6	1.7	1.3	1.4	-0.1	0.8	0.2	1.4	5.5	1.6	-1.0	-1.0	2.3	4.1	0.5	1.8
South Jutland	-1.4	0.7	-1.4	-1.9	-0.3	1.2	0.1	1.5	7.6	3.5	1.3	0.4	5.3	6.0	0.0	0.0
Ribe	-0.4	2.5	0.0	-0.9	0.0	1.3	0.2	1.4	9.2	5.0	3.0	2.1	8.8	8.8	3.2	2.6
Vejle	-1.1	1.6	0.4	0.7	0.3	1.2	0.0	1.5	7.1	3.4	1.0	0.0	6.3	6.2	1.4	2.1
Ringkøbing	-1.4	1.8	-1.4	-1.2	0.1	0.9	-0.3	1.4	10.5	6.1	3.4	2.3	9.2	8.8	1.7	2.5
Århus	-3.9	0.3	1.4	2.7	0.4	0.8	-0.2	1.6	7.5	4.2	1.2	0.9	11.7	5.3	2.4	5.2
Viborg	-4.0	1.6	-1.6	-1.6	0.2	0.9	0.0	1.7	6.5	2.9	0.8	0.1	2.8	5.4	-0.8	0.1
North Jutland	-4.6	1.7	-0.1	-0.5	0.0	1.0	0.1	1.7	7.2	2.9	0.8	-0.4	2.6	5.6	0.8	0.8
Denmark	0.0	0.0	0.0	0.0	0.4	0.9	-0.1	1.6	6.4	2.1	-0.3	-0.8	6.7	3.0	-0.4	0.8

Source: Table supplied by Sven Illeris

Storstrøm). The somewhat higher level of international migration during 1976–78 also assisted the population upturn in these counties. Together, the two migration components helped to offset the major fall in natural change found everywhere.

The slight improvement in the Copenhagen region's overall population change rate in 1984–86 was primarily the result of international migration. This was in spite of the fact that the internal migration balance picked up considerably between 1976–78 and 1980–82. The effect at that time was offset by a downturn in international migration and by a further fall in natural increase. Since 1980–82 the internal migration balance has moved against the Copenhagen region once more. The experience of Århus since 1976–78 has been similar to that of Copenhagen, except that its internal migration balance has continued to rise into the mid 1980s. West Zealand and Storstrøm have also experienced significant increases in their in-migration rates since the early 1980s, though still lower than those of 1976–78, and in their international migration balances.

International migration gave all counties a small boost in their popula-tion numbers during the mid 1980s, helping to offset a further small fall in the natural increase rate. Indeed, as outlined above, it was this component which caused the general acceleration in the national growth rate, rather than natural change. In all counties of Jutland (except Århus), the 1980s brought a setback for the internal migration balance from the relatively strong inward movement of 1976–78. However, there was little further deterioration between 1980–82 and 1984–86, and for Viborg, North Jutland and Vejle there was no return to the serious levels of net loss experienced during the 1960s. The same was not true for Ribe and South Jutland.

More detailed data at the municipality scale, not surprisingly, reveal a more complicated pattern than this. For instance, urban municipalities outside Copenhagen experienced net migration losses during the early 1970s, but since then these areas have gained through migration. The highest rates of growth in the other municipalities (i.e. the least urban) were generally concentrated in their 'most urbanized' municipalities. During the early 1970s it was the municipalities with less than 50 per cent of their inhabitants in towns with at least 2,000 population which showed the highest rates of net migration. The 'most rural' municipalities experienced net losses throughout the 1970s and 1980s.

Further insight into the changing nature of migration trends can be gained by examining the characteristics of those involved, particularly by age and occupational composition. Table 7.3 compares the net internal migration experience of the two geographical extremes of Denmark by reference to broad age groups. It shows clearly the general pattern, found in most countries, of a net inward flow of school leavers and young adults from the most peripheral counties to the metropolitan region. The net flow is in the opposite direction for all the other age groups identified, not just for retirement and pre-retirement groups but also for those of family age and their children. Indeed the numbers of older people involved, in net terms at least, appear to be relatively modest compared to the latter.

Trends over time in migration by age are also fairly clear cut, particularly for the Copenhagen region (Table 7.3). By comparison with 1965, in 1977

Table 7.3 Denmark: Internal net migration by age groups, selected years for Copenhagen region and Viborg and North Jutland counties

Age	Copenhagen region				Viborg + North Jutland counties			
	1965	1977	1981	1985	1965	1977	1981	1985
0–14	−2 328	−3 388	−1 392	−2 183	194	755	72	477
15–19	3 518	1 211	1 514	1 608	−1 683	−461	− 523	− 529
20–24	3 148	1 157	2 372	2 419	−1 557	−508	− 846	− 903
25–29	− 999	−1 303	− 408	− 914	7	483	130	149
30–44	−1 367	−2 547	−1 063	−2 067	143	494	− 13	448
45–64	− 504	−1 326	− 893	−1 377	30	149	125	234
65+	− 213	− 400	− 252	− 309	39	61	47	− 37
Total	1 255	−6 596	− 122	−2 823	−2 827	973	−1 008	−156

Source: Table supplied by Sven Illeris

the metropolitan region experienced a higher net loss of the traditional net out-migrant age groups and a lower net gain of the teenage and young adult groups. In general, this change had gone into reverse by 1981 but had begun to reassert itself again by 1985. The only exception is that between 1981 and 1985 the net in-migration of the 15–24 age groups increased in absolute terms partly due to the larger size of these age groups due to the baby boom of the mid 1960s but no doubt also influenced by changes in the distribution of opportunities for training, jobs and career development.

The two peripheral counties generally present a mirror-image of the Copenhagen region's experience of the migration turnaround between 1965 and 1977. By 1981, however, their attractiveness to the traditional in-migration age groups appears to have fallen to lower levels than those of the mid 1960s, though their net retention of teenagers and young adults continued to be better than at that time. Nevertheless, by 1985 there had been a further upturn in the net gain of the traditional in-migrant age groups, though not accompanied by any reduction in the loss of young adults. This prevented the overall migration balance for these two peripheral counties from climbing out of deficit and back towards the significant net inflow of 1977, but marked a substantial improvement on the aggregate level of migration loss recorded in 1981.

As regards the social composition of migration exchanges, some evidence has been compiled by G. Illeris (1984). She found that all groups of the population were involved in the changed patterns of migration during the early-mid 1970s. Selectivity operated in favour of professional or white-collar workers in the population, and in consequence these sectors were perhaps over-represented. The working class were also mobile but to a lesser extent (Illeris, G. 1984; Court 1985a). In 1977 the dominant trend was out-migration from the largest towns to other parts of the country; especially in the case of workers in 'urban' (service) occupations, salaried employees (i.e. managerial and technical) and the self-employed in 'urban' occupations.

A number of factors have therefore combined to produce the initial turnaround in population trends and the subsequent fluctuations in the scale and spread of population deconcentration. The dramatic change between the late 1960s and the mid 1970s in the fortunes of the

Copenhagen region *vis-à-vis* the rest of the country, though reinforced by the above-average decline in the former's rate of natural increase and the latter's generally greater rise in international immigration, was primarily the result of the major switch in the direction of net internal migration flows. These comprised a combination of lower rates of movement by school-leavers and young adults to the Copenhagen region and higher levels of exodus from it by all other broad age groups including families with children. The early 1980s brought a substantial decline in the rate of deconcentration, reflected in a convergence of net migration rates for both counties and municipality types, but the new pattern had tended to reassert itself again by the middle of the decade. These latest developments, however, have not been so uniform across the country as those of the mid 1970s, with the islands and east Jutland generally faring better than the more peripheral parts of Jutland.

Towards an explanation of counterurbanization in Denmark

The explanation for these trends lies not in one factor alone (Illeris 1979b), but in the interaction of several processes working at the same time, though not necessarily together or with the same degree of importance (Court 1985a). The nature of the processes which have promoted changes in the geography of employment is examined in the next section in an attempt to estimate their influence on the changes in population distribution. This also investigates the degree to which population growth is the cause or the consequence of a changed distribution of employment opportunities. The operation of the housing market, its relationship to job location and its effects on the distribution of population also merit examination. Particular attention needs to focus on regional variations in housing investment in the form of construction and house prices. State influence has helped to further mould the structure of opportunities open to individuals; not only policies aimed directly at altering the spatial distribution of population and economic activity, but also some policies that are not spatial in orientation or rationale but nevertheless have a spatial impact.

The changing geography of production

The nature and location of job opportunities changed during the period between 1970 and 1983, the latest year for which data are available at the time of writing. The array of choices open to individuals with respect to work expanded as a result of changes in the nature of production and in the labour market. Location became more flexible as a result of economic, technological and other structural changes.

At the beginning of the 1960s over half the industrial jobs were located in the capital region, compared with only one third of the population. Two-thirds of the country's jobs were concentrated in the four largest urban areas; Copenhagen, Århus, Odense and Ålborg. Only one-seventh of all manufacturing jobs were located in the five peripheral counties in north, west and south Jutland, where a quarter of the population were living. During the 1970s industrial development was characterized by a displacement from the east towards the west of the country (Sørensen 1984a; 1984b; Hartoft-Nielsen 1984) and from large towns towards small towns, both in the number of jobs and industrial establishments (Maskell 1983; 1985; Court 1988).

Despite manufacturing declining nationally during the period, there were places which were favoured by both these developments; principally the small-town municipalities in the periphery of Jutland. Maskell (1985) found that between 1972 and 1982 the Copenhagen region suffered a decline of 48,532 jobs (−40.7 per cent) and 625 firms (−36.3 per cent) in manufacturing (Table 7.4). In the same period the rural periphery of the country showed an increase of 9,408 (9.9 per cent) in manufacturing jobs. Maskell suggested that this rapid relocation was not primarily the result of migration but the net outcome of closures and contractions in eastern centres, and openings and expansions in the peripheral parts of Jutland. Wickmann and Birch (1983), in their study of small businesses, found that the peripheral regions were characterized by a much higher degree of 'entrepreneurship', measured in terms of propensity of people to set up their own firms.

It is unlikely that this shift in the location of manufacturing from bigger to smaller settlements was the consequence of state intervention. Most of the decentralization resulting from government policy in Denmark involved only short-distance moves. Most of the projects taking advantage of government incentives consisted of expansions of local companies, e.g. Brandtex A/S in Brande, or new establishments. Only a few firms have moved into the development areas from the developed regions, and these are most typically branch plants (Court 1987). It therefore seems likely that government intervention, at least in the sphere of regional industrial policy, has had little importance in the redistribution of population.

Employment in private and public services

In the private sector of service employment growth was experienced throughout the settlement system in the 1970s (see Table 7.5), with the exception of the small villages where shops, for example, were closing down. Economies of scale caused a concentration into fewer and larger settlements. The most dynamic branches, i.e. business and financial services, are highly concentrated in the Copenhagen area and other major centres of population. However, even these branches of the service sector have decentralized some of their activities to small-town areas (Illeris, S. 1984a; 1988b).

It has been suggested by Matthiesen (1981, 63) that the administrative reform of 1970 is partly the cause of the 'accelerated process of deurbanization' (*sic*). This reform introduced a decentralization of tasks and control. The level of public services was high and increased throughout the 1970s. Likewise the number employed in the public sector also grew considerably; from 18.5 per cent of the workforce in 1970 to 36.7 per cent in 1983. Although there is no general agreement about the

Table 7.4 Denmark: Manufacturing industry, 1972–82, by region

Region	Total employment				Number of enterprises			
	Distribution 1972	1982	Change 1972–82 number	%/year	Distribution 1972	1982	Change 1972–82 number	%/year
Islands	58	50	−62 837	−3.0	55	48	−775	−2.3
of which: Copenhagen region	38	30	−48 532	−3.7	35	28	−625	−3.0
Jutland	42	50	+ 2 511	+0.1	45	52	+101	+0.3
of which: Peripheral Jutland	24	31	+ 9 408	+0.9	27	33	+193	+1.0
Denmark	100	100	−60 326	−1.6	100	100	−674	−1.0

Source: Maskell, P., 1985

Table 7.5 Denmark: Service employment, 1970–80, distribution and change by region (%)

Region	Distribution 1980			Change 1970–80		
	Retail Trade	Finan. & bus. servs.	Total	Retail Trade	Finan. & bus. servs.	Total
Copenhagen Region	36	49	42	− 6	+25	+28
East of Storebælt	12	8	10	+11	+82	+45
Funen	9	7	8	+ 5	+76	+44
Vejle & Århus counties	17	15	17	+ 3	+63	+48
Rest of Jutland	27	20	23	+11	+79	+51
Denmark total	100	100	100	+ 2	+46	+39
Number (000)s	207	173	1 626			

Note: The 1970–80 growth is probably over-estimated, due to different methods of data collection
Source: Illeris, 1988a

consequences of the reforms and changes which took place around 1970, it is clear that a higher degree of equality in public service distribution was obtained, and this contributed to the changes which occurred in the settlement system. All the municipalities had to fulfil certain tasks, which in effect created rapid urban growth within former rural areas (Court 1985a).

Two opposing tendencies have been at work in the public sector for a number of years. Concentration into fewer institutions with more specialized functions has taken place within many subsectors, most notably hospitals and primary schools. However, at the same time, the expanding demand for the services of other subsectors has led to a reduction of the threshold population, and hence to a more decentralized location pattern.

In recent years the concentration tendencies have slowed down, partly as a consequence of the high costs involved in the construction of new public facilities, and partly due to an increased political interest in closer contact between institutions and the community. At the same time, local services, for instance kindergartens and secondary schools, have become the most important growth sectors across the country (Illeris, S. 1984a).

The changed patterns of capital investment help to explain the greater retention of school-leavers and young adults by more peripheral areas, which constituted one important element of the overall migration turnaround noted earlier. For instance, they were associated with larger numbers being taken into the education system. The decentralization of educational opportunities and increased commuting possibilities meant that fewer had to move from the peripheral areas in order to obtain an education. At the same time, the length of time spent in education became longer, with many young adults establishing families before their education was complete and becoming bound to the area for various reasons. Thus the time between their own completion of education and their children starting school became shorter, and previously it had been these years, in particular, when mobility was high. There was also a greater variety of employment opportunities in the peripheral areas. Many young people obtained their education locally and stayed in the area to take up local jobs. Others who had migrated returned. This was particularly true of those with middle-range training (Johansen 1983). Hence it could well be that population change in certain areas was not caused so much by the decision to migrate as by the decision to stay put, because of the increased employment and educational/training opportunities available within a given time-distance from the home (Court 1985a; 1988).

Residential property market

The relationship between household and job location is important in inter-regional migration. A strong relationship between a buoyant labour market and those areas with a high rate of house price increase and/or a high rate of investment in the construction of housing would be expected (Court 1985a). For some groups of the population, for instance the retired, this relationship may not be so important. In such cases other factors must be decisive; people moving to be nearer to relatives or simply to find the peace and quiet that city life fails to provide.

During the 1960s and early 1970s there was a vigorous construction of new dwellings. Table 7.6 shows how the pattern of construction changed after 1973, when there was a rapid decrease to 1976, and again from 1979 to 1982. The latter decline, which especially hit the construction of owner-occupied detached housing, was an obvious effect of the economic crisis (although the growing number of small childless households also played a part). On the other hand, there was increased construction of rented multi-family buildings and of relatively cheap low-density housing, for instance terraced and semi-detached houses. Illeris, S. (1984a) suggests that the lack of population growth in the peripheral regions, small settlements, and in the outer rings of the metropolitan areas during the early 1980s may be partly explained by the different composition of house building at that time.

A shift-share analysis by Christoffersen and Illeris (1982) shows that from 1979 to 1981 few changes took place in the geographical distribution of construction of each housing type. Thus those areas of the country where detached houses dominated, i.e. the peripheral areas, small settlements and the outer rings, were hardest hit by the decline in house building. On the other hand, those parts of the country, i.e. the major urban areas, in particular their inner rings and central municipalities where other dwelling types dominate, suffered little from the decline of house-building. Moreover, an examination of population development in the Copenhagen region by Illeris (1983) showed that the number of inhabitants stabilized across the range of existing housing stock and among all age groups, and not just in the areas closest to the city centre. His analysis of the Copenhagen region supports the conclusion that the decrease in house building heavily influenced the distribution of population during the early 1980s.

The costs involved in purchasing/renting a property are also important. Most migrants move into a dwelling of the existing housing stock rather

Table 7.6 Denmark: Construction of new dwellings, 1970–86, by dwelling type

Year	Detached one-family	Other one-family	Multi-family	Total[1]
1970	24 124	5 215	19 908	49 247
1973	33 941	4 084	14 300	55 566
1976	24 672	5 197	8 792	39 218
1979	19 614	6 730	3 900	31 064
1982	3 702	4 859	6 549	16 177
1983	4 859	9 981	5 915	22 071
1984	8 530	10 990	6 032	20 803
1985	7 678	8 863	5 198	22 613
1986*	10 539	9 961	5 728	27 729

Notes: [1] Includes a small number of residences in institutions etc.
    * Estimate
Source: Bygge- og anlægsvirksomhed (Statistiske Efterretninger), various years

than a new dwelling. Therefore house prices are more likely to be of even greater significance to most potential migrants than the level of new building. If the price trends of one-family housing are considered, then until the early 1970s prices were marginally higher in the Copenhagen region than in the rest of Denmark. After 1971–72 the trend was reversed, and the prices in the rest of Denmark increased more rapidly than in the Copenhagen region. This gap widened during the mid to late 1970s to reach their highest point in 1980. During the years 1981–82 the prices again declined throughout Denmark until 1983 when they increased again, although more steeply in the Copenhagen region (Court 1985a).

It is, however, difficult to establish the precise nature of the cause–effect relationships in house construction and price trends. A geographical relationship exists between the processes operating in the housing and labour markets, with the two markets operating partially to reinforce one another. Those areas with employment growth in west Jutland were also the areas of a high rate of investment in the construction of housing and/or a high rate of house price increases. It could be argued that since the main criterion of entry to the housing market is income, the changes which occurred in the housing market were, for most people, determined by developments in the labour market during the 1970s and early 1980s. However, migration was also dependent on the ability of people to find housing, which could cause problems if major differences existed between labour markets in terms of the price and availability of housing. Therefore counterurbanization could be seen as the outcome of the ways in which both the labour and housing markets operated (Court 1988).

The role of the State

The influence of the State cannot be ignored, since it has permeated Danish economic and social life increasingly throughout the postwar period; a feature by no means unique to Denmark. The spatial impact of policies, whether intentional or otherwise, can have a marked effect on the distribution of population through the structure and location of economic activity and public services. So, too, can changes in the structure of the governmental systems themselves. The administrative reform of 1970 was certainly a significant force for urban growth outside the metropolitan region at both regional and local levels. Under the new administrative arrangements there was a tendency to make the largest settlement of each new unit into the 'growth pole'. This was especially the case in those new counties that lacked a big city and in those municipalities that had no existing settlement above a certain size. All the municipalities were given a certain range of tasks to perform, stimulating rapid urban growth within former rural areas both through the jobs directly created and, as mentioned earlier, through increasing the scope of the services provided (Court 1985a).

A major reform of the planning system occurred around the same time as the administrative reform. This involved the setting up of a three-tier hierarchy with national, regional and municipal economic, structural and land-use plans. The pace of counterurbanization may also have been affected by certain planning legislation. According to Abild (1985) and Møller (1985) the Urban and Rural Zone Act (*By- og Landzoneloven*), which came into force in 1969, hindered the growth of the most rural areas. This act is restrictive in that it prohibits, for example, the conversion of empty agricultural buildings for small industrial firms. Planning since 1970 has focused on the development of a deconcentrated settlement system. The trend towards a decrease in the growth of the capital region and the three municipalities with cities of between 100,000 and 200,000 inhabitants was actually formulated as a target in the national plan (Matthiesen 1981). However, counteracting this was the tendency towards reurbanization during the late 1970s (Matthiesen 1980) and early 1980s.

The objective of these combined policies was to create an equal development for the whole country in an attempt to level out some of the differences between the large towns and the rest of the country. The first regional development act was passed in 1958 (with revisions in 1972 and 1985). Its aim was to counteract the concentration of economic activity and employment in the Copenhagen region, Århus and Vejle, and at the same time to encourage the industrial development of the more peripheral areas of the country. However, in recent years central government have argued that there are insufficient resources for developing all parts of the country, hence the attention on 'growth centres' of approximately 5,000 inhabitants (Court 1987).

Only a few governmental functions have migrated to peripheral regions. Likewise, as was noted earlier, very few private firms have moved to the development areas as a result of government incentives. In any case in recent years the overall rise in unemployment and the decelerating growth of the Copenhagen region have caused regional issues to recede into the background, whilst the more general structural national economic problems have been given priority (Court 1987).

Conclusions

The pattern of population change in Denmark has changed markedly since the 1960s, particularly from the switch of the Copenhagen region from substantial growth into overall decline. The 1970s also saw a transformation in the migration balances of remote rural regions and a continuation of growth in regions of low settlement density adjacent to deconcentrating urban centres. The early 1980s showed signs that counterurbanization was slowing down, suggesting that there would perhaps be a return to large city growth, albeit not to the same extent as previous phases of urbanization. However this appears to have been a transitory phase in the development of the settlement system, with the resumption after 1984 of growth in the medium and small towns of Denmark.

This chapter has identified a number of reasons for the recent changes in population distribution. It is not surprising to discover that the turnaround was the product of several forces working simultaneously, and not necessarily with synergy. Any explanation of population change, and in particular redistribution, has to be sought in terms of the wider societal and economic forces. The relationships between urbanization and spatial development patterns on the one hand, and changes in the macro-economic and social organization on the other, are unlikely to submit to any single set of explanatory variables or to a unitary theoretical paradigm. Illeris (1980) attempted to bring some structure into the discussion of the possible causes and effects with particular reference to market-economy countries. His factors were merely hypotheses and he stressed that research was needed if their relative importance were to be established (Burtenshaw and Court 1986).

It is now clear that patterns of industrial development changed significantly during the early 1970s. Counties in west Jutland which experienced high rates of population growth at that time also showed positive developments in terms of the number of industrial jobs and firms. The Copenhagen region showed the most dramatic decline in industrial development, as well as in population. Though manufacturing employment trends tended to lag behind the population trends, this time lag was partly caused by factors relating to migration and did not necessarily mean that the changes in population distribution 'caused' the interregional shifts in employment. The changes in the nature of production, and as a consequence the labour market, were important contributory agents influencing the structure of opportunities. A fairly strong relationship has also been shown between areas with a buoyant labour market and those with dynamic housing situations, though in this case too it is difficult to ascribe causality.

In the absence of data on local employment trends since 1983, it is difficult at this stage to give firm conclusions reflecting the latest developments in the distribution of population and economic activity or to speculate on future prospects. Official policy is wedded to the strategy of 'growth pole of small poles', by which every municipality should focus on one settlement as a growth centre for services and manufacturing. This is pursued in combination with the more obvious policy of establishing a settlement hierarchy through the regional plans. The main objective of planning efforts over the next decade is towards a more deconcentrated settlement system. However, counteracting this are initiatives aimed at encouraging the regeneration of some parts of the inner cities, which are partly guided by increased activity in the renewal of the older building stock.

These observations prompt new questions into the nature of small and medium-sized towns, and more importantly their linkages with large towns and cities. It would appear that increased locational flexibility has removed or weakened constraints, so that firms and households may now select from a wider range of settlement sizes without incurring increased production costs, reducing marketing gains, or sacrificing life-style options. More research is needed into the role of the property market and its decision makers in population and thereby labour force distribution. Linked to this is the need for greater information on the role of commuting in regional population development.

Acknowledgement

The author wishes to thank Sven Illeris for all his help and useful comments.

Further reading

On the development of the Danish urban system see: Illeris, S. 1984: The Danish settlement system: development and planning, in Bourne, L.S. *et al.* (eds.) *Urbanisation and settlement systems: international perspectives* (Oxford: Oxford University Press), 226–38. Developments in population growth and migration in the Copenhagen region, including core–ring differences, are described by Matthiesen, C.W. 1980: Trends in the urbanization process: the Copenhagen Case. *Geografisk Tidsskrift* 80, 98–101. Population deconcentration trends since the 1960s are described and analysed in considerable detail for the whole of Denmark in two papers: Matthiesen, C.W. 1981: Settlement change and political response, *Geografisk Tidsskrift* 81, 55–66 and Illeris, S. 1984: Danish regional development during economic crisis, *Geografisk Tidsskrift* 84, 53–62. For a general overview of regional development and spatial inequalities see: Court, Y. 1987: Denmark, in Clout, H. (ed.), *Regional development in Western Europe*, Third Edition (Chichester: David Fulton Publishers), 307–18.

8

Federal Republic of Germany:

The intensification of the migration turnaround

THOMAS KONTULY and ROLAND VOGELSANG

Germany was one of the early countries to undergo the Industrial Revolution. In the 1840s it experienced a rapid spatial concentration or urbanization of its population. Industry and population condensed in a few locations in what is now the Federal Republic of Germany (FRG). In areas such as the 'Ruhrgebiet', the Saar, and Hamburg rapid population growth started between 1843 and 1871, while industrialization was delayed in the southern regions which remained predominantly rural. An uninterrupted trend of urbanization, measured as increasing regional population concentration at the state (*Land*) level, can be seen from 1871 to the Second World War (Kontuly *et al.* 1986). With the post-war recovery, population concentration continued once again.

German language sources report minor changes in the level of spatial demographic deconcentration during the 1970s in the FRG, and conclude that these variations represent a continuation of a past rather than the beginning of a new long-term trend (Koch 1980; Koch and Gatzweiler 1980; Gatzweiler 1982). These sources discuss the counterurbanization phenomenon more indirectly than directly. Only Koch (1980) analyses the applicability of the counterurbanization thesis for the Federal Republic and other Western European countries, and argues that migration changes seen during the 1970–75 period do not constitute sufficient empirical proof for the beginning of the phenomenon. Koch and Gatzweiler (1980) recognize that the attractiveness of large West German urban agglomerations appears to decrease slightly during 1974–75 compared to the 1960s. But even though rates of in-migration to attractive urban regions and out-migration from certain peripheral areas slowed during the mid-1970s, they argue it is too early to speak of a reversal in migration trends similar to that observed in the US. Gatzweiler (1982) finds West German interregional migration patterns between 1970 and 1979 exhibiting signs of a movement from densely to sparsely populated regions, and this represents a change in the traditional distribution of regional migration balances in the FRG, but he concludes that it is too soon to postulate this as a long-term trend.

This chapter concentrates on three points. The first argues that a trend in the direction of counterurbanization starts in the FRG during the 1960s and strengthens during the 1970s and 1980s. Counterurbanization is evident in the FRG when evaluating the phenomenon using total population changes and/or net internal migration. The second point relates the counterurbanization trend to changes in the internal migration patterns of several age groups of the West German population. Point three suggests explanations for the new directions of age-specific internal migration.

Approach

Our study of counterurbanization in the Federal Republic of Germany first considers the issue of spatial scale. Then, the set of general definitions used as guidelines throughout this chapter are discussed. A short explanation of the data sources follows. Our analysis of the regional deconcentration of the West German population then focuses on an evaluation of the counterurbanization phenomenon utilizing total population change and separate considerations of each of the components of demographic change.

Spatial scale

Counterurbanization must not be confused with the suburbanization of the West German population, a process intensifying in the FRG since World War Two. In order to distinguish counterurbanization and urbanization patterns from the process of suburban decentralization, functional urban regions (FURs) are the geographic unit used in the chapter. Unlike comparable functional region schemes defined for the USA, this West German FUR system contains 58 areas, the 'BfLR-Bereiche', which cover the entire country (Figure 8.1).

Functional urban regions were specified by the Bundesforschungsanstalt für Landeskunde und Raumordnung (BfLR), the West German Federal Research Institute for Regional Geography and Regional Planning, and represent nodal regions defined as 'high-order' central places plus their surrounding hinterland (Kroner 1976; Kroner and Kessler 1976). The 'BfLR-Bereiche' scheme was used as a basic regional delimitation system until 1978. Thereafter, the BfLR employs a 75-region breakdown, i.e., the Planning Regions or 'Raumordnungsregionen'; refer to a recent publication such as BfLR (1986).

Raumordnungsregionen correspond for political reasons more closely with the boundaries of the states (Länder) and are therefore more useful for planning and administrative purposes. In some cases state boundaries traverse through FURs. In our opinion, the Planning Regions are too small in land area for approximating a functional urban system, and using this regional scheme would create problems in which the interregional counterurbanization process overlaps with intra-regional and/or suburban decentralization. For this reason, this chapter employs the BfLR-Bereiche functional urban scheme in an evaluation of changing West German interregional demographic patterns.

In the Federal Republic no single core region dominates the urban system. Rather than a predominant metropolitan agglomeration or an

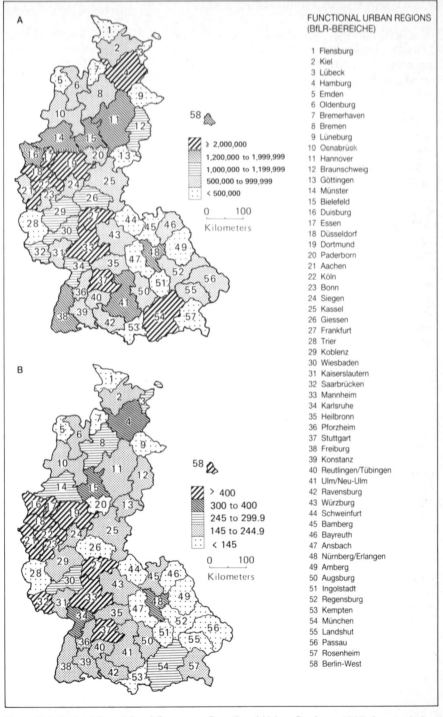

Figure 8.1 Federal Republic of Germany: Functional Urban Regions, 1985. A: population size; B: population density 1985 (persons per km²).

influential national capital region such as London, Brussels, Copenhagen, Helsinki, Oslo, Paris, Stockholm, or Vienna, West Germany exhibits numerous spatially dispersed urban complexes (Figure 8.1). In addition to the Rhine–Ruhr agglomeration of Essen, Düsseldorf, Dortmund, and Köln and the Rhine–Main and Neckar regions centred on Frankfurt, Mannheim/Ludwigshafen, and Stuttgart, there are the geographically separated large population centres of Hamburg in the north, München in the south and Nurnberg/Erlangen in the east. The West German urban system exhibits a varied spatial distribution of small, medium, and large-sized regions. Most of the smallest urban areas are found along the international borders.

A general correspondence exists between the classification of FURs by population size (Figure 8.1A) and by regional population density (Figure 8.1B). Most but not all of the large-sized functional urban regions are also the most densely populated. Differences exist because certain FURs are overbounded. For example, München (FUR 54) is found in the highest population size class (Figure 8.1A) but because of overbounding is found in the average population density category (Figure 8.1B). Similar discrepancies exist for other regions such as Hamburg (FUR 4), Hannover (FUR 11), Münster (FUR 14), and Freiburg (FUR 38). Each of these FURs has a very dominant single central city and consequently a larger hinterland of its own. The general correspondence between regional population size and density will be important to remember when we analyse the relationships between total and age-specific net internal migration and regional population size.

Counterurbanization as interregional population deconcentration

In this chapter, counterurbanization refers to a redistribution of population from larger settlements and more densely populated areas to smaller centres and less densely settled areas (Champion 1985). We interpret the counterurbanization process in the Federal Republic of Germany as an interregional deconcentration of population and employ functional urban regions as the basic spatial unit.

Two formal definitions of the counterurbanization phenomenon will be applied in this chapter. First, counterurbanization is defined as a negative association between the total population change (growth) rate and the population sizes of functional urban regions (Fielding 1982; 1986a). Second, counterurbanization is described in the form of a negative relationship between the net internal migration rate and the population sizes of functional urban regions (Fielding 1982; 1986a).

Data sources

The Bundesforschungsanstalt für Landeskunde und Raumordnung provided total population change and its disaggregation into components of demographic change by the 58 functional urban regions for the 1970 to 1985 time period (BfLR 1986; 1987). Major definitional alterations at the 'community' level between 1968 and 1975 created gaps in the regional total population data series for the years before 1970. For this reason, population sizes of FURs in 1950, 1960, and 1968 were reconstructed based on data for smaller regional units (Kontuly *et al.* 1986).

Yearly net internal migration by FUR for 1970 to 1984 were also furnished by the BfLR (BfLR 1986; 1987). German migration data are collected from population registers, and regarded as being of extremely high quality. The 1970 to 1984 total net internal migration data are disaggregated by German and foreign movers; total net internal migration is also subdivided into six age-groups.

Stratifications of the young and the intermediate age-groups changed between 1973 and 1974. The BfLR used the following age categories from 1970 through 1973: less than 16 years old, 16 to 20, 21 to 34, and 35 to 49. After 1973 the classification was changed to the following: less than 18 years old, 18 to 24, 25 to 29, and 30 to 49. The 50 to 64 years and the 65 and over age-groupings remained unchanged during the study period. Age-group changes between 1973 and 1974 created disturbances in the urbanization and counterurbanization patterns for the 30 to 49 and the under 18 year olds; these changes will be discussed later in the chapter.

Recent patterns of overall population change

Total regional demographic change in the FRG will be evaluated using three approaches. The first investigates variations in the absolute levels of population change and the annualized population growth rates for five size categories of functional urban regions. The second examines temporal variations in the spatial distribution of population growth rates, while the third statistically tests associations between the total population change rate and the population size/population density of FURs.

Levels of population change and rates of change

In the first approach both absolute levels of population change and annualized change rates are summarized using five population size categories of functional urban regions. Size categories are constructed so that the middle or third interval represents average regional population size and so that two distinct categories lie above and two lie below the mean. Formally, each of the class intervals in Tables 8.1 and 8.2 are defined using the mean (arithmetic) 1985 regional population size and the standard deviation of 1985 population size. The five class intervals in each of the maps in Figures 8.1 and 8.2 are established using the same method, but utilizing the population mean of each period.

The national size of the West German population increased between 1950 and 1980 but declined thereafter (Table 8.1). The population growth rate of the 1950s was the result of a high level of natural increase and the immigration of expellees from former territories of the Third Reich and of refugees from East Germany. Construction of the 'Berlin Wall' in 1961 reduced the number of immigrants entering the FRG from the German Democratic Republic. Natural increase remained high in the FRG until 1968, and has declined ever since. In 1985, the death rate exceeded the birth

Table 8.1 Federal Republic of Germany: Total population change, 1950–85, by Functional Urban Regions grouped according to 1985 population size

FUR size group (million people)	1950–60	1960–68	1970–80	1980–85
Population change (000s)				
2.0 and over	3 166.2	1 703.7	475.1	−309.1
1.2–1.99	975.6	651.5	20.3	− 93.8
1.0–1.19	435.2	460.3	14.1	− 40.1
0.5–0.99	483.3	1 165.1	415.5	78.7
Under 0.5	− 311.9	347.5	61.2	19.5
Total FRG	4 748.4	4 328.1	986.2	−344.8
Change rate (% per year)				
2.0 and over	1.74	1.03	0.21	− 0.27
1.2–1.99	0.93	0.72	0.02	− 0.16
1.0–1.19	0.75	0.92	0.02	− 0.13
0.5–0.99	0.38	1.09	0.29	0.11
Under 0.5	−0.55	0.76	0.10	0.06
Total FRG	0.90	0.95	0.16	− 0.11

rate and the country experienced natural decrease.

A net in-migration of foreign workers caused the West German population to increase rapidly during the second half of the 1960s and the first half of the 1970s. Then, in response to a high national rate of unemployment and a declining economic growth rate, strict controls were imposed in 1973 on the entrance of 'guest' workers. Foreign net in-migration increased once again during the late 1970s, when families and dependents of foreign workers (in particular the Turkish) were allowed to enter the Federal Republic. At present, these controls remain in place as far as immigration of foreigners from outside the European Community is concerned.

Variations in the absolute levels of regional population change between 1950 and 1985 not only reflect the broad, national demographic factors described above but also comprise shifts down the urban size classes (Table 8.1); a shift in which population growth in small-sized FURs replaces the expansion of large regions. Annualized rates of population change between 1950 and 1985 show clearly a kind of hierarchical shift (Table 8.1). The positive correspondence, during the 1950s, between the regional demographic change rate and FUR population size indicates a dominance by large-sized regions. Urban areas with sizes equal to or greater than two million people experienced the highest growth rate in the 1950s (1.74 per cent). Rate of growth declines as regional size categories decrease, with regions of less than one-half million people exhibiting the lowest rate of population change (−0.55 per cent). This positive correspondence during the 1950s between FUR population size and FUR growth rate indicates an urbanization pattern, or a redistribution of population from smaller-sized and less densely populated urban regions to larger and more densely settled areas.

A trend toward counterurbanization begins in the FRG during the 1960s

(Table 8.1). Urban regions in the one-half million to one million population size class exhibit the fastest growth rate during the 1960s (1.09 per cent), while the largest-sized urban regions rank just second (1.03 per cent). A similar pattern continues during the 1970s, with the smallest size class now ranking third above the 1–1.19 million and the 1.2–1.99 million size categories. Through the first half of the 1980s, growth rates decline as population size categories increase.

Focusing exclusively on rates can be misleading when large growth rates translate into small absolute population increases (Engels and Healy 1979). This condition does not hold for the Federal Republic during the time periods after 1960, when the dominance of large-sized regions begins to break down. A comparison of annualized rates of population growth with changes in absolute levels (Table 8.1) reveals that between 1960 and 1985 FURs in the over 2 million size class expanded by approximately 1.87 million people while urban regions between 0.5 and 0.99 million grew by 1.66 million.

A shift of demographic growth down the urban size classes can also be seen in the performance of the smallest category of urban regions (under 0.5 million), which improves its relative ranking to third place during the 1970s and in the 1980s shows the second highest growth rate (0.06 per cent). During the first half of the 1980s, only the two smallest categories of FURs show positive growth rates, while the average and above average-sized regions exhibit negative rates of change (Table 8.1). The correspondence between FUR population size and the FUR growth rate becomes a negative association during the 1980s reversing the pattern of the 1950s.

Regional distribution of population growth rates

The shift of population growth to small-sized urban regions during 1960–85 manifests itself in the form of a reduction of the concentration of growth in the west-central and the south-west regions and the shift to a more even spatial distribution throughout the Federal Republic (Figure 8.2). In the 1950s rapid population growth concentrated primarily in the Rhine–Ruhr agglomeration (FURs 16–19, 22 and 23), in the Rhine–Main and Neckar regions (FURs 27, 33, 37 and 40). Four of the eight regions exhibiting the highest growth-rates were in the largest size class, while all of the regions in the north and a continuous strip of FURs running from north to south along the eastern border showed low growth rates.

Population growth moved to large urban regions in the centre (FURs 26, 27 and 43) and in the south (FUR 54) of the country during the 1960s. The Rhine–Ruhr complex showed relative decline and a spatial dispersion of above-average growth began to certain regions which traditionally experienced low growth rates (FURs 5, 20 and 51) and belonged to the small size category. Patterns during the 1970s reinforced those of the 1960s, with a greater dispersal of growth to the smaller FURs in the north-west and the south-east. This wider regional dissemination of growth to small-sized FURs continued during the 1980s, with above-average growth concentrating in the south and to a lesser degree in the north of the country. A corridor of average or below average growth, excluding Bonn (FUR 23),

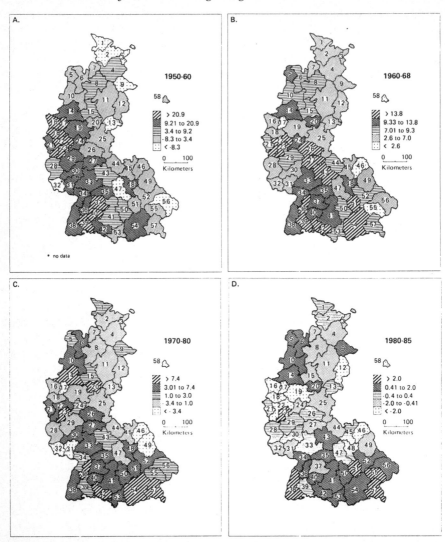

Figure 8.2 Federal Republic of Germany: total population change, 1950–85, Functional Urban Regions (per cent).

now runs through the centre of the Federal Republic.

A major difference between the regional growth patterns of the 1980s compared to those of the 1960s and 1970s is the more pronounced decline of the Rhine–Ruhr area, which now includes Köln (FUR 22), and the relative decline of the other large urban regions such as Frankfurt (FUR 27) and Stuttgart (FUR 37). Newer, large FURs with contemporary employment bases which expanded rapidly during the 1960s and 1970s stopped growing, whereas some small and more peripheral FURs gained relatively

(Figure 8.2). A combination of the relative stagnation of the newer, large FURs and the continuous decline of older industrial regions in the Rhine–Ruhr accounts for the negative change rate of the two million-plus size category during the 1980s (Table 8.1).

Statistical analysis of total population change

This section tests more rigorously for the existence and timing of counterurbanization tendencies in the FRG, using measures of statistical associations between the population size/population density of FURs and their regional population growth rates. As explained earlier, these statistical tests represent applications of one of Fielding's definitions of counterurbanization (Fielding 1982; 1986a). Figure 8.3 summarizes these relationships for the 1950 to 1985 time periods; regression lines drawn on these graphs indicate the general nature of the relationships and the way it changes over time. West Berlin, with its exceptional political situation and boundary, appears as an outlier in each of the statistical tests relating regional population density and the regional population growth rate, necessitating its removal from graphs a1, b1, c1, and d1 in Figure 8.3 and the related analysis.

A positive relationship, indicative of continuing urbanization or spatial concentration of regional population, existed during the 1950s. Both the association using population density (a1) and the one employing population size (a2) are positive and statistically significant at the 5 per cent level. The 1960s and 1970s appear as transition periods in an evolution from an urbanization to a counterurbanization pattern; all four of the trend lines show a negative slope (b1, b2, c1, and c2) but none are statistically significant. Using this statistical approach, counterurbanization appears during the 1980s (d1 and d2), with both negative trend lines significant at the 5 per cent level (Figure 8.3).

Frequency distributions of the regional population density and the regional population size variables are not statistically normal, but transformations of each of these variables enabled us to approximate normal distributions. Statistically significant positive relationships in a1 and a2 of Figure 8.3 remained unchanged, when transformed population size or density was correlated with the demographic growth rate. The counterurbanization or negative associations in d1 and d2 also remained invariant. Note that, in these analyses, we are not seeking to explain population change in the West German urban system, but are merely using correlations with density and size in order to identify the prevailing trends towards urbanization and counterurbanization.

In summary, this evaluation of overall population change indicates that an urbanization pattern existed in the FRG during the 1950s, and that counterurbanization became evident in the 1980s. Patterns during the 1960s and 1970s represent an evolution from a trend of urbanization to one of counterurbanization. A spatial demographic deconcentration of the West German population occurred in the 1980s; a deconcentration which may be related to the shifting of population growth down the urban size classes.

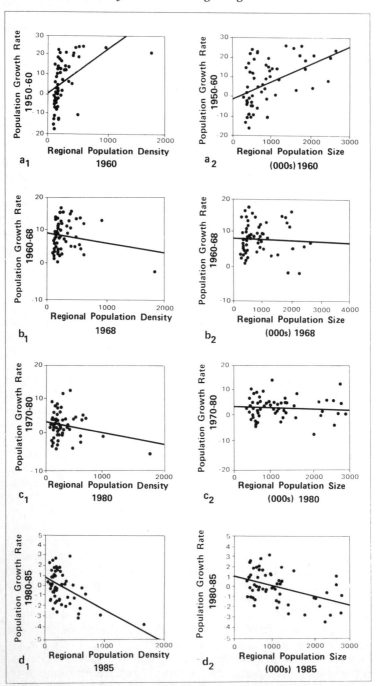

Figure 8.3 Federal Republic of Germany: relationship between population growth rate and population density/size, 1950–85, for Functional Urban Regions. Note that population growth rate is per cent for whole period, regional population density is expressed in persons per km².

Components of population change, 1970–85

The direct reasons for the evolution into the clear counterurbanization of the 1980s can be obtained by comparing the population change components in the later period with those of the 1970s for the five FUR size groups used in Table 8.1. A lower birth rate in the 1980s compared to the 1970s reduced population growth in the FURs fairly uniformly, with four of five regional size categories showing larger rates of natural decline in the 1980s (Table 8.2). Variations in net international migration by foreigners significantly affected the largest size category of regions. Net immigration by foreigners represented a major source of West German regional population growth during the 1970s, and a major portion of this increase ended up in the largest-sized regions. During the 1970s, the population of the Federal Republic increased by 1.35 million due to the net immigration of foreigners, with urban regions of over 2 million people accounting for 0.54 million of this net addition. In the first half of the 1980 the latter experienced the largest net loss of foreigners (−0.11 per cent), a net reduction of 0.12 million (Table 8.2).

The shifting of regional growth down the rank of West German urban size classes between 1970 and 1985 was also caused by changes in the internal redistribution of the population. In the categories of average and above average-sized FURs each show negative net internal migration during the 1980s while the two smallest-sized categories of FURs exhibit positive net internal migration.

Levels and rates of change for demographic components

Detailed changes in regional growth patterns for large versus small-sized FURs during the 1970s and 1980s can be seen in a comparison of the levels of average annual population change and the annualized rates of the components of demographic change for the 2-million-plus versus the 0.5–0.99 million group (Table 8.2). Almost all of the demographic components influenced the change from positive growth in the 1970s to population decline during the first half of the 1980s for the largest-sized category of urban regions. The net international migration by non-Germans changed from an annual average immigration of 53,900 between 1970 and 1980 to an emigration of 24,800 between 1980 and 1985. A further reduction in natural change and negative net internal migration also contributed to the 1980s population change rate (Table 8.2). Net internal out-migration was not limited to the older industrial regions in the Rhine–Ruhr agglomeration, i.e. Essen (FUR 17), Düsseldorf (FUR 18), and Dortmund (FUR 19). Köln (FUR 22), Frankfurt (FUR 27), and Stuttgart (FUR 37) also show net internal out-migration during the first half of the 1980s; in addition, all other FURs in this size-category (Hamburg [FUR 4], Mannheim [FUR 33], and München [FUR 54]) experience large reductions in net internal in-migration.

Functional urban regions in the 0.5–0.99 million size class were also impacted by the continued decline of the birth rate and changes in the direction of net migration by foreigners between the 1970s and the 1980s.

Table 8.2 Federal Republic of Germany: Components of population change, 1970–80 and 1980–85, by FUR size groups

FUR size group (million people)	Natural change		Net international migration		Net internal migration						Total population change	
					Total		Germans		Foreigners			
	70–80	80–85	70–80	80–85	70–80	80–85	70–80	80–85	70–80	80–85	70–80	80–85
Annual average (000s)												
2.0 and over	−36.0	−40.7	6.6	−23.0	76.9	1.9	23.0	26.7	53.9	−24.8	47.5	−61.8
1.2–1.99	−24.6	−24.3	−13.3	−3.1	39.9	8.7	8.5	9.9	31.4	−1.2	2.0	−18.7
1.0–1.19	−11.4	−12.5	−4.4	−2.3	17.2	6.8	3.9	4.3	13.3	2.5	1.4	−8.0
0.5–0.99	−3.0	−9.5	11.6	23.2	32.9	2.0	6.8	7.7	26.1	5.7	41.5	15.7
Under 0.5	−5.9	−8.1	−0.8	7.4	12.8	4.6	2.6	3.5	10.2	1.1	6.1	3.9
Annual rate (%)												
2.0 and over	−0.16	−0.18	0.3	−0.10	0.34	0.01	0.10	0.12	0.24	−0.11	0.21	−0.27
1.2–1.99	−0.21	−0.21	−0.11	−0.03	0.33	0.07	0.07	0.08	0.26	−0.01	0.02	−0.16
1.0–1.19	−0.18	−0.20	−0.07	−0.04	0.27	0.11	0.06	0.07	0.21	−0.04	0.02	−0.13
0.5–0.99	−0.02	−0.06	0.08	0.16	0.23	0.01	0.05	0.05	0.18	−0.04	0.29	0.11
Under 0.5	−0.10	−0.13	−0.01	0.12	0.21	0.08	0.04	0.06	0.17	0.02	0.10	0.06

But positive net internal migration more than doubled between the two periods, increasing from an annual average of 11,600 between 1970 and 1980 to 23,200 for 1980–85. The smallest size category of FURs mirrors the changes of this group, with the difference being that the negative net internal migration of the 1970s turns positive during the 1980s (Table 8.2).

As a result of low birth rates and current restrictions on the entrance of foreign workers from outside the European Community, internal migration has become the primary component of regional demographic change. The large net in-migration of foreign workers offset the declining birth rate of the native German population during the early 1970s. Then, the imposition of controls on the immigration of guest workers, in 1973, resulted in net foreigner emigration in each year from 1974 to 1977. At the end of the 1970s, family members and dependents of these foreign workers were allowed to enter the Federal Republic. This net immigration of foreign family members affects regional levels of natural change to the present day, because foreigners still possess higher birth rates than the native German population. The constraints of the 1973 restrictions were felt during the first half of the 1980s; net international migration by foreigners has remained negative since 1982.

Between 1970 and 1974, regional variations in the natural change rate (the difference between the birth and death rate) assisted the trend toward counterurbanization. High rates of natural increase in small-sized, sparsely populated regions with large proportions of Roman Catholics aided a regional deconcentration of the population. After 1974, the relatively high natural increase rate of foreigners counteracted this counterurbanization tendency, for foreign workers and their families concentrated in large German cities and large, densely populated urban regions (Gatzweiler 1983).

The contribution of net foreign migration to counterurbanization or urbanization trends varied widely between 1970 and 1984. Because of their locational concentration within the country, the net movement of foreigners into or out of large-sized urban regions corresponds with periods of either immigration into or emigration out of the Federal Republic (Kontuly and Vogelsang 1988a).

Statistical analysis of net internal migration

A second series of statistical tests for the existence and timing of counterurbanization in the Federal Republic focuses on internal migration, since this aspect of demographic change currently assumes prime importance, and will remain the principal demographic component in the future as birth rates remain low and current restrictions on the immigration of foreigners continue. The counterurbanization phenomenon will be tested in the form of a statistical association between the total net internal migration rate (TNIMR) and the regional population size RPS of FURs; then, TNIMR will be subdivided by German (GNIMR) and foreign (FNIMR) internal movers and related to RPS.

Correlation coefficients expressing these associations on an annual basis between 1970 and 1984 are graphed in Figure 8.4. (Urbanization and

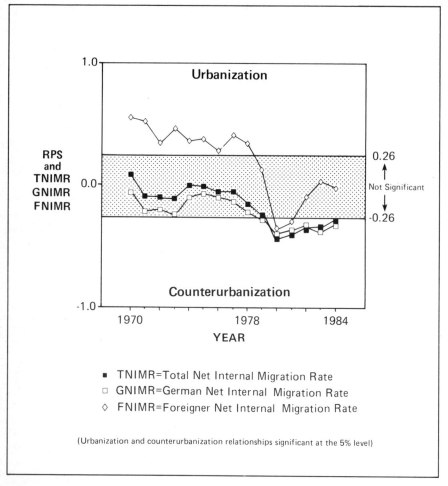

Figure 8.4 Federal Republic of Germany: correlation coefficients between regional population size (RPS) of FURs and the net internal migration rate, 1970–84 for total, German and foreign populations.

counterurbanization relationships are statistically significant at the 5 per cent level). In 1970 the total net internal migration variable shows a pattern which is neither urbanization or counterurbanization. By 1980 counterurbanization had become evident and the relationship remained in this direction through 1984. The timing of the counterurbanization phenomenon when measured as a statistically significant negative relationship between the net internal migration rate and the population size of FURs parallels the findings of the test summarized in Figure 8.3, which identified the beginning of a deconcentration trend in total population during the first half of the 1980s.

Figure 8.4 also shows the results of separate tests for the internal migration of Germans and foreign nationals. Because of the minor importance of foreigners in internal migration, the pattern traced by the German internal migration variable (GNIMR) in Figure 8.4 closely follows the one relating to the total population.

The internal migration of foreigners within the FRG is minimal (Gatzweiler 1982), on the average accounting for only 5 per cent of yearly internal moves. The internal migration of foreigners remains focused on large metropolitan regions from 1970 through 1978, as shown by an urbanization direction of movement (Figure 8.4). After 1978, the direction varies between counterurbanization (in 1980 and 1981) and neither urbanization nor counterurbanization (in 1982–84).

Its trend toward regional population deconcentration started in 1976 and reached the critical statistical threshold in 1979. Since that year it has remained in this counterurbanization direction through 1984. The internal movement of foreigners thus postponed the counterurbanization pattern of the German population by one year. The migration of foreigners, whether representing international (Kontuly and Vogelsang 1988a) or internal movement, dampens the counterurbanization pattern of the German population.

Our evaluation (Kontuly and Vogelsang 1988b) of the volume or level of net internal migration provides additional verification of a counterurbanization trend in the FRG during the 1970 to 1984 period. The migration turnaround discussed in that study conforms with the changes summarized in Tables 8.1 and 8.2 of this chapter. Structurally weak, densely populated urban regions, such as in the Rhine–Ruhr agglomeration and the Saarland, were not specifically responsible for this turnaround, for these areas were experiencing net out-migration in each of the years from 1970 to 1984.

Statistical testing for the existence of counterurbanization defined as a negative relationship between the total net internal migration rate and population size of FUR revealed the phenomenon began in 1980 and continued through 1984. An analysis of absolute net migration volume provides additional verification of this finding (Kontuly and Vogelsang 1988b). The results of the latter study eliminate the possibility that in the correlation analysis of net internal migration rates with population size, small-sized urban regions carry undue weight in affecting the statistical relationships and thereby distort our results.

An age-based explanation of counterurbanization trends

A disaggregation of net migration by age, in an earlier study (Kontuly *et al.* 1986), revealed during the 1970s a counterurbanization pattern of movement for the 50 years and older group and an urbanization direction of movement for the 18 to 29 year olds. Detailed case studies of migration in several types of urban regions confirmed the importance of analysing age-selective movement, and provided a direction for the investigation of explanations for urbanization and counterurbanization patterns in the Federal Republic (Vogelsang and Kontuly 1986). Our analysis of age-specific total migration (Kontuly and Vogelsang 1988a) showed that a

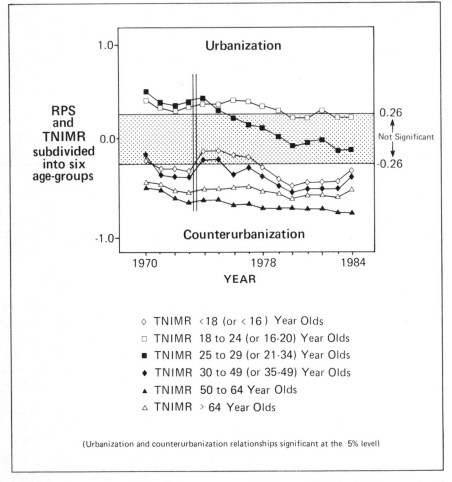

Figure 8.5 Federal Republic of Germany: correlation coefficients between regional population size (RPS) and total net internal migration rate (TNIMR), 1970–84, by age groups. Note that the age-group definitions changed in 1974; those in brackets relate to 1970–73 (see text).

counterurbanization pattern of movement filtered down from older to younger age-groups of the population. Useful insights into changing urbanization and counterurbanization trends were revealed and, more importantly, causes were suggested for the intensification of counter-urbanization in the FRG.

A third series of statistical tests focuses on the timing and intensity of counterurbanization for different age-groups of the population, through an evaluation of the relationships between age-specific net internal migration rates and the population size of FURs during the 1970 to 1984 time period (Figure 8.5). As discussed earlier in this chapter, these statistical tests represent applications of definitions of counterurbanization which provide clues to the explanations of the phenomenon. Several different explanations will be suggested later in this chapter for the age-specific migration changes revealed. The migration data set combines the internal movement of both Germans and foreigners in the age-specific net internal migration variable, but it should be remembered that Germans account for 95 per cent of the moves underlying the associations shown in Figure 8.5.

Changes in age-group delimitations between 1973 and 1974 resulted in a disturbance of the counterurbanization patterns for certain age-groups. The double-line drawn on Figure 8.5 allows for a clear division of the time periods before and after this definitional change. Between 1971 and 1973, the under 18 (or under 16) year-olds closely follow the counterurbanization pattern of the 30 to 49 (or 35–49) age-group. We can therefore treat these two groups as essentially a single category of family migrants, whilst realizing that a growing number of single-parent families are represented in this group. Probably a result of the definitional changes between 1973 and 1974, both age-groups move into the not significant portion of the diagram, which signifies neither an urbanization nor a counterurbanization pattern. The disturbance is partly artificial and only temporary, for the 30 to 49 year-olds once again move in a counterurbanization direction starting in 1976 and the under 18 year-olds return to this pattern of movement in 1978. Both family migrant age-groups continue following a counterurbanization pattern through 1984. In addition, the pre-retirement (50 to 64) and retirement (over 64) age-groups move in a counterurbanization direction throughout the period.

The urbanization pattern of movement of both the 18 to 24 (16–20 before 1974) and the 25 to 29 (21–34) age-groups stops during the study period. Definitional changes create no distortion in the movement patterns of these two age-groups (Figure 8.5). The 25 to 29 year-olds move out of a clear urbanization pattern in 1976; thereafter their movement patterns tend toward counterurbanization. The 18 to 24 year-olds continue moving in an urbanization direction until 1980; thereafter they move in neither a significant urbanization or counterurbanization direction, except for the year 1982.

Age-specific internal migration patterns therefore changed dramatically between 1970 and 1984. In 1984 no age-group moved in a statistically significant urbanization direction. The 30 to 49 and the under 18 year-old groups, which include primarily family migrants, moved in a counterurbanization direction as did retirement and pre-retirement movers, represented by the 50 and over age-groups. Also, the 25 to 29 year-olds began approaching a counterurbanization pattern of movement during the second half of the 1970s and the first part of the 1980s.

Diverse explanations are necessary to understand these changing patterns of age-specific migration. The filtering-down of a counterurbanization direction of movement from the 50 and over age-groups to family movers (the 30 to 49 year-olds plus their children) appears related to both a deconcentration of employment opportunities to small-sized, sparsely populated regions and an increasing preference for residences located in areas with abundant natural amenities. The internal movement of the 30 to 49 year-olds remains oriented to regions with sufficient job opportunities.

Employment openings are being created in small-sized regions as the result of several factors including the net in-migration of the 50 and over population, the West German government's policy of deconcentrating higher education opportunities, and the improvement of social, recreational, and infrastructure facilities. Pleasant environmental conditions, the availability of moderately priced dwellings, and low house lot prices in sparsely populated regions appear to be influencing the migration patterns of the 30 to 49 year-olds. The residential preferences were expressed by the 50 and over age-groups (Kontuly and Vogelsand 1988a). Also, we believe that the life-style preferences of the 18 to 29 year-olds regarding unemployment, part-time jobs and shared employment options are filtering up to family migrants.

Both return migration and employment deconcentration appear as possible explanations for the filtering down of a counterurbanization direction of movement to the 25 to 29 year-olds. Employment availability provides the main attraction to migrants in the age-group. Returning home upon finishing university studies, during a period of high national unemployment, could provide an explanation for the reversal of this age-group's urbanization pattern of movement (Gatzweiler 1982). A second explanation could be the deconcentration of industrial and service employment to smaller, less densely populated urban regions, as mentioned in the discussion of family migrants.

Educational and employment opportunities influence the migration patterns of the 18 to 24 year-olds. Their changing movement patterns also appear related to return migration, a deconcentration of employment opportunities to small-sized regions, and to the regional decentralization of higher education.

Conclusions and implications

The German literature which evaluates the counterurbanization phenomenon argues that the migration changes evident in the Federal Republic during the 1970s are not of sufficient magnitude to confirm such a deconcentration trend (Koch 1980; Koch and Gatzweiler 1980; Gatzweiler 1982). Applying several definitions of the phenomenon, which utilize both total population change and the net internal migration rate, this chapter formally documents West German counterurbanization during the 1980s. The findings of this chapter supplement the conclusions of this body of German literature. In addition to identifying a trend toward regional population deconcentration in the 1970s, this chapter shows such a tendency began in the 1960s. The patterns of the 1960s and 1970s then strengthened and evolved into the strong counterurbanization trend evident during the first half of the 1980s. The spatial deconcentration of the West German population represents a long-term phenomenon which required 25 years to materialize fully. In contrast to the experience of most other Western European countries and the United States, the counterurbanization phenomenon can be seen to have strengthened in the Federal Republic of Germany throughout the 1960 to 1985 time period.

Reasons suggested for the changing age-specific internal migration patterns of Germans involve the three major perspectives used for explaining the counterurbanization phenomenon, i.e. demographic restructuring, employment deconcentration, and the role of government policy. We have given the demographic restructuring hypothesis considerable attention in this chapter. Residential preferences for high amenity locations in small, sparsely populated urban regions filtered down from the pre-retirement and retirement age-groups (50 years-old and over) to the family migrants (30 to 49 year-olds) and possibly to the 25 to 29 age-group. Life-style preferences for part-time and shared employment also filtered up from the 18–29 age-groups to the family migrants; more time will be spent at a residential rather than at an employment location, so choice of residence will assume greater importance in the future. The changing preferences of these age-groups represent a major component in the explanation of the counterurbanization phenomenon in the Federal Republic.

The working-age population remains constrained by the location of jobs, but the latter are becoming more widely available across national space. New employment opportunities exist in small, sparsely populated regions due to the growth of the pre-retirement and retirement-aged population and in response to the Federal Government's dispersal of higher education and social, recreational and infrastructure facilities to peripheral regions. This suggests both the economic deconcentration and the government policy perspectives as additional and complementary explanations for West German counterurbanization.

The interaction of the post-1980 decline of large urban regions with contemporary economic bases and the possibly widespread deconcentration of employment opportunities to small, sparsely populated urban areas remains unclear and these represent important topics for future research. Employment and unemployment data are available for several regional scales in the Federal Republic, but not for the functional urban region scheme. A systematic exploration of the importance of the employment deconcentration perspective as an explanation for counterurbanization would require a major reconstruction of the economic data to correspond with our FUR scheme.

Government policies clearly influence international migration, but the impact on internal population redistribution is not as clear-cut. The 1965 Regional Planning Act (Raumordnungsgesetz) provided a framework and the guiding principles for regional development. It attempted to provide an equivalent standard of living to all West Germans (bundesgesetzblatt 1965), a provision 'guaranteed' in the Constitution. The Act can be interpreted as the regional consequence of one of the most important bills of rights. However, in practice, it is of very limited consequence.

The Regional Planning Programme of 1975 (Bundesraumordnungsprogramm) went one step further toward realizing the general aims of the Act by focusing on improving infrastructure and economic and environmental conditions in disadvantaged rural areas, and on providing a healthier environment in overpopulated and environmentally stressed areas (BRBS 1975). The redistributional effects of the 1975 Programme appear to be at least partially responsible for the growth of employment and population in certain small, sparsely populated urban regions through certain improvements in infrastructure.

Future impacts of the 1975 Programme on the smaller urban regions are uncertain, because more recently attention has shifted to aiding structurally weak industries in densely populated areas. At present, regional Programmes aiding sparsely populated areas are more than counterbalanced by the financial assistance extended to certain branches of manufacturing located in densely populated regions. In addition, special financial agreements between the federal government and the state of North-Rhine–Westfalia, designed to assist in the structural transformation of the Rhine–Ruhr, exceed the amount of money spent on regional programmes for the small, sparsely populated regions. In conclusion, the new trend of population deconcentration in the FRG cannot be associated with the financial assistance provided by either the federal government or the states (Länder).

Government policies strongly influenced the size of the foreign migration stream into or out of the Federal Republic, and since foreigners tend to concentrate in large cities and densely populated urban regions, these policies indirectly impacted upon the urbanization/counterurbanization phenomenon. Cyclical downturns in the national economic growth rate and the corresponding increase in the national unemployment rate, which motivated the imposition of controls on the influx of foreign workers in 1973, led to the net emigration of foreigners during the first half of the 1980s mainly from large-sized urban regions (Kontuly and Vogelsang 1988a). Future levels of the foreign migration stream will vary with changes in the national economic growth rate. In the short run, the net emigration of foreign workers, their families, and dependents will most likely continue and will primarily affect the large urban regions.

In 1984, family migrants, pre-retirement and retirement-aged migrants were all moving in a counterurbanization direction. For each group, the trend is of a long-term nature. The 50 and over age-groups were already moving in a counterurbanization direction in 1970, and allowing for the disturbance in migration patterns caused by changes in age-group definitions, it is likely that both the 30 to 49 and the under 18 age-groups have been moving according to a counterurbanization pattern since 1971.

The West German population continues to age. In the future, the numbers aged 30 years and over will expand while those under 30 will contract. Demographic forecasts suggest that by 1990, 62 per cent of the West German population will be 30 years of age or over, while 38 per cent will be less than 30 (Steins 1984). The regional patterns of movement of the 30 and over age-groups, reinforced by the ageing of the national population, suggest that counterurbanization tendencies will predominate in the future.

With a counterurbanization trend verified for the Federal Republic, several explanations for changing age-specific migration patterns require additional research, elaboration and testing. First, it is important to discover the national and regional extent of a possible deconcentration of industrial and service employment to small, sparsely populated regions. Secondly, the role of regional development policies in this redistribution needs to be clarified. A third task is to establish the importance of return migration to the changing patterns recently observed for the 18 to 24 and the 25 to 29 year-olds. Finally, research should try to determine the importance of non-employment related preferences for the working-age population, and to specify the trade-offs made in the locational decision-making process between employment and amenity factors.

Further reading

The main themes in this chapter can be followed up in more detail in three other studies by the authors, as follows:

Kontuly, T., Wiard, S. and Vogelsang, R. 1986: Counterurbanization in the Federal Republic of Germany, *Professional Geographer* 38, 170–81. This derives general operational guidelines for evaluating and testing for counterurbanization in the FRG and analyses population growth rates for functional urban regions for three periods between 1950 and 1979.

Vogelsang, R. and Kontuly, T. 1986: Counterurbanization in der Bundesrepublik Deutschland, *Geographische Rundschau* 38, 461–8 (in German). This discusses the use of the word in the German literature and explains why it is not widely adopted. Case studies of four categories of functional urban regions illustrate the processes of net migration for different age-groups of the population. It also outlines the consequences of the counterurbanization process for regional planning.

Kontuly, T. and Vogelsang, R. 1988: Explanations for the intensification of counterurbanization in the Federal Republic of Germany, *Professional Geographer* 40, 42–54. This evaluates the impact of international migration on regional population concentration and deconcentration in the Federal Republic and discusses the filtering down of a counterurbanization pattern from older to younger age-groups of the population.

9

France:

Decentralization and deconcentration in the wake of late urbanization

HILARY P.M. WINCHESTER and PHILIP E. OGDEN

Counterurbanization in France can be understood only in the context of the very distinctive demographic and urban history of the country. France was unusual amongst Western countries in its slow rate of population growth during the nineteenth century (van de Walle 1979) and until the Second World War (Ogden and Huss 1982). Two related consequences of this have been the late development of urbanization, and the restricted growth of industrial cities. The French form of industrialization was influenced by slow population growth, and was geographically dispersed and related to local resources (Aldrich 1987). France therefore contained few major urban-industrial agglomerations (Hohenberg and Lees 1985), and none which could effectively compete with Paris. Paris has been hugely dominant in the development of France, and is a classic example of a primate city, not only in terms of population size, but in its functions, status and influence.

Despite the very late onset of demographic and urban growth in the postwar period, there is a wealth of evidence to show that French urbanization and counterurbanization have been telescoped in time. This chapter focuses on the evidence for counterurbanization rather than urbanization. Counterurbanization was first indicated in France by the results of the 1975 census (Courgeau 1978; Courgeau and Lefèbvre 1982; Gérard 1976; Honoré 1978), while the first major study of counterurbanization in France was that by Bauer and Roux (1976). The 1975 census showed that the proportion of the French population living in rural areas diminished only slightly from the 1968 level (30.1 per cent) to 27.1 per cent, while the growth of urban areas slowed. These trends were clearly reinforced by 1982, when the rural population remained almost proportionally constant at 26.7 per cent, but urban growth diminished from 1.1 per cent p.a. between 1968 and 1975 to only 0.4 per cent p.a. between 1975 and 1982 (Boudoul and Faur 1982; INSEE 1982a). These patterns are by no means geographically uniform, however. It is the centres of cities which have experienced the greatest population loss, while the rural *communes* which have gained population are those close to the built-up areas. Since 1975, France has displayed some of the classic features of counterurbanization recorded in other developed countries. There has been a profound turnaround in the spatial pattern of growth, with rural *communes* experiencing population gain after a century of loss. The 1982 census showed significant changes in urban and rural populations brought about by net migration rather than natural change; these changes are significantly related to changes in the availability of and the demand for jobs and housing.

The role of counterurbanization since 1975 is less clear than it might be, because it is occurring at a time of economic recession, slow population growth, and reduced mobility rates, including a reduction in out-migration from the largest cities of Paris and Lyon (Courgeau and Pumain 1984). This chapter also shares with others in this volume a scepticism about identifying counterurbanization as a clear-cut break with the past. The idea of a rural renaissance, or *rurbanisation* (Mougenot 1982; Pitte 1986), needs to be treated with care. It has been cogently argued by a number of writers that many of the recent changes in population distribution may be seen as an extension of urbanization through large-scale decentralization, a *périurbanisation* (Bauer and Roux 1976; Taffin 1986). As Noin and Chauviré (1987) have insisted, France has become a profoundly urban nation in the late twentieth century, and some of the counterurban trends are more apparent than real, because of quirks in the available data sources, and problems over the definition of 'urban' and 'rural'.

The influence of the historical legacy

French demographic and urban development provides a complex back-cloth to the recent experience of counterurbanization. Low fertility rates profoundly influenced patterns of urbanization. Cities grew slowly, and mainly as a result of in-migration from rural areas. Over much of France, industrialization and urbanization occurred separately, and industrial agglomerations were the exception rather than the norm. The pattern of dispersed industrial development in the north of the country still affects the present use of those areas, which are less desirable than many other rural districts, and so are experiencing less counterurbanization than the sunny and unsullied south (Berger *et al.* 1980). On the other hand, the slow growth of cities before the war, and their exceptionally rapid development after the war, have caused problems of housing and infrastructure which have stimulated the recent urban exodus.

The pattern of slow demographic and urban growth altered very dramatically in the postwar period. From 1945, France experienced an exceptionally high level of population growth (Dyer 1978). At the same time, industrial development was extremely rapid, and new jobs were becoming available in the service sector (Durand 1972). Population and employment growth was accompanied by a sharp acceleration of urban growth, which exceeded 1.8 per cent p.a. between 1954 and 1968 (Pumain and St-Julien 1984). All towns gained population, but until 1968 the larger cities gained proportionally more than the smaller ones. The primacy of Paris and its region was reinforced by high levels of growth; the Ile de France region grew by 1.8 per cent p.a. between 1954 and 1962, and 1.5 per cent p.a. between 1962 and 1968, compared with growth rates of around 1 per cent p.a. for France as a whole between 1954 and 1968. Urban growth resulted not only from natural increase but also from a continued and accentuated rural depopulation (Pitié 1971). This pattern of urbanization took place markedly later than in many other countries of western Europe: in 1954, 43.0 per cent of the French population still lived in rural areas, a proportion which was rapidly reduced to 30.1 per cent by 1968. The recency of this rural–urban migration has left many French urban dwellers with family and property links with rural areas which have frequently been maintained by patterns of second-home ownership, retirement migration, and, more recently, by counterurbanization.

Postwar urbanization inevitably was tacked on to the existing urban structure. Many of the old city cores contained ageing and decaying dwellings (see, for example, the study of Bordeaux by Clout [1984]), a situation exacerbated by rent control policies. Most growth was therefore concentrated at the edges of the cities; a response to the enormous pressure on the housing stock was the construction of huge blocks of flats, the *grands ensembles*, on vacant land at the urban periphery. These housing estates, often characterless, poorly built, and badly serviced, provided homes for more than a million people. As a result, most French cities have a dearth of good quality housing, particularly in individual units rather than flats; good housing at a reasonable price is mostly available outside the city boundaries.

Unchecked postwar urbanization, in Paris and elsewhere, gave rise to a proliferation of urban and regional policies designed to balance regional inequalities and to plan the urban system (Clout 1987; House 1978; Laborie *et al*. 1985). These policies were initially designed to encourage development in large cities as counter-magnets to the primacy of Paris, the *métropoles d'équilibre*. By the mid-1970s, the focus of attention had shifted down the hierarchy to smaller towns, the *villes moyennes*; these policies have aimed to stimulate industry, encourage environmental conservation, and improve housing. This direct stimulus to growth at the lower end of the urban hierarchy has been assisted by the designation of nine new towns between 1969 and 1973; these have been centres of urban growth outside the major cities. Furthermore, a number of subsidies for industrial development are available only outside the metropolitan areas (Laborie *et al*. 1985). Indirect stimulus to decentralization was also provided by the urban policies of the late 1960s and early 1970s which brought about urban renewal in major city centres (Chaline 1984), although later policies have emphasized rehabilitation and conservation (Kain 1982). The particular problems associated with housing, including the poor quality of the *grands ensembles*, have also recently become the focus of improvement policies (Tuppen and Mingret 1986), which have provided a further indirect stimulus to urban out-migration.

Data sources and the approach to the study of counterurbanization

The process of counterurbanization is used here, as in the rest of this volume, to indicate population growth at the lower end of the urban hierarchy and in rural areas, contrasting sharply with the recent French experience of urbanization. Bourne (1980) and others have offered a number of perspectives on counterurbanization, two of which are particularly applicable to the French case. First, voluntary movements away from the disamenities of the city to the perceived attractions of the countryside are highly likely, given both the housing difficulties of the city and the freshness of links with rural areas. Secondly, the effects of policy, both intentional and unintentional, can be expected to have played a significant role, as outlined above.

Our analysis of counterurbanization in France relies heavily on the census of 1982, and to a lesser extent on the earlier censuses of 1954, 1962, 1968 and 1975. This is because, unlike many of the other countries, France has an inadequate system for making comparable annual population estimates at different geographical scales. The censuses provide a mine of useful data on population change and the relative contribution of natural change and net migration to overall change. They also yield information on the socio-economic and demographic features of the population and of migrants.

At the same time, some weaknesses of the census should be noted, particularly in relation to periodicity and coverage. First, analyses of change over time are restricted to arbitrary intercensal periods, which may not coincide with shifts in trends. Secondly, while the censuses provide detailed migration tabulations, these are based on the place of residence at or around the time of the previous census (in 1982, the migration question asked about place of residence on 1 January 1975), without any intermediate moves being recorded. In addition, the data on socio-economic and demographic characteristics suffer from some limitations, notably the presentation of data at a household level rather than for the individual, and also are not easy to link up with detailed information on employment trends.

One particularly strong advantage of the census in the present context, however, is the ability to present data for a range of different spatial units and frameworks. For a direct test for the existence of counterurbanization, it is very useful that data can be assembled for functionally defined urban regions, the *zones de peuplement industriel et urbain* (ZPIU). These are defined on the basis of daily journeys to work, non-agricultural employment, and the number and size of industrial and commercial enterprises. The ZPIU usually contain an urban heart covering one or more *communes*, as well as adjacent rural *communes* which form part of the functional urban region. In 1982, 89.5 per cent of the population of France, some 48.6 million people, lived within the functional urban regions. Furthermore, substantially more than half of the population which lived in rural areas were in rural *communes* which formed part of a functional urban region (8.7 million of 14.4 million) (INSEE, 1982b). The building block for all urban and rural areas is the administrative unit of the *commune*. Urban districts, *unités urbaines*, include individual towns, *villes isolées*, and contiguous built-up areas which extend over more than one *commune*, *agglomérations urbaines*. Urban districts contain at least 2,000 people in the main settlement, while areas outside urban districts are classified as rural. Data on population change for categories of urban areas by size have been among the most useful for preliminary identification of the population turnaround (Fielding 1986a).

Data on growth and the components of change are also available for the units of the national administrative structure, based on the *commune*. There is a nested hierarchy of administrative units from the *commune* to the nation, which builds up through *cantons*, *départements* and planning regions. In the case of Paris, the City of Paris itself is a *commune*, but is also the equivalent of a *département*; it is divided into 20 *arrondissements*, each of which is further divided into four *quartiers*. Data available for the administrative units such as *départements* are generally less useful than for the functional urban units, since average population change in an administrative area is likely to mask potentially significant differences between urban and rural areas.

In this chapter, the evidence for the rate and structure of population change in France is examined at a number of levels. At the regional and departmental level, recent population changes reveal the general spatial patterns of natural and migratory population movement. Next, the evolution of population for rural settlements and for size categories of urban settlements is examined to give basic evidence of the turnaround of growth. Finally, the patterns of change for the functional urban regions are examined, and for both their rural and urban components. The analysis is essentially a national-level survey, although two case studies of the Paris Basin and the *département* of Isère in south-east France are examined in more detail. Later sections of this chapter analyse the demographic and socio-economic features of counterurbanization, and relate the patterns of population distribution to changes in housing and employment. A large number of empirical studies of French counterurbanization and the explanations offered for this process by French authors are reviewed in the light of wider theoretical considerations in the counterurbanization debate.

Recent patterns of overall population change

There is some evidence of counterurbanization in the geographical patterns of population change between 1975 and 1982 at the *département* level (Figure 9.1). The clearest indication is in the pattern of decentralization from Paris and its three immediately adjacent suburban *départements* (Noin *et al.* 1984). Two other areas of population loss occur at a regional scale, indicative of structural economic change. The larger zone consists of eleven largely rural *départements* in the centre and south, which are areas of traditional declining peasant agriculture where population loss has been occurring continuously since the later nineteenth century. The smaller zone includes those industrial areas of the north-east which have suffered particularly badly during the economic recession of the 1970s and early 1980s (Thumerelle 1980). The highest rates of population growth are found in the wider Paris Basin and in the long-established growth areas of the south-east. An indication of counterurbanization trends is found in the diffuse areas of moderate population growth which include most of

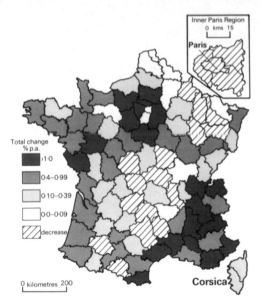

Figure 9.1 France: population change, 1975–82, by *département*. Source: INSEE, 1982a.

Table 9.1 France: Population change, 1962–82, by type of commune

Type of commune	Change rate (% per annum)			Shift in rate* (% point)	Population 1982 (000s)
	1962–68	1968–75	1975–82		
All France	+1.1	+0.8	+0.5	−0.4	54 102
All urban *communes*	+1.8	+1.2	+0.3	−0.9	14 425
Rural *communes*	−0.4	−0.1	+0.9	+1.0	39 677
Communes belonging to *unités urbaines* by size:					
Paris agglomeration	+1.4	+0.6	+0.1	−0.6	8 673
200 000 and over	+2.1	+1.2	+0.2	−1.0	11 014
100 000–199 999	+2.5	+1.2	+0.2	−0.9	4 055
50 000– 99 999	+2.1	+1.6	+0.2	−1.3	3 659
20 000– 49 999	+2.0	+1.3	+0.3	−1.0	3 570
10 000– 19 999	+1.7	+1.5	+0.6	−0.9	2 653
5 000– 9 999	+1.4	+1.3	+0.9	−0.4	2 902
Under 5 000	+1.1	+1.1	+1.0	−0.1	3 150

Note: * Between 1968–75 and 1975–82. Note that figures may not sum because of rounding
Source: INSEE, Recensement Général de la Population de 1982: Villes et Agglomérations Urbaines, Table 4, pp. 166–7

Brittany, Normandy and the western littoral. Moreover, many of the predominantly rural *départements* in central France, Brittany, and parts of the Pyrenees, show a fractional population gain, contrasting with their history of population loss.

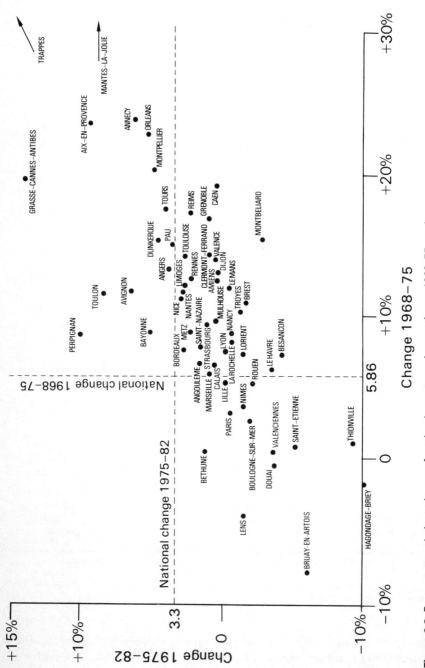

Figure 9.2 France: population change for the largest agglomerations, 1968–75 and 1975–82, compared with national population change. Source: Pumain, 1983.

Analysis of population change by settlement size groups reveals a clear trend towards counterurbanization by 1975–82. It is clear from Table 9.1 that there has been a major shift from decline to growth in the rural areas since 1975. Growth began in the larger rural settlements in the late 1960s. This has gradually extended down the size hierarchy, so that by 1975–82 only the very tiny rural communities, those with populations of less than 200 people, experienced population decline. Conversely, the urban areas have declined sharply in their rate of growth, from 1.8 per cent p.a. in 1962–68, to 0.3 per cent p.a. in 1975–82. The rate of growth of urban areas shows an almost perfect inverse correlation with settlement size. Growth is very firmly concentrated in towns of less than 20,000, while the largest agglomerations are growing very slowly indeed.

Further evidence of counterurbanization stems from the slowdown in growth of the large urban agglomerations (defined as urban agglomerations with a population of at least 100,000 in 1975). This recent slow growth is even more marked than the slowdown in population growth as a whole (Figure 9.2). All but four of the large agglomerations which grew between 1968 and 1975 expanded more slowly in the subsequent intercensal period, and many cities experienced population loss where previously there had been gain. Urban population loss has affected all sizes of cities from Paris (population 8.5 million in 1982) to Boulogne (99,000 in 1982), and cities in all regions. Industrial cities have been badly hit, but cities as diverse as St Etienne, Nîmes, and Rouen have suffered population loss (see Pumain and St-Julien (1978) for a classification of cities). The cities which have sustained high growth through both intercensal periods fall into two categories; first, those of the outer Paris region, including some new town developments; and secondly, the distinctive Mediterranean cities of leisure and pleasure (Pumain 1983; Pumain and St-Julien 1984).

The slowing of growth in the largest cities is particularly marked in their central districts. Table 9.2 compares growth in the central district (the central urban *commune*) with overall growth in the urban region for the ten

Table 9.2 France: Population change, 1968–82, for the ten largest urban areas and their central *communes*

Urban area	Urban area (*Unités urbaines*)			Central *commune*	
	Population 1982 (000s)	change 1968–75 (%)	change 1975–82 (%)	change 1968–75 (%)	change 1975–82 (%)
Paris	8 510	3.6	−0.5	−11.1	− 5.8
Lyon	1 170	7.5	−0.1	−13.5	− 9.6
Marseille	1 080	5.9	0.9	2.3	− 3.9
Lille	935	5.1	−0.1	− 8.8	−10.7
Bordeaux	628	7.5	2.6	17.5	− 6.7
Toulouse	523	14.1	2.5	0.7	− 8.1
Nantes	465	11.8	2.5	− 0.9	− 6.2
Nice	449	11.4	2.7	6.5	− 2.3
Toulon	410	11.3	8.4	8.7	− 2.5
Grenoble	392	16.9	0.8	2.3	− 6.0

Source: Adapted from Boudoul and Faur, 1982, Tables 5 and 6

largest cities in France in the periods 1968–75 and 1975–82. For six cities, gain in the central area from 1968 to 1975 turned to loss in the ensuing period, and for another two cities the existing population loss intensified. In a number of cases, this population loss may be associated with large-scale clearance projects in advance of renewal in city centres (Chaline 1984), as well as with free market forces. In the two largest cities of Paris and Lyon, however, where central city decline was well established by 1968–75, population loss diminished in intensity from 1975 to 1982, and there is evidence of city-centre rehabilitation and gentrification (Winchester and White 1988). Population trends are therefore bringing about a convergence of the growth experience of the different sizes of larger cities, as the process of counterurbanization moves down the urban hierarchy.

It is clear from the evidence presented above that population loss has particularly affected the central areas of large cities in the last intercensal period, and that population gain has occurred in rural areas and small towns. The classification of population change within, nearby, and entirely outside the functional urban regions, the ZPIU, is particularly useful in interpreting these patterns of recent population change. Table 9.3a shows the rate of population change for rural *communes* belonging to a ZPIU compared with those totally outside a ZPIU. The growth of rural *communes* within a ZPIU was greater from 1975 to 1982 than for any other category of rural or urban area (cf. Table 9.1). At the other extreme, those rural *communes* not belonging to a ZPIU still showed population decline during the period 1975–82, although at a much reduced level. This provides eloquent testimony to the spatial variation of counterurbanization, which

Table 9.3 France: Population change for rural *communes*, 1962–82, by relationship with ZPIU

a. Population change rate (% per annum)

Relationship with ZPIU	1962–68	1968–75	1975–82
All rural *communes*	−0.4	−0.1	+0.9
Those belonging to ZPIU	+0.1	+0.8	+1.6
Those not belonging to ZPIU	−1.1	−1.3	−0.2

b. Proportion of *communes*, by change type (%)

Relationship with ZPIU	Increasing		Decreasing	
	Total	By more than 15%	Total	By more than 15%
All rural *communes*	55.5	23.4	44.5	9.0
Those within ZPIU	74.1	7.8	25.9	3.1
Those not within ZPIU:				
(a) near to ZPIU*	55.1	22.9	44.9	8.8
(b) entirely outside ZPIU	39.1	11.0	60.9	14.7

Notes: ZPIU = Zone de Peuplement Industriel ou Urbain;
　　　　 *where at least one *commune* in a *canton* belongs to a ZPIU
Source: (a) INSEE, 1982b, 111; (b) calculated from Boudoul and Faur, 1982, Table 7

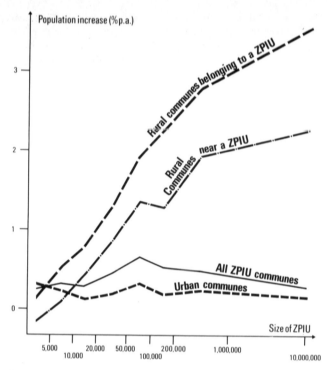

Population increase (% p.a.)

Rural communes belonging to a ZPIU

Rural Communes near a ZPIU

All ZPIU communes

Urban communes

Size of ZPIU

Figure 9.3 France: population change by type of *commune*, 1975–82, by size of ZPIU. Source: Boudoul and Faur, 1982.

is affecting accessible rural areas, while large tracts of remoter rural areas are still being depopulated.

The performance of rural *communes* also depends on the size of the ZPIU to which they belong, or which they are near to (Figure 9.3). Rates of population growth, both within and near the ZPIU, are highest around the largest metropolitan zones, the centres of which are losing population. The spatial pattern of the fast-growing rural *communes* reveals that they lie on average 10 km from the central city in the cases of Tours and Poitiers, 12 km for Rennes and Montpellier, 15 km for Toulouse and 20 km for Lyon. In the case of Paris, this diffuse urbanization, *périurbanisation*, is now occurring about 40 km from the centre, compared with 25 km at the last intercensal period (Noin and Chauviré 1987, 165). Finally, Table 9.3b shows the summary disposition of rural *communes* by location in relation to a ZPIU, and the proportion of each group exhibiting gain or loss in the last intercensal period. Of the rural *communes* entirely outside a ZPIU, only 39 per cent gained population, and only 11 per cent gained by more than 15 per cent over the period. There is still, therefore, a heartland of population decline, particularly in mountainous and isolated areas where it is still accurate to talk of an empty France, *'la France du vide'* (Béteille 1981).

Detailed analyses of population change by size of urban area and by functional urban region reveal the twin patterns of deconcentration and decentralization. Deconcentration is evident from the fact that since the mid-1970s, population growth has occurred in regions that have been losing population for decades, as well as from the substantial reduction in growth rates sustained by most of France's large urban agglomerations. Decentralization is shown by the extension of urbanization into the rural areas of many functional urban regions, and by the inclusion of large numbers of rural *communes* in the statistical definition of the functional urban regions for 1982.

Components of population change

Recent trends in population change identified above have been brought about by the combined effects of both net migration and natural change. At a national level, both components of population change have altered significantly since the 1960s. The mean annual rate of natural change fell from 0.67 per cent in 1962–68 to 0.58 per cent in 1968–75 and then to 0.40 per cent in 1975–82, principally due to lower fertility rates. Net immigration has declined even more sharply from 0.47 per cent p.a. in 1962–68 to 0.23 and 0.06 in the subsequent two intercensal periods, mainly as a result of changes in migration policy relating to the recruitment of labour from Mediterranean Europe and North Africa (de Ley 1983).

Within France, the contribution of net migration and natural change exhibit very different patterns, with no clear-cut relationships between the two. Figures 9.4a and 9.4b show the relative contribution of natural change and migration at the level of the *département* from 1975 to 1982. The pattern of natural change (Figure 9.4a) shows a marked regional variation, with a demographically buoyant north, where rates of natural increase exceeded 0.3 per cent p.a., and a south with generally very low rates of natural increase or natural decrease, resulting from the cumulative effects of long-term population decline (Ogden 1985, 26). The rural areas which have declined for so long have suddenly experienced a dramatic reversal of migration flows since 1975 (Figure 9.4b), by the process of deconcentration mentioned in the previous section. This reversal has occurred even in some *départements* of the Auvergne which had lost population for the preceding hundred years. Brittany provides a good example of the reversal in rural population trends: all four *départements* gained population by net in-migration, and in every case at a higher rate between 1975 and 1982 than in the previous intercensal period. However, at the same time, natural growth decreased in all four *départements* (Dean 1987; Perry *et al.* 1986). In-migration was also particularly marked in the *départements* of the south-east and was substantial in much of the south-west. Traditional areas of attraction which maintained their net inflow were the outer *départements* of the Paris Basin and lower Seine. Conversely, almost the whole of north-east France lost population by out-migration.

The spatial pattern of the components of population change between 1975 and 1982 has shown some significant alterations from the regional trends of the two preceding intercensal periods (Ogden 1985; Ogden and Winchester 1986). The industrial regions of the north and east have lost

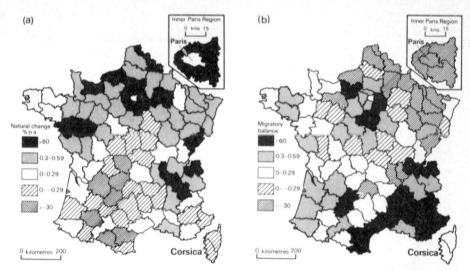

Figure 9.4 France: components of population change, 1975–82, by *département*: (a) Natural change; (b) Net migration, % per annum. Source: INSEE, 1982a.

migrants although fertility rates are still high. The Mediterranean regions are now the most attractive for migrants, with a gain at the regional level of over 1.0 per cent p.a. Before 1968, the western regions exhibited migration loss, but since that date the migration balance has become and has remained positive through population deconcentration. Growth has slowed in the Paris Basin, and the out-migration and decentralization from the largest cities is evident at the national scale. Furthermore, this movement of younger people to rural areas both within and outside the ZPIU is beginning to bring about a rejuvenation of age structures, and there is limited evidence of a steadying and reversal of natural decline. When rural population growth occurs as the result of both in-migration and natural increase, then it might be said that there is genuine evidence of a 'rural revival'.

The extent of the difference in net migration rates between the period 1975–82 and previous periods is revealed more fully in Figure 9.5, where data are presented for rural *communes* by size and for urban *communes* grouped into agglomerations. With the exception of the very smallest, all size groups of *communes* under 20,000 population experienced net in-migration. Furthermore, the net out-migration from the larger urban areas is indicative of a turnaround in migration trends as well as a slowing of natural increase (Pumain and St-Julien 1984, 311–12). As Fielding (1986a, 36–9) observed, the large upward shifts in net migration balance for the rural areas, and the decline in net migration to the urban areas, clearly place France in the group of countries where 'counterurbanization has replaced urbanization as the dominant trend'. Some authors tend towards the view that these trends are greatly exaggerated by the underbounding of urban areas (see, for example, Noin and Chauviré 1987, 163). On the other hand, while some rural growth may well be a product of

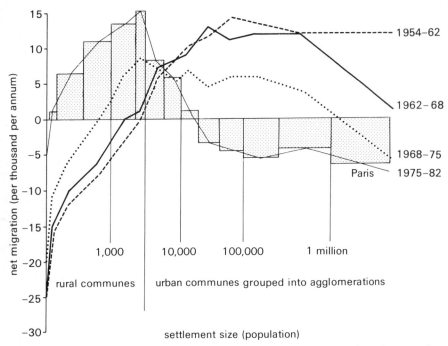

Figure 9.5 France: the relationship between net migration rate and settlement size, 1954–82. Source: Fielding, 1986a, p. 38.

périurbanisation, as indicated by Figure 9.3, it is Fielding's view (1986a, 38) that 'any change (to Figure 9.5) to allow for this bias would not be enough to alter the basic shape of the curve'. He argued that the descriptive model of the transition from urbanization to counterurbanization, involving a reversal in the relationship between net migration rates and settlement size, is 'largely supported by the facts of French urban development over the period 1954–82'.

The balance of natural change and migration may be usefully explored at the more localized scale of the Ile de France and Isère. The Ile de France planning region consists of central Paris, the three 'inner' *départements*, which form the suburban *petite couronne*, and four outer *départements* of the *grande couronne* (see Figure 9.6). The Paris region has gained population over a period of many years; however, the rate of growth at the regional level was much lower from 1975 to 1982 (0.3 per cent p.a.) than from 1968 to 1975 (0.9 per cent p.a.) (Fleury 1982). This growth was particularly associated with buoyant natural increase and a continued net immigration from abroad. Significantly, however, between 1975 and 1982 there was a net loss of over 400,000 people through internal migration to other French regions, although the Ile de France continued to play a major role in gross inter-regional migration, being the origin or destination of 44 per cent of all moves in France between 1975 and 1982 (Boudoul and Faur 1986, 299). These movements included out-migration to the rural periphery, to

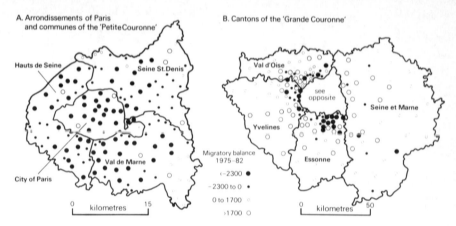

Figure 9.6 France: migration change in the Ile-de-France, 1975–82.

immediately neighbouring regions, and to regions much further afield. The only positive migration balances occurred from the regions of the north and north-east which were undergoing industrial restructuring.

Within the region, an analysis of natural increase and net migration shows a redistribution of population in a remarkably consistent pattern of decentralization from the region's core to its periphery. The critical component of population change was net migration: the City of Paris experienced particularly heavy net out-migration (Figure 9.6A). For Paris, this was part of a longer-term decline of the central city (Bonvalet and Lefèbvre 1983; Bonvalet and Tugault 1984) and the decline was in fact less marked in 1975–82 than in 1968–75 (178,000 out-migrants compared with 360,000). Population loss was particularly intense in the four central *quartiers*, and only 9 of the 80 *quartiers* actually gained population, these being in areas of recent urban renewal in, for example, the 13th or 19th *arrondissements*. Renewal in other areas, in the *quartier* of Les Halles in the first or second *arrondissements*, for example, led to population decline of 20–30 per cent as public buildings replaced housing.

Net out-migration also prevailed throughout the three inner *départements* (Figure 9.6A) where the great majority of *communes* lost population by this mechanism. By contrast, most of the *cantons* of the four outer *départements* gained population (Figure 9.6B). The degree of geographical uniformity in the patterns of Figures 9.6A and 9.6B is remarkable, with the spillover of areas of out-migration into the *grande couronne* reflecting the rapid spread of decentralization between 1975 and 1982. The major zones of growth were only those areas outside the continuously built-up area (Fleury 1982; Bélliard and Boyer 1983), and the new towns (Burgel 1986), suggesting the importance of both voluntary and guided decentralization.

The second case study, Isère, reveals a more recent process of rural migration gain, with a lagging pattern of natural growth. Isère is a large and physically diverse *département* in the Rhône–Alpes region with a notable concentration of 390,000 people around the chief city of Grenoble.

Table 9.4 Isère: Components of population change, 1962–82, for *communes* by population size (% per annum)

Commune population 1982	Population change			Natural change			Net migration		
	62–68	68–75	75–82	62–68	68–75	75–82	62–68	68–75	75–82
Under 50	−5.3	−3.4	−0.1	−0.6	−0.9	−1.3	−4.7	−2.6	+1.2
50– 99	−3.1	−2.9	+0.6	−0.3	−1.1	−0.9	−2.8	−1.8	+1.5
100– 199	−3.2	−1.7	+2.0	−0.2	−0.6	−0.4	−3.0	−1.2	+2.4
200– 499	−1.3	−0.3	+2.4	−0.0	−0.3	−0.2	−1.3	−0.0	+2.6
500– 999	−0.1	+0.8	+3.3	+0.2	+0.1	+0.1	−0.3	+0.7	+3.2
1 000– 1 999	+0.6	+1.6	+2.3	+0.3	+0.3	+0.2	+0.2	+1.3	+2.1
2 000– 4 999	+2.0	+1.8	+2.2	+0.7	+0.5	+0.5	+1.3	+1.3	+1.7
5 000– 9 999	+2.6	+2.5	+1.2	+1.0	+0.9	+0.7	+1.6	+1.6	+0.5
10 000– 19 999	+8.6	+3.8	+2.0	+1.6	+1.6	+1.3	+7.1	+2.2	+0.7
20 000– 49 999	+7.1	+2.9	+0.0	+1.4	+1.5	+1.1	+5.7	+1.4	−1.1
100 000–199 999	+0.6	+0.4	−0.8	+1.2	+0.9	+0.7	−0.6	−0.5	−1.5

Source: Recensement Général de la Population de 1982, Isère

From the late nineteenth century, Isère lost significant numbers of people who left the land to find more rewarding opportunities in the towns of Isère or elsewhere (Winchester 1984; 1989). From the 1930s, as metal-lurgical and engineering industries developed, the *département* began to gain population through in-migration, both from neighbouring *départe-ments* and also from Italy. During the 1960s and early 1970s, this process accelerated as the *département* gained growth industries decentralized from Paris, and as leisure and tourism achieved mass popularity after the 1968 Winter Olympics. During the last intercensal period, the process continued although at a lower rate, and the *département* gained 35,000 people through net in-migration.

The relative buoyancy of Isère as a whole masks the dominant trend over the last half-century of polarization in population distribution between Grenoble itself and its nearby valleys on the one hand, and the rural periphery on the other. During the 1960s, the majority of rural *communes* in Isère lost population by out-migration. The areas which experienced the greatest rates of depopulation were the high-altitude *communes* and those distant from the major cities. The lack of desirability of these areas was reinforced by an over-dependence on agricultural employment, and by low levels of amenity and service provision. Decades of steady out-migration had left them with a distorted age–sex structure, small total population and an excess of deaths over births (Winchester 1984). Many of the worst-affected *communes* appeared at the time to have no hope of any economic or demographic revival, as their individual populations fell to double figures, as net migration rates reached −5 per cent p.a., and as a rapid cycle of demographic and economic decline became established. Table 9.4 empha-sizes the excessive population losses for small rural *communes* in the 1960s, caused particularly by migration.

Table 9.4 also clearly indicates the recent migration turnaround of those same rural *communes*. The rural *communes* as a whole grew by 20 per cent between 1975 and 1982. All categories of rural *communes* gained population, except the smallest *communes* with fewer than 50 people in 1982. Even this latter category had a positive migration balance over this period, as did all other size categories of *communes* under 20,000 people. For the smaller *communes* of under 500, this represented a dramatic shift in migration trends from the two previous intercensal periods. However, *communes* of fewer than 500 people were still experiencing natural decline, which was particularly severe for the smaller settlements as a result of the ageing of their population brought about by their history of prolonged depopulation. It is also important to remember that these aggregate figures for rural *communes* conceal a certain number of residual, geographically well-defined, zones of a continuing lack of attraction (Winchester 1989). Nevertheless, it is quite clear from the data in Table 9.4 that the period 1975–82 marked a major shift from the predominant experience of the post-war years. An interesting comparison may be drawn with Dean's (1987) study of Brittany, where migration trends show a similar reversal, but where the rural areas have a long history of natural growth.

Characteristics of the migrants

The trends to decentralization and deconcentration outlined above may be further amplified by consideration of the demographic and socio-economic characteristics of the counterurbanizing population. The origins, age and socio-economic status of the migratory population are considered first at a national level, and then for the two case-study areas just described.

International migration has played a minor role in France's population growth in recent years, but this change from previous experience has probably contributed to the development of counterurbanization. During the post-war period the destinations of immigrants have been urban rather than rural (Guillon 1986); it is likely that the decline in immigration has meant a lesser ability to compensate for the effects of internal net out-migration on urban areas than in the 1960s. At the same time, the policy of family reconstitution and the acceptance of refugees from south-east Asia has brought in a wider age range of international migrants whose preferred destinations are likely to be more diverse than in previous periods. The socio-economic composition of international migrants is still, however, made up of a disproportionate number of manual workers (69 per cent of foreigners compared with 33 per cent of French). As such, they form a replacement population both in terms of the jobs they occupy and in terms of their spatial distribution.

The census provides information on the age of population who changed residence between 1975–82. It is well established that the peak propensity to migrate occurs in young adulthood and is related to changes in the life cycle. The age at which people were most migratory in France from 1975 to 1982 was very young, under 20 years of age for women and between 20 and 24 years for men (Courgeau 1985). Between those dates, 48 per cent of the French population changed their place of residence; for the 25–34 year age-group, the migration rates were 77 per cent for women and 75 per cent for men. The migration rates decline sharply for the age-groups over 34 years; 42 per cent of men aged 35–54 changed residence, and only 37 per cent of women (INSEE 1982a). The recent general lowering of mobility rates has not affected the age structure of migration (Boudoul and Faur 1986, 294).

The age structure of migrants varies greatly between in-migrants and out-migrants, between rural and urban areas, and for different sizes of ZPIU (Figure 9.7). Between 1968–75 and 1975–82, *communes* which lie outside the ZPIU (Figure 9.7) experienced a reduction in the rate of gross out-migration across all age-groups, together with an increase in the rate of gross in-migration for virtually all age-groups and particularly for people aged 25–39. At the other end of the settlement spectrum, in the Paris ZPIU, there was a slight drop in gross in-migration rates, but virtually no change in out-migration rates. In net terms, the Paris ZPIU recorded a migratory loss for all but 15–19 and 20–24 year-olds in 1975–82, with especially high net out-migration by people around retirement age and by the family-rearing groups and their children (Boudoul and Faur 1986, 298). The two other examples in Figure 9.7 for the medium-sized ZPIUs of 10–20,000 and

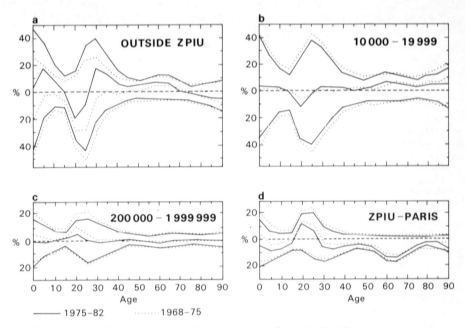

Note: The upper lines represent in-migration; the lower lines out-migration;
the intermediate net migration.

Figure 9.7 France: age-specific migration rates, 1968–75 and 1975–82, by size of ZPIU.
Source: Boudoul and Faur, 1986, p. 298.

the larger agglomerations of 200,000–2 million lie between these two
extremes.

This pattern of age-specific migration has, not surprisingly, had a
differential effect on the regions. Dean's (1987) detailed study of Brittany
showed that the greatest propensity for both in- and out-migration
occurred in the 25–34 age group, but net losses from Brittany were very
marked in this category, especially for women. Conversely, Brittany gained
mainly in the mature age-groups, with a significant retirement component
(Dean 1987, 317). This pattern is not replicated in all areas of the provinces;
within Isère, for instance, in-migration is dominated by young people
especially compared with local migrants (30 per cent of regional in-
migrants were aged 25–34, compared with 17 per cent of local migrants).
Despite these regional differences, the age structure of the counterurbanizing population is clearly dominated by the population of working
age and their children, with a retirement element in certain favoured areas.
The increased in-migration of these groups in remoter rural areas is
particularly significant in the context of reduced migration propensities in
the country as a whole.

The census data provide some evidence of the socio-economic status of
the counterurbanizing population, although the data have limitations,

Table 9.5 France and Isère: Socio-economic composition of households, 1982 (%)

Socio- economic group	Total households		All newly established or relocated households in rural *communes*		Households in new owner-occupied housing in rural *communes*	
	France	Isère	France	Isère	France	Isère
Farmers	4.2	3.0	6.6	3.5	7.4	3.3
Self-employed	6.3	7.2	8.6	10.4	9.4	11.1
Professional and upper managerial	7.7	8.7	6.5	8.6	7.3	10.0
Intermediate professions	12.9	15.8	15.3	20.3	18.9	24.5
Clerical	11.3	9.4	8.9	8.3	8.9	7.0
Manual	25.1	27.6	34.3	35.3	36.7	36.9
Retired	25.2	22.0	15.9	10.8	9.4	5.8
Other	7.2	6.3	3.8	2.9	2.0	1.3

Source: INSEE: Recensement Général de la Population de 1982; Principaux Résultats; INSEE: Recensement Général de la Population de 1982, Isère

with statistics referring to households rather than individuals, and with the best estimate of the newly relocated households also including newly formed households setting up home for the first time. Table 9.5 shows the socio-economic composition of those households which moved into or became established in rural *communes* between 1975 and 1982, compared with the socio-economic composition of the population as a whole in 1982. Most notable is the over-representation of farmers, the intermediate professional class and manual workers among the recent arrivals in rural *communes*. The high-status groups are adequately represented, but the professional and upper managerial classes are better represented in new moves to urban areas than to rural. It is clear that the 'new' population is by no means all of high status. The under-represented groups are the retired, who are less mobile than average, and those in non-manual occupations, which are predominantly clerical, and may be under-represented on a household basis because of the predominance of women in these jobs.

This pattern of migration by socio-economic group is replicated in Isère with some slight differences (Table 9.5). Isère has a higher proportion of high-status occupations than France as a whole, with fewer retired persons or farmers. The new rural population in Isère accordingly consists of relatively more of the high-status households, particularly in the intermediate professional category. A high proportion (35 per cent) of new rural dwellers are, however, manual workers and their families. The housing conditions of the new rural dwellers further clarify this picture. It is possible to distinguish those new rural dwellers living in new (post-1975) owner-occupied housing from those living in older and rented housing. This category of new rural dwellers in new housing does indicate a higher representation of high-status groups, but they are by no means a dominant category. The socio-economic group that is best represented in new rural housing are the manual workers, while the retired are noticeably under-represented.

Underlying factors in French counterurbanization

The evidence for counterurbanization must be seen in the context of French urban and demographic development and the theoretical explanations of the process. These general explanations cannot include the idiosyncracies of every national system, but more importantly, they tend to ignore a factor of particular significance to France – the role of housing availability. This obviously forms a significant link in the relocation decision, whatever the imperatives of employment and government policy; indeed, the availability of a desired type and situation of housing may form a prime locational factor in its own right. This section examines the role of the housing market, then considers changes in the structure and location of employment, and finally explores the impact of government policy on counterurbanization.

The role of the housing market

The second section of this chapter outlined the constraints on housing supply, type, and quality, brought about by French post-war urbanization. These constraints, and the accompanying price inflation of quality urban housing, have pushed new housing developments to the periphery of urban areas. The very rapid growth of population in the rural *communes* belonging to ZPIUs suggests very strongly that a large component of the rural revival is the result of new peri-urban housing. Furthermore, the rapid economic development of France in the post-war period has brought about a profound upgrading of life-styles for the population as a whole, so that the majority of French households, including manual workers and the intermediate professions, can now afford to live in the location and the accommodation that they prefer.

The significance of new housing in France is undeniable. Of the households which have set up home in rural areas since 1975, almost 900,000 are living in new houses, accounting for approximately a third of the new dwellings built since 1975. This massive spate of new building has taken place particularly in the *communes* belonging to ZPIUs. It is difficult to establish the extent to which this new housing is a result of changed patterns of demand compared with changed patterns of supply. However, a wealth of empirical local studies is available which throws some light on this topic. In reviewing these studies, and examining the patterns of change in the Ile de France and Isère, it appears that there is a geographical differentiation in the nature of counterurbanization in France.

Many studies of counterurbanization in France cite the demand for individual housing as the prime explanatory factor (see, for example, Bauer and Roux 1976; Mayoux 1979). Demand has been particularly strong for houses (*pavillons*) rather than flats. This demand is coupled with the desire to escape from city pressures and to improve the quality of life by returning to live in the country. It is indeed possible that these explanations may be more significant in France than in some other countries like Britain, because of the more recent urbanization of French society and the stronger rural links of present urban dwellers (Boudoul 1986). The supply of such housing has largely been met by the private sector, while the provision of social housing by the state has been sharply reduced. Further attention needs to be paid to the elucidation of the role of housing developers, financial institutions and public authorities in housing developments (see, for example, David and Freschi 1979; Jaillet and Jalabert 1982; Taffin 1986).

The move to a new house does not necessarily mean a move to a new job, and within France the development of increasingly sophisticated transport systems has raised the level of personal mobility and commuting. Thus, Terrier (1986, 333) has noted that there was a 28 per cent increase in the total distance covered by commuters between 1975 and 1982, reflecting the growth of the number of people in the workforce, an increase in the proportion of people travelling to work, and an increase in the average distance travelled from 18.4 to 19.5 km. Some 50 per cent of the employed population work outside their *commune* of residence; and while 75 per cent travel over distances of less than 15 km, a significant and growing proportion (especially in the Paris region) travel over 50 and even over 100 km. Changes in housing demand and supply, linked with increasing daily personal mobility, are thus of crucial importance in explaining the pattern of urban decentralization around both Paris and other large cities in the provinces.

In the Isère case-study area too, the role of housing factors and commuting appears very significant in the redistribution of population. In 1982, new rural dwellers made up 21 per cent of all households in the *département* compared with 15 per cent in France as a whole, and over half of this group lived in new houses (39 per cent nationally). The majority of this housing is owner-occupied, and David *et al.* (1986) ascribe this association between new rural dwellers and new housing to a diffuse form of urbanization linked to the widespread building of quality individual houses. This peri-urban development entails an increase in commuting distances; there is very little evidence of the relocation of employment in Isère.

Effects of economic restructuring

One of the major explanations offered for counterurbanization is the restructuring of employment opportunities. Restructuring of economic production, together with associated employment losses, certainly under-lies regional migration trends from north to south (Figure 9.4b). Within France, the decentralization of industry has been brought about partly through the new spatial division of labour and partly through the active intervention of the state in national and regional economic planning (Clout 1987). The impact of decentralized industry on migration in the north of France is well documented, and it is considered by Limouzin (1980) to be the major factor in the population turnaround, which has further stimulated rural business. Industrial relocation in the lower Seine was found by Fruit (1985) to be extremely significant in explaining counterurbanization, in that in many cases a move to the country actually brought about a location nearer employment. Similarly, Ganiage (1980), in a study of the Beauvaisis in the northern part of the Paris Basin, attributed population growth to the policy of industrial decentralization and regional grants; and in particular to the implantation of major firms such as Lockheed, Nestlé and Givenchy which has provided thousands of jobs and has thus transformed the local economy. This 'industrial colonization' has important links with the housing demand considered earlier: new industries have attracted professional and managerial people who could afford to purchase or to build their own detached houses.

Those writers who have emphasized the role of the decentralization of industry from the core are essentially describing a process operating in the wider Paris Basin, although Perry *et al.* (1986, 158) also considered it to be significant within Brittany. The decentralization of industry has been most marked within a 200 km radius of Paris, even though the available levels of grant aid are lower there than in the rest of the country. It appears that industrialists, and particularly the managers, require proximity to Paris to maintain access to the city, and are loathe to be relegated to genuinely rural areas. It is therefore plausible, as Winchester (1989) has argued elsewhere, that employment-led counterurbanization may be better developed in the wider Paris Basin than in other, more peripheral, parts of the country. The overconcentration of power, population and wealth in the country's core is likely to have a significant impact on the regional experience and causes of counterurbanization, just as previously on the experience of urbanization.

The role of employment decentralization in recent migration outside the Paris Basin appears to be relatively minor. In the case of Isère, for instance, the creation of employment is significantly less than the spread of new housing and households. Data on employment creation are generally scarce, but fortunately an employment survey in this *département* (INSEE 1984) sheds some light on the issue. Of 45 rural and small-town *cantons*, 23 increased private-sector employment over the period 1978–80, but this barely compensated for the loss of similar jobs in the other 22 *cantons* (INSEE 1984). In almost all cases, the increase in employment occurred in the areas relatively accessible to Grenoble, either in the immediate suburbs or slightly further afield. Two areas of particularly marked employment growth were the *cantons* of La Verpillière and Le Bourg D'Oisans; the former containing part of the designated area of the new town of L'Isle D'Abeau, the latter the rapidly growing ski and recreation resorts of Alpe d'Huez and Les Deux Alpes. New housing and new households have spread more widely than new employment; 40 of the 45 *cantons* experienced positive migration flows, although many still have a fragile economic base (Winchester 1989). The new spatial division of labour is barely affecting Isère, and there is no very strong evidence of the national decentralization of the production-line processes of industrial conglomerates. There is some evidence of fairly minor employment decentralization to the suburbs, which, however, appears to be following population rather than *vice versa*.

The restructuring and decentralization of industry have therefore had an impact which has been mainly limited to particular regions of the country, as Dean (1988) has indicated in his analysis of inter-regional flows of the economically active population between 1975 and 1982. He finds that 'the new spatial division of labour provides a less convincing theoretical

perspective for the composition of migration to the southern regions ...
[where] quality of life factors ... appear more important' (Dean 1988, 96).
New industrial developments in engineering, electronics, and information
industries have, however, occurred in cities such as Grenoble, Toulouse
and Montpellier, initiated by decentralization of nationalized industries in
the post-war period, and sustained by buoyant economic growth (Pumain
and St-Julien 1978). The economic impetus of these growth industries has
contributed to the population decentralization around the cities of
southern France, and to the demand for high-quality housing in those
areas. The planned decentralization of industry does not equate to the
neo-marxist idea of the deliberate exploitation of the periphery by the
forces of capital. The evidence for movements of jobs into the rural
periphery at the behest of big business is extremely flimsy. The exploitative
new spatial division of labour propelled by big business, whereby the
production process is relegated to the cheaper, more docile periphery, is
not a justifiable explanation of counterurbanization in France as a whole.

Impact of government policy

A third group of explanations for counterurbanization considers both the
unintended effect of various national policies and the direct impact of state
intervention. The direct impact of state intervention can be seen in explicit
policies of decentralization of population and employment since the mid
1960s. These policies include the decentralization of industry from Paris
and subsidized relocation elsewhere, mainly, as indicated above, in the
Paris Basin. Planned population decentralization has helped develop new
growth centres and new towns away from the existing metropolitan
centres. At the level of the largest cities, the *métropoles d'équilibre*, the impact
of designation has been to implement city centre renewal, new towns, new
industrial zones, and new mass-transit systems. The combined impact of
these developments has inevitably encouraged population decentralization
around those cities. Furthermore, the policy for the smaller towns, the *villes
moyennes*, has encouraged both industrial development and urban conservation; both these factors have enhanced the residential desirability of
the smaller towns. The planning of the urban system has had the overall
effect of encouraging growth at the lower end of the urban hierarchy.

Other government policies have affected the regions, as most sectoral
policies have a spatial impact. In particular, the very well developed and
explicit support for the maintenance of the rural sector may have slowed
the rural exodus (Winchester and Ilbery 1988). Policies for the rural areas
have been designed to support primary employment to maintain population, while national park policies aim to keep permanent population away
from the remotest areas. The likely effect of these policies on population
distribution would be to enhance growth at the lower end of the urban
hierarchy, but not in the remotest rural districts; however, it is almost
impossible to assess the extent of their impact. As with all regional policies,
it is very difficult to assess what would have happened had they not been
in existence.

Conclusions and implications

The 1982 census provided dramatic evidence for a reversal of post-war urbanization trends, and more limited and indicative evidence of the types of people involved and the associated changes in economic structures. The population redistribution has essentially consisted of a marked slowing of urban growth, while massive decentralization has occurred to rural areas incorporated within functional urban regions. A deconcentration of population has also occurred by in-migration to remoter rural areas, including some areas which had lost population by out-migration for a century or more. By 1982, net migration gains were highest for rural *communes* and for small urban areas, while the largest cities lost migrants. This contrasts sharply with the situation in 1962 when urbanization was the norm. Nevertheless, there are still significant areas of rural out-migration and population decline, particularly in the most remote and inhospitable areas.

Counterurbanization appears to be principally a movement of people of working age with their households. Retirement migration is significant for some of the provinces, while the cities still attract young adults. The decentralizing population consists not only of high-status groups, but also very significant numbers of manual workers. There is a clear association between new rural dwellers and new high-quality housing in peri-urban districts. The importance of the housing factor and its concentration in peri-urban areas indicates that the French movement of counterurbanization can hardly be considered a clean break with the past.

The association between new rural dwellers and new employment is more difficult to analyse. Some new rural dwellers are able to maintain their existing employment by lengthening commuting distances and by using the improved systems of mass transport available to many of the metropolitan centres. Others have been able to take advantage of the diffusion of employment which has occurred within and around the Paris Basin. However, there appears to be little evidence of employment decentralization affecting rural areas which are genuinely remote, although there is some local decentralization around most cities.

The recent nature of counterurbanization in France means that there has been little time for policy reactions to it; policies which may affect it are confused and contradictory. There is control over the architecture of dispersed housing in the regions, but little apparent control over its actual development. Recently, controls have been introduced on dispersed developments along the coast, but at the same time the fiscal restrictions on second-home ownership have been relaxed.

As for the future, the dearth of annual statistics on migration means that there is no firm basis from which to assess whether any reduction in the pace of counterurbanization has occurred since 1982, nor even to gauge whether the trends towards decentralization and deconcentration observed from comparisons between 1968–75 and 1975–82 were continuing to accelerate during the latter period. Further evidence will not become available until the results of the next census. The physical provision of good-quality housing in rural areas would suggest that the new rural population will certainly be maintained. There is increasing evidence that counterurbanization is working down the social hierarchy, and that inner cities are again attracting high-status groups. It remains to be seen how this re-evaluation of rural and urban space will affect the social groups and the spatial locations involved.

Further reading

The first commentary on counterurbanization in France was Bauer, G. and Roux, J.-M. 1976: *La rurbanisation ou la ville éparpillée* (Paris: Seuil). This volume recognized diffuse urbanization at a very early stage and concentrates particularly on life-style and housing explanations of the phenomenon.

One of the best statements is: Berger, M., Fruit, J.-P., Plet, F. and Robic, M.-C. 1980: Rurbanisation et analyse des espaces ruraux péri-urbains, *L'ÉSpace Géographique* 4, 303–13. This article considers the appropriateness or otherwise of the term *rurbanisation*, and offers a thoughtful and critical commentary on the work by Bauer and Roux (1976).

A very clear statement of the results of the 1982 census is contained in a brief and well illustrated article, written by census officials: Boudoul, J. and Faur, J.-P. 1982: Renaissance des communes rurales ou nouvelle forme d'urbanisation? *Économie et Statistique* 149, I–XVI. In the English language literature, a broader view of the census results is provided by Ogden, P.E. and Winchester, H.P.M. 1986: France, in Findlay, A. and White, P. (eds) *West European population change* (London: Croom Helm), 119–41.

A summary of the statistical evidence on counterurbanization in France is given in: Ogden, P.E. 1985: Counterurbanization in France: the results of the 1982 population census, *Geography* 70, 24–35. Comments on the role of employment change are succinctly presented in: Dean, K.G. 1988: Inter-regional flows of economically active persons in France, 1975–82, *Demography* 25, 81–98.

Two useful case-studies of contrasting regions are: Dean, K.G. 1987: The disaggregation of migration flows: the case of Brittany, 1975–1982, *Regional Studies* 21, 313–25, and Winchester, H.P.M. 1989: The structure and impact of the postwar rural revival: Isère, in Ogden, P.E. and White, P.E. (eds) *Migrants in modern France: population mobility in the later nineteenth and twentieth centuries* (London, Unwin Hyman), 142–59. The latter also contains a useful historical overview of immigration to and internal migration within France.

10

Italy:

counterurbanization as a transitional phase in settlement reorganization

G. DEMATTEIS and P. PETSIMERIS

Italy has a long history of urban life, but until after the Second World War urbanization proceeded only slowly. In Italy modern urbanization overlies a dualistic structure of medieval origin. In the North and Centre there was a burgeoning of urban growth between the eleventh and thirteenth centuries, creating a dense and continuous network of towns (Hohenberg and Lees 1985). In the South the feudal system suffocated this pheno-menon and only a few coastal cities grew up, Naples emerging as the most important; until the first half of this century vast areas remained rural hinterlands (Compagna 1967). With the first phase of industrialization a further geographical differentiation in the urban network began. Between the second half of the nineteenth century and the beginning of the twentieth century the new sources of economic growth affected principally the northern and eastern part of the country. This period saw the formation of the 'industrial triangle', whose apexes (Turin, Milan and Genoa) became the cores of great urban agglomerations. Meanwhile, the North East and Centre had a more balanced growth divided between the higher levels of the hierarchy (Venice, Bologna and Florence) and the smaller towns inherited from the close-knit medieval network. The only exception was Rome which, as the capital, grew rapidly after 1870 in the midst of a rural and relatively underdeveloped hinterland. Despite these developments, however, little more than one-third (35.5 per cent) of Italy's population lived in towns of over 20,000 inhabitants at the 1936 Census (Carozzi and Mioni 1970).

The process of urban concentration accelerated during the period of rapid industrial growth in the 1950s and 1960s, reaching a peak in the period 1958–64. At this time, although the birth rate exceeded the death rate everywhere, demographic growth occurred in only 23 per cent of Italian territory, mainly in the urban and industrial areas, whereas almost all rural areas and most small towns were losing population due to migration. During the 1970s, however, the areas with increasing popula-tion widened to cover 55 per cent of the national territory. These growth zones included non-metropolitan areas and smaller towns, even those more distant from the main cities. At the same time, the areas of faster population concentration in the 1950s and 1960s began to experience a gradual slowing in their growth and in certain cases, especially in the North West, began to lose population. In the South, on the other hand, the renewed growth of small towns and rural areas was accompanied by a continued growth of the major cities (Cencini *et al.* 1983; Dematteis 1986a, 1986b; Cori 1986).

The purpose of this chapter is to provide more detail about these recent developments, both in terms of the patterns of population and in the form of an interpretation in the context of the counterurbanization debate. As the next section shows, this is by no means an easy task because statistical series for urban systems do not exist in Italy and because there is very little information available on migration except at the broad regional level. We are therefore forced to rely very heavily on the commune level and data for overall population change. As a result, it is impossible for us to make the rigorous tests for the 'clean break' notions of counterurbanization that this book is aiming for. Nevertheless, following an examination of some of the factors responsible for the observed trends towards population deconcentration, we are able to combine this evidence with information drawn from more local studies to provide the basis for drawing conclusions about the nature of the apparent counterurbanization tendencies. In brief, we reckon that counterurbanization is not a long-term phenomenon, but neither is it necessarily making way for a further phase of urbanization in the traditional sense of the word.

Data and approach

Statistical series for urban systems do not exist in Italy. Official records supply data on the basis of the administrative divisions i.e. the 20 regions, divided into 95 provinces which are made up of 8,086 communes. This is the basis on which the results of the Census carried out every ten years – most recently in 1981 – are published. In addition, information is available from the Public Records Office on resident population in each commune on 31 December of each year together with information on moves and net balance over the previous twelve months.

The use of provincial and regional data has drawbacks as far as the analysis of urbanization processes are concerned as they cover very large and usually heterogeneous areas. Only in a very few cases does a province coincide with a large urban system. The use of this kind of subdivision also leads to the loss of important information for the understanding and interpretation of the processes occurring.

The commune is therefore the unit of analysis most suited to our purposes, although not ideal. The main drawback of the use of this information presented at this level is the enormous difference in size between communes. In certain cases entire cities, such as Genoa and Rome, fall within a single commune, whereas in others like Milan and Naples the commune includes only the central core leaving the surrounding concentric rings divided between many other communes.

Some studies have attempted to identify functional urban regions, but each suffers from certain weaknesses in relation to present purposes.

Cafiero and Busca (1970) identify a certain number of metropolitan areas on the basis of size, demographic density and number of non-agricultural workers. This definition cannot, however, be used for the present study, because it covers only a limited part of the urban network and, moreover, is based on purely formal criteria. Other subdivisions have been made by Hall and Hay (1980) and Berg *et al.* (1982) in an attempt to identify in Italy urban systems which were comparable with other European countries. It proved impossible to make exact analogies as data on journeys to work were not available, and hence the solutions adopted by these authors have rather shaky foundations. Since then, commuting data have been forthcoming from the 1981 Census and have been used by Sforzi and others to divide the country into 177 Functional Urban Areas (ISTAT-IRPET 1986), but this research is too recent for complete data series to have been prepared.

On the other hand, for planning purposes, certain Italian regions have defined so-called 'metropolitan areas' within their boundaries. These relate to Turin, Milan, Genoa, Rome and Naples, the five main urban concentrations. These newly defined areas consist of between 14 and 106 communes and lend themselves to a comparative analysis of the demographic variations between central city and periphery, i.e. between core and ring.

In the analysis which follows, we examine population change for the five 'metropolitan areas' when we come to explore trends in more detail, but for the main part of our study we use data at the commune level. This is the only one to allow comparison across the whole country and over a reasonable period of time. It should also be noted that this level has already provided important results in the study of urban growth (Cencini *et al.* 1983; Vitali 1983). We shall, however, also make use of data at provincial and regional level for dealing with certain questions, particularly the analysis of the components of population change. As a result of using this variety of spatial frameworks, none of which is ideally suited for the study of counterurbanization, we need to exercise caution in interpreting the significance of the patterns which we observe.

Recent patterns of population change

The deconcentration process

Adopting the most general definition of counterurbanization as a phenomenon of deconcentration (Berry 1976), a first measure of population change can be derived from the application of an index of concentration to the whole country and to individual regions at given dates. This was done by Celant (1986), who used the Gini index applied to the population of the communes for the period 1970–85. According to this study, the initial values of the concentration index show regional variations which reflect the history and structure of the country. The highest values correspond to regions which contain the major cities (Lombardy, Piedmont, Liguria, Latium and Campania), while the lowest correspond to regions characterized by a weak urban network (Molise, Calabria and Basilicata).

The recent behaviour of the index, however, has been less predictable.

Observing the pattern from 1970 to 1985, the regions can be classified into the following five groups:

A – regions characterized by a marked deconcentration trend throughout the whole period (e.g. Lombardy);
B – regions showing signs of concentration up to the mid 1970s, followed by deconcentration (e.g. Venetia);
C – regions where population deconcentration became clearly apparent only during the 1980s (e.g. Tuscany);
D – regions where concentration continued until the late 1970s followed by a period of stabilization (e.g. Marche);
E – regions characterized by an increasingly urban concentration trend through the period, though with some signs of a deceleration in this process in the 1980s (e.g. Sicily).

In Figure 10.1 changes in the concentration index are shown for a typical

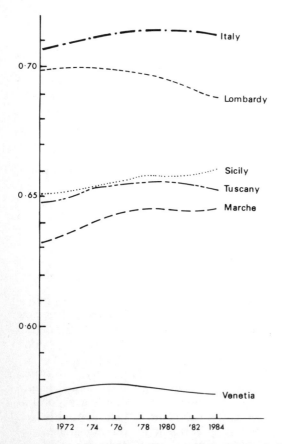

Figure 10.1 Italy and five representative regions: index of population concentration by communes, 1970–85. See Table 10.1 and text.

Table 10.1 Italy: Classification of regions according to trends in population concentration, 1970–85, by macro-region

Type (see text for details)	North West	North East and Centre	South
A	Liguria Lombardy		
B	Piedmont	Venetia Friuli V.J. Latium	
C		Emilia R. Tuscany	Campania Apulia
D	V. d'Aosta	Trentino A-A Marche	
E		Umbria	Abruzzi Molise Basilicata Calabria Sicily Sardinia

region in each of these five groups and compared with the index for the country as a whole, which is most like type C in trend. (Note that the national index appears so high up the chart because some of the regions with the highest levels of concentration are omitted, particulary Piedmont, Liguria and Latium – all with indices of over 0.75.) In Table 10.1 the regions are subdivided by type for three parts of Italy. This illustrates a certain correspondence between early deconcentration (type A) and the industrially 'mature' regions in the North West, between more recent deconcentration (types B, C and D) and the regions of the North East and Centre, and finally between continued concentration (type E) and the South.

Population growth and city size

A more analytical indicator than the concentration index is the relationship between rates of population growth and the size of urban centres. Fielding (1982) suggested correctly that this kind of analysis should be based on net migration. In the absence of these data, however, and given that the level of natural increase has been relatively slight over the last fifteen years, it is possible to obtain useful results even from examining the rates of overall population change and relating them to the size of communes.

Ten regions, representative of the various situations in the country, were chosen and their annual demographic change in 8 size groups was calculated for the periods 1971–81 and 1981–85. As the graphs in Figure 10.2 show, all the curves increase initially and then decrease, indicating that to a certain extent population deconcentration was already underway in the 1970s. Comparing the two periods we see in addition that this process had advanced further by the first half of the 1980s.

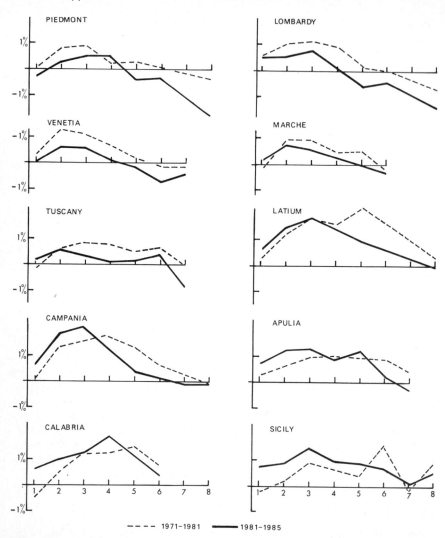

Figure 10.2 Italy: population change in ten typical regions, 1971–81 and 1981–85, by size of communes. Communes are grouped according to population size in 1981. Key to groups (population in thousands): 1: Under 5; 2: 5–10; 3: 10–20; 4: 30–50; 5: 50–100; 6: 100–250; 7: 250–500; 8: 500 and over.

Within these general trends strong regional differences emerge. For the northern regions we find that already in the 1970s the maximum growth occurred in the relatively low size groups (numbers 1–3 in Figure 10.2), whereas for the larger cities (numbers 6–8), the rates of change were already close to zero or negative. In central Italy (Tuscany, Marche and Latium) these tendencies were less evident and in the South even less so.

In 1981–85 the annual growth rates for all size groups in the regions of the North and Centre tend to be lower than in 1971–81. This is because, due to a steady decrease in the birth rate, the average rate of population growth fell practically everywhere, particularly in the North. This did not occur in the South because the fall in the birth rate was compensated for by a change in migration from net loss to net gain.

As previously, a broad contrast can be drawn between the experiences of the three parts of Italy in 1981–85 (Figure 10.2). In the two regions of the earliest and most intense urbanization (Piedmont and Lombardy) communes of over 500,000 inhabitants registered higher rates of decline, reinforcing the trend of the previous period. In Piedmont the greater growth of the 30–50,000 size group was due to the growth of areas surrounding the metropolitan area of Turin. In the southern regions there was a marked rise in the growth rates of smaller towns in 1981–85 by comparison with the 1970s. By this time the curve for Campania had moved closer to a counterurbanization pattern, but only in Apulia was the increase in growth rate for smaller towns accompanied by a corresponding reduction in rates of change in the larger cities. The other regions of the South were apparently experiencing a generalized demographic growth rather than a process of population deconcentration or counterurbanization.

In conclusion, the curves representing population change against commune size show patterns that can be interpreted differently in different regions. They range from a strong counterurbanization relationship (downward curve) in Lombardy, to the intermediate situations found in other parts of the North and Centre, and to the completely different pattern in the South.

Even in regions with typical counterurbanization patterns as described by Fielding (1982), however, we must bear in mind that the data do not relate to urban systems but to communes. The latter correspond to functional urban regions only in relatively few cases, the majority either forming merely a part of a larger urbanized area or representing smaller essentially rural settlements lying within the broader sphere of influence of an urban centre. For this reason the growth of small and medium towns does not necessarily indicate that counterurbanization processes are occurring. Instead it could result from a further concentration of population in the suburban outer areas of the large urban systems, though later we will see that this is not particularly important in most areas.

Types of population change for communes

Further light on the nature of population change at the commune level is shed by the work of Cencini *et al.* (1983), who examined trends between 1958 and 1980 primarily in the parts of Italy which were considered marginal as regards accessibility and economic development (see also Dematteis 1986a; 1986c). These areas were identified on the basis of communes recording population loss in all three periods 1958–64, 1968–74 and 1974–80 and correspond closely with the mountain zones and inland hill areas, with the important exception of the lower part of the intensively cultivated Po river plain from Vercelli to the delta. These areas of 'depopulation' (shown as Type C zones in Figure 10.3) were distinguished

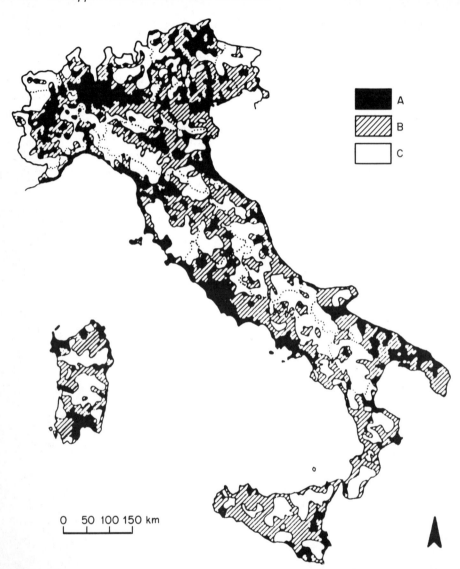

Figure 10.3 Italy: three types of communes classified on the basis of population trends between 1958 and 1980. A: Growth during 1958–64; B: Decline during 1958–64 and recovery during 1968–80; C: Decline during 1958–64 and 1968–80. Source: Dematteis, 1986a, Figure 2.

from areas of 'consolidated growth' (Type A) which recorded population growth in at least the first of the three periods – these tending to coincide with 'central areas', principal cities and metropolitan areas as well as areas of greatest industrial or tourist development – and areas of 'repopulation' (Type B) which experienced population loss in 1958–64 and growth in one or both of the subsequent periods – communes largely falling in an intermediate geographical location and tending to occupy locations peripheral to the Type A zones.

Merely mapping the distribution of these three types of communes in Figure 10.3 gives a clear idea of the geographical extension of the areas of population growth that has taken place since the early 1960s, because the areas of 'repopulation' (Type B) account for 37 per cent of the national territory and 35 per cent of the total number of communes, though only a quarter of Italy's population. In addition, however, population statistics aggregated for these groups of communes reveal a marked reduction in the rate of population loss experienced by the Type C zones, for though, by definition, they declined in all three periods, their overall rate of loss fell from 10.3 per cent in 1968–74 to only 4.0 per cent in 1974–80 (Table 10.2). Moreover, this experience was shared by all five of the macro-regions shown in Table 10.2.

The impression of the spreading of population growth more widely over Italy since the period of strong concentration in the 1950s and early 1960s is reinforced by the convergence of growth rates between the different types of zones recognized in Figure 10.3 and Table 10.2. For Italy as a whole, in 1958–64 some 25 percentage points separated the overall change rate of the Type A communes (13.6) from that of the Type C communes (−11.6), but this margin fell somewhat to 18 points in 1968–74 and then dropped even more sharply to just under 8 points in the later 1970s (Table 10.2). In fact, it can be seen that the Type B communes were in aggregate the fastest growing in 1974–80, but this does not undermine the observation of the general narrowing of the spread of growth rates. Since the early 1960s, therefore, the growth of the Type A zones, in aggregate, slowed markedly,

Table 10.2 Italy: Population change for types of zone, 1958–80, and by macro-region for Type C

Zones and macro-regions	Population change (%)			Shift in change rate (% point)	
	1958–64 (A)	1968–74 (B)	1974–80 (C)	(B) − (A)	(C) − (B)
Italy, by zone type					
Zone A	13.6	7.7	3.9	−5.9	−3.8
Zone B	− 5.1	− 1.6	5.2	+3.5	+6.8
Zone C	−11.6	−10.3	−4.0	+1.3	+6.3
Italy total	3.8	2.9	3.3	−0.9	+0.4
Zone C, by macro-region					
North West	−10.7	− 8.0	−5.2	+2.7	+2.8
North East	−12.4	− 8.6	−3.4	+3.8	+5.2
Central	−13.9	−10.4	−3.8	+3.5	+6.6
Northern Mezzogiorno	−12.5	−13.0	−3.5	−0.5	+9.5
Southern Mezzogiorno and Islands	− 9.5	−11.5	−4.0	−2.0	+7.5
Zone C total	−11.6	−10.3	−4.0	+1.3	+6.3

Source: After Dematteis, 1986c, Table 1

as the highest percentage growth rates pushed out into the Type B zones and the population losses of the Type C zones diminished considerably after the early 1970s.

Metropolitan growth

As has been mentioned previously, lack of statistics for appropriate areas makes it impossible to undertake a nationwide comparison of trends since the early 1950s for metropolitan and non-metropolitan areas or for individual functional urban regions by size. The nearest that we can get to this is to examine population trends for the 'metropolitan areas' defined for planning purposes for Italy's five largest cities. Table 10.3 allows a comparison of the trend in change rates between the 1970s and the first half of the 1980s for each metropolitan area. These change rates can be compared with those for the non-metropolitan remainders of the regions in which they are situated, as well as with the national growth rate. Moreover, it is possible to break the metropolitan areas into their core and ring components, thereby enabling their development to be assessed in the context of the type of urban life-cycle model described by Berg *et al.* (1982).

The transformation in the fortunes of these metropolitan areas between 1971–81 and 1981–85 is clear, even though the onset of lower growth may well have dated from before 1971. The average growth rate of all five metropolitan areas combined stood at 0.40 per cent a year in the 1970s, not much below the national level, but had fallen to just under zero in the early 1980s, a considerably larger drop than for the country as a whole (Table 10.3). In the first period, Rome and particularly Naples grew faster than the national population and only Genoa was in decline, but by 1981–85 three metropolitan areas were recording heavy population losses and only Naples, maintaining its impressive rate of growth, grew more rapidly than the national rate.

In terms of the relative performance of the core and ring components of each metropolitan area, it can be seen from Table 10.3 that even in the first

Table 10.3 Italy: Population change, 1971–85, for five metropolitan areas and their regions (% per year)

Type of area	Turin	Milan	Genoa	Rome	Naples	Italy
1971–81						
Core	−0.44	−0.73	−0.66	0.21	−0.12	—
Ring	1.44	1.34	0.67	3.09	1.86	—
Metropolitan area	0.23	0.20	−0.55	0.51	0.94	0.40
Rest of region	0.02	0.53	0.04	0.97	0.64	0.46
Region	0.11	0.41	−0.25	0.67	0.80	0.45
1981–85						
Core	−1.83	−1.39	−0.89	−0.12	−0.13	—
Ring	0.83	0.69	−0.12	2.22	1.67	—
Metropolitan area	−0.79	−0.35	0.82	0.18	0.91	−0.00
Rest of region	−0.25	0.15	−0.23	1.09	0.80	0.36
Region	−0.47	−0.03	−0.51	0.50	0.86	0.28

period the prevailing state is one of advanced suburbanization (absolute decentralization). All but Rome recorded losses in their cores and gains in their rings – and the different position of Rome results only from a statistical anomaly due to the fact that its central administrative area is far more extensive than for the other cities. The main changes in the 1980s are those affecting the three northern metropolitan areas, which all experienced not only a marked increase in the losses from their cores but also a deterioration of the performance of their rings. It is the latter – the inability of the rings to absorb as many people from the declining cores – as much as the acceleration in the cores' decline that was responsible for Turin and Milan joining Genoa in a state of disurbanization (decentralization in decline) in the early 1980s. By contrast, the rings for Rome and Naples continued their strong growth in 1981–85 and were easily able to compensate for the relatively low rate of population loss sustained by their cores.

The position of the non-metropolitan regional remainders is not easy to interpret. By definition, these areas lie outside the functional regions of the five cities and, though it is not possible to rule out some metropolitan boundary spillover, the number of communes affected is likely to be few. This appears to be confirmed by the actual population growth rates for these regional remainders, particularly in the three northern cases (Table 10.3). Those for Turin and Genoa were barely able to maintain their population levels in the 1970s, let alone match the national rate of growth or absorb net in-migration from their respective metropolitan areas, while in 1981–85 they were losing population alongside them. Counterurbanization, if indeed it is operating in this context, would seem to involve a long-distance shift in population, no doubt at least partly associated with a regional restructuring away from the North West. The non-metropolitan territory around Milan continued to grow in the 1980s, though by less than the country as a whole, indicating a relative loss in its share of the national population. Only around Rome and Naples were the non-metropolitan areas growing rapidly in the 1980s – in these cases contributing strongly towards the overall growth of their regions and probably not relying to a great extent on inward movement from their major cities.

Summary

These analyses of population change indicate that population redistribution trends in Italy have gone into the reverse during the last twenty years. According to the Gini index the level of population concentration, as measured at the scale of the individual communes across the whole of Italy, peaked in the mid 1970s, after which deconcentration became the prevailing tendency. Between the early 1960s and late 1970s there was a marked increase in the number of communes experiencing population growth, while those which were depopulating throughout this period saw their aggregate level of population loss decline significantly. This was true for all the macro-regions of Italy, but in relation to the development of the urban system contrasts are evident between the North, the Centre and the South. In the North the relationship between population growth and

settlement size had already adopted a strong counterurbanization relationship in the 1970s, but this did not take place in the Centre until the
early 1980s and there was still considerable large-city growth in the South
in the 1980s. The limited population data available for metropolitan areas in
the 1970s and 1980s reinforce these regional differences, with a particular
contrast between the northern examples of Turin and Genoa, with their
metropolitan areas and regional remainders both in decline in the 1980s,
and Naples, with strong growth in both metropolitan area and surrounding region.

Components of population change

In order to interpret correctly processes of concentration of population, it is
important to assess the relative importance of the migratory and natural
change. As we have no data on net migration for towns by size group we
shall attempt to give a general analysis at macro-regional level. This will
serve as a background to a more qualitative interpretation of trends in the
relationship between population growth and settlement size.

After the 1950s and 1960s when there was rapid population growth in
the Centre and North and depopulation in the South, the situation was
reversed. Between 1971 and 1981 the population of the South grew by 6.2
per cent compared with only 3.5 per cent for the rest of Italy. In 1981–85 the
population change in the Centre and North fell to zero while the South
grew by 3.3 per cent, a higher annual rate than in the early 1970s.

As far as natural change is concerned, in 1978 the North West switched
to an excess of deaths over births and only two years later the same
occurred in the North East followed by the Centre in 1983. The South
continued to show a natural increase but a steadily declining one, going
from 6.4 per thousand in 1981 to 4 per thousand in 1985.

The change due to migration has also undergone an evolution. The
North West, which in the 1950s and 1960s had a very large net increase in
population from migration, saw its migration balance gradually fall to
practically zero by the 1980s. The Centre and North East maintained a
steady net annual in-migration of around 2–3 per thousand from 1975 to
1985, but the South, after a long period of net loss due to out-migration,
reversed the trend in 1982 when it registered a net increase of 6 per
thousand.

Between the 1970s and 1980s, therefore, new features emerged – the
greater natural growth of population in the South than in the North and
the inversion of the migration pattern. As a result, the higher rate of
population growth in the South in the 1980s was due not only to natural
increase but also to migration. The latter chiefly comprises a 'return
migration' of those who moved north to the industrialized regions of Italy
for work and then returned home after retiring or as a result of reductions
in the labour force requirements of industry in those areas. Indeed, at
national level too, Italy changed in the 1980s from being a country of net
emigration to one of slight net international population gain.

In the light of these general trends the lack of a clear relationship
between population growth and settlement size in the South can in part be

explained by the fact that both natural increase and return migration have been relatively evenly distributed among large and small towns. This uniform growth has taken place alongside internal migration which is still directed mainly towards the principal cities and their suburban areas. The result is a continued increase in the population of the larger towns and cities accompanied by an acceleration in the growth of the smaller towns and villages.

The situation in the North is a little more complex. Here the influx of population from the South has ceased and, due to the fall in birth rate, the natural change rate is negative. Moreover, return migration within this part of Italy is almost negligible; the outflow of retired people moving from the city back to smaller towns is insufficient to explain the loss of population from the large cities. This phenomenon of counterurbanization appears to be a redistribution of population between towns at different levels in the size hierarchy, due mainly to short-distance moves and a reduction in the attraction of the large cities for those living in their surrounding regions. Migration from outlying areas to the cities still occurs, but only to a limited extent and on a very selective basis, involving mainly young adults with average to higher levels of education (Petsimeris 1988).

Factors in population redistribution

Counterurbanization is more than population deconcentration. Though metropolitan expansion cannot be ruled out as a factor and its importance cannot be gauged precisely from the available data, it is clear from the foregoing analyses that the areas of recent population recovery are widely scattered and include parts of Italy most distant from the largest cities. Moreover, we do not need to rest our case relating to these new patterns of population change merely on the examination of the patterns themselves, because we can document associated changes which give some indication of the nature of the developments which have been taking place. In short, the population trends represent the spatial consequence of important economic, technological and social transformations which have affected all industrialized Western countries over the last twenty years.

Employment change and population redistribution

As far as the spatial organization of labour in Italy is concerned, the big industrial conurbations entered a phase of functional restructuring in the middle 1970s. This involved the progressive substitution of labour-intensive processes by capital-intensive ones through automation, the decentralization of jobs towards more peripheral locations, the reorganization of multi-plant forms and the contracting-out of production processes. As these changes affected initially the larger cities and increased the number of jobs in smaller towns, we should expect that the changes in industrial employment will be parallel to the population changes observed in Figure 10.2. Evidence of this type could help to support the hypothesis that counterurbanization depends at least in part on the spatial redistribution of industrial employment – something that is frequently referred to as de-industrialization, though not entirely correctly since the cutback in employment is often associated with a re-industrialization involving new investment and extra production.

Figure 10.4 compares the evolution of population and manufacturing jobs for representative regions of North, Central and South Italy (Piedmont, Marche and Calabria). From the two periods we can observe the evolution of urbanization and industrialization over time. The period 1951–61 corresponds to the phase of maximum concentration of population and employment, while the period 1971–81 relates to the phase of counterurbanization/de-industrialization. Piedmont is a typical example of mature industrial development characteristic of the 'central' economic formation of the North West, with the principal plants of large multi-nationals like Fiat and Olivetti. Marche is a typical example of the Italian 'peripheral area', with diffused recent industry and labour-intensive manufacturing carried out by small businesses located in non-metropolitan

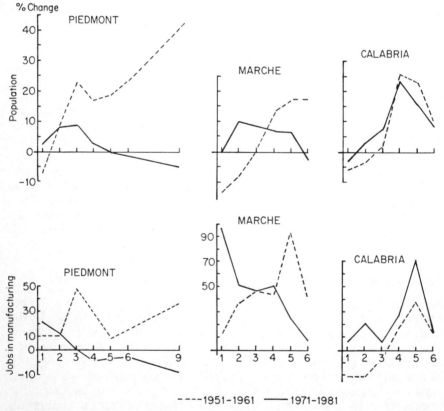

Figure 10.4 Italy: change in population and manufacturing employment, 1951–61 and 1971–81, by size of communes. Communes are grouped according to population size at the start of the period. Key to groups (population in thousands): 1: Under 5; 2: 5–10; 3: 10–25; 4: 25–50; 5: 50–100; 6: 100–250; 7: 250–500; 8: 500–1000; 9: 1000 and over. Source: Dematteis, 1986c, Figure 3.

areas where in the 1970s non-unionized part-time labour and the absence of social conflict was an important comparative advantage for small and medium-size industries. Calabria is an example of the southern 'marginal' and little-industrialized region with a chronic surplus of manpower.

It can be observed from Figure 10.4 that there is a close relationship in each case between the curve representing the relationship between manufacturing employment growth and commune size and that of the relationship between population change and commune size. In the two more industrialized regions a marked inversion is seen between the two periods. The positive correlation observed during the phase of centraliza-tion in 1951–61 (though admittedly rather weak for manufacturing jobs in Piedmont) was replaced by a negative, downward-sloping line in the 1971–81 phase of counterurbanization. The latter process appears to be more advanced in Piedmont, where de-industrialization is found for all groups of communes with more than 10,000 inhabitants. In Calabria, where there is practically no industrialization, concentration is dominant in both periods, with the only main differences being some upward movement in the growth rates of the three smallest settlement categories.

Unfortunately it is not possible to make the same empirical analysis for employment in the service sector, since the figures for the 1971 Census cannot be compared with those for 1981. It is nevertheless certain that in the same period tertiary employment rose far more than previously in the smaller towns in peripheral areas and also in outlying towns in the South (Cappellin and Grillenzoni 1983). This implies that the counterurbanization process is also associated with a spatial redistribution of the less skilled tertiary sector.

Housing and government policy

Another factor which may partially explain the loss of population in Italy's major cities is the housing market. Since the early 1970s this has been characterized by a high and differentiated demand and a weak and rigid supply, especially in rented accommodation (Secchi 1984). Despite de-industrialization and population decline in the main cities, demand there has remained high for various reasons, such as the existing unsatisfied housing demand, the erosion of residential property by tertiary activities, the higher standards expected by the emerging social classes and the breaking-up of the extended family into smaller nuclei. It seems, however, that the larger the city, the smaller the supply of housing on the market, with the situation being particularly severe in the city centres. Moving outwards towards the periphery and rural peri-urban fringe, it becomes easier to find accommodation or obtain permission to build new houses. Certainly, the population trends are reflected in the geographical evolution of the housing stock, which over the post-war period has tended to grow fastest in the metropolitan areas but in the 1970s was growing more slowly there than in the less densely inhabited areas (Table 10.4).

Government policies have also had some influence on the housing situation. In particular, the control on rents has had the effect of reducing local residential mobility. The stricter application of town planning

Table 10.4 Italy: Growth of the housing stock, 1951–81, by type of commune

Type of commune	Overall density of housing (Dwelling/ha)	Change in stock 1951–81 (%)	1971–81 (%)	Share of increase 1971–81 (%)
Metropolitan	2.78	+127	+19	26
Large urban	1.24	+108	+26	16
Small urban	0.73	+ 83	+28	22
Non-urban	0.36	+ 64	+32	36
Italy	0.73	+ 92	+26	100

Note: Communes are as classified by the Italian Ministry for Urban Areas on the basis of housing characteristics
Source:CRESME, 1987, p. 29

legislation in the larger towns has helped to favour building construction in the smaller ones. There is no evidence, on the other hand, that the regional policies specifically designed to help the less developed areas have influenced these general trends, either at national level (e.g. schemes to help the Mezzogiorno) or in individual regions (Celant and Morelli 1986).

Some importance must, however, be attached to the policy of the dispersal of service infrastructures, particularly relating to communications, education and health, which was carried out in Italy in the 1960s and 1970s. This greatly reduced the previous considerable inequalities in service provision between town and country and between industrial and agricultural areas, giving the North, most of the Centre and part of the South a certain homogeneity in terms of those territorial conditions which function as external economies for industrial decentralization. Even though it has come later and been less pronounced than elsewhere, Italy has seen during the late 1960s and the 1970s a process of urbanization of the country typical of mature industrial capitalism and countries with a welfare state. This process precedes that of counterurbanization but must not be confused with it, even though it is probably an essential condition for renewed demographic growth in more peripheral locations.

The importance of local socio-historical and cultural conditions

The recovery of smaller towns has also been influenced by the nature of the local business milieu and the related legacy of social and cultural characteristics. This seems to have played a particularly important role in the recent emergence of new economic growth in the 'Third Italy' of the North East and Centre. There is a high correlation between the areas of recent peripheral development in Italy and the traditional geographical distribution of autonomous or semi-autonomous forms of agricultural work – share-cropping, smallholdings, small rented properties and mixed farms (Bagnasco and Pini 1981).

These types of tenancy are usually associated with dispersed settlements and traditional urban networks with a high density of small and medium-sized towns. In many cases the extended family, as a unit of production in the small agricultural tenancy, is the basic social institution which, adapting to the new needs of decentralized and diffused industrial production, has fed the process with a labour force already divided into small management units capable of assuming a limited entrepreneurial role (Paci 1980). The diffused settlement structure has at the same time meant that this workforce can be increased at a low cost, as property is usually owner-occupied or self-built, families are self-sufficient in food needs, there is the possibility of part-time agricultural work and urbanization costs are low. These conditions, together with the system of self-help and services within the single family units, the non-proletarianization of the workforce (most of whom are self-employed), the acceptance of the work ethic and the market as a principal means of social integration, all contributed to reducing class conflict and assuring flexibility in the work-force, such as the willingness to accept overtime and dangerous or unguarded work.

The principal source of the local entrepreneurial skills responsible for the activation of industrial development in rural areas seems to have been the traditional urban middle class involved in crafts and commerce, which has always been well represented in the towns, even the small ones, of central and north-eastern Italy. Moreover, because of their essentially individual and localized demands, these peripheral systems lend themselves particularly well to decentralized forms of government and control, capable of offsetting, within certain limits, the lack of central government (Trigilia 1980). Therefore they effectively present themselves in the political dimension as alternatives to the metropolitan systems, where in the 1970s social conflict took on a highly ideological nature and was thus far more difficult to resolve.

Conclusions and prognostications

Having examined the components and possible factors contributing to counterurbanization we may ask ourselves to which general spatial model Italy can be said to belong. The data presented here and those statistics examined in other studies (Dematteis 1986a; Celant 1988; Petsimeris 1988) appear to correspond fairly well to the cyclical model suggested by Berg *et al.* (1982) as far as the passage from urbanization to suburbanization and then to disurbanization is concerned, but signs of re-urbanization are totally absent. As it is a purely descriptive model we cannot interpret this absence nor make reasonable forecasts for the future completion of the cycle in Italy.

In a previous piece of research (Cencini *et al.* 1983), it was suggested that the renewed growth of the smaller towns followed a pattern of spread of population from metropolitan areas outwards into the regional hinterland. The continued recovery of the parts of Italy most distant from the largest cities has led us to reject this hypothesis and to adopt an interpretation based on the concept of threshold, i.e. connected with certain conditions favourable to the growth of smaller towns after a phase of marginalization and stagnation. A map of the geographical distribution of towns with increasing population shows clearly that they are widely scattered and, if we exclude the external metropolitan fringe, are not correlated to the proximity of large cities. This appears to result from the way that changes occurring at the international level (e.g. economic crisis, new technologies, new divisions of labour) have a differentiated territorial impact depending on the diversity of regional and local conditions (infrastructural, demographic, socio-cultural, etc.). The spatial discontinuity seems to depend on the 'threshold' values of these conditions. For instance, as a rule in Italy the borderline between zones of demographic recovery and zones in the phase of depopulation follows the separation between densities of more than 100 persons/km^2 and zones of low density (usually less than 50 persons/km^2).

The explanation based on thresholds of local conditions can be combined with a more general explanation of counterurbanization: that it represents a temporary phase of transition from a hierarchical spatial organization of settlement to a partially non-hierarchical one (Dematteis 1985b). This interpretation has as its starting point the fact that the territorial redistribution of population among settlements of various sizes and locations corresponds to a general process of decentralization involving those activities and functions which, until twenty years ago, tended to be concentrated in the main urban and metropolitan areas. The reduction in the relative importance of economies of agglomeration means that all the functional interdependencies which were once contained within a single compact urban system now tend to be more spatially dispersed.

As a consequence, the spatial structure of urban and metropolitan areas should extend to a macro-regional scale, and therefore be based on the specialization and complementary functional relationships between the various places. The structure can be represented in graphs with a high level of connectivity. This type of spatial organization, based on interconnected nets, will tend to substitute for the hierarchy still prevalent today, founded on a historical pattern of relations at various levels (tree graphs) modified and simplified during the course of this century by the processes of polarization–agglomeration (star graphs) occurring since the 1960s.

If this is true, the functional unit of reference today can no longer be the single town or single urban system (core plus ring) but the settlement network at a regional or interregional scale and - for the quaternary functions - at the international scale. The urban multiplier effect, being distributed among the various settlements in the networks (according to the local specializations), would continue to weaken the classic relationship (assumed in the accumulative urban growth model) between the growth and size of the single settlement. This process should now work to the advantage of the small and medium-sized centres, in as much as the redistribution of functions and employment between the secondary nodes of the network, penalized in the preceding phase of urban polarization, now mean that they are gaining new population.

This recovery, however, is not occurring everywhere, but only where the previously mentioned threshold permits. Its intensity does not depend as before on the distance from main cities but is increasingly influenced by the particular features of the place, especially its ability to produce local innovations and to penetrate international markets (Camagni 1986).

This interpretation is very close to that proposed by Pred (1977), and also by Fielding (1982) in relation to the new spatial division of labour. While these authors emphasize the processes of hierarchical decentralization within multi-plant firms, the analysis of the Italian situation leads us to give greater weight to processes of local self-organization (Dematteis 1986b) and deconcentration through the sub-supply market. By this we mean that the network of smaller towns does not play a purely passive role, benefiting from the larger cities, but also plays an active role as the location of small and medium-sized companies which are competitive at international level and able to organize their growth in local systems (Garofoli 1983; Becattini 1987).

We should not imagine that this growth can continue without limits or even become an alternative to that of the major cities (as the word counterurbanization would suggest). The current changes would seem to be simply a phase of adjustment in the geographical distribution of employment. In Italy this process is particularly evident in the northern and central regions where it represents a re-evaluation of the dense network of small towns with infrastructural potential overshadowed in previous phases. Nevertheless, the new reticulated organization of space is only a modification of the Christaller-type functional articulation and it does not modify the city/periphery hierarchy based on a traditional dominance/dependence relationship (Camagni and Pompili 1987). Small towns, freed from the constrictions of the demand thresholds of the surrounding market area, can support a far wider range of activities and functions, but not all. At the same time, the largest cities are strengthening their position in quaternary functions (financial control, innovations, programming, decision-making and cultural trend-setting). So if the single smaller town frees itself from direct dependence on the nearest large city to become an integrated node in a larger network, it becomes altogether dependent on a vaster metropolitan network increasingly integrated at international level.

This leads us to presume that the present phase of territorial adjustment characterized by processes typical of counterurbanization will be only a short- or medium-term phenomenon. It will not necessarily make way for a new phase of urbanization as the urban life-cycle model predicts. It is more likely that over the next ten or twenty years we shall see irregular fluctuations of concentrated and diffused growth. There will be considerable differences between regions and local areas because the functional specialization and different types of comparative advantage on which the new urban network is based leads to different local responses to changes in the economic climate and general policies. These differences will tend to cushion the possible tendencies towards urbanization or disurbanization due to national or international economic cycles.

It remains to be seen whether Italy will evolve towards a situation of increased control or dominance by the metropolitan system over the peripheral network which is still largely independent, or whether from the latter some strong urban systems could emerge, capable of rising, at least for some functions, to metropolitan level. It would appear that the networks of Veneto, Emilia Romagna and northern Tuscany are moving in this direction. Another question yet to be answered is the future of the towns of the South, which are at the moment excluded from both the

European metropolitan level and the endogenous development of advanced industry. An alternative to an underdevelopment permanently dependent on government subsidy would seem to be the decentralization of productive capital from the Centre and North towards the medium-sized towns of the South which are at present the most dynamic.

Further reading

Several accounts of the changing Italian urban system are available in English. A good introduction is provided by Cori, B. 1984: The national settlement system of Italy, in Bourne, L.S., Sinclair, R. and Dziewonski, K. (eds) *Urbanization and settlement systems: international perspectives* (Oxford: Oxford University Press), 283–300. An outline of population trends is provided by King, R. 1986: Italy, in Findlay, A. and White, P. (eds) *West European population change* (London: Croom Helm), 163–86. The Italian experience of counterurbanization is specifically addressed by Dematteis, G. 1986: Urbanization and counterurbanization in Italy, *Ekistics* 53, 316/317, 26–33; also Dematteis, G. 1986: Counterurbanization in Italy, in Bourne, L.S., Cori, B. and Dziewonski, K. (eds) *Progress in settlement systems geography* (Milan: F. Angeli), 161–94. More detailed analyses (in Italian) can be found in Cencini, C. *et al.* 1983: *L'Italia emergente: indagine geodemografica sullo sviluppo periferico* (Milan: F. Angeli) and Vitali, O. 1983: *L'evoluzione urbana in Italia 1951–1977* (Milan: F. Angeli). For a detailed case-study, see Petsimeris, P. 1988: *L'urbanisation au Piedmont: analyse géographique des transformations sociofonctionelles d'une région mûre*, thèse de doctorat de 3me cycle, Université de Caen.

11

Japan:

the slowing of urbanization and metropolitan concentration

NORIKO O. TSUYA and TOSHIO KURODA

Introduction

Japan, the first non-Western country to experience industrialization, has one of the world's highest levels of urbanization. In 1980 approximately 76 per cent of the 117 million Japanese were living in cities (*shi-bu*). This proportion is similar to the corresponding figures for such Western countries as the United States, Canada, West Germany, and France (United Nations 1987). A vast majority of the Japanese urban population lives in the metropolitan regions centring around three major cities of Tokyo, Osaka, and Nagoya. Among these regions, the one around Tokyo has the highest share, with approximately 25 per cent of the total population in 1980, followed by the metropolitan node of Osaka with a share of 14 per cent, while the third, Nagoya, has an 11 per cent share. Altogether, approximately one half of the 1980 population lives in these three major metropolitan regions.

Urbanization in Japan has therefore been primarily a process of population concentration in the three major metropolitan regions. During the late 1950s and the 1960s, the rate of concentration was especially high due mainly to a large population influx from rural agricultural regions. However, this urban concentration slowed down considerably during the early 1970s and virtually stopped after the oil crisis because of a considerable decline in net in-migration. Meanwhile, a new migratory process characterized by intra-urban migration (movement from core cities to suburbs within metropolitan regions) developed during the 1960s and the early 1970s. After a virtual balancing of in- and out-migration during the late 1970s, the trend toward urban concentration reappeared in the early 1980s as population inflow into the major metropolitan regions (especially to the region centring around Tokyo) started increasing again.

In the following sections, we examine in detail patterns of recent population changes in Japan as well as socio-demographic and economic changes associated with the population changes. Specifically, in the next section, we outline the approach for this study of urbanization and counterurbanization in Japan, defining the geographic basis and identifying problems associated with the definition, in addition to discussing the availability of data and major data sources. In the third section, we look at the trend of post-war population changes, focusing upon the patterns of population concentration/deconcentration as well as migration. We then examine socio-demographic and economic characteristics of migrants such as the sex ratio and the age structure in the fourth section. In the fifth section, we investigate possible causes of population movement, touching upon impacts of population redistribution policies in post-war Japan. The chapter concludes with a discussion of the implications of our findings.

Approach

Analyses of urbanization and counterurbanization depend very much upon the definition of 'urban areas'; there is more than one definition used in Japan. The most common and widely accepted definition of urban area is the area within the city boundary, called *shi-bu*. *Shi-bu*, however, often includes agricultural areas with relatively low population density, and accordingly some of the population living within the administrative boundaries of cities are not exactly 'urban'. Therefore, starting from the 1960 population census, the Japanese government adopted an additional definition of urban areas based on population density. 'Densely Inhabited Districts' (DIDs) are the areas (districts) with a population density of 4000 inhabitants or more per km^2 and a total population of 5000 or more. In 1980 approximately 76 per cent of the Japanese population lived in *shi-bu* and 60 per cent in DIDs.

Analyses of urbanization and counterurbanization can also be made by examining patterns of population distribution in terms of metropolitan and non-metropolitan regions. In Japan, there are 47 prefectures (*ken*) which are basic geographical divisions for local administrative purposes, and these prefectures in turn constitute twelve larger regions (Figure 11.1). Among the twelve regions, we can consider Minami-kanto, Nishi-kinki, and Tokai as metropolitan and the remaining nine regions as non-metropolitan. The three metropolitan regions are also known as Tokyo, Hanshin, and Chukyo metropolitan regions respectively. Centring around the three major cities of Tokyo (the nation's capital), Osaka, and Nagoya respectively, these regions have been the economic, cultural, and political centres in post-war Japan. Urbanization trends in post-war Japan can therefore be measured and analysed in terms of several alternative frameworks – *shi-bu*, DIDs, metropolitan/non-metropolitan regions, or the twelve regions and their constituent prefectures.

Concerning the availability of data, Japan has had quinquennial population censuses since 1920 except for 1945, the final year of World War II, and vital statistics have also been available annually since the turn of this century. Annual reports on internal migration in Japan have also been compiled since 1954 from residence registration records called 'Basic Residence Registers'. These sources allow us to carry out reasonably accurate analyses of urbanization and migration in Japan.

However, two problems with these sources must be mentioned, relating to analyses of changes over time and to the limited detail of migration

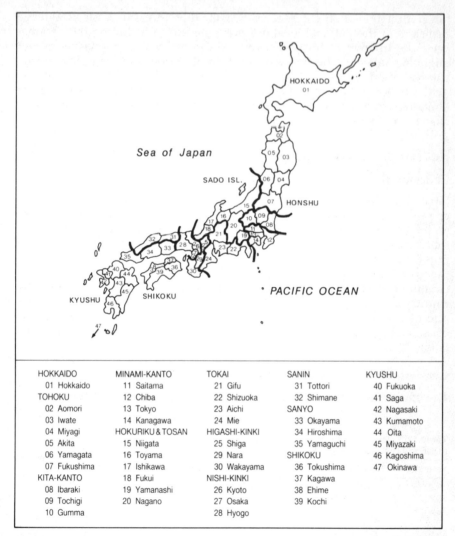

Figure 11.1 Japan's administrative divisions: 12 regions and 47 prefectures. Note: Metropolitan Japan is defined as the three regions of Minami-kanto, Nishi-kinki and Tokai.

HOKKAIDO	MINAMI-KANTO	TOKAI	SANIN	KYUSHU
01 Hokkaido	11 Saitama	21 Gifu	31 Tottori	40 Fukuoka
TOHOKU	12 Chiba	22 Shizuoka	32 Shimane	41 Saga
02 Aomori	13 Tokyo	23 Aichi	SANYO	42 Nagasaki
03 Iwate	14 Kanagawa	24 Mie	33 Okayama	43 Kumamoto
04 Miyagi	HOKURIKU & TOSAN	HIGASHI-KINKI	34 Hiroshima	44 Oita
05 Akita	15 Niigata	25 Shiga	35 Yamaguchi	45 Miyazaki
06 Yamagata	16 Toyama	29 Nara	SHIKOKU	46 Kagoshima
07 Fukushima	17 Ishikawa	30 Wakayama	36 Tokushima	47 Okinawa
KITA-KANTO	18 Fukui	NISHI-KINKI	37 Kagawa	
08 Ibaraki	19 Yamanashi	26 Kyoto	38 Ehime	
09 Tochigi	20 Nagano	27 Osaka	39 Kochi	
10 Gumma		28 Hyogo		

statistics. Specifically, in 1953 a large-scale annexation of towns (*machi*) and villages (*mura*) to cities (*shi-bu*) occurred owing to the government policy that encouraged such reorganization for benefits resulting from larger administrative capacities. Consequently, the proportion living in *shi-bu* increased sharply between 1950 and 1955 censuses, and the data prior to this annexation and following it are not exactly comparable.

Secondly, detailed analyses of migration can sometimes be hampered due to lack of such basic demographic data as age of migrants. Only a limited number of prefectures collect the information on age of migrants for compilation at the prefectural level, therefore the Basic Residence Registers at the national level are prevented from including the national age data. In spite of this, however, we can estimate age–sex-specific net migration rates for the five-year intercensal periods, applying the census survival method to the quinquennial census data (for details of the method, see Japan Statistics Bureau 1984, 57). We must keep these limitations in mind as we examine the recent patterns of overall population change in Japan.

Recent patterns of population change

Concentration into *shi-bu* and DIDs

Japan has been undergoing a process of urbanization ever since the country embarked on her industrialization in the early twentieth century and the pace of urbanization has generally corresponded with the tempo of that industrialization. As shown in Table 11.1, the proportion of the total population living in *shi-bu* doubled between 1920 and 1940 and, following the disruption of the war years and the boundary changes of 1953, continued to increase rapidly during the late 1950s and 1960s, when the country experienced very rapid economic development. In the 1970s, the rate of population concentration into both the *shi-bu* and DIDs slowed considerably, reaching something of a plateau by the end of the 1970s (Table 11.1).

Concentration into metropolitan Japan

The rapid urbanization during the late 1950s and the 1960s was due

Table 11.1 Japan: Proportion of population living in cities (*shi-bu*) and in Densely Inhabited Districts (DIDs), 1920–85

Year	Total population	Proportion in *Shi-bu*	Proportion in DIDs
1920	55 963 053	18.0	—
1925	59 736 822	21.6	—
1930	64 450 005	24.0	—
1935	69 254 148	32.7	—
1940	73 114 308	37.7	—
1945	71 998 104*	27.8	—
1947	78 101 473*	33.1	—
1950	84 114 574	*37.3*	—
1955	90 076 594	56.1	—
1960	94 301 623	63.3	43.7**
1965	99 209 137	67.9	48.1**
1970	104 665 171	72.1	53.5
1975	111 939 643	75.9	57.0
1980	117 060 396	76.2	59.7
1985	121 048 923	76.7	60.6

Note: Data for *shi-bu* for 1950 and 1955 are not comparable (see text)
   * Excludes Okinawa-ken
   ** Excludes Okinawa-ken because DIDs were not yet established there
Source: Statistics Bureau, Management and Coordination Agency (1987) 1985 Population Census of Japan, Volume 1: Total Population

Table 11.2 Japan: Population and per cent distribution by region, 1950–1985

Region	1950	1955	1960	1965	1970	1975	1980	1985
POPULATION (1 000):								
Hokkaido	4 296	4 773	5 039	5 172	5 184	5 338	5 575	5 679
Tohoku	9 022	9 334	9 326	9 108	9 031	9 233	9 572	9 730
Kita-kanto	5 191	5 225	5 139	5 183	5 382	5 797	6 199	6 512
Minami-kanto	13 051	15 424	17 864	21 017	24 113	27 039	28 699	30 273
Hokuriku and Tosan	8 052	8 043	7 964	7 877	7 856	8 107	8 357	8 537
Tokai	8 867	9 489	10 086	10 926	11 778	12 726	13 315	13 806
Higashi-kinki	2 607	2 637	2 626	2 706	2 863	3 135	3 376	3 548
Nishi-kinki	9 000	10 174	11 405	13 070	14 538	15 696	16 146	16 533
Sanin	1 513	1 543	1 488	1 401	1 343	1 350	1 389	1 411
Sanyo	5 284	5 449	5 456	5 470	5 655	6 016	6 197	6 338
Shikoku	4 220	4 245	4 121	3 975	3 904	4 040	4 163	4 227
Kyushu*	13 012	13 739	13 787	13 304	13 017	13 460	14 071	14 455
Metropolitan**	30 918	35 088	39 355	45 013	50 430	55 464	58 160	60 612
Non-metropolitan***	53 197	54 989	54 947	54 196	54 235	56 476	58 900	60 437
All Japan	84 115	90 077	94 302	99 209	104 665	111 940	117 060	121 049
PER CENT DISTRIBUTION								
Hokkaido	5.1	5.3	5.3	5.2	5.0	4.8	4.8	4.7
Tohoku	10.8	10.4	9.9	9.2	8.6	8.3	8.2	8.0
Kita-kanto	6.2	5.8	5.5	5.2	5.1	5.2	5.3	5.4
Minami-kanto	15.6	17.1	18.9	21.2	23.0	24.2	24.5	25.0
Hokuriku and Tosan	9.6	8.9	8.5	7.9	7.5	7.2	7.1	7.1
Tokai	10.6	10.5	10.7	11.0	11.3	11.4	11.4	11.4
Higashi-kinki	3.1	2.9	2.8	2.7	2.7	2.8	2.9	2.9
Nishi-kinki	10.7	11.3	12.1	13.2	13.9	14.0	13.8	13.7
Sanin	1.8	1.7	1.4	1.4	1.3	1.2	1.2	1.2
Sanyo	6.3	6.1	5.9	5.5	5.4	5.4	5.3	5.2
Shikoku	5.0	4.7	4.4	4.0	3.7	3.6	3.6	3.5
Kyushu*	14.2	14.4	13.7	12.5	11.5	11.1	11.1	11.9
Metropolitan**	36.8	39.0	41.7	45.4	48.2	49.5	49.7	50.1
Non-metropolitan***	63.2	61.0	58.3	54.6	51.8	50.5	50.3	49.9

Notes: * Includes Okinawa-ken
      ** Total of the three metropolitan regions of Minami-kanto, Tokai, and Nishi-kinki
      *** Total of the remaining nine regions above

Sources: Bureau of Statistics, Office of the Prime Minister (1982) 1980 Population Census of Japan; Statistics Bureau, Management and Coordination Agency (1987) 1985 Population Census of Japan, Volume 2, Part 1

primarily to a major increase in the degree of population concentration in the three major metropolitan regions of Minami-kanto, Nishi-kinki and Tokai centred on the cities of Tokyo, Osaka and Nagoya respectively (Table 11.2). The rate of concentration was especially high during the 1960s, when these three regions together grew by over 11 million people, while the aggregate population of the other nine regions in Japan fell somewhat. In the 1970s, however, non-metropolitan Japan experienced a significant population recovery, adding over 2 million people in both intercensal periods and slowing the rate of concentration into three metropolitan regions, particularly after the oil crisis of 1973–74. Even in the latter half of the 1970s, however, the proportion of the population living in the metropolitan regions did not decrease and between 1980 and 1985 the pace of concentration again quickened. By the 1985 the population of the three metropolitan regions had overtaken that of the rest of Japan, having almost doubled from just over 30 million in 1950, when they accounted for little more than one-third of the nation's people. The most substantial element of this growth was provided by the Minami-kanto region, which added 17 million to its population over this 35-year period and grew faster than the other two metropolitan regions in all seven intercensal periods.

Population change and its components

It is possible to break down the overall population change figures into two components – natural increase and a residual element. At the national level the latter principally comprises international migration and changes in census coverage. Both these, however, are reckoned to be relatively small. Though the number of exits from Japan increased markedly from the mid 1960s and reached around 4 million in 1980, only a small proportion of these, usually amounting to less than 50,000 a year, left for the purposes of emigration, long-term business stays or studying abroad, while similarly the number of non-Japanese who entered Japan with the intention of staying for more than one year was always less than 50,000 in the 1960s and 1970s (National Institute for Research Advancement 1982, 213–64). Census coverage in post-war Japan has generally been very high – a net error of less than 1.5 per cent according to post-enumeration surveys – so it is considered that underenumeration would not seriously affect our analysis of population trends (Institute of Population Problems 1985, 33). In analysing population change at subnational scales in Japan, therefore, we can consider that this residual element is due mostly to migration and that the latter is primarily the product of internal migration within Japan rather than the effects of international movements.

Table 11.3 presents a summary of population changes for the metropolitan and non-metropolitan regional groupings, broken down into the two components of natural increase and net migration. The data on overall population-change rate confirm the marked fall in the growth rate of metropolitan Japan since the early 1960s and especially its much lower rate of population increase since the mid 1970s. For the nine non-metropolitan regions in aggregate, the 1970s were distinctly different from the three previous intercensal periods, but in the 1980s their combined growth rate

Table 11.3 Japan: Components of population change in metropolitan and non-metropolitan regions, 1950–1985

Periods	Metropolitan/ Non-metropolitan	Population change		Natural increase		Net migration	
		000s	%	000s	%	000s	%
1950–55	Metropolitan	4 169	(13.5)	2 043	(6.6)	2 126	(6.9)
	Non-metropolitan	1 790	(3.4)	3 997	(7.5)	−2 207	(−4.1)
1955–60	Metropolitan	4 264	(12.2)	1 876	(5.3)	2 389	(6.8)
	Non-metropolitan	−39	(−0.1)	2 899	(5.3)	−2 937	(−5.3)
1960–65	Metropolitan	5 657	(14.4)	2 646	(6.7)	3 011	(7.7)
	Non-metropolitan	−749	(−1.4)	2 384	(4.3)	−3 133	(−5.7)
1965–70	Metropolitan	5 417	(12.0)	3 409	(7.6)	2 008	(4.5)
	Non-metropolitan	39	(0.1)	2 272	(4.2)	−2 233	(−4.1)
1970–75	Metropolitan	5 034	(10.0)	4 011	(8.0)	1 023	(2.0)
	Non-metropolitan	2 241	(4.1)	2 677	(4.9)	−436	(−0.8)
1975–80	Metropolitan	2 698	(4.9)	2 871	(5.2)	−173	(−0.3)
	Non-metropolitan	2 427	(4.3)	2 272	(4.0)	155	(0.3)
1980–85	Metropolitan	2 452	(4.2)	2 113	(3.6)	339	(0.6)
	Non-metropolitan	1 537	(2.6)	1 777	(3.0)	−240	(−0.4)

Sources: Statistics Bureau, Management and Coordination Agency (1985) Population of Japan, Final Report of the 1980 Population Census; Institute of Population Problems, Ministry of Health and Welfare (1987) Latest Demographic Statistics 1986, Institute of Population Problems Research Series, No. 248

fell back more sharply than for metropolitan Japan, so that the gap between them widened again after being very close in 1975–80.

In terms of the change components, Table 11.3 shows that population increases in the metropolitan regions were due more to in-migration than natural increases during the 1950s and the early 1960s. In the late 1960s the impact of migration started declining sharply, and during 1975–80 the metropolitan regions as a whole experienced an excess of out-migration over in-migration. After 1980 population inflow into the metropolitan regions started increasing again, but the amount of the inflow was much smaller than that in the 1950s and the 1960s. In contrast, throughout the post-war years except for the period 1975–80, the non-metropolitan regions continued to experience net out-migration, making natural increase the sole factor of their population increases. The amount of net out-migration from the non-metropolitan regions was especially large during the 1950s and the 1960s.

From these findings, we therefore can consider that the rapid urbanization during the late 1950s and the 1960s was caused primarily by heavy population inflow into the metropolitan regions and also by natural increases in the metropolitan regions. A considerable part of these natural increases in the metropolitan regions are though to be caused by relatively high fertility of in-migrants since many of them were, as we will see later, in the prime of their reproductive ages (in their 20s and early 30s).

Migration trends

Examining changes in the amount of net migration by the twelve regions, we can further see that all three metropolitan regions experienced heavy population inflow during the late 1950s and the 1960s, the largest being the Minami-kanto region (Table 11.4). In the 1970s, however, the volume of net migration into the metropolitan regions decreased substantially, and this tendency became especially noticeable after 1975. The most salient example is the Nishi-kinki region, which even experienced a considerable net loss during 1975–85. Meanwhile, during the 1970s some of the regions adjacent to these metropolitan regions (such as Kita-kanto and Higashi-kinki) started having net population inflow although the volume was relatively small. However, during the early 1980s the net migration balances of the three metropolitan regions moved back in a positive direction, with the increase in Minami-kanto being especially noticeable.

Analysing changes in migratory flows between the metropolitan and non-metropolitan regions as well as within them, we can discover an additional picture behind the rapid urbanization during the late 1950s and the 1960s and the subsequent slowing-down of this urbanization trend. Figure 11.2 shows changes in the relative importance of the four types of inter-prefectural migration: (1) from the non-metropolitan to metropolitan regions; (2) within the metropolitan regions; (3) from the metropolitan to non-metropolitan regions; and (4) within the non-metropolitan-regions. From Figure 11.2, we can see that during the late 1950s and the early 1960s the migratory flow from the non-metropolitan to metropolitan regions had the highest share. However, in the mid 1960s the share of within-metropolitan migration surpassed that of non-metropolitan to metropolitan migration, and then continued to maintain a similar level of share.

Table 11.4 Japan: Net migration by region, 1950–1985

Region	1950–55	1955–60	1960–65	1965–70	1970–75	1975–80	1980–85
Hokkaido	44	−53	−178	−284	−160	−17	−84
Tohoku	−474	−583	−663	−453	−207	−40	−142
Kita-kanto	−336	−344	−168	−30	104	137	106
Minami-Kanto	1 473	1 563	1 859	1 356	887	187	500
Hokuriku and Tosan	−496	−416	−384	−324	−113	−47	−28
Tokai	36	105	247	157	103	−44	16
Higashi-Kinki	−107	−110	−21	38	113	114	73
Nishi-kinki	618	721	906	495	328	−318	−131
Sanin	−62	−117	−126	−89	−314	4	−7
Sanyo	−136	−213	−183	−44	52	−49	−22
Shikoku	−237	−297	−273	−184	−15	2	−23
Kyushu*	−403	−805	−1 135	−863	−178	49	−87

Note: The unit for these figures is 1 000
 * Includes Okinawa-ken

Sources: Bureau of Statistics, Office of the Prime Minister (1984) 1980 Population Census Monograph Series No. 2: Migration; Statistics and Information Department, Ministry of Health and Welfare (1985) Vital Statistics 1984 Japan, Volume 1; ———— (1986) Vital Statistics 1985 Japan, Volume 1

Meanwhile, the share of metropolitan to non-metropolitan migration formed almost a mirror image of that of non-metropolitan to metropolitan migration, converging in the mid 1970s. During 1975–80, the shares of these two types of migration almost balanced themselves off at about the level of 23 to 25 per cent. During the early 1980s, the share of migratory flow from the non-metropolitan to metropolitan regions again began to exceed that of the flow in the opposite direction. The share of migration within non-metropolitan regions declined somewhat during the late 1950s and the early 1960s and then started increasing gradually.

From these findings, we therefore can conclude that the rapid urbanization during the late 1950s and the 1960s in Japan was caused mainly by a massive population inflow into the three metropolitan regions from the non-metropolitan regions. On the other hand, the slowing-down of urban concentration in the 1970s (especially after 1975) was due primarily to substantial decreases (and sometimes a net loss) in the net population inflow into these metropolitan regions, with regions adjacent to the metropolitan regions experiencing some net population inflow. These substantial decreases in the net population inflow were caused mainly by decreases in migration from the non-metropolitan to metropolitan regions, coupled with increases in migration from the metropolitan to non-metropolitan regions. In the early 1980s, in-migration into the major metropolitan regions, especially the Minami-kanto region, again started increasingly slowly.

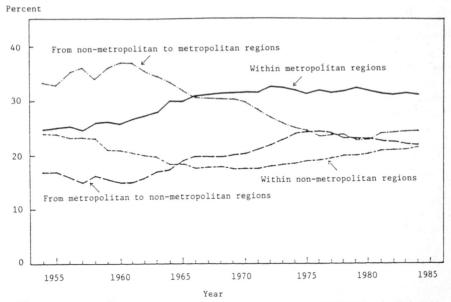

Figure 11.2 Japan: composition of inter-prefectural migration, 1954–84, by metropolitan type. Source: Japan Statistics Bureau, Management and Coordination Agency, Migration Report based on Basic Residence Registers, various years.

Developments in the Minami-kanto region

To investigate further these recent changes in urbanization and internal migration in Japan, we now look specifically into population changes in the Minami-kanto region which, including Tokyo, has been the largest centre of urbanization and population concentration in modern Japan. Table 11.5 presents changes in population during 1950–85 for the four prefectures comprising the Minami-kanto region. It can be seen that the prefecture of Tokyo (which includes the city of Tokyo and extensive parts of its commuting environs) experienced a very high rate of population growth during the 1950s while the corresponding rates for the adjacent prefectures of Saitama and Chiba were relatively low. However, this trend was reversed in the 1960s, with the main focus of population growth shifting from Tokyo to the adjacent prefectures; that is, while the prefectures of Saitama and Chiba experienced a sudden spurt in the rate of population growth between 1960 and 1975, the corresponding rate for Tokyo dwindled substantially. Meanwhile, the prefecture of Kanagawa, which includes the major city of Yokohama as well as many smaller cities and towns in commuting distance of the city of Tokyo, has succeeded in maintaining a high rate of population growth throughout the post-war years until the mid 1970s. After 1975 the prefectures in the Minami-kanto region had considerable decreases in their rates of population growth, except for the prefecture of Tokyo whose growth in population had already come to a virtual halt in the mid 1960s (Table 11.5). Reflecting these population changes, Tokyo prefecture's share of the region's population which had risen to 54 per cent in 1960 thereafter declined steadily to reach 39 per cent in 1985, while the corresponding shares of Saitama, Chiba and Kanagawa continued to grow throughout the period 1960–85.

These patterns of population change are dominated by migration flows, as would be expected in such a dynamic context. As shown by the final panel of Table 11.5, the basic trend of population movement in the Minami-kanto region during the 1950s was migration into the core metropolitan prefectures of Tokyo and Kanagawa, while the other two prefectures grew principally because of natural increases. By contrast, migration into Tokyo prefecture fell dramatically in the early 1960s and switched into net loss after 1965, whereas higher levels of net in-migration were experienced by the other three prefectures, with particularly impressive increases in Saitama and Chiba. With the much lower level of net migration into the region as a whole in 1975–80, the migration balances for these three prefectures shrank markedly to the stage where the contribution of migration to overall population growth fell to about half in Saitama and Chiba and to less than a quarter in Kanagawa. During the early 1980s the two core prefectures experienced a modest rebound in net migration, with more substantial recovery being in Tokyo even though net outflow continued there.

We can therefore conclude that the rapid concentration of the Japanese population into the Minami-kanto region during the late 1950s and 1960s was produced first by heavy in-migration to large metropolitan cities like Tokyo and Yokohama. However, during the 1960s, while the region as a

Table 11.5 Japan: Population change and net migration for prefectures in Minami-kanto Region, 1950–1985

Year	Saitama	Chiba	Tokyo	Kanagawa	Total Minami-kanto
Population (000s)					
1950	2 146	2 139	6 278	2 488	13 051
1955	2 263	2 205	8 037	2 919	15 424
1960	2 431	2 306	9 684	3 443	17 864
1965	3 015	2 702	10 869	4 431	21 017
1970	3 866	3 367	11 408	5 472	24 113
1975	4 821	4 149	11 674	6 398	27 042
1980	5 420	4 735	11 618	6 924	28 699
1985	5 864	5 148	11 829	7 432	30 273
Population share in the region (%)					
1950	16.4	16.4	48.1	19.1	100.0
1955	14.7	14.3	52.1	18.9	100.0
1960	13.6	12.9	54.2	19.3	100.0
1965	14.3	12.9	51.7	21.1	100.0
1970	16.0	14.0	47.3	22.7	100.0
1975	17.8	15.3	43.2	23.7	100.0
1980	18.9	16.5	40.5	24.1	100.0
1985	19.4	17.0	39.1	24.5	100.0
Population change (%)					
1950–55	5.4	3.1	28.0	17.3	18.2
1955–60	7.4	4.6	20.5	17.9	15.8
1960–65	24.0	17.2	12.2	28.7	17.7
1965–70	28.2	24.6	5.0	23.5	14.7
1970–75	24.7	23.2	2.3	16.9	12.1
1975–80	12.4	14.1	− 0.5	8.2	6.1
1980–85	8.2	8.7	1.8	7.3	5.5
Net migration change (%)					
1950–55	− 1.5	− 3.1	21.1	10.0	11.3
1955–60	2.3	0.0	14.5	11.9	10.1
1960–65	17.3	11.5	4.8	20.6	10.4
1965–70	19.0	17.2	− 2.8	14.1	6.5
1970–75	14.5	14.5	− 5.0	7.4	3.7
1975–80	6.0	8.1	− 4.9	2.2	0.7
1980–85	4.0	4.5	− 1.3	3.2	1.7

Sources: Statistics Bureau, Management and Coordination Agency, 1985; Population Census of Japan, Volume 1; Bureau of Statistics, Office of the Prime Minister, 1955 Population Census of Japan, Volume 1; ———, 1980 Population Census of Japan, Volume 1; ———, 1970 Population Census of Japan, Volume 1

whole kept receiving a large population influx, the direction of the population flow shifted from the core metropolitan to the adjacent prefectures, indicating a trend of 'dispersed' urban concentration (i.e., migration from core metropolitan to suburban areas). When the pace of population concentration into this region slowed down considerably during 1975–80, the main impact was the substantial fall in net in-migration to Saitama,

Chiba and, to a lesser extent, Kanagawa. Although the amount of migration into Tokyo and Kanagawa increased somewhat during the early 1980s (consequently increasing the net migration into the region), it did not reach the level it had during the earlier period of rapid population concentration.

Summary

Urbanization in post-war Japan was dominated by a process of rapid population concentration into three metropolitan regions during the late 1950s and 1960s. This was caused first by heavy population inflow from non-metropolitan to core metropolitan prefectures and then by migration from core metropolitan to adjacent prefectures. During the 1960s Tokyo began to be affected by the 'doughnut' phenomenon, in which most metropolitan growth takes place not in the urban core but around its periphery, as had already emerged in other large cities round the world like London, Paris, New York and Boston (Wilkinson 1965, 168–71; Kanekiyo 1983) – a process that deepened in Japan in the early 1970s, even though Tokyo remained the country's economic and political centre (Yazaki 1970, 34–5). Partly because of this metropolitan decentralization, the pace of population concentration slowed down considerably during the 1970s, especially between 1975–80. Moreover, urbanization reached a virtual plateau after 1975, due mainly to a dramatic decline in net migration into the major metropolitan regions. This, however, was not enough to produce population deconcentration, nor can a phenomenon of counterurbanization be clearly identified – findings which agree in general with those of Vining (1982) and Kawashima (1982).

Characteristics of migrants

According to the previous analysis internal migration is clearly the major component behind the urbanization process and the changing pattern of population distribution in post-war Japan. It is generally recognized in Japan, as much as in other developed countries, that the volume and direction of migration differ considerably according to the socio-demographic and economic characteristics of migrants. This raises questions as to which groups in the population are primarily responsible for the population shifts which have been observed, particularly the slowdown in net migration from non-metropolitan to metropolitan regions in the 1970s.

Unfortunately, as mentioned earlier, the scope for analysis on the characteristics of migrants is severely restricted because national-level data on migration were not collected until the 1970 population census, and also because the Basic Residence Registers do not have nationwide information on migrants' age. In the 1970 census, however, information was collected for the first time on age and sex of people who changed their residence during the one year prior to the census (i.e., from October 1969 to September 1970), thus making some analyses of basic characteristics of migrants possible. Similar information was collected again in the 1980 census. For years before 1970 and for longer time periods, it is possible to estimate age–sex-specific net migration rates by prefecture for each five-year intercensal period utilizing the cohort survival method based on data from the censuses.

Table 11.6 presents the rate of migration by age and sex of inter-prefectural migrants in Japan for the one-year period prior to the 1970 and 1980 censuses. The rate is the proportion of the population in each five-year age-group at the time of the census who changed their usual place of residence during the one-year period prior to the census. From Table 11.6, we can see that the rate of inter-prefectural migration is considerably higher for males than for females, and this sex-dependent difference is due primarily to the higher propensity of migration for males aged 15 or older. More importantly, we can also notice that there are significant age-dependent variations in the migration rate. Specifically, inter-prefectural migration is high among people aged 15–24, with those in their early 20s showing the highest rate. From these findings, we can therefore deduce that urbanization in post-war Japan was due mainly to the movement of young population, especially males aged 15–24, and that concentration of migration in young males aged 15–24 was due mainly to university admission or finding employment.

In order to further analyse population movement among different prefectures, we have used the cohort survival method to estimate age–sex-specific net migration rates by prefecture for each five-year inter-

Table 11.6 Japan: Inter-prefectural migration rates by age and sex of migrants during the one-year period prior to the 1970 and 1980 censuses (per cent)

Age	1970		1980	
	Male	Female	Male	Female
0	2.2	2.2	1.9	1.9
1– 4	3.5	3.5	3.0	3.0
5– 9	2.2	2.2	2.1	2.1
10–14	1.4	1.4	1.3	1.3
15–19	8.8	6.5	6.5	4.6
20–24	9.6	7.2	8.0	5.4
25–29	7.0	5.9	5.4	4.8
30–34	4.8	3.3	3.7	3.0
35–39	3.3	2.1	2.8	2.0
40–44	2.6	1.5	2.1	1.1
45–49	2.3	1.2	1.6	0.8
50–54	1.9	1.0	1.3	0.8
55–59	1.5	1.0	1.1	0.7
60–64	1.1	1.0	0.8	0.7
65–69	0.8	1.0	0.7	0.8
70–74	0.7	1.0	0.6	0.8
75–79	0.6	0.9	0.6	0.8
80–84	0.6	0.8	0.6	0.8
85+	0.7	0.7	0.6	0.7
Total	4.2	3.1	3.0	3.1

Sources: Bureau of Statistics, Office of the Prime Minister, 1970 Population Census of Japan, Volume 7, Part 1; Statistics Bureau, Management and Coordination Agency, 1980 Population Census of Japan, Volume 6

censal period between 1950 and 1980. We find that core metropolitan prefectures such as Tokyo and Osaka have been experiencing a large net inflow of population aged 15–24 throughout the post-war period although the scale of this influx has generally been declining over time. Moreover, during the 1960s these core metropolitan prefectures started experiencing a considerable outflow of population older than age 24 (especially males in their late 20s and early 30s) and this out-migration trend became increasingly strong during the early 1970s. The first panel in Figure 11.3 presents the male age-specific net migration profiles for the prefecture of Tokyo as an example of this type of migration profile, showing clearly the emergence of heavy net losses of young family-age men in the 1960s, and the progressive decline and later onset of the teenage influx across the three periods highlighted.

The cohort-survival analysis allows the identification of at least two other types of prefectures based on their age-specific migration profiles. One comprises prefectures adjacent to these core metropolitan prefectures and is illustrated in Figure 11.3 by the case of Saitama, which is located along the northern boundary of the Tokyo prefecture. This did not experience any significant net migration over all the age groups of both sexes during the 1950s, but recorded a considerable inflow of population aged 15–34 during the 1960s and the early 1970s, with the inflow declining substantially during the late 1970s. The other comprises non-metropolitan prefectures far from the core metropolitan prefectures and is exemplified in Figure 11.3 by Kagoshima, the southernmost prefecture on the island of Kyushu (see Figure 11.1). This has been experiencing a large outflow of population aged 15–24 throughout the period 1950–80, but began experiencing a considerable inflow of population aged 25–34 during the 1970s.

From these findings on changes in the age pattern of inter-prefectural migration, we can therefore conclude that the rapid population concentration in the metropolitan regions during the late 1950s and the 1960s was caused primarily by massive in-migration of young population (especially males aged 15–24) from non-metropolitan agricultural regions. It is also found that during the 1960s and the early 1970s substantial intra-metropolitan migration of population older than age 24 occurred indicating an emergence of the 'doughnut' phenomenon (suburbanization). The slowing-down of urban concentration during the 1970s was due largely to the net out-migration of population aged 25–34 from metropolitan to non-metropolitan regions, while migration of those aged 15–24 into metropolitan regions continued on a smaller scale.

There is also some evidence that return migration has helped to produce these distinctive age profiles of migration and may have contributed to the phasing of trends over time. According to studies that analysed population movement in post-war Japan by birth cohort based on the data from the Basic Residence Registers (some prefectures have compiled the age-specific migration data) as well as a national survey on internal migration by Japan Bureau of Census (Kawabe 1983; 1984; 1985), it was found that some young people who had migrated into the metropolitan regions during the 1960s returned to non-metropolitan regions after living in large cities (such as Tokyo and Osaka) for a decade or so. In

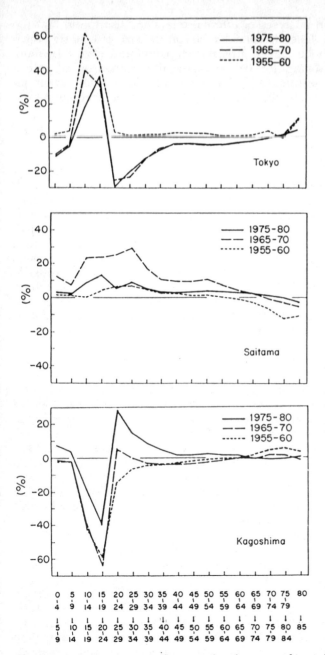

Figure 11.3 Japan: age-specific net migration rates for males in three prefectures, 1955–60, 1965–70 and 1975–80. Source: Japan Statistics Bureau, Management and Coordination Agency, Tokyo, 1984, Jinko Idou (Internal Migration). 1980 Population Census Monograph Series No. 2, 58–64.

addition, these cohort analyses of internal migration also found that the volume of migration depends considerably on the size of cohorts which constitute the most mobile age groups at each period under consideration, and that after controlling for cohort sizes, the propensity of return migration increased during the 1970s although the rate of urban in-migration was still substantially higher than the rate of out-migration from urban areas.

Causes of migration

There are numerous macro (social structural) as well as micro (individual) factors considered to be instrumental in motivating people to migrate. These factors can also be divided into those connected with the situations at the origin and destination of migration, as well as the relative situation of the origin and destination. However, the causal mechanism through which these factors influence people to migrate (or not to migrate) remains unclear since these factors are interrelated; it is therefore almost impossible to untangle the relationship between these factors. Keeping in mind these difficulties involved in assessing causes of migration, we now review the main reasons which have been put forward to explain the pattern and tempo of population redistribution in Japan since the 1950s.

Rural–urban migration

The dominant pattern of internal migration in modern Japan has been a movement from rural areas to cities, generally with the purpose of obtaining non-agricultural jobs (Minami 1967; ESCAP 1984, 134–6; Japan Statistics Bureau 1984, ch. 4). Starting from the latter half of the 1950s, Japan experienced rapid economic development, showing almost a straight line of economic growth (an average annual growth rate of 10 per cent) during the late 1950s and the 1960s. Although the growth rate was somewhat higher after 1960s, the overall economic growth during the late 1950s and the 1960s was undeniably dramatic. Corresponding with this rapid economic growth, the proportion of the employed population in agriculture showed significant decreases. In 1950 approximately 45 per cent of the employed population was in agriculture, the proportion going down to 38 per cent in 1955, further to 30 per cent in 1960, and to only 18 per cent in 1970 (Japan Statistics Bureau 1979; 1982). The rapid economic development in Japan during the late 1950s and the 1960s provided ample non-agricultural job opportunities and since most of the non-agricultural jobs were in urban areas, this rapid shift of the employed population from agriculture to non-agriculture was accompanied by massive population concentration into urban metropolitan regions. Hence, the rapid urbaniza-tion during the late 1950s and the 1960s can be thought to have been produced mainly by migration of the labour force from rural agricultural regions due to increasing job opportunities in urban areas in response to the Japanese economy's dramatic development.

This primacy of employment-related motives in migration to large urban areas and the surrounding metropolitan areas was still found to be prominent among in-migrants to urban areas during the 1970s (Japan Statistics Bureau 1984, 69–71). For example, according to the 1972 Tokyo Migration Survey, both sexes move to Tokyo primarily to find jobs (either a first job or a better one) regardless of the years of in-migration. In all, job-related moves were found to constitute around 60 per cent of the motives for migration to Tokyo – a finding which parallels the results of other studies in Tokyo and other Japanese cities (Japan Statistics Bureau 1984, 69–71; White 1982, 31).

In addition to the rapid economic development which created abundant non-agricultural employment opportunities in metropolitan regions, there seem to be three other supplementary factors facilitating the rapid urban concentration during the late 1950s and the 1960s: increasing wage differences between agriculture and non-agriculture employment; development of labour-efficient agriculture; and the post-war breakdown of the *ie* (or house) system. First, relative attractiveness of non-agricultural employment increased during the 1950s and the early 1960s due to the difference between agricultural and non-agricultural wages (Minami 1967). According to Minami, the inclination to move out of agriculture to non-agricultural industries depends greatly on the wage differentials between agriculture and non-agriculture, the' ratio of which increased substantially during the late 1950s and the early 1960s due primarily to rapid increases in real wages of non-agriculture. The growth of labour unions also promised better work conditions for those choosing industrial employment, making the shift to non-agriculture even more attractive (White 1982, 18).

Secondly, introduction of farm machinery brought about labour-efficient agriculture which in turn made it possible to meet the strong labour demand from the urban industrial sector (ESCAP 1984, 136). Although it can be argued that lack of sufficient agricultural labour supply (due to rapid out-migration of population from agriculture) compelled the advancement of agricultural technology, it is also true that agricultural mechanization advanced swiftly during the period of Japan's rapid economic development. This made the successive outflows of population from agriculture possible without an abrupt reduction of the number of farm households (Nagaoka *et al.* 1977, 39).

Thirdly, in the new constitution which was adopted immediately after World War II, the new civil code declared the end of the *ie* system that had put its primary function on preservation of biological and cultural lineage (Taeuber 1958, 100–3). Under the *ie* system, primogeniture had been the norm of succession, and eldest sons were therefore obliged to stay in their native households (this was especially true in rural areas), succeed their fathers in their business, and take care of parents in their old age. However, the post-war breakdown of the *ie* system ensured the rule of equal inheritance among all children, and concurrently facilitated migration out of rural areas not only of younger children but also of eldest sons (and their families) (ESCAP 1984, 136). In summary, these three factors (wage differences between agriculture and non-agriculture, mechanization of farm machinery, and breakdown of the *ie* system) are all thought to have

224 Noriko O. Tsuya and Toshio Kuroda

contributed to the post-war migratory flood in the late 1950s and the early 1960s.

Population dispersion

During the 1960s we also witnessed an emerging trend of population dispersion from core to adjacent prefectures within the metropolitan regions. As this intra-metropolitan dispersion continued into the early 1970s, population started dispersing further into regions outside (but adjacent to) metropolitan regions (such as Kita-kanto and Higashi-kinki). This growing 'doughnut' phenomenon, together with rural population turnaround, led to the slowing-down of migratory flows into metropolitan regions during the mid to late 1970s, which in turn produced a virtual halt of the urbanization process.

It has often been argued that the slowing-down of migration into the metropolitan regions, a major cause of the cessation of urbanization, reflects diminishing attractiveness of some of the factors that had previously 'pulled' people (especially younger population) into urban areas. First, it has been pointed out that narrowing of the differences in living standards between metropolitan and non-metropolitan regions resulted in diminishing relative attractiveness of urban residence and life-style. For example, during the 1970s differences in starting wages between rural communities and cities contracted greatly and a balancing trend of urban–rural income differentials emerged (ESCAP 1984, 136). During the late 1970s the rate of income growth in the prefecture of Tokyo was also lower than the national average (Mera 1987).

Secondly, it is also argued that the deterioration of metropolitan environments due to industrial pollution and overcrowded housing conditions is also responsible for the 'doughnut' phenomenon and rural population turnaround. Journalism has alleged that prolonged commuting time, the high cost of living, and environmental pollution were pushing people out of urban residence (e.g., *Asahi Shimbun*, 1 February 1977; *Japan Times International*, 27 November 1976). On the other hand, according to the 1972 Tokyo survey on migration, major reasons for out-migration from the prefecture of Tokyo in the early 1970s were employment (approximately 39 per cent) and the housing situation (27 per cent) (Japan Statistics Bureau 1984, 70–1). Moreover, dividing this migratory outflow by destination of out-migration, it was found that a vast majority of inter-regional migration was due to employment-related reasons while movement to the adjacent prefectures (such as Kanagawa, Saitama and Chiba) were due to scarce housing (44 per cent) as well as to job-related reasons (31 per cent). In addition, around 7 per cent of migrants to the adjacent prefectures cited environmental problems as the reason for moving out of Tokyo. We therefore can see that while the job-related motives were still dominant, housing and environmental factors became increasingly important as causes of out-migration, especially of suburbanization during the early 1970s.

Moreover, at a more aggregate level it is also argued that this slowing-down of migratory inflows was, to a large extent, simply the consequence of dispersed industrialization which was brought about by diminishing advantages of industrial concentration in the larger cities and by the efforts made by provincial areas to achieve industrial development (Nishikawa 1973, 112–14). However, as we have seen in the third section, unlike many developed countries in North America and northwestern Europe, Japan did not experience significant net population outflow from the metropolitan regions during the 1970s. Instead, in- and out-migration almost reached a balance during the late 1970s.

With regard to this, Vining (1982) also pointed out that although net population inflow to metropolitan regions slowed down due to industrial dispersion from urban centres, significant net population outflow from metropolitan regions (population dispersion away from the metropolitan areas, which he called 'migration to the periphery') did not take place because of difficulties to expand or establish industries in non-metropolitan regions due primarily to their unfavourable conditions of location, such as lack of level land and problems of severe cold weather.

Reconcentration in the 1980s

By contrast with the wealth of studies which have examined the slowdown in metropolitan growth in the 1970s, the recovery of net migration into the metropolitan regions in the 1980s, especially in the Minami-kanto region, has been little analysed. This is in spite of the fact that this phenomenon has received extensive popular as well as policy attention. Nevertheless, the available evidence suggests some correlation with employment trends. The share of national employment located in the Minami-kanto region, having decreased slightly during 1975–80, increased again during 1980–85. This region had 26.1 per cent of persons employed in all Japan in 1975; the proportion went down to 25.9 per cent in 1980, but recovered to 27.2 per cent in 1985 (Japan Statistics Bureau 1987). These changes seem to imply that the Minami-kanto region is again 'pulling' people due to improvements in employment conditions in the region. Although it is not yet clear whether this reappearance of urban population concentration will be a secular trend or a temporary phenomenon, it will certainly affect not only the pattern of population distribution but also economic and social aspects of society in the future.

The role of national planning and policy

As in most other developed countries, so too for Japan, it can be suggested that the effects of government policy – both direct and indirect – have influenced trends towards population concentration and dispersion. National policies in post-war Japan have pursued the goal of balanced economic and social development of the nation, and the notion of balanced population distribution became increasingly important in the scope of national planning during the 1960s and 1970s. Several European countries are more advanced than Japan in the maturity and efficacy of their national population distribution policies, yet Japan has come up with some policy innovations of her own (White 1982).

Japan's national planning and policies have passed through several distinct phases since World War II. Until the late 1960s the main spatial focus was on the correction of interregional economic imbalances, particularly through the development of about two dozen designated growth centres (Yazaki 1970, 28; Itoh 1978). This growth-centre idea was incorporated in the First Comprehensive National Development Plan (or *Zenso*, short for *Zenkoku Sogo Kaihatsu Keikaku*) of 1962. The primary objective of the Zenso, however, was to facilitate national-scale planning for industrial distribution and public investment through maximization of economic efficacy and development (Shiramasa 1978). Even so, it achieved gradual success in regional job creation and equalization of wages (White 1982, 24; Muramatsu and Kuroda 1974).

The growth-centre idea was largely discarded upon formulation of the New National Comprehensive Development Plan (*Shinzenso*). The New Plan was adopted in 1969 as a guiding principle for national development until the mid 1980s, with the notion of national land-use determination and the assumption of rapid economic growth (an average GNP growth of 8 per cent annually). According to the New Plan, administrative and information functions were to be concentrated in large metropolitan cities whereas production and distribution were to be dispersed elsewhere, being linked together by a high-speed communication and transportation network (Economic Planning Agency 1972).

However, in the early 1970s the country was hit by rapid inflation and an industrial recession, climaxing in the oil crisis of 1973. It also witnessed an increasing popular questioning of the meaning of rapid economic growth that produced various environmental problems. The government responded to this situation with the Third Comprehensive National Development Plan (*Sanzenso*) of 1977. The Sanzenso still adopted the notion of national land-use planning, but also emphasized stable and slow economic growth, incorporating popular demands and environmental protection. Importantly, the Third Plan also gave special attention to population redistribution, with the primary objective of balanced distribution through adoption of the 'Integrated Residence Policy' which aimed at luring population away from large metropolitan cities and promoting the development of smaller local communities (National Land Agency of Japan 1979). A reading of the plan gives an impression that economic growth was given much less emphasis, with the clear intention of facilitating more dispersed population distribution. However, the plan did not specify how to establish the industrial structure underlying the population distribution (Shiramasa 1978) and many interested parties, including local planners and leaders, doubted the effectiveness of this policy (White 1982, 25). One study (Glickman 1979, chs. 6–7) indicates that government plans to redistribute population and industrial activities had by then exerted little influence on actual patterns of redistribution, in comparison with the influences from the free market and with the effects of taxation and revenue-sharing policies.

Evaluation of the effectiveness of the Sanzenso does not seem to be fully settled. We have already noted that Japan in fact experienced a considerable slowing-down of urban concentration during the late 1970s, but we have also witnessed the subsequent resurgence of in-migration and urban concentration, especially to the Minami-kanto region. In order to counter-act this and to further promote balanced development and dispersion of metropolitan concentration, the government adopted in 1987 the Fourth Comprehensive National Development Plan (*Yonzenso*). The Fourth Plan, like the Second and the Third, emphasizes the idea of integrated residence and environmental protection, and aims at development of smaller local communities through communication with large metropolitan centres, and newly expresses the need for an active contribution toward the internation-al urban system (National Land Agency of Japan 1987). It is, however, too early to see the effects of the Fourth Plan, but it would be interesting to monitor and examine the prospective responses to this plan from various sectors of society.

Conclusions and implications

The rapid urbanization during the late 1950s and the 1960s in Japan was primarily a process of population concentration in the three major metropolitan regions centring around the cities of Tokyo, Osaka and Nagoya. This heavy concentration was caused first by the large migratory flows into major metropolitan cities in these regions. During the 1960s, however, while the regions as a whole kept receiving large population inflows, the direction of the flows changed from core metropolitan to the adjacent prefectures, indicating an emergence of the 'doughnut' pheno-menon (suburbanization).

During the 1970s (especially after the oil crisis), however, urban concentration slowed down considerably. This was due mainly to substantial decreases (and sometimes a net loss) in the net population inflow into the metropolitan regions, which was in turn caused by the enlarging 'doughnut' in the regions adjacent to the metropolitan regions as well as by a rural population turnaround. Nevertheless, these changes were not large enough to reverse the urbanization process nor to produce a reduction in the proportion of the national population accounted for by the three metropolitan regions. Moreover, the early 1980s witnessed a renewed increase of migration into the metropolitan regions, especially to the metropolitan node of Tokyo.

Examining socio-demographic features of migrants, it has been found that population aged 15–34 (the largest age-group of which was males aged 15–24) formed a large majority of the heavy migratory flows into the metropolitan regions during the late 1950s and the 1960s. While these young people kept migrating into large metropolitan cities, substantial numbers of other people started moving into the areas adjacent to the core metropolitan prefectures during the 1960s and the early 1970s, thus creating suburbanization and the 'doughnut' phenomenon. Cohort analy-ses also suggest that the rural population turnaround in the 1970s was caused mainly by return migration of people who migrated at age 15–24 into metropolitan regions during the 1960s back to non-metropolitan regions after staying in large cities for a decade or so.

As regards the causes of population movement in post-war Japan, it appears that many factors have been involved. There seems little doubt that non-agricultural job opportunities offered by urban areas have been the primary cause of the rapid urban concentration of population (especially young population aged 15–24) during the late 1950s and the 1960s, facilitated further by widening wage differentials between agricultural and non-agricultural jobs, mechanization of agriculture, and breakdown of the *ie* system. On the other hand, the slowing-down of urban concentration during the 1970s reflects: diminishing relative attractiveness of urban residence and life-style owing to the narrowing of regional differences in living standards; overcrowded housing conditions and environmental issues (which are primarily causes of intra-metropolitan migration); and dispersed industrialization due partly to a series of national policies and planning for balanced industrial and population distribution.

From these findings, we therefore conclude that rapid urbanization in post-war Japan was brought about by heavy inflows of young population into the metropolitan regions to obtain non-agricultural employment. The subsequent slowing-down of this concentration (due to growing suburbanization and rural population turnaround) occurred as relative advantages of the metropolitan living standard diminished and housing conditions in core metropolitan areas became congested. This implies that a high level of development and urban population concentration, beyond a certain saturation point, are pre-conditions for counterurbanization (or slowing-down of urban concentration). At the same time, the Japanese experience during the 1970s also suggests that population distribution can to some extent be influenced by population redistribution policies, but population distribution seems to be influenced even more strongly by industrial distribution. It therefore seems unlikely that substantial population redistribution beyond the metropolitan boundary would take place unless conditions are favourable for the location of industry.

In this sense, the recent reappearance of population concentration in the metropolitan regions, especially the metropolitan node of Tokyo, is considered as being partly a result of contained industrial dispersion within metropolitan regions. This is also an indication of the limitations of governmental policies and planning, implying that population movement cannot be manipulated beyond a certain point. Restricted by geographical conditions and strongly influenced by industrial distribution, the future pattern of population distribution in Japan will never be truly 'dispersed'; whatever is done, some remote areas will continue to lose population. However, it is important to aim for a slow-down in the recent reconcentration (especially in the Tokyo metropolitan node) and for a reasonable balance between metropolitan and non-metropolitan populations because population distribution and movement have strong influences on the social, economic and political future of the country.

Further reading

The Japanese experience of the metropolitan migration turnaround is described and compared with that of other countries by Vining, D.R. 1982: Migration between the core and the periphery, *Scientific American* 247 (6), 36–45. An introduction to the dynamics of population growth in the Japanese urban system is provided by Yamaguchi, T. 1984: The Japanese national settlement system, in Bourne, L.S., Sinclair, R. and Dziewoński, K. (eds) *Urbanization and settlement systems: international perspectives* (Oxford: Oxford University Press), 261–79. A systematic analysis of urban change based on functionally defined regions is available in Kawashima, T. 1982: Recent urban trends in Japan: analysis of functional urban regions, in Kawashima, T. and Korcelli, P (eds) *Human settlement systems* (Laxenburg, Austria: International Institute for Applied Systems Analysis), 21–40. A more detailed account of urban change can be found in Glickman, N.J. 1979: *The growth and management of the Japanese urban system* (New York: Academic Press). Migration flows up to 1983 are described and analysed by Ogawa, N. 1986: Internal migration in Japanese postwar development, *Research papers Series* 33 (Tokyo: Nihon University Population Research Institute).

12

Conclusion:

temporary anomaly, long-term trend or transitional phase?

A.G. CHAMPION

This book has focused on the major transformation in the geography of population change which has taken place in the advanced Western world over the past two or three decades. As documented in Chapter 1, the most impressive features are the speed with which the metropolitan migration reversal and rural population turnaround took place in individual countries and the number of countries which experienced changes along these lines at around the same time. From the first observations of a rural renaissance in the United States, researchers were quick to show that almost all of the more developed countries in North America and non-Communist Europe, along with Japan and Australia, were being affected by forms of population deconcentration that involved wider geographical shifts than traditional suburbanization. The strong degree of uniformity in the apparent nature and timing of these developments across national boundaries, coinciding with the evidence of major economic restructuring and social transformation cited by these studies, seemed to confirm speculation that a new 'post-industrial' era was dawning and that the urbanization process associated with the passing industrial phase was on the wane. Yet, a decade further on, the situation appears to be much more varied and volatile. More recent studies have shown that in some countries the pace of population redistribution from major metropolitan centres to more rural regions was proceeding more slowly in the 1980s than during the previous decade and that, in at least one case, it had reached a peak even before the new phenomenon had been discovered. On the other hand, in one or two countries there are signs of a renewed acceleration of population deconcentration in the mid 1980s, while in others the process has progressively intensified since the 1970s. From a policy viewpoint as well as an academic perspective, it is extremely important to know what is likely to emerge out of this current period of uncertainty and its confusing signs and, in particular, to discover whether the counterurbanization trend of the last two decades is merely a temporary phenomenon or represents the prevailing tendency of the future.

The primary aim of this book has been to feed extra information into the counterurbanization debate in order to help towards answering this question. It has drawn on the findings of research undertaken on nine different countries over the past fifteen years, drawing on results from the 1980/82 round of population censuses and on a wealth of local case-study material. The authors of the national essays were charged with the task of reviewing the actual trends observed in their countries and of setting their observations into the context of the academic literature on the conceptual and methodological problems of studying counterurbanization. More specifically, they were required, first, to assemble data relating to the scale and timing of the deconcentration tendency; secondly, to account for it in direct terms such as the demographic components of change and the socio-demographic characteristics of the people involved; thirdly, to identify the types of factors which were considered to form the most likely explanations for the switch in migration flows away from the major metropolitan regions; and thereby, lastly, to draw conclusions about the nature of counterurbanization insofar as it is a distinctive feature in the particular national context. The role of this final chapter is to draw together the results of this exercise and assess their significance.

Extent and timing of counterurbanization

The national case studies have generally corroborated the observations of the multinational comparative surveys reviewed in Chapter 1. Thus they have confirmed the widespread occurrence of the slowdown in the rate of population concentration experienced by advanced Western countries in the 1970s. They have shown that in most countries the largest metropolitan centres and capital region either recorded absolute population decline or net out-migration for at least part of that decade. It is also clear that their peripheral regions and the more rural sections within them moved into a stronger demographic position at this time, in many cases reversing a long-established pattern of population decline. As regards more recent events, the case studies again broadly confirm the findings of the multinational surveys, not only in indicating a weakening of the deconcentration tendency or even a return to more traditional centripetal shifts but also in revealing a lower degree of uniformity in population redistribution trends between, and to some extent within, individual countries.

It is inevitable that the national case studies should present a much more varied and complex picture than was suggested by the review in Chapter 1. In detail, of course, the experience of every country can be found to be unique, or at least it can appear so. In this latter context, the contributors to this volume have not been able to get round the fact that each country has its own way of collecting and presenting data and, in particular, has a different level of interest in and perception of the structure of urban and regional systems. Indeed, this problem was not completely overcome in the multinational comparative surveys, even those like Hall and Hay (1980) which went to great lengths to apply a common definition for identifying functional regions but still had to wrestle with building-blocks of different sizes and variations in the availability of commuting data. The important thing is that the contributors have been aware of these problems and have therefore been in a position to allow for their effects when interpreting the results of the analyses which they have undertaken.

This being so, it can be stated with reasonable confidence that, despite the general tendency towards a reduction in metropolitan growth and a revival of more rural areas in the 1970s, there are considerable differences between countries in the extent of population deconcentration and in its phasing over time. In relation to the scale of counterurbanization, for instance, a major contrast can be drawn between countries like the UK and Denmark, where the largest urban regions recorded absolute population losses for virtually the whole of the past two decades, and the case of Japan, where even though the margin between metropolitan and non-metropolitan regions narrowed markedly, the former continued to experience the faster population growth throughout. In between these extremes, the FRG, France and Italy all saw absolute population losses from their largest cities at some point over the last twenty years, while Australia, Norway and the United States each saw its aggregate metropolitan growth rate dip below that for the rest of the country but not become negative, not even for metropolitan areas with over one million people.

The spatial extent of the population deconcentration impact has also been seen to vary considerably between countries. In Chapter 4 Hugo has highlighted the degree to which the turnaround in Australia has been concentrated in the more accessible areas, though this must be seen in the context of the huge scale of this country and its large coverage of very sparsely inhabited desert. Similarly, the rather muted expression of deconcentration in more distant parts of Norway and Japan may in part reflect the nature of their terrain, their lack of cheaply developed land and their inaccessibility from even medium-sized cities. In most other countries, by contrast, the rural population turnaround appears a very significant phenomenon, embracing not only the more remote regions but also relatively small settlements within them. Court shows that this is particularly true for Denmark, perhaps not surprising given the much smaller distances involved. It is also found from the analyses of population growth rates for different sizes of settlements in the FRG, the UK and France, except where the smallest rural communities are identified individually rather than being grouped into broader urban-centred labour market areas. The same appears to be the case in the north of the United States and in northern Italy, though the separate analyses for other parts of these countries suggest that relatively strong big-city growth has been continuing there alongside a resurgence of non-metropolitan and rural areas.

In terms of phasing over time, the early 1970s does stand out as very significant for counterurbanization in several countries. In the United States the principal changes in non-metropolitan growth rates occurred immediately after the turn of the decade, shown so dramatically by the early studies reviewed in Chapter 1. Likewise, the most substantial developments in population deconcentration in Denmark and Norway took place in the first few years of the decade. This period also saw the counterurbanization trend running at its peak rate in the UK, but here the origins can be traced back further, because as shown in Chapter 5 the largest cities were not growing as fast as the nation as a whole even during the 1950s and the lower end of the settlement-size ladder had already made a substantial recovery by the 1960s. By contrast, the peak level of deconcentration seems to have occurred in the later 1970s in France, Japan and Australia and it is notable that, while the process slowed down or went into reverse in most countries in the early 1980s, it appears to have intensified in the FRG and Italy. Moreover, the mid 1980s have brought signs of a renewed acceleration in Denmark and the UK following a period of slower deconcentration.

This degree of variation between the nine countries included in this survey might be thought to undermine the rationale for this study, but in reality it can be viewed as highlighting the research challenge and as providing extra opportunity for analysis. All the contributors to this book are convinced that a significant development took place in the geography of population change in their countries at some point during the last two decades or so, even though in one or two cases, notably Norway, this development was apparently rather weak and ephemeral. Compared with the record of traditional urbanization processes, the differences between countries in the extent and timing of counterurbanization seem relatively insignificant. It therefore seems highly inconceivable that the events in each country should be caused by completely different sets of factors, but much more likely that the processes involved vary in strength and impact between countries under the influence of conditioning factors such as the geographical layout of national territory, the previous history of urbaniza-tion and the recent pace of economic growth. This, at any rate, is the viewpoint that has formed the basis of this book, which assumes the existence of a fairly general phenomenon of counterurbanization and uses the experiences of the individual countries to piece together a clearer picture of it. Using the analogy of the jigsaw puzzle, it is recognized that not all the pieces necessarily belong to the same puzzle, but the strategy is to draw selectively from the different national case studies in order to work towards a 'pure' version of the phenomenon.

The components of the population shifts

After describing the extent and timing of counterurbanization, the second task set for the national case studies has been to identify the components of the population shifts in direct accounting terms, using the term 'compo-nents' more widely than traditional demographic usage to include age structure and employment characteristics. In brief, they were asked to confirm – to the extent that appropriate data were available – that internal migration formed the principal element in population deconcentration and in fluctuations in its intensity over time, and they were also requested to examine the influence of natural change and international migration on population trends. Their examination of age structure was aimed at assessing the relative importance of retirement migration as opposed to movements by those of working age, while data on economic activity and employment would provide some pointers to the reasons underlying these movements.

As regards the purely demographic components, natural change and international migration appear to have had some influence on population deconcentration in some countries. Natural change has certainly contributed to the fall in the actual rate of growth in the major cities, because of the decline in birth rate which occurred fairly consistently across most countries after the early 1960s and in Japan from around 1975. On the other hand, this downward shift has principally served to give greater prominence to these cities' migration losses which had previously been offset by stronger natural increase. It has not played an important role in promoting counterurbanization, because the reduction in natural change rates in the cities has not tended to be greater than nationally, except in Italy and Japan. If anything, there has been a tendency towards the convergence in birth rates between the more urban and more rural parts of most countries, which has worked against population deconcentration because rural areas have traditionally been characterized by higher fertility. Moreover, in several countries including the UK, France and Denmark, the highest levels of natural increase are no longer associated with the largest cities or most rural areas but with some of the intermediate locations which received large numbers of young migrants in the 1950s and 1960s. Natural change has therefore contributed to the nationwide deconcentration patterns of the past two decades only in certain instances.

The role of international migration is given considerably more attention by the case studies, suggesting that its significance has been underestimated in previous studies of counterurbanization. At the same time, it is a complicated phenomenon which fluctuates considerably over time in its net levels and patterns and which affects places differently. According to the case studies, the arrival of international migrants has tended to bolster national core regions and the largest settlements in any destination area. Its effect can be seen most clearly in the New World contexts of the United States and Australia, where immigrants have tended to locate in the major metropolitan centres. Its principal relevance for counterurbanization is where the extra pressures which immigration puts on these cities in terms of congestion costs or ethnic conflict have led to an acceleration of migration out of these places to other areas in the same country. This factor takes on additional significance if for any reason the supply of immigrants diminishes, particularly once the internal migration streams have built up their own momentum. The pivotal position of Sydney and Melbourne in the Australian migration network has been clearly documented in Chapter 4. In the American context this factor has taken on a new dimension with the increasing number of Hispanic immigrants, which have contributed to the rapid growth of the South and West regions while at the same time tending to reinforce the populations of the larger metropolitan centres there. In the European context, the rundown in the numbers of 'guest workers' in the FRG and France from the mid 1970s, and particularly after 1978, may well have contributed to the faster relative decline of their major urban regions and thereby increased the apparent rate of national population deconcentration. Moreover, the return of these workers to their home countries and the closing of foreign job opportunities to potential new immigrants has contributed to the observed shift in population growth rates there, as exemplified in this volume by the strong growth of both town and countryside in the south of Italy.

Nevertheless, as the case studies make it clear, it is the switches in the patterns and rates of internal migration that have been very largely responsible for the observed tendency towards population deconcentration. In all countries the net migration from more peripheral areas to the major metropolitan centres declined steeply between the 1960s and 1970s, even if it did not actually go into reverse in every case. In every country, the most heavily urbanized region, or at least its largest cities, experienced heavy internal migration loss at some stage between the early 1960s and early 1980s – Greater London and South East England particularly in the late 1960s and early 1970s; the large metropolitan areas in Australia and the North of the United States through most of the 1970s, as also for the Copenhagen metropolitan region and the Oslo capital region; the Paris agglomeration and the Japanese metropolitan areas (the latter to a very limited extent, admittedly) principally in the late 1970s; and the three metropolitan areas of north-west Italy in the early 1980s. Similarly, the subsequent recovery of the major city regions in the United States, Denmark and the UK appears to correspond with a marked narrowing of the migration-rate differentials between settlement size categories and a tendency for convergence towards a zero migration balance, while for Norway and Japan the margin in favour of the metropolitan regions re-opened in the early 1980s.

Concerning the significance of retirement migration, it is clear from the studies which have provided data on migration by age that the centrifugal tendencies have not been caused entirely, or even largely, by movements of the elderly. It is true that many of the places that grew faster in the 1970s are in areas traditionally associated with retirement migration and also that the number and general mobility of elderly people have increased over time. Nevertheless, retirement migration was already a well-established phenomenon before the 1970s and, moreover, continuously high levels of in-migration are needed merely to replace the previous generation of retirees because of their high death rate. Instead, the major change from the 1960s appears to be the increasing tendency for younger age-groups to take on a 'retirement pattern' in their net migration flows. This is documented particularly clearly by Kontuly and Vogelsang, who have detected in the FRG a significant swing towards counterurbanization among the 30–49 year-olds and their children during the later 1970s. For France, Winchester and Ogden find that net in-migration to the Paris region in 1975–82 was restricted to adults under 30 years old, while Frey demonstrates that non-metropolitan America switched from net loss to gain of 25–34 year-olds between the later 1960s and the later 1970s. Frey is also able to point to the pervasiveness of the counterurbanization trends among population sub-groups by showing that blacks were as heavily involved in these migration switches as non-blacks.

Few national case studies present hard information on the employment status of migrants or on the relationship between population and employment trends. Nevertheless, there is sufficient evidence to refute the suggestions made early in the counterurbanization debate that the rural population turnaround was largely caused, if not by the elderly, by others who were not gainfully employed, including early retirees, those dependent on unemployment benefits or other welfare payments, and drop-outs or hippies in search of alternative life-styles. Though Hugo argues that the role of welfare payments has not been given enough attention in the Australian literature, it is clear from the British evidence that a massive redistribution of jobs in favour of non-metropolitan areas took place during the 1970s. Similarly, Italian data on the growth of jobs in manufacturing indicates a marked upswing between the 1950s and 1970s in the attractiveness of smaller settlements, at least in northern and central regions. Moreover, the studies on Denmark, Norway, Japan and the United States put forward sound arguments which relate the rise and fall of the rural population turnaround to the fluctuating fortunes of the primary production sectors (particularly agriculture and energy) and to the changing levels of investment in new manufacturing plant, while ascribing the subsequent recovery of certain major cities to the more recent developments in employment in the service sector, especially in financial services and information-processing activities.

Explanations for the migration turnaround

It is one thing to produce a direct explanation of recent population in terms of an accounting framework like demographic components and relationship to employment change, difficult though even this can be in terms of assembling the appropriate data as mentioned previously. It is, however, quite another thing to be able to identify the underlying factors and even harder to bring forward concrete proof of the precise role which they have played and of their importance relative to each other. The case-study authors were not requested to mount their own in-depth enquiries into this area – indeed this would no doubt have taken a great deal of time or dissuaded them from contributing to this volume! – but instead were asked to draw upon the results of their previous research and upon the conclusions of other studies on counterurbanization in their countries. The outcome is a list of specific explanations which will be presented first, in keeping with the 'jigsaw puzzle' strategy outlined earlier in the chapter, before attempting to look for underlying processes.

At various stages in this book, the turnaround is seen as being the product of one or more of the following:

1   The expansion of commuting fields round employment centres.
2   The emergence of scale diseconomies and social problems in large cities.
3   The concentration of rural population into local urban centres.
4   The reduction in the stock of potential out-migrants living in rural areas.
5   The availability of government subsidies for rural activities.
6   The growth of employment in particular localized industries like mining, defence and tourism.
7   The restructuring of manufacturing industry and the associated growth of branch plants.
8   Improvements in transport and communications technology.

9 The improvement of education, health and other infrastructure in rural areas.
10 The growth of employment in the public sector and personal services.
11 The success of explicitly spatial government policies.
12 The growth of state welfare payments, private pensions and other benefits.
13 The acceleration of retirement migration.
14 The change in residential preferences of working-age people and entrepreneurs.
15 Changes in age structure and household size and composition.
16 The effect of economic recession on rural–urban and return migration.
17 The first round in a new cyclic pattern of capital investment in property and business.

Though several of these may be considered to be no more than conjecture as yet, the list seems so long and varied that the reader is bound to ask why the turnaround took the academic world very much by surprise when it was first identified in the mid 1970s. By the same token, it is perhaps equally surprising that the turnaround has itself been able to go into reverse in several countries since then or at least slacken in its intensity. Drawing on the evidence of the national case studies and the wider counterurbanization literature, however, it seems possible that a resolution of this apparent paradox may be found in the way in which these individual explanations relate to more fundamental types of processes and in the fact that the latter may change both qualitatively and quantitatively over time. The rest of this section attempts to substantiate these points.

The first stage in the argument is to note that, faced with a plethora of potential explanations, various commentators have evolved their own classificatory frameworks in order to present a more coherent picture of the underlying processes and in some cases to produce a more manageable set of hypotheses for testing. In one of the earliest reviews of alternative perspectives on urban decline and population deconcentration, Bourne (1980) arranged explanations into five 'schools of thought' which he labelled (1) structural and technological change and the search for economic efficiency; (2) cultural predispositions and the amenities–disamenities hypothesis; (3) the implicit or unintended policy hypothesis; (4) systematic exploitation, power and conflict; and (5) uncertainty and the random space economy. By contrast, Moseley (1984) adopted a straight-forward dichotomy between people-led and job-led explanations, while others have arrayed hypotheses along a unidimensional scale; for instance, from 'voluntarist' to 'non-voluntarist' (Bolton 1988, in relation to the degree of freedom in personal choice of place of residence), from 'economic' to 'socio-environmental' (Perry *et al.* 1986, concerning the factors considered by migrants) and from 'micro-scale' to 'macro-scale' (Coombes *et al.* 1989, regarding the level of decision-making in the organization of production).

In the context of the aims of this book, however, probably the most telling point is that made by Fielding (1982, 19–20) to the effect that counterurbanization should be considered strictly as a process rather than a pattern and that, as such, it constituted only one of several processes that might potentially be responsible for population deconcentration, the other candidates being industrial factor costs, state intervention, the changing social composition of the population and the new geography of production. In doing this, Fielding was following Berry's (1976) interpretation of the counterurbanization process, which, as described in Chapter 2, was essentially concerned with the changing residential preferences of residents and entrepreneurs and is thus broadly equivalent to Bourne's (1980) second 'school of thought' mentioned above. Though the use of the term 'counterurbanization' to denote both the overall pattern of population change and one of the processes behind it is a sure recipe for semantic confusion, this basic distinction has been adopted and developed usefully by Frey in his analysis of metropolitan change in the United States, as reported in Chapter 3. Here he distinguishes what he calls the 'deconcentration' perspective from two other groups of explanations, the regional restructuring perspective and period explanations. He then goes on to show, by comparing the patterns actually recorded with those expected on the basis of the alternative hypotheses, that deconcentration constituted the dominant dimension of population redistribution trends in the 1970s.

Once it is established that deconcentration constitutes only one element of the changing geography of population, then it becomes easier to account for fluctuations over time in the pace of centrifugal shifts and in the degree to which the latter can 'explain' observed spatial variations in overall population change rates. In the first place, the other elements of population change are likely to vary over time in their absolute strength and may also alter in their geographical incidence, being perhaps more conformable with the deconcentration dimension at certain times than at others. Secondly, it would not be surprising to find that the intensity of deconcentration itself waxed and waned. Several of the aspects of the migration turnaround listed earlier would seem susceptible to cyclic factors; indeed, some to the extent that Frey would consider them as period explanations.

This point can be taken further by suggesting, along the lines of Illeris (1988b), that the counterurbanization component of population change is the outcome of a form of 'tug-of-war'. It is possible to conceive of three groups of forces – those leading to dispersal, those pulling towards concentration, and lastly those which may have different geographical effects at different times. The first two are likely to vary over time in both their absolute intensity and their strength relative to each other, while the last group will change sides from time to time. Reference back to the national case-studies can reveal several examples of this latter type including fluctuations in such things as international migration, energy costs, and age structure. These have served to give freer rein to widespread preference for lower-density settlement at certain times, such as when energy costs are falling or the number of young families is increasing, whereas at other times they have tended to curb it.

The nature of the counterurbanization phenomenon

It is not wise to make a definite statement on the nature of counterurbanization until much more is known about the role of the individual explanations listed in the previous section. On the other hand, if the conceptualizations of Frey and Illeris are anywhere near correct, it is possible to offer some tentative conclusions. These provide some clues as to the way in which national settlement systems are likely to develop in the future and help to clarify some of the main areas for further research.

Drawing both on the findings of the national case studies and on the wider literature, one is led to the following conclusions. In the first place, over the past two decades, most advanced Western countries have experienced some degree of centrifugal tendency by which their populations have become more uniformly distributed across national territory, even if this is only true when measured at the finer spatial grains of individual municipalities or census wards. This change constitutes deconcentration in the broadest sense of the term as adapted by Berry (1976) from Tisdale's (1942) definition of urbanization, but a great deal of confusion can be avoided if this overall shift in population distribution can be denoted by the more general term *dispersal*.

Secondly, it is concluded that *counterurbanization* constitutes one particular form of population dispersal. This is taken to mean a redistribution of population from larger to smaller places across the urban system, where places are defined on a functional basis and are relatively self-contained in terms of the daily movements of their residents. Though this definition is not always easy to implement, particularly in heavily urbanized multi-nodal regions, its intent is clear, namely that traditional suburbanization and local metropolitan decentralization are not considered to be aspects of counterurbanization.

Thirdly, following Fielding's (1982) approach, counterurbanization can be said to be fully developed when a strong negative correlation exists between size of settlement and a measure of its population growth. For the latter, however, overall population change rate is preferred to net migration rate, allowing the counterurban shifts to be disaggregated later into their natural change, international migration and internal migration components. Moreover, in order to avoid confusion, the term 'counterurbanization' should be restricted to the relevant *patterns* of population change and trends in these, in the same way that the geographical definition of 'urbanization' refers to the levels and trends in the distribution of people between different types of areas; the same term should not be used to denote a causal process.

Counterurbanization, thus defined, constitutes the phenomenon which needs to be explained and whose nature research should be seeking to discover. As observed in the previous section of this chapter, it cannot be traced to one single factor like changes in residential preferences, but seems to result from a plethora of relatively specific explanations. In coming to a better understanding of the nature of counterurbanization, it is considered helpful to follow Frey's example in recognizing three groups of factors – those which comprise period explanations, those which relate to regional restructuring, and those which are stimulated by the search for lower-density environments. The latter include the factor of residential preferences, but also embrace a wider range of forces such as the greater space requirements of modern industry and the fact that infrastructural improvements have increasingly bestowed on more rural areas many of the advantages which formerly were found only in larger cities. Frey labels these the 'deconcentration perspective' and makes it clear that this is not necessarily the only force behind the migration turnaround, since under certain conditions it may be reinforced by the effects of regional restructuring and period factors. To summarize, *deconcentration* is seen as one of the underlying processes which leads to *counterurbanization*, which is a particular form of population *dispersal*.

This formulation of the factors affecting population distribution, while it does not get to grips with the role of the many individual explanations, does help to explain the emergence of counterurbanization between the 1950s and 1970s. The switch away from urbanization can now be attributed not only to a major shift in favour of the centrifugal forces embraced by the deconcentration perspective, but also to a set of temporary (period) factors which substantially favoured rural and non-metropolitan locations at that time and to a process of regional restructuring.

In relation to the latter, Fielding (1989) describes how there emerged a new spatial division of labour involving the spatial separation of command functions from execution and of white-collar employees from blue-collar. He also suggests that at this time more detailed changes were taking place that differentiated technical and professional workers from other white-collar workers, and skilled manual workers from the semi-skilled and unskilled. The results of this corporate restructuring were the de-industrialization of the major cities, the branch-plant boom in lower-cost and more remote sites and a limited degree of dispersal of higher-paid workers to places fairly close to the main metropolitan centres.

This framework also helps to make sense both of the subsequent decline in the pace of counterurbanization and of local deviations from the pattern of population change which the deconcentration perspective alone would lead one to expect. It highlights the fact that the deconcentration process itself diminished in strength in most countries towards the end of the 1970s and into the 1980s, no doubt partly because economic recession reduced the need for centrifugal moves and stifled the opportunities for mobility. It is also clear from the national case-studies that the period factors which had favoured more rural areas in the early 1970s faded away or indeed swung actively against dispersal over the next few years. Finally, the regional restructuring process seems to have taken on a new lease of life, with Fielding (1989) noting that from the mid 1970s the organization of production began to shift away from Fordist models of major corporate expansion towards more flexible approaches.

These recent developments, however, are not seen as part of a simple return to the urbanization process of the early post-war period. Instead, they appear to involve the breakdown of any clear relationship between net migration and settlement size and seem to be leading to the re-emergence of broader regional patterns of growth and decline. Particularly rapid growth is associated with what Fielding (1989) calls 'prestige environments' which are often scenically attractive and usually have a social base and a past history appropriate for an emergent entrepreneurial culture and information-based economic development. In some cases such as south-east France, southern FRG and north-central Italy, this growth is working alongside the deconcentration process and moving people into medium-sized and smaller centres, though the latter are not evenly distributed over national territory. Elsewhere, in the UK, Norway and Denmark for instance, the effect is being concentrated in and around the major metropolitan centre. In this way, the greater variety of the counterurbanization experience found both within and between countries in the 1980s can be attributed partly to the way in which restructuring has taken place and to the extent to which it has paralleled or counteracted an attenuated deconcentration process.

The emerging settlement system

How far does this reconstruction of the experience of the 1970s and 1980s help us to anticipate what is in store for advanced Western countries during the rest of this century and beyond? In particular, is the counterurbanization experience of the past two decades a temporary anomaly, or does it look like developing into a long-term trend as a replacement for urbanization? Alternatively, does it represent a transitional stage in a shift towards some new type of settlement system which may currently exist in embryonic form only?

The information presented in this book and drawn together in this final chapter does not point unequivocally in one direction. On the other hand, the main weight of the evidence does not favour the idea of counterurbanization being a temporary blip in an ongoing process of urbanization. It has been shown that deconcentration is a powerful force and that there are good reasons why it should have intensified during the post-war period and penetrated further across national space. While other factors seem to have given it an extra boost during the 1970s, it is the slowing of deconcentration in the 1980s, insofar as it occurred, that seems more likely to be the anomaly.

On the other hand, it is difficult to visualize counterurbanization as a long-term trend in the way that rapid urbanization was for over a century in most of these countries. This is because of the very nature of the phenomenon, because, defined as a negative association between net migration and settlement size, counterurbanization contains the seeds of its own destruction in a way that was not true of urbanization. Whereas the latter can be considered a cumulative process in that the largest places grow fastest and thereby increase their attractive power, counterurbanization is self-defeating because the fate of the smallest places that, by definition, are the most attractive is that they should grow most rapidly and thus decline in their attractiveness. In theory, therefore, the pace of counterurbanization will tend to decline over time as places become more evenly matched in size. In this sense, counterurbanization is merely the means by which a traditional pattern of population concentration is transformed into a more dispersed distribution. No indication is given about the way in which settlement patterns will evolve at a later date, except presumably that then there is likely to be very little relationship between growth rate and size of place.

Among the case-study chapters, the most detailed impression of what such a future settlement pattern would involve is provided in Chapter 10 by Dematteis and Petsimeris, who suggest that counterurbanization represents a temporary phase of transition from a hierarchical spatial organization of settlement to a partially non-hierarchical one. According to this view, the functional interdependencies which were once contained within a single compact urban system are now becoming more dispersed, with the result that the spatial structure of urban and metropolitan areas is extending to the macro-regional scale. Under this emerging type of spatial organization based on interconnected nets and complementary functional relationships between places, the functional unit of reference is no longer the single town or urban area but a settlement network operating at a regional or interregional scale. The urban multiplier effect, being distributed among the various settlements in the networks according to the local specializations, would continue to weaken the classic relationship between the growth and size of individual settlements. To the extent that it remains possible to identify individual settlements on the basis of the daily journeys made by residents, their growth will be partly a function of the dynamism of the wider regional network and partly influenced by the particular features of the place, especially its ability to produce local innovations and penetrate international markets. Because not all regions will be able to develop similarly vibrant networks and also because the individual settlements within them will not be equally successful, a very varied pattern of population change performance can be anticipated.

Already, using the evidence not only of Italy but several other countries too, it is possible to build up a picture of this new type of settlement system (Fielding 1989). In brief, it is one dominated in functional terms – and probably also in population size ranking – by one centre which is normally the national capital and which is most fully integrated into the global information economy and the exclusive club of world cities which it is generating. Closely associated with this centre in functional terms, and probably but not necessarily in spatial terms, are the prestige environments which are responsible for the major part of the export earnings of the leading sectors. The remainder of national territory may be involved in the mass-production branch-plant economy for certain types of production sector which continue to be organized along essentially Fordist lines. In general, however, these areas will be geared much more to domestic markets and become increasingly consumer-orientated as retirement and tourist areas, where lower-level service activities and specialized craft industries are likely to prove important complements to local economies based on continuing primary production and on non-basic manufacturing.

At first glance, this new type of settlement system does not appear to represent such a major departure from previous experience as those interpretations of counterurbanization which suggest that the majority of people will be living in an essentially rural environment scattered widely across national territory (see Chapter 2). On the other hand, the above scenario does not say anything about the local distribution of the inhabitants of individual settlements, which could well become increasingly dispersed unless strict land-use planning controls were to prevent this from happening. Moreover, given that most countries are currently characterized by some very large and densely settled urban agglomerations, there is plenty of scope for major population shifts during the transitional period of counterurbanization, particularly if the forces of both deconcentration and restructuring are pulling in broadly the same direction. This has important implications for government attitudes towards spatial policy, which have only fairly recently switched direction from their promotion of dispersal to the protection and rejuvenation of the economic base and population of the larger cities. The inexorable shift away from traditional patterns of urbanization suggests that the main emphasis in government policy should be directed towards easing the transition to the new patterns and towards channelling development in such a way as to maximize the advantages of the new system whilst ensuring that the negative impacts on both the areas of growth and the areas of decline are kept within acceptable bounds.

On the other hand, there are inevitably many uncertainties about the nature of the new settlement system and the speed with which it will emerge. The scenario outlined above does not completely resolve a number of issues which have been raised in the counterurbanization debate of the last few years, particularly those relating to the 'clean break' question. It has been shown that the 'prestige environments' which formed the principal growth areas of the 1980s are not necessarily completely separate from the major metropolitan concentrations. Moreover, even if a newly emerging growth area is largely separate from the original core region, it rarely comprises a set of essentially freestanding medium-sized and small settlements but instead a relatively strongly integrated network of interdependent places. There is always the possibility that the latter will evolve into the 'industrial agglomerations' of the future, just as the settlements of the early Industrial Revolution period must initially have appeared as a form of scatteration away from the traditional urban centres.

Such sources of uncertainty are, of course, the life-blood of intellectual inquiry, and indeed a major research challenge lies ahead. In the first place, there remains much work to be done on the nature and role of the individual explanations which have been suggested as the cause of the migration turnaround of the 1960s and 1970s. Secondly, further efforts need to go into identifying the relationships that exist between these factors in order to discover how directly they relate to underlying processes such as deconcentration and restructuring. Thirdly, looking to the future, it is important to obtain a more detailed knowledge of the ingredients of the deconcentration process and the way in which individual householders, private entrepreneurs and political bodies responsible for location decisions weigh up the various considerations relating to the urban–rural dimension. Fourthly, the progress which has already been made in understanding the changes taking place in the organization of economic activity and its implications for urban and regional restructuring must be maintained. Finally, in reaching concrete conclusions not only about the nature of changes but also about the likely scale of their impact in geographical terms, there is no substitute for the continuous monitoring of their quantitative aspects, with all the implications which this has for the availability of research funds and appropriate data sources.

Further reading

One of the earliest reviews of the explanations for urban decline is: Bourne, L.S. 1980: Alternative perspectives on urban decline and population deconcentration, *Urban Geography* 1, 39–52. Fielding's first review of the counterurbanization debate can be found in Fielding, A.J. 1982: Counterurbanization in Western Europe, *Progress in Planning* 17, 1–52. For a more recent statement, see Fielding, A.J. 1989: Migration and urbanization in Western Europe since 1950, *The Geographical Journal* 155, 60–69. Illeris's views on the factors influencing population dispersal are outlined in more detail in: Champion, A.G. and Illeris, S. 1989: Population redistribution trends in Western Europe: a mosaic of dynamics and crisis, in Hansen, J.C. and Hebbert, M. (eds.) *Unfamiliar territory: the reshaping of European geography* (Aldershot: Gower).

Bibliography

Abild, C. 1985: Landbyernes kamp. Århus Stiftendende, May 15.

ABS 1976: *Census of population and housing 1976*. Canberra: Australian Bureau of Statistics.

——1981: *Census of population and housing 1981*. Canberra: Australian Bureau of Statistics.

——1986a: *Internal migration, Australia, 12 months ended 30 June 1985*. Canberra: Australian Bureau of Statistics: Catalogue No. 3408.0.

——1986b: *Census of population and housing 1986*. Canberra: Australian Bureau of Statistics.

——1988: *Internal migration, Australia, 12 months ended 31st May 1987*. Canberra: Australian Bureau of Statistics. Catalogue No. 3408.0.

Agresta, A. 1985: The migration turnaround: end of a phenomenon? *Population Today* 13:1, 6–7.

Ahnström, L. 1986: The turnaround trend and the economically active population of seven capital regions in western Europe. *Norsk Geografisk Tidsskrift* 40, 55–64.

Aldrich, R. 1987: Late-comer or early starter? New views on French economic history. *The Journal of European Economic History* 16, 89–100.

Andersson, Å. 1985: *Kreativitet. Storstadens framtid*. Värnamo: Prisma.

Bagnasco, A. and Pini, R. 1981: Sviluppo economico e trasformazioni sociopolitische dei sistemi territoriali a economia diffusa: economia e struttura sociale. *Quaderni della Fondazione G. Feltrinelli* 14, 3–125.

Båtevik, F.O. 1987: *Arbeidsreiser og busetnadsmønster i Sogn og Fiordane*. Master's thesis, Institutt for Geografi, Universitetet i Bergen.

Bauer, G. and Roux, J.-M. 1976: *La rurbanisation ou la ville éparpillée*. Paris: Seuil.

Beale, C.L. 1975: *The revival of population growth in non-metropolitan America*. Economic Research Service, US Department of Agriculture, ERS 605.

——1977: The recent shift of United States population to non-metropolitan areas, 1970–75. *International Regional Science Review* 2, 113–22.

Beale, C.L. and Fuguitt, G.V. 1978a: The new pattern of non-metropolitan population change. In Taeuber, K., Bumpass, L. and Sweet, J. (eds.), *Demography* (New York: Academic Press).

——1978b: Population trends in non-metropolitan cities and villages in subregions of the United States. *Demography* 15, 605–20.

——1985: Metropolitan and non-metropolitan growth differentials in the United States since 1980. Madison, Wisc.: Centre for Demography and Ecology Working Paper 85-6.

Becattini, G. (ed.) 1987: *Mercato e forze locali: il distretto industriale*. Bologna: il Mulino.

Bell, M. 1978: Non-metropolitan population growth in South Australia. Unpublished BA (Hons.) thesis, Flinders University of South Australia.

Belliard, J.-C. and Boyer, J.-C. 1983: Les 'nouveaux ruraux' en Ile-de-France. *Annales de Géographie* XCII, 433–51.

Berg, L. van den, Drewett, R., Klaassen, L.H., Rossi, A. and Vijverberg, C.H.T. 1982: *Urban Europe Volume 1: A study of growth and decline*. Oxford: Pergamon.

Berger, M., Fruit, J.-P., Plet, F. and Robic, M.-C. 1980: Rurbanisation et analyse des espaces ruraux péri-urbains. *L'Espace Géographique* 4, 303–13.

Berry, B.J.L. 1967: Functional economic areas and consolidated urban regions of the US, *Final Report of the Social Sciences Research Council study of metropolitan area classification*. New York: Social Science Research Council.

——1970: The geography of the United States in the year 2000. *Transactions of the Institute of British Geographers* 51, 21–54.

——1976: The counterurbanization process: urban America since 1970. In Berry, B.J.L. (ed.) *Urbanization and counterurbanization* (Beverly Hills, California: Sage Publications), 17–30.

——1980: Urbanization and counterurbanization in the United States. *Annals of the American Academy of Political and Social Science* 451, 13–20.

Béteille, R. 1981: *La France du vide*. Paris: LITEC.

BfLR 1986: *Informationen zur raumentwicklung*. Helf 11/12. Bonn–Bad Godesberg: Bundesforschungsanstalt für Landeskunde und Raumordnung.

——1986 and 1987: Private communications. Bonn–Bad Godesberg: Bundesforschungsanstalt für Landekunde und Raumordnung.

Bolton, N. 1988: The rural population turnaround: a case study of North Devon. Unpublished Ph.D. thesis (Plymouth: Plymouth Polytechnic).

Bonvalet, C. and Lefèbvre, M. 1983: Le dépeuplement de Paris 1968–1975. Quelques éléments d'explication. *Population* 38, 941–8.

Bonvalet, C. and Tugault, Y. 1984: Les racines du dépeuplement de Paris. *Population* 39, 463–82.

Borchert, J.R. 1967: American metropolitan evolution. *Geographical Review* 57 (3), 301–32.

Boudoul, J. 1986: Navettes, mobilité résidentielle, périurbanisation: rapport introductif. *Espace, Populations, Sociétés* 1986–II, 303–4.

Boudoul, J. and Faur J.-P. 1982: Renaissance des communes rurales ou nouvelle forme d'urbanisation? *Economie et Statistique* 149, I–XVI.

——1986: Trente ans de migrations intérieures. *Espace, Populations, Sociétés* 1986–II, 283–92.

Bourne, L.S. 1980: Alternative perspectives on urban decline and population deconcentration. *Urban Geography* 1, 39–52.

Bourne, L.S. and Logan, M.I. 1976: Changing urbanization patterns at the margin: the examples of Australia and Canada. In Berry, B.J.L. (ed.), *Urbanization and counterurbanization* (Beverly Hills, California: Sage Publications), 111–43.

Bourne, L.S., and Simmons, J.W. 1979: *Canadian settlement trends: an examination of the spatial pattern of growth 1971–76*. Major Report 15 (Toronto: Centre for Urban and Community Studies, University of Toronto).

Bowie, I.J.S. 1987: *The urban and non-urban populations of Australia 1800–1981*. Bathurst: Mitchell College of Advanced Education.

BRBS 1975: Raumordnungsprogram für die grossräumige Entwicklung des Bundesgebietes. Bonn: Bundesminister für Raumordnung, Bauwesen und Städtebau.

Britton, M. 1986: Recent population changes in perspective. *Population Trends* 44, 33–41.

Brox, O. 1980: Mot et konsolidert bosettingsmonster. *Tidsskrift for Samfunnsforskning* 21, 227–44.

Bundesgestzblatt 1965: *Raumordnungsgestz*. TI.I, S2. Bonn.

Burgel, G. 1986: Les villes nouvelles. *Espace, Populations, Sociétés* 1986–II, 377–84.

Burnley, I.H. (ed.) 1974: *Urbanization in Australia: the postwar experience*. Cambridge: Cambridge University Press.

——1981: Population change and social inequalities in sparsely populated regions in Australia. In Lonsdale, R.E. and Holmes, J.H. (eds.), *Settlement systems in sparsely populated regions; The United States and Australia* (New York: Pergamon), 105–24.

Burtenshaw, D. and Court, Y. 1986: Suburbanization or counterurbanization; the case of Denmark. In Heinritz, G. and Lichtenberger, E. (eds.), *The take-off of suburbia and the crisis of the central city* (Stuttgart: Franz Steiner Verlag Wiesbaden), 54–69.

Byfuglien, J. 1986: The analysis of the settlement pattern in relation to planning problems. *Norsk Geografisk Tidsskrift* 40, 187–94.

Cafiero, S. and Busca, A. 1970: *Lo sviluppo metropolitane in Italia*. Rome: Svimez.

Camagni, R. 1986: Innovation and the urban life cycle: production, location and income distribution aspects. In Nijkamp, P. (ed.), *Technological change, employment and spatial dynamics* (Berlin: Springer Verlag), 382–400.

Camagni, R. and Pompili, T. 1987: *Potere economico come 'comando' sulle risorse in un contesto territoriale*. VIII AISRE Conference, Cagliari, mimeo.

Cappellin, R. and Grillenzoni, C. 1983: Diffusion and specialization in the location of service activities in Italy. *Sistemi Urbani* 5, 2, 249–82.

Carozzi, C. and Mioni, A. 1970: *L'Italia in formazione: ricerche e saggi sullo sviluppo urbanistico del territorio nazionale*. Bari: De Donato.

Castells, M. 1985: High technology economic restructuring and the urban regional process in the United States. In Castells, M. (ed.), *High technology, space and society* (Beverly Hills, California: Sage Publications), 11–40.

Celant, A. 1988: *Nuova citta Nuova campagna*. Acts of XXIV Italian Geographical Congress, Bologna: Patron.

Celant, A. and Morelli, P. 1986: *La geografia des divari territoriali in Italia*. Firenze: Sansoni, (Chap. 4 & 5).

——1986c: Counterurbanization in Italy. In Bourne, L.S., Cori, B. and Dziewonski, K. (eds.), *Progress settlement systems geography* (Milan: F. Angeli), 161–94.

Cencini, C., Dematteis, G. and Menegati, B. (1983: *L'Italia emergente: indagine geodemografica sullo sviluppo periferico*. Milan: F. Angeli.

Chaline, C.H. 1984: Contemporary trends and policies in French city planning: a chronicle of successive urban policies, 1950–1983. *Urban Geography* 5, 326–36.

Champion, A.G. 1981a: Counterurbanization and rural rejuvenation in Britain: an evaluation of population trends since 1971. Seminar Paper 38 (Newcastle upon Tyne: Department of Geography, University of Newcastle upon Tyne).

——1981b: Population trends in rural Britain. *Population Trends* 26, 20–3.

——1983: Population trends in the 1970s. In Goddard, J.B. and Champion, A.G. (eds.), *The urban and regional transformation of Britain*. London: Methuen, 187–214.

——1985: Urban–rural differences in population change in Great Britain. *Espace, Populations, Sociétés* 1985–1, 128–43.

——1987a: Momentous revival in London's population. *Town and Country Planning* 56(3), 80–2.

——1987b: Recent changes in the pace of population deconcentration in Britain. *Geoforum* 18(4), 379–407.

——1989: Counterurbanization: the British experience. *Geographical Perspectives*, forthcoming.

Champion, A.G. and Congdon, P.D. 1988: An analysis of London's population change rate. *Built Environment* 13, 193–211.

——1989: The migration turnaround in London and its relation to employment and housing markets. In Congdon, P. and Batey, P. (eds.), *Advances in Regional Demography* (London: Belhaven), 180–204.

Champion, A.G., Coombes, M.G. and Openshaw, S. 1984: New regions for a new Britain. *Geographical Magazine* 56, 187–90.

Champion, A.G., Green, A.E., Owen, D.W., Ellin, D.J. and Coombes, M.G. 1987: *Changing places: Britain's demographic, economic and social complexion.* London: Edward Arnold.

Champion, A.G. and Illeris, S. 1989: Population redistribution trends in Western Europe: a mosaic of dynamics and crisis. In Hansen, J-C and Hebbert, M. (eds.), *Unfamiliar territory: the reshaping of European geography* (Aldershot: Gower).

Cheshire, P. and Hay, D. 1986: The development of the European urban system, 1971–81. In Ewers, H.-J., Goddard, J.B. and Matzerath, H. (eds.), *The future of the metropolis: Berlin, London, Paris, New York: Economic aspects* (Berlin/New York: de Gruyter), 149–70.

Christoffersen, H. and Illeris, S. 1982: *Den regionale udvikling i Danmark 1979–81.* Copenhagen: Amtkommunernes og Kommunernes Forskningsinstitut.

Cleveland, W.S. 1979: Robust locally weighted regression and smoothing scatterplots. *Journal of the American Statistical Association* 74, 829–36.

——1981: LOWESS: A program for smoothing scatterplots by robust locally weighted regression. *The American Statistician* 35, 54.

Clout, H.D. 1984: Bordeaux: urban renovation, conservation and rehabilitation. *Planning Outlook* 27, 84–92.

——(ed.) 1987: *Regional development in Western Europe.* 3rd edition. London: David Fulton.

Cochrane, S.G. and Vining, D.R. 1986: Recent trends in migration between core and peripheral regions in developed and advanced developing countries. *Working Papers in Regional Science and Transportation* 108 (Philadelphia: Regional Science Department, University of Pennsylvania).

Commonwealth Bureau of Census and Statistics 1962: *Census of the Commonwealth of Australia, 30 June 1954, Volume VIII – Australian statisticians report.* Canberra: Government Printer.

——1967: *Census of the Commonwealth of Australia, 30 June 1961, Volume VIII – Australian statisticians report.* Canberra: Government Printer.

Compagna, F. 1967: *La Politicia della citta.* Bari: Laterza.

Cook, B. 1980: Migration patterns of the elderly. Paper presented to the fifth annual meeting of the Regional Science Association, Australian and New Zealand Section, Tanunda, South Australia.

Coombes, M.G., Dalla Longa, R. and Raybould, S. 1989: Counterurbanization in Britain and Italy: a comparative critique of the concept, causation and evidence, *Progress in Planning* 32, 1–70.

Coombes, M.G. Dixon, J.S., Goddard, J.B., Openshaw, S. and Taylor, P.J. 1982: Functional Regions for the Population Census of Great Britain. In Herbert, D.T. and Johnston, R.J. (eds.), *Geography and the urban environment: progress in research and applications* 5 (Chichester: Wiley), 63–112.

Cori, B. 1984: The national settlement of Italy. In Bourne, L.S., Sinclair, R. and Dziewoński, K. (eds.), *Urbanization and settlement systems: international perspectives* (Oxford: Oxford University Press), 283–300.

——1986: The national settlement system of Italy: a general view. In Bourne, L.S., Cori, B. and Dziewoński, K. (eds.), *Progress in settlement systems geography* (Milan: F. Angeli), 97–135.

Courgeau, D. 1978: Les migrations internes en France de 1954 à 1975, I. Vue d'ensemble. *Population* 35, 525–45.

——1985: Changements de logement, changements de département et cycle de vie. *L'Espace Géographique* 4, 289–306.

Courgeau, D. and Lefèbvre, M. 1982: Les migrations internes en France de 1954 à 1975, II. Migrations et urbanisation. *Population* 37, 341–69.

Courgeau, D. and Pumain, D. 1984: Baisse de la mobilité résidentielle. *Population et Sociétés* 179.

Court, Y. 1984: *Counterurbanization: a review and bibliography*. Research Seminar Series. Portsmouth Polytechnic, Department of Geography.

——1985a: Interpretation of the turnaround: population redistribution in Denmark 1970–83. Paper presented at IBG Population Study Group Conference, Liverpool, September, mimeo.

——1985b: Recent patterns of population change in Denmark. *Geography* 70, 353–6.

——1986: Denmark. In Findlay, A. and White, P. (eds.), *West European population change* (London: Croom Helm), 81–101.

——1987: Denmark. In Clout, H. (ed.), *Regional development in Western Europe*, 3rd ed. (Chichester: David Fulton Publishers), 307–18.

——1988: Alternative explanations of counterurbanization: the case of Denmark, 1970–83. Unpublished Ph.D. thesis, Department of Geography, Portsmouth Polytechnic.

CRESME 1987: *Le aree urbane in Italia*. Rome: CRESME. Unpublished report for the Ministero per le Aree Urbane.

Cross, D.F.W. 1988: The characteristics of non-metropolitan population growth in England and Wales, 1971–1986, with special reference to Southern England. Unpublished Ph.D. thesis, King's College, London.

David, J. and Freschi, L. 1979: Incidences demographiques et foncieres de la rurbanisation: le cas de Champagnier (Isère). *Revue de Géographie Alpine* 67, 29–49.

David, J., Herbin, J. and Meriaudeau, R. 1986: La dynamique démographique de la zone de montagne française: le tournant historique des années 1970. *Espace, Populations, Sociétés* 1986–II, 365–76.

Dean, K.G. 1986: Counterurbanization continues in Brittany. *Geography* 71, 151–4.

——1987: The disaggregation of migration flows: the case of Brittany, 1975–1982. *Regional Studies* 21, 313–25.

——1988: Interregional flows of economically active persons in France, 1975–1982. *Demography*, 25, 81–98.

Dean, K., Brown, B. and Perry, R. 1984a: The conceptualisation of counterurbanization. *Area* 16, 9–14.

Dean, K.G., Shaw, D.P., Brown, B.J.H., Perry, R.W. and Thorneycroft, W.T. 1984b: Counterurbanization and the characteristics of persons migrating to West Cornwall. *Geoforum* 15, 177–90.

de Ley, M. 1983: French immigration policy since May 1981. *International Migration Review* 17, 196–211.

Dematteis, G. 1985a: Contro-urbanizzazione e deconcentrazione: un salto di scala nell-organizzazione territoriale. In Innocenti, R. (ed.), *Piccola citta e piccola impresa* (Milan: F. Angeli), 101–18.

——1985b: Contro-urbanizzazione e strutture urbane reticolari. In Bianchi, G. and Magnaghi, I. (eds.), *Sviluppo multiregionale: teorie, metodi, problemi* (Milan: F. Angeli), 121–33.

——1986a: Urbanization and counterurbanization in Italy, *Ekistics* 53, 316/317, 26–33.

——1986b: L'ambiente come contingenza e il mondo come rete. *Urbanistica* 85, 112–17.

——1986c: Counterurbanization in Italy. In Bourne, L.S., Cori, B. and Dziewonski, K. (eds.), *Progress in settlement systems geography* (Milan: F. Angeli), 161–94.

Department of Social Security 1988: *Social security pensioners and beneficiaries as a proportion of the population and the labour force: Australia, 1977–1987*. Canberra: Statistical Services and Analysis Section, Performance Monitoring Branch.

——n.d. *Social security pensioners and beneficiaries as a proportion of the population and the labour force: Australia, 1976–1986.* Canberra: Department of Social Security.

Dewdney, J.C. 1968: Age-structure maps of the British Isles. *Transactions, Institute of British Geographers* 43, 9–18.

Drakakis-Smith, D. 1984: Underdevelopment in the tropics: the case of North Australia. *Singapore Journal of Tropical Geography* 5 (2), 125–39.

Drewett, R., Goddard, J. and Spence, N. 1976: Urban Britain: beyond containment. In Berry, B.J.L. (ed.), *Urbanization and counterurbanization* (Beverly Hills, California: Sage Publications), 43–79.

Durand, P. 1972: *Industrie et régions.* Paris: La Documentation Française.

Dwyer-Leslie and Maunsell 1983: *River Murray irrigation overview.* Study for South Australian government, River Murray Irrigation Overview Steering Committee, February, 4 volumes.

Dyer, C. 1978: *Population and society in twentieth century France.* London: Hodder and Stoughton.

Economic Planning Agency 1972: *New comprehensive national development plan.* Tokyo: Ministry of Finance Printing Bureau.

Emanual, C. and Dematteis, G. 1987: *Reti urbane minori e deconcentrazione metropolitana nella Padania Centro-occidentale.* VIII AISRE Conference, Cagliari, mimeo.

Engels, R.A. 1986: The metropolitan non-metropolitan population at mid-decade. Paper presented at the Population Association of American Annual Meeting at San Francisco, CA, mimeo.

Engles, R.A. and Forstall, R.L. 1985: Tracking the non-metropolitan population turnaround to 1984. Paper presented at the Population Association of America Annual Meeting, Boston, MA.

——1985b: The experience of the non-metropolitan population turnaround during the 1980s. Paper presented at the Population Association of America Annual Meeting, Boston, MA, March 28.

Engels, R. and Healey, M.K. 1979: Rural renaissance reconsidered. *American Demographics* 1(5), 16–20.

ESCAP (Economic and Social Commission for Asia and the Pacific) 1984: *Population of Japan.* Country Monograph Series No. 11. New York: United Nations.

Farley, R. 1984: *Blacks and whites; narrowing the gap?* Cambridge, Mass.: Harvard University Press.

Fielding, A.J. 1982: Counterurbanization in Western Europe. *Progress in Planning* 17, 1–52.

——1983: Counterurbanization in Western Europe: recent empirical and theoretical contributions to the debate. Paper presented at the Anglo-Dutch Migration Symposium, Soesterberg, The Netherlands, 14–16 September.

——1986a: Counterurbanization in Western Europe. In Findlay, A. and White. P. (eds.), *West European population change* (London: Croom Helm), 35–49.

—1986b: Counterurbanization. In Michael Pacione (ed.), *Population geography: progess and prospects* (London: Croom Helm), 224–56.

Fleury, M. 1982: Fort ralentissement de la croissance démographique de l'Ile de France: résultats provisoires du recensement. *Aspects économiques de l'Ile de France*, 5, 3–9.

Forstall, R.L. 1975: Trends in metropolitan and non-metropolitan population growth since 1970. Washington, DC: Population Division, US Bureau of the Census.

——1981: Is America becoming more metropolitan? *American Demographics* 3 (11), 18–22.

——1987: Population and estimated net migration by region and metropolitan status, 1960–85. Paper presented at the Annual General Meeting of the

Association of American Geographers, Portland, Oregon.

Forstall, R.L. and Engels, R.A. 1984: Growth in non-metropolitan areas slows. US Bureau of the Census, Washington, DC, mimeo.

Foss, O., Sørlie, K. and Texmon, I. 1987: All folketallsvekst i storbyene! *nordREFO* 17: 2–3, 111–32.

Fothergill, S. and Gudgin, G. 1979: Regional employment change: a sub-regional explanation. *Progress in Planning* 12, 155–219.

Frey, W.H. 1986: Lifecourse migration and redistribution of the elderly across US regions and metropolitan areas. *Economic Outlook USA* 13:2 (Second Quarter).

——1987: Migration and depopulation of the metropolis: regional restructuring or rural renaissance? *American Sociological Review* 52, 240–57.

Frey, W.H. and Speare, A. Jr. 1988: *Regional and metropolitan growth and decline in the United States*. A 1980 Census Monograph. New York: Russell Sage.

Fruit, J.-P. 1985: Migrations résidentielles en milieu rural péri-urbain: le pays de Caux central. *Espace, Populations, Sociétés* 1985–1, 150–59.

Fuguitt, G.V. 1985: The non-metropolitan population turnaround. *Annual Review of Sociology* 11, 259–80.

——1987: Reversal of the US non-metropolitan turnaround? Contribution to panel discussion at the Annual Meeting of the Association of American Geographers, Portland, Oregon, 24 April.

Fuguitt, G.V. and Beale, C.L. 1989: *Rural and small town America*. A 1980 Census Monograph. New York: Russell Sage.

Fuguitt, G.V., Heaton, T.B. And Lichter, D.T. 1988: Monitoring the metropolitanization process. *Demography* 25, 115–28.

Fuguitt, G.V. and Tordella, S.J. 1980: Elderly net migration: The new trend of non-metropolitan population change. *Research on Aging* 2, 191–204.

Ganiage, J. 1980: La population de Beauvaisis: transformations économiques et mutations démographiques, 1790–1975. *Annales de Géographie*, 89, 1–36.

Garofoli, G. 1983: *Industrializzazione diffusa in Lombardia. Sviluppo territoriale e sistemi produttivi locali*. Milan: F. Angeli.

Gatzweiler, H.-P. 1982: *Neuere Binnenwanderungstendenzen im Bundesgebiet*. Bonn–Bad Godesberg: BfLR.

——1983: *Ausländerentwicklung in den großstädten*. Bonn–Bad Godesberg: BfLR.

Gerard, M.-C. 1976: Recensement de 1975: l'extension des 'grandes banlieues'. *Economie et Statistique* 80, 63–71.

Glickman, N.J. 1979: *The growth and management of the Japanese urban system*. New York: Academic Press.

Goddard, R.G. 1983: Rural renaissance – but where? Paper presented at 53rd Congress of the Australian and New Zealand Association for the Advancement of Science, Perth.

Gordon, P. 1979: Deconcentration without a 'clean break'. *Environment and Planning A* 11, 281–9.

Grafton, D.J. and Bolton, N. 1987: Counterurbanization and the rural periphery: some evidence from North Devon. In Robson, B.T. (ed.), *Managing the city* (London: Croom Helm), 191–210.

Gravier, J.F. 1947: *Paris et le désert français*. Paris: le Portulan.

Guillon, M. 1986: Les étrangers dans les grandes agglomérations françaises, 1962–1982. *Espace, Populations, Sociétés* 1986–II, 179–90.

Hall, P. 1971: Spatial structure of metropolitan England and Wales. In Chisholm, M. and Manners, G. (eds.), *Spatial policy problems of the British economy* (Cambridge: Cambridge University Press), 96–125.

Hall, P. and Hay, D. 1980: *Growth centres in the European urban system*. London: Heinemann.

Hall, P., Thomas, R., Gracey, H. and Drewett, R. 1973: *The containment of urban*

England: 1. Urban and metropolitan growth processes or Megalopolis denied. London: George Allen & Unwin.

Hamnett, C. and Randolph, W. 1983: The changing population distribution of England and Wales, 1961–81: clean break or consistent progression? Built Environment 8, 272–80.

Hansen J.C. 1975: Population trends and prospects in marginal areas of Norway. In Kosinski, L.A. and Prothero, R.M. (eds.), People on the move. Studies on internal migration (London: Methuen), 255–75.

——1979: Bosettingsmønster og regionalpolitikk – harmoni eller konflikt. Plan og Arbeid, 62–73.

——1983: Regional policy in an oil economy: the case of Norway. Geoforum 14, 353–61.

——1985: Regional disparities in present-day Norway. Norsk Geografisk Tidsskrift 39, 109–24.

——1986: The urban turnaround – the beginning of a U-turn? In Cawley, M. (ed.), New approaches to the development of marginal regions. Demographic issues; migration and ethnic minorities (Galway: University College), 3: 5–35.

——1987: Fornorsking av modeller for regional utvikling. Sosiologi i dag, 17:3–4, 131–47.

Hansen, V. 1960: Some characteristics of a growing suburban region. Saertryk af Geografisk Tidsskrift 59, 214–25.

Hartoft-Nielsen, P. 1984: Industrienstrukturens regionale udvikling i 1970'erne. In Illeris, S. and Pedersen, P.O. (eds.), Industrienkoncentration eller spredning (Copenhagen: Amtskommunernes og Kommunernes Forskningsinstitut), 22–49.

Hawley, H. 1971: Urban society: an ecological approach. New York: The Ronald Press Co.

——1978: Urbanization as process. In Street, D. and Associates (ed.), Handbook of contemporary urban life (New York: Jossey Bass), 3–26.

Heaton, T.B. 1983: Recent trends in the geographical distribution of the elderly population. In Riley, M.W., Hess, B.B. and Bond, K. (eds.), Aging in Society (Hillsdale, NJ: Lawrence Earlbaum Associates), 95–113.

Heaton, T.B., Lichter, D.T. and Fuguitt, G.V. 1982: The geographic redistribution of blacks and non-blacks: thirty years in perspective. Madison, WI: Center for Demography and Ecology Working Paper 82–29.

Hepworth, M.E. 1987: Information technology and spatial systems. Progress in Human Geography 11(2), 157–80.

Hodge, G. 1983: Canadian small town renaissance: implications for settlement systems concepts. Regional Studies 17, 19–28.

Hohenberg, P.M. and Lees, L.H. 1985: The making of urban Europe 1000–1950. Cambridge, Mass.: Harvard University Press.

Holmes, J.H. 1981: Sparsely populated regions of Australia. In Lonsdale, R.E. and Holmes, J.H. (eds.), Settlement systems in sparsely populated regions: The United States and Australia. (New York: Pergamon), 70–104.

Holt-Jensen, A. 1987: Konsolideringshypotesen og turnaroundtrenden i 1980-og 1990-årene. Geografi i Bergen 110, Institutt for Geografi, Norges Handelshogskole og Universitetet i Bergen.

Honoré, G. 1978: L'exode rurale tend-il à se ralentir? Cahiers de Statistique Agricole 41, 1–4.

Hooson, D.J.M. 1960: The distribution of population as the essential geographical expression. Canadian Geographer 17, 10–20.

House, J.W. 1978: France: An applied geography. London: Methuen.

Hoyt, H. 1939: The structure and growth of residential neighbourhoods in American cities. Washington, DC: Federal Housing Administration.

Hugo, G.J. 1983a: *Population change in urban and rural areas 1976–1981*. 1981 Census project paper 7, National Institute of Labour Studies, Flinders University of South Australia.
——1983b: *Interstate migration in Australia, 1976–81*. 1981 Census project paper 1, National Institute of Labour Studies, Flinders University of South Australia.
——1984: *Patterns and components of regional population change 1976–1981*. 1981 Census project paper 3, National Institute of Labour Studies, Flinders University of South Australia.
—1986a: *Australia's changing population: trends and implications*. Melbourne: Oxford University Press.
——1986b: Population aging in Australia: implications for social and economic policy. *Papers of the East–West Population Institute*, No. 98. Honolulu: East–West Center.
——1987: Australia's changing non-metropolitan population. Reference No. 8: 1–29 in *Rural Australia Symposium 1987; contributed papers to the National Symposium*, Federal Department of Primary Industry and the Rural Development Centre, University of New England, IRDC Publication No. 151.
——1988: Australia's mobility transition. Paper presented to session on the Demography of Australia: A Bicentennial Perspective, Population Association of America's annual meetings in New Orleans 21–23 April, 1988.
——1989a: Elderly migration: contexts, issues, policies and problems. In Rogers, A. and Serow, W. (eds.), *Elderly migration: an international comparative study*, ch. 16 (Boulder: University of Colorado).
——1989b: Counterurbanization in Australia. *Geographical Perspectives*.
Hugo, G.J., Rudd, D.M., Downie, M., Macharper, A. and Shillabeer, A. 1981: *A demographic profile of the present and likely future population of the South Coast – Fleurieu Peninsula regions of South Australia with particular emphasis on the aged population*. Discipline of Geography, Flinders University of South Australia.
Hugo, G.J. and Smailes, P.J. 1985: Urban–rural migration in Australia: a process view of the turnaround. *Journal of Rural Studies* 1, 11–30.
Illeris, G. 1984: *Nettovandringer i Danmark*. Kulturgeografi 4, Afløsningsopgave, Geografisk Institut, Copenhagen University.
Illeris, S. 1964: The functions of Danish towns. *Geografisk Tidsskrift* 63, 203–36.
——1967: Urban sprawl in Denmark – a preliminary note. *Tidjschrift voor Economische en Sociale Geografie* 58, 146–52.
——1978: Urbanization in Denmark. *Geographica Polonica* 39, 49–64.
——1979a: The Danish settlement system. In IGU Commission on National Settlement Systems (ed.), *The National Settlement Systems II* (Warsaw: Polish Academy of Sciences, Institute of Geographical and Spatial Organization), 47–71.
——1979b: Recent developments of the settlement system of advanced market economy countries. *Geografisk Tidsskrift* 78/9, 49–56.
——1980: *Research on changes in the structure of the urban network*. Copenhagen: Amtkommunernes og Kommunernes Forskningsinstitut.
——1982: De nye realiteter i den regionale udvikling. *Byplan* 34, 1–5.
——1983: Befolkningsudviklingen i den aeldre del af Hovedstadsregionen 1973–82. *AKF-Nyt* 4.
——1984a: Danish regional development during economic crisis. *Geografisk Tidsskrift* 84, 53–62.
——1984b: The Danish settlement system: development and planning. In Bourne, L.S. (ed.), *Urbanization and settlement systems: international perspectives* (Oxford: Oxford University Press), 226–38.
——1987a: Centralisation ou décentralisation? Répartition de la population et des activités économiques au Danemark. *Revue Belge de Géographie* 109, 165–82.

——1987b: The urban turnaround revisited: a preliminary note. Paper presented to IGU Commission on Urban Systems, Dublin, June 1987.

——1988a: Counterurbanization revisited: the new map of population distribution in Central and North-western Europe. In Bannon, M., Bourne, L. and Sinclair, R. (eds.), *Urbanization and urban development*. (Dublin: University College).

——1988b: *Local economic development in Denmark*. Copenhagen: Amtkommunernes og Kommunernes Forskningsinstitut.

Imset, Ø. 1982: Bosettingsmonsteret i Finnmark er ikke konsolidert. *Meddelelser 67*, Geografisk Institutt, Norges Handelshøyskole og Universitetet i Bergen.

INSEE 1982a: Recensement general de la population de 1982: principaux resultats. Sondage au 1/20 France metropolitaine. Paris: INSEE.

——1982b: Recensement general de la population de 1982: composition communale des zones de peuplement industriel ou urbain. Paris: INSEE.

——1984: Indicateurs de fragilite des zones rurales: Isere-chiffres a la cantonade. *Notes et Documents de l'INSEE Rhone–Alpes* 21.

Institute of Population Problems 1985: *Re-estimates of population by age and sex and vital rates in postwar Japan*. Tokyo: Institute of Population Problems, Ministry of Health and Welfare.

ISTAT-IRPET 1986: *I mercati del lavoro in Italia*. Seminar on Identificazione dei Sistemi Territoriali, Rome, mimeo.

Itoh, Z. 1978: Kokudo kaihatsu keikaku to seikatsuken-koso no rekishi (Japan's land development plan and the history of integrated residence policy). *Jurist 11*, 38–44.

Jaillet, M.-C. and Jalabert, G. 1982: La production de l'espace urbain peripherique. *Revue Géographique des Pyrénées at du Sud-Ouest* 53, 7–26.

Japan Statistics Bureau 1979: *Population of Japan: summary of the results of 1975 Population Census of Japan*. Tokyo: Prime Minister's Office.

——1982: *1980 Population Census of Japan*. Volume 2. Tokyo: Prime Minister's Office.

——1984: *Jinko Idou (Internal Migration)*. 1980 Population Census of Japan Monograph Series No. 2. Tokyo: Prime Minister's Office.

——1987: *Social indicators by prefecture*. Tokyo: Prime Minister's Office.

Jarvie, W.K. 1981: Internal migration and structural change in Australia 1966–71: some preliminary observations. In *Papers of the Australian and New Zealand Section of the Regional Science Association*, 6th meeting, 25–55.

——1984: Internal migration in Australia 1966–71 to 1971–76. Ph.D. thesis, School of Social Sciences, Flinders University of South Australia.

Johannisson, B. and Spilling O. (eds.) 1986: *Lokal naeringspolitikk – entreprenørskap og nettverksstrategier i noen norske og svenske kommuner*. Olso: Universitetsforlaget.

Johansen, C.U. 1983: *Hvad blev af dem? En analyse af mobiliteten blandt tidligere uddannelsessøgende i Ribe og Vejle Amter*. Esbjerg: Sydjysk Universitets Forlag.

Jones, R. (ed.) 1975: *Essays on world urbanization*. London: George Philip.

Jones, H., Caird, J., Berry, W. and Dewhurst, J. 1986: Peripheral counterurbanization: findings from an integration of census and survey data in northern Scotland. *Regional Studies* 20, 15–26.

Jones, H., Ford, N., Caird, J. and Berry, W. 1984: Counterurbanization in societal context: long-distance migration to the Highlands and Islands of Scotland. *Professional Geographer* 36, 437–44.

Kain, R. 1982: Europe's model and exemplar still? The French approach to urban conservation 1962–1981. *Town Planning Review* 53, 403–22.

Kanekiyo, H. 1983: Migration transition in the United States. *Journal of Population Studies (Jinkogaku Kenkyu)* 6, 15–21.

Kanstad, T. and Kindseth, O. 1983: Senterstruktur og bosettingsmønster. *Rapport 3*, Bodo: Nordlandsforskning.

Kawabe, H. 1983: Population distribution and internal migration since 1960. *Journal of Population Studies (Jinkogaku Kenkyu)* 6, 7–14.

——1984: Kokunai jinko ido no saikento (re-evaluation of internal migration in Japan). *Summary of Proceedings of the 1984 Annual Meeting of the Human Geographical Society of Japan* (Kyoto: Human Geographical Society of Japan), 8–11.

——1985: Some characteristics of internal migration observed from the cohort-by-cohort analysis. *Journal of Population Problems (Jinko Mondai Kenkyu)* 175, 16–30.

Kawashima, T. 1982: Recent urban trends in Japan: analysis of functional urban regions. In Kawashima, T. and Korcelli, P. (eds.), *Human settlement systems* (Laxenburg, Austria: International Institute for Applied Systems Analysis), 21–40.

Keeble, D.E. 1980: Industrial decline, regional policy and the urban–rural manufacturing shift in the United Kingdom. *Environment and Planning A* 12, 945–62.

Kennett, S.R. 1983: Migration within and between labour markets. In Goddard, J.B. and Champion, A.G. (eds.), *The urban and regional transformation of Britain* (London: Methuen), 215–38.

Kennett, S. and Spence, N. 1979: British population trends in the 1970s. *Town and Country Planning* 48, 221–3.

Klaassen, L.H., Molle, W.T.M. and Paelinck, J.H.P. 1981: *Dynamics of urban development*. Aldershot: Gower.

Koch, R. 1980: 'Counterurbanization' auch in Europa? *Informationen zur Raumentwicklung* 2, 59–69.

Kock, R. and Gatzeiler, H.-P. 1980: *Migration and settlement: 9. Federal Republic of Germany*. Laxenburg, Austria: IIASA.

Kontuly, T. and Vogelsang, R. 1988a: Explanations for the intensification of counterurbanization in the Federal Republic of Germany. *Professional Geographer* 40, 42–54.

——1988b: The migration turnaround in the Federal Republic of Germany. *Geographical Perspectives*, forthcoming.

Kontuly, T., Wiard, S. and Vogelsang, R. 1986: Counterurbanization in the Federal Republic of Germany. *Professional Geographer* 38, 170–81.

Kroner, G. 1976: Programmregionen der bundesraumordnung und regionale Arbeitsmarkte. *Informationen zur Raumentwicklung*, 11/12.

Kroner, G. and Kessler, H.R. 1976: Vorschlag einer raumlichen Gliederung des Bundesgebietes nach der Erreichbarkeit von Oberzentren. *Informationen zur Raumentwicklung* 1.

Laborie, J.-P., Langumier, J.-F. and De Roo, P. 1985: *La politique française d'aménagement du territoire de 1950 à 1985*. Paris: La Documentation Française.

Law, C.M. 1967: The growth of the urban population in England and Wales, 1801–1911. *Transactions, Institute of British Geographers* 41, 125–43.

Law, C.M. and Warnes, A.M. 1976: The changing geography of the elderly in England and Wales. *Transactions, Institute of British Geographers* NS1, 453–71.

Lawton, R. 1982: People and work. In House, J.W. (ed.), *The UK space* (London: Weidenfeld & Nicolson), 103–203.

Lichtenberger, E. 1976: The changing nature of European urbanization. In Berry, B.J.L. (ed.), *Urbanization and Counterurbanization* (Beverly Hills, California: Sage Publications), 81–107.

Lichter, D.T., Fuguitt, G.V., Heaton, T.B. and Clifford, W.B. 1981: Components of change in the residential concentration of the elderly population, 1950–1975. *Journal of Gerontology* 36, 480–9.

Lichter, D.T., Heaton, T.B. and Fuguitt, G.V. 1986: Black and white population redistribution in the United States. *Social Science Quarterly* 76, 21–38.

Lindblad, J. 1976: Where the dropouts are. *Bulletin*, 27 March, 32–9.

Limouzin, P. 1980: Les facteurs de dynamisme des communes rurales françaises: methodes d'analyse et résultats. *Annales de Géographie* 89, 549–87.

Long, J.F. 1981: *Population deconcentration in the United States.* Special Demographic Analysis CDS–81–5. (Washington, DC: US Government Printing Office.)

Long, L.H. 1988: *Migration and residential mobility in the United States.* A 1980 Census Monograph. New York: Russell Sage.

Long, L.H. and DeAre, D. 1982: Repopulating the countryside: a 1980 Census trend. *Science* 217, 111–16.

Long, L.H. and Hansen, K.A. 1979: *Reasons for interstate migration.* Current population reports, no. 81. Washington DC: US Bureau of Census.

Longino, C.F. Jr., Wiseman, R.F., Biggar, J.C. and Flynn, C.B. 1984: Aged metropolitan–non-metropolitan migration streams over three census decades. *Journal of Gerontology* 39, 721–9.

McCarthy, K.F. and Morrison, P.A. 1978: *The changing demographic and economic structure of non-metropolitan areas in the 1970s.* Santa Monica: Rand Corporation, P6062.

McDonald, H. 1986: Integration is the watchword, and it really works. *Far Eastern Economic Review*, 14 August, 53–4, 63.

McQuinn, P. 1978: *Rural retreating: a review and an Australian case study.* Armidale: Department of Geography, University of New England.

Maher, C. 1985: The changing character of Australian urban growth. *Built Environment* 11 (2), 69–82.

Maher, C. and McKay, J. 1986: *1981 internal migration study final report: internal migration in Australia.* Canberra: Department of Immigration and Ethnic Affairs.

Males, W., Poulter, D. and Murtough, G. 1987: Off-farm income and rural adjustment. *Quarterly Review of the Rural Economy*, June 9(2), 160–9.

Maskell, P. 1983: *Industriens regionale omlokalisering 1970–1980.* Copenhagen: Handelhøjskolen.

——1985: Redistribution of Denmark's manufacturing industry 1972–82. *Scandinavian Housing and Planning Research* 2, 79–83.

Matthiesen, C.W. 1980: Trends in the urbanization process: the Copenhagen case. *Geografisk Tidsskrift* 80, 98–101.

——1981: Settlement change and political response. *Geografisk Tidsskrift* 81, 55–66.

——(ed.) 1983: *Urban policy and urban development in the 80s; Danish experience in a European context.* Bygeografisk Skriftserie Rapport 16. Copenhagen: Geografisk Centralinstitut.

——1985: *Dansk byers vaekst.* Copenhagen: Det Kongelige Dansk Geografisk Selskab & C.A. Reitzels Forlag.

Mayoux, J. 1979: *Demain l'espace. L'habitat individuel péri-urbain.* Rapport de la mission d'étude présidée par Jacques Mayoux. Paris: La Documentation Française.

Menzies, B.J. and Bell, M.J. 1981: *Peri-urban development: a case study of the Adelaide Hills.* Research monograph No. 2. Adelaide Extension Research and Evaluation Unit, Department of Agriculture.

Mera, K. 1987: Chika josho ni miru chiiki kakusa:toshin no gyomuchiiki ga chika wo sendo (Regional differences in terms of increases in land prices: industrial districts in cities leading land price changes). *Japan Economic Research Center Report* 550, 25–33.

Minami, R. 1967: Population migration away from agriculture in Japan. *Economic Development and Cultural Change* 15, 183–201.

Mogensen, G.V., Mørkeberg, H. and Sundbo, J. 1979: *Småbyer i Landdistrikter,* Publikation 86. Copenhagen: Socialforskningsinstituttet.

Møller, J. 1985: Lov hindrer udvikling i landsbyer. *Politiken*, 23 March.

Morrison, P.A. and Wheeler, J.P. 1976: Rural renaissance in America? *Population Bulletin* 31 (3), 1–27.

Moseley, M. 1984: The revival of rural areas in advanced economies: a review of some causes and consequences. *Geoforum* 15, 447–56.

Mougenot, C. 1982: Les mécanismes sociaux de la rurbanisation. *Sociologia Ruralis* 22, 264–78.

Muramatsu, M. and Kuroda, T. 1974: Japan. In Berelson, B. (ed.), *Population policy in developed countries* (New York: McGraw Hill), 704–30.

Murphy, P. 1979: Migration of the elderly and non-metropolitan change. Unpublished paper presented to Regional Science Association (Australia and New Zealand section) fourth annual meeting, Albury-Wodonga.

Myklebost, H. 1979: Befolkningsutviklingen i Norge 1950–1975. *Ad Novas – Norwegian Geographical Studies* 14, Oslo: Universitetsforlaget.

——1984: The evidence for urban turnaround in Norway. *Geoforum* 15, 167–76.

Nagaoka, A., Nakatoh, Y. and Yamaguchi, F. (eds.) 1977: *Nihon nogyo no chiiki kozo (Regional structure of agriculture in Japan)*. Tokyo: Taimeido.

National Institute for Research Advancement 1982: *Kokusai jinkoidou ni kansuru chosa-kenkyu no tameno junbi-chosa (Preparatory report for a study of international migration)*. Tokyo: Shakai Kogaku Kenkyusho.

National Land Agency of Japan 1975: *Showa 50-nendo kokudo no rivo ni kansuru nenji hokoku (The 1975 Report on utilization of the nation's land)*. Tokyo: Ministry of Finance Printing Bureau.

——1979: *Sanzenso: The third comprehensive national development plan*. Tokyo: Ministry of Finance Printing Bureau.

——1987: *Daiyoji zenkoku sogo kaihatsu keikaku (The fourth comprehensive national development plan)*. Tokyo: Ministry of Finance Printing Bureau.

Nishikawa, S. 1973: Saikin junen no chiiki-kan rodo ido (Labor migration between regions during the past ten years). *Kenzai Hyoron* 22, 104–15.

Noin, D., Chauviré, Y. *et al.* 1984: *Atlas des Parisiens*. Paris: Masson.

Noin, D. and Chauviré Y. 1987: *La population de la France*. Paris: Masson.

Noyelle, T.J. and Stanback, T.M., Jr. 1984: *The economic transformation of American cities*. Totowa, NJ: Rowman and Allanheld.

Ogden, P.E. 1985: Counterurbanization in France: the results of the 1982 population census. *Geography* 70, 24–35.

Ogden, P.E. and Huss, M.-M. 1982: Demography and pronatalism in France in the nineteenth and twentieth centuries. *Journal of Historical Geography* 8, 283–98.

Ogden, P.E. And Winchester, H.P.M. 1986: France. In Findlay, A. and White, P. (eds.), *West European population change* (London: Croom Helm), 119–41.

Ohls-Packalén, G. 1987: Hovudstadsregionernas befolkningsutveckling åren 1971–1985. *NordREFO* 17:2–3, 25–37.

OPCS 1981a: *Census 1981, Preliminary Report, England and Wales*. London: HMSO.

——1981b: The first results of the 1981 Census. *Population Trends* 25, 21–9.

——1984: *Census 1981: Key statistics for urban areas, Great Britain*. London: HMSO.

Oscarsson, G. 1987: Storstadstilväxten – Obalansens orsaker och möjliga åtgärder. *NordREFO* 17:2–3, 38–68.

Owen, D.W., Coombes, M.G. and Gillespie, A.E. 1986: The urban–rural shift and employment change in Britain, 1971–81. In Danson, M. (ed.), *Redundancy and recession: restructuring the regions* (Norwich: Geo Books), 23–47.

Paci, M. (ed) 1980: *Famiglia e mercato del lavoro in un'economia periferica*. Milan: F. Angeli.

Paterson, I.G., Kirkham, D.O. and Gilmore, K.C. 1978: *The changing rural environment – a study of rural retreats, new life styles and land use in southern Tasmania*. Environmental Studies Occasional Paper No. 6. Hobart: University of Tasmania.

Pedersen, P.O. 1984: De regionale udvikling i 1970 'ernes Danmark – samspillet mellem bosaetningsmønster, arbejdspladsstruktur og uddannelsessystem set i de langsigtet perspektiv. *NordREFO* 3, 35–53.

Perry, R., Dean, K. and Brown, B. 1986: *Counterurbanization: international case studies of socio-economic change in rural areas*. Norwich: Geo Books.

Petsimeris, P. 1988: *L'urbanisation au Piedmont: analyse géographique des transformations sociofonctionnelles d'une région mûre*. Thèse de doctorat de 3me cycle, Université de Caen.

Pitié, J. 1971: *L'exode rural*. Paris: PUF.

Pitte, J.-R. 1986: Une renaissance pour le milieu rural. *L'Aménagement Foncier Agricole et Rural* 50 (Spécial), 3–9.

Planstyrelsen and Boligministeriet 1982: *The human settlements situation and related trends and policies*. Copenhagen.

Pred, A. 1977: *City systems in advanced economics*. London: Hutchinson.

Prinsley, D.M., Kidd, B., Howe, A.L. and Cameron, K. 1979: *The experience of retirement migration to Phillip Island and its impact on the community*. Occasional Paper in Gerontology, National Research Institute for Gerontology and Geriatric Medicine, University of Melbourne.

Pumain, D. 1983: Déconcentration urbaine. *Population et Sociétés* 166.

Pumain, D. and St-Julien, T. 1978: *Les dimensions du changement urbain*. Paris: CNRS.

——1984: Evolving structure of the French urban system. *Urban Geography* 5, 303–25.

Randolph, W. and Robert, S. 1981: Population redistribution in Great Britain, 1971–81. *Town and Country Planning* 50, 227–31.

Rasmussen, T.F. 1986: Byregionenes rolle for den regionale balanse og ubalanse. In Knudsen, J.P. and Aamo, B.S. (eds.), *Regional utvikling mot ar 2000* (Oslo: Cappelen), 208–24.

Richter, K. 1985: Non-metropolitan growth in the late 1970s: the end of the turnaround? *Demography* 22, 245–63.

Robert, S. and Randolph, W. 1983: Beyond decentralization: the evolution of population distribution in England and Wales, 1961–81. *Geoforum* 14, 75–102.

Scott, A.J. and Storper, M. (eds.) 1986: *Production, work, territory: the geographical anatomy of industrial capitalism*. Boston: Allen & Unwin.

Scott, P. 1964: The hierarchy of central places in Tasmania. *The Australian Geographer* IX (3), 134–47.

Secchi, B. 1984: *Il zacconta urbanistico: la politica della casa e del territorio in Italia*. Turin: Einaudi.

Shiramasa, G. 1978: Ichizenso kara sanzenso he: sono keifu to kadai (From the first to the third comprehensive national development plan: their genealogy and prospects). *Jurist* 11, 45–51.

Smailes, P.J. and Hugo, G.J. 1985: A process view of the population turnaround: an Australian rural case study. *Journal of Rural Studies* 1, 31–43.

Sørensen, I.M. 1984a: Det industrielle Danmark. *Dansk Industri* 2, 15.

——1984b: Industrien er flyttet vestpå. *Dansk Industri* 2, 5.

South Australian Department of Lands 1986: *Department of Lands Annual Report 1985–1986*. Adelaide: Government Printer.

Spence, N.A., Gillespie, A., Goddard, J., Kennett, S., Pinch, S. and William, A.M. 1982: *British cities: analysis of urban change*. Oxford: Pergamon.

Spilling, O.R. and Isaksen, A. 1987: Regionale strukturendringer i naeringslivet. *Plan og Arbeid* 5, 36–41.

Statistisk Sentralbyrå (1985): *Standard for kommuneklassifisering*. Oslo: Kongsvinger.

Sternlieb, G. and Hughes, J.W. 1975: *Post-industrial America: Metropolitan decline and inter-regional job shifts*. New Brunswick, NJ: Centre for Policy Research.

——1977: New regional and metropolitan realities of America. *Journal, American Institute of Planners*, July, 227–41.

Stiens, G. 1984: Auswirkungen der Bevölkerungsentwicklung bis zum Jahr 2000 in räumlicher Differenzierung. *Informationen zur Raumentwicklung*, 12, 1204.

Systat, Inc. 1987: *Systat graphics for the MacIntosh*. Evanstan, Illinois: Systat, Inc.

Taeuber, I.B. 1958: *The population of Japan*. Princeton, NJ: Princeton University Press.

Taeuber, I.B. and Taeuber, C. 1971: *People of the United States in the twentieth century*. A Census Monograph. Washington, DC: US Bureau of the Census.

Taeuber, K.E. 1975: Racial segregation: the persisting dilemma. *Annals of the American Academy of Political and Social Sciences* 422, 87–96.

Taeuber, K.E. and Taeuber, A.F. 1965: *Negroes in cities*. Chicago: Aldine Publishing Co.

Taffin, C. 1986: L'essor périurbain. *Espace, Populations, Sociétés* 1986–II, 305–12.

Terrier, C. 1986: Les déplacements domicile-travail en France. *Espace, Populations, Sociétés* 1986–II, 333–42.

Thumerelle, P. 1980: Crise economique et décroissance démographique: l'exemple de la région Nord-Pas de Calais. *Annales de Géographie* 89, 144–56.

Tisdale, H. 1942: The process of urbanization. *Social Forces* 20, 311–16.

Törnqvist, G. 1987: Kreativitetens geografi. In Aalbu, H. (ed.), *Kompetansespredning om vekststrategi* (Oslo: Norsk Samfunnsgeografers Forening, Skrifter 15), 25–56.

——1989: City systems and the new information technology. In Hansen, J.C. and Hebbert, M. (eds.), *Unfamiliar territory – the reshaping of European geography* (London: Gower), forthcoming.

Trewartha, G.T. 1953: The case for population geography. *Annals, Association of American Geographers* 43, 71–97.

Trigilia, C. 1980: Struttura di classe e sistema politico: neocorporativismo o neolocalismo? *Inchiesta* 46/47, 37–59.

Tuppen, J.N. and Mingret, P. 1986: Suburban malaise in French cities: the quest for a solution. *Town Planning Review* 57, 187–201.

United Nations 1987: *1985 Demographic Yearbook*. New York: United Nations.

van de Walle, E. 1979: France. In Lee, W.R. (ed.), *European demography and economic growth* (London: Croom Helm), 123–43.

Vernon, R. 1960: *Metropolis 1985*. New York: Harvard University Press.

Vining, D.R. 1982: Migration between the core and the periphery. *Scientific American* 247(6), 36–45.

Vining, D.R. and Kontuly, T. 1978a: Population dispersal from major metropolitan regions: an international comparison. *International Regional Science Review* 3, 49–73.

Vining, D. and Kontuly, T. 1978b: Population dispersal from major metropolitan regions: Great Britain is no exception. *International Regional Science Review* 3, 182.

Vining, D.R. and Pallone, R. 1982: Migration between core and peripheral regions: a description and tentative explanation of patterns of 22 countries. *Geoforum* 13, 339–410.

Vining, D., Pallone, R. and Plane, D. 1981: Recent migration patterns in the developed world. *Environment and Planning A* 13, 243–50.

Vining, D.R., Pallone, R. and Yang, C.H. 1982: Population dispersal from core regions: a description and tentative explanation of the patterns in 20 countries. In Kawashima. T. and Korcelli, P. (eds.), *Human settlement systems: spatial patterns and trends* (Laxenburg, Austria: International Institute for Applied Systems Analysis).

Vining, D.R. and Strauss, A. 1977: A demonstration that the current deconcentration of population in the United States is a clean break with the past.

Environment and Planning A 9, 751–8.

Vitali, O. 1983: *L'evoluzione urbana in Italia 1951–1977*. Milan: F. Angeli.

Vogelsang, R. and Kontuly, T. 1986: Counterurbanisation in der Bundesrepublick Deutschland. *Geographische Rundschau* 38, 461–8.

Wait, S. 1979: Retirement migration: a case study of Mildura. BA (Hons.) thesis, Monash University.

Wardwell, J.M. 1977: Equilibrium and change in non-metropolitan growth. *Rural Sociology* 42, 156–79.

Warnes, A.M. and Law, C.M. 1984: The elderly population of Great Britain: locational trends and policy implications. *Transactions, Institute of British Geographers* NS 9, 37–59.

Webber, R. and Craig, J. 1976: Which local authorities are alike? *Population Trends* 5, 13–19.

Weber, A.F. 1899: *The growth of cities in the nineteenth century*. New York: Macmillan.

Weekley, I. 1988: Rural depopulation and counterurbanization: a paradox. *Area* 20, 127–34.

Wells, H.G. 1902: *Anticipation of the reaction of mechanical and scientific progress upon human life and thought*. London: Chapman & Hall.

White, J.W. 1982: *Migration in metropolitan Japan: social change and political behavior*. Japan Research Monograph 2. Berkeley, California: Institute of East Asian Studies, University of California.

Wickmann, J. and Birch, A. 1983: *Ungskoven i dansk erhvervsliv*. Copenhagen: Håndvaerksrådet.

Wilkinson, T. 1965: *The urbanization of Japanese labour, 1863–1955*. Amherst: University of Massachusetts Press.

Williams, M. 1972: *The making of the South Australian landscape*. London: Academic Press.

Wilson, F.D. 1984: Urban ecology, urbanization and systems of cities. *Annual Review of Sociology* 10, 283–307.

Winchester, H.P.M. 1984: Out-migration from Isère in a period of rapid urbanization, 1962–68. In Ogden, P.E. (ed.), *Migrants in modern France: four studies* (Queen Mary College, University of London, Occasional Paper 23), 67–86.

——1989: The structure and impact of the postwar rural revival: Isère. In Ogden, P.E. and White, P.E. (eds.), *Migration in modern France: population mobility in France in the later nineteenth and twentieth centuries* (London: Unwin Hyman).

Winchester, H.P.M. and Ilberry, B.W. 1988: *Agricultural change: France and the EEC* (London: John Murray).

Winchester, H.P.M. and White, P.E. 1988: The location of marginalised groups in the inner city. *Environment and Planning D* 6, 37–54.

Wright, J. 1982: Migration of school leavers: a case study in the Southeast of South Australia. Unpublished BA (Hons.) thesis, School of Social Sciences, Flinders University of South Australia, Adelaide.

Yamaguchi, T. 1984: The Japanese national settlement system. In Bourne, L.S., Sinclair, R. and Dziewoński, K. (eds.), *Urbanization and settlement systems: international perspectives* (Oxford: Oxford University Press), 261–79.

Yazaki, T. 1970: *The socioeconomic structure of the Tokyo metropolitan complex*. Translated by Mitsugu Matsuda. Hawaii: University of Hawaii Social Science Research Institute.

Index